Beta: Quiet Girls Can Run the World

Rebecca Holman

Beta: Quiet Girls Can Run the World

There is more than one way to be the boss

CORONET

First published in Great Britain in 2017 by Coronet
An imprint of Hodder & Stoughton
An Hachette UK company

3

A CIP catalogue record for this title is available from the British Library

Hardback ISBN: 978 1 473 65618 5
Trade Paperback ISBN: 978 1 473 65619 2
Ebook ISBN: 978 1 473 65620 8

Typeset in Sabon MT by Palimpsest Book Production Ltd, Falkirk, Stirlingshire

Printed and bound in Great Britain by Clays Ltd, St Ives plc

Hodder & Stoughton policy is to use papers that are natural, renewable
and recyclable products and made from wood grown in sustainable forests.
The logging and manufacturing processes are expected to conform
to the environmental regulations of the country of origin.

Hodder & Stoughton Ltd
Carmelite House
50 Victoria Embankment
London EC4Y 0DZ

www.hodder.co.uk

CONTENTS

You know that woman who isn't speaking in the meeting you're at? She's the only person who hasn't shared her thoughts on the presentation you've just watched (and you're kind of glad: you've been in the room for ninety minutes now and definitely have better things to do with your day). But her silence is in contrast to the rest of the room, and you can't work out if it's because she's intimidated (there's a lot of big personalities here), bored, disinterested, or she just doesn't have anything to say because she isn't that bright.

What you can't see is that while everyone else in the room is 'engaging in a robust exchange of views', she's making notes and thinking things through. While they're getting sucked into a pointless argument, she's trying to solve the problem. And, to save time, she'll probably email her thoughts after the meeting to the person who presented. She realises she may not get credit for solving the problem like that, but it's the easiest way to do it.

She's the Beta woman and she's getting stuff done all over your office and you probably hadn't noticed. In a world that champions shouting loudest, both IRL and online, we're told that female success in the workplace is allowed to look only a certain way: big, brash and Alpha. The reality is that any individual woman is far more complex than that, so why be so reductive?

Let's rewind. It's seven years ago. I'm in the pub on a Friday night with my new team. Two weeks before, I became their boss when I landed a job editing a women's website that had been wildly successful and was now in sharp decline. It would have taken a Herculean effort to turn it around, and as I was a relatively inexperienced, very timid editor, no one was sure if I was up to the job. Least of all me.

Apparently this was the first thing we'd all agreed on. 'They think you won't last, that you'll be out in six months,' one of my new team conspiratorially told me, in an ill-judged, booze-fuelled attempt at bonding. I stared at him aghast, my mouth hanging open. 'But I think they're wrong. There's a lot more going on there,' he added quickly, when he realised his attempt to be named Employee of the Month had backfired. 'Still waters run deep, and all that.' As he rambled on, my face felt hot and I flushed. What if they were right? If they all thought that, surely they *must* be right.

If it hadn't been Friday night I would have resigned immediately. Instead I got annihilated and did some pretty horrific snot-crying on the night bus home, accompanied by a dark cloud of self-doubt that lasted far beyond my hangover.

Two years later, it's about 11 a.m. on a Tuesday morning in November. I'm in the back of a taxi and I'm struggling to breathe. Twenty minutes earlier I was in the office, having just taken some new medication for the migraines that had been plaguing me for months. Almost instantly my chest and the back of my throat had tightened in an allergic reaction.

I'm attempting to call my doctor while trying to work out whether to get the driver to take me home or to the hospital. But my overriding thought is, I've got to get back to my desk or to my laptop before anyone notices I've gone. Any anxiety I feel over the allergic reaction, or any concern at having had three migraines every week for the last eight, is overridden by the fear that I'll be found out for what I am: not passionate enough, not committed enough, not anything enough for my job. That I don't deserve it.

A migraine isn't a good enough reason not to reply immediately to an email, and a trip to A and E no excuse for missing a deadline. Therefore I'm failing.

Last year I worked something out. I realised that, although I have very few of the obvious qualities one imagines an editor will possess – at least in the Meryl Streep, *Devil Wears Prada* vein (sharp suit, icy stare) – I'm okay at my job. Scratch that: I'm good at my job. But I only got okay, then good at it, when I worked out that embracing who I was and what I was good at, rather than pretending to be someone else, was the only thing that was going to work. The minute I stopped questioning whether I was the right person for the role and focused on doing the job, everything fell into place. Basically, I embraced my inner Beta.

But you don't have to do it my way – spending the best part of a decade sweaty-palmed in meetings, panicking every Sunday night and penning imaginary resignation letters twice weekly . . .

As it happens, I'd never seen myself as an editor. I'd always known I wanted to write, and as I studied journalism and applied diligently for work experience, I pictured myself as a staff writer somewhere – researching stories, doing interviews, and filing my copy to a shadowy editor figure, who didn't really feature in my fantasies of what adult life would look like. Because, as we're told, there's only one type of person who becomes the boss, and I certainly wasn't it.

After I graduated, I started working for a publishing agency in south London. We had a small team, and worked across lots of different projects. I was a decent writer, worked hard and was happy to muck in, so eventually I was made editor of my own little title (I was also the deputy editor, staff writer and editorial assistant). Then I worked on a bigger magazine, and eventually I was made editor again, with my own small team to manage.

And then the recession hit. We lost the contract for our magazine, I lost my job and, aged twenty-six, I had to work out how to be a writer, editor, and maybe even a boss outside the confines of the safe little space I'd worked in for the last four years.

With each new freelance gig, or job, I took on, I was convinced that this would be the one where I'd find my feet, where I'd feel from the outset that I was being taken seriously. But, of course, the world doesn't work like that. How highly you rate your own ability has nothing to do with the job you're in, and everything to do with your own sense of self. What I didn't realise was that, although I'd start each job disappointed that I hadn't morphed into the professional *Wunderkind* I wanted to be, I was gradually learning what success meant to me.

But I didn't understand that at the time. Instead I spent

the rest of my twenties and my early thirties feeling like a bad editor and a bad boss. So, what changed? In part, I got a bit older and stopped worrying. No one was trying to have me fired so I couldn't have been doing that bad a job, right? (Classic Beta self-deprecation, right there . . .)

And I got more experienced – I learnt more stuff. On the day I joined the place I work now, someone asked me a technical question to which I knew the answer. More than that, I was the only person around who did know the answer. Somehow, I'd gone from always feeling like the youngest and least experienced member of the team to the most experienced. Or, to put it another way, it took me until I was thirty-one to grasp that there were occasions when I was the most experienced person in the room.

But experience isn't really about knowing the answers. It's about being okay with not knowing the answers. And the real breakthrough for me came when I stopped reacting to what I thought other people were thinking (which is a ridiculous and pointless guessing game) and started focusing on what I wanted to achieve. Easier said than done, but if you nail that, it's truly liberating.

A huge part of this was about my embracing the Beta. Feeling okay about admitting when I didn't know something (which is easier when you realise that no one else has a clue either), or when I was making a decision based on gut instinct (because gut instinct is part of the reason they hired me) and embracing the fact that I'd probably get it wrong sometimes (there's nothing more Beta than being able to own your mistakes with good grace).

But that's all useful stuff for life in general, so why are we focusing on the workplace here?

It's only in the last sixty years or so that women have entered the workplace in any sort of meaningful way. My mother was probably one of the first generation of women who went to work as a matter of course. For her, Alpha or Beta didn't come into it. She worked in a male-dominated environment and rarely with other women. Finding her place at the office had its own challenges, but the idea that she could be more than one 'type' of woman never occurred to her. The fact that she was there, and thriving, was enough.

Almost forty years after she first joined the workplace, we're still struggling to find more than two blueprints for how a woman should be. For example, we're endlessly told that our job needs to be the centre of our universe; it has to be our passion. Clocking off at 5 p.m. isn't an option (unless you're clocking off at five to pursue your secret-passion project, which one day you intend to make your full-time career). Success at work only looks one way. And a successful woman? She's shouting louder than everyone else in the room. She's bloody-minded and argumentative because these are all signs that she's passionate about the project at hand and cares about its success above all else. *Ergo*, she's good at her job.

And where does that leave the rest of us? Those of us who ask questions before making decisions, for whom compromise isn't a dirty word but a way to make things work and drive things forward? Is wanting evenings and weekends to be about something more than a screen and work a sign of laziness? Are we by default bad at our jobs? Do we not care enough? Because that's kind of how the narrative goes right now.

But there's a good reason why women's roles in the workplace lack so much nuance – and it's why this book is about Beta women and work, not about Beta people. Men don't need to figure out where they fit in the workplace to the same extent: the workplace was created to fit around them. Men have had centuries to fine-tune how their individual personality types can survive and thrive in an office environment. Women have had just sixty years to get it right, and when we're still fighting to be paid the same amount as our male counterparts, it's no wonder that when we do smash through the glass ceiling, or even attempt to get near it, our roles become one-dimensional.

Who's got time to blaze a trail on their own terms when we've got all of this to contend with? It's exhausting.

So that's where we are: 47 per cent of the workforce reduced to being the secretary or the shoulder-pad-wearing bitch-boss. But that's not my reality and I'm guessing it's not yours either.

How do you know if you're an Alpha or a Beta woman? It's tricky, because almost every careers coach, psychologist or, indeed, woman I spoke to had a different answer when I asked them if they could explain what Alpha and Beta were, and which camp they fell into. And the fact is, we're all on a spectrum of Alpha and Betaness, but we need to start somewhere.

When I'm talking about Alpha and Beta women, this is always what I think of: you have two women in your office, both great at their jobs, but with very different personalities. One is Alpha Woman, and she possesses many of the traits we readily associate with success. She is impeccably dressed, perfectly groomed and highly organised. She is always on time and is always prepared for every meeting or presentation. She is decisive and will be the first to share her opinion in a meeting (the rest of the room will often defer to that opinion, such is her authority). She has no apparent fear of confrontation. She is highly competitive, whether she's running a marathon or working her way through the Booker Prize shortlist before anyone else. She has boundless levels of energy and enthusiasm, her social-media output is perfectly curated – in fact, she is excellent at promoting her own work and achievements via every available medium. She's focused, single-minded and will push things through even when other people don't agree with her (which means she can also be dogmatic, and will kick up a fuss when she doesn't get her own way). She's the woman in the office whom men will describe as 'scary' or 'a bitch' when they don't get their own way with her. She may be inspiring, she may be intimidating, but she's certainly Alpha. She starts the conversation, she sets the agenda. Others follow.

Got it? Right.

What about Beta? She may appear (but not always) to be less organised than her Alpha peer, but this is mainly because if she is less than prepared for a meeting, she'll certainly 'fess up to it rather than styling it out, as Alpha would. (Alpha Woman would never show weakness; Beta Woman is constantly revealing hers.) Beta Woman is an excellent team player and collaborator, and her team love her, but she's also extremely self-deprecating. When she speaks up in a meeting (the idea that a Beta Woman will sit in silence and never share her opinion is a myth: she just considers what she says beforehand), she'll qualify

8

everything as 'opinion' rather than 'fact'. She's laid-back and feels she hasn't enough energy to be 'on' all the time, unlike her Alpha colleague. She's a hard worker – diligent – but when she's finished work for the day, she's finished. When she makes decisions they are considered and thought-out, and she tries to be as accommodating and flexible as she can, to ensure that the needs – and agendas – of as many people as possible are met. Men in the office who don't get what she's about might describe her as a 'pushover' or a 'lightweight'.

None of us will be all of either Alpha or Beta: for example, I've written what is basically the Beta description about myself, but I know I share some traits with Alpha. And plenty of classic Alpha women will, I'm sure, identify with some aspects of a Beta personality. But which of these women looks like success? Is it the quieter, considered Beta, or the decisive, make-things-happen Alpha?

It's the Alpha every time, but that's wrong. Not because the Alpha isn't doing a great job, but because we should all be able to succeed on our own terms – however loudly we shout.

I'm only just working this out, which is part of the point of this book: it's my way of finding out if I can be truly successful on my own terms, without emulating other people's model for success. But also, and more importantly, I want to champion the aforementioned Beta girl, because she's doing a great job, and no one tells her so often enough. I want to sing her praises from the rooftops, and remind us all that success can look however you want it to.

And we're going to need Beta Woman more than ever because the world is changing, fast. We need people who can lead with emotional intelligence, be flexible to new ideas and adapt their plans when required, leaving their ego at the door. Beta Woman's time is now.

So, here's to the collaborators, the pragmatists and the people who believe that being nice works, and that getting your own way isn't always the most important thing. Here's to the unsung workforce of Beta women who are being great bosses, great leaders, and are still sometimes at the front of the charge to the pub at 5.01 p.m. Because I'm sure being a superwoman is great, but it doesn't always look like the most fun.

1.

'So who is the Beta woman? How is she different from the Alpha woman? Why are you so determined to force all working women into two unhelpful and reductive boxes?' I hear you ask.

Let's start with the latter, because it's the simplest to answer. I want to talk about Beta women not because I think all women either are or aren't one – as I've already said, it's a spectrum, with some women displaying more Alpha or Beta tendencies than others – but because I want to speak up for every woman who isn't professing to be the shout-the-loudest, dogmatic, in-the-gym-at-the-crack-of-dawn, working-all-the-hours-she-can-possibly-manage-on-very-little-sleep boss-lady. Even if she isn't your boss yet, she soon will be because she's the Alpha female, and that is how it works. And in an age of Instagram #goals and constant one-upmanship, Alpha has become shorthand for hardcore. Six-kids-and-CEO-of-a-medium-sized-multinational hard-core. Silencing-an-entire-room-of-subordinates-with-one-glance hardcore. The early-morning-spinning-class-badge-of-honour hardcore.

I should probably have gone to interview a bunch of women at a terrifying dawn gym class for this book but, suffice to say, I only ever get up before dawn if it's to catch a cheap flight somewhere hot.

Let's be clear. Some (plenty?) of women operate in that way and are perfectly happy. The problem is that operating on full pelt has become the goal we should all be aspiring to, and that's where I take issue. Why else would there be reams of articles on the internet dedicated to the morning routines, exercise regimes, travel beauty tips and wardrobe hacks of preternaturally successful women? Yes, there are plenty of meme-friendly mantras about being yourself and finding what makes you happy, but we don't live in a world where 'being content' is a marker of success. A marker of success is zipping across town in an Uber to three different networking events before heading home to finish work and grab a refreshing four hours' sleep before it all begins again. It's exhausting and unsustainable for most mere mortals, yet anything less, and we haven't quite nailed life.

So by Beta, I mean the rest of us – the non-Alphas.

We all know who the apparent Alpha women in our lives and newsfeeds are, but who are the non-Alphas? We're the women for whom no promotion is worth getting out of bed before seven-thirty on a Monday morning. We're the women who may or may not love our jobs (although I have to confess to adoring mine) but want the opportunity to succeed and do well, so we work hard. It's women like me, who fear that they're not hardcore enough but that the time and energy they'd waste on pretending to be hardcore could be better used elsewhere . . . like on their actual job.

Just found out you've got to run a team and you're concerned that the only management style that works is the Shouting and Fear Method™? Been told you're too passive in that shouty weekly meeting where nothing ever gets decided? Can't be bothered to hang around in the office till 8 p.m. because that's what everyone else does, or Instagram your Sunday-afternoon 'mini brainstorm for next week!' session (because you're in the pub on a Sunday afternoon, where you belong, and you got all of your work finished on Friday anyway)? Then, my friend, you might just be a non-Alpha. Welcome to the club.

In this 24/7, Instagram-filtered, heavily curated world, we're told to go hard or go home – but why do we assume that going hardcore is always the best way? What are the differences between Alpha and Beta traits, and does it stand that Alpha characteristics make one more successful?

When I asked all the women I interviewed for this book if they were an Alpha or a Beta, almost no one had a straight answer for me. No one said they were an outright Alpha. Most felt they were Alpha in some aspects of their lives and Beta in others. And, equally, someone with emotional intelligence can be an excellent leader whether they're an Alpha or a Beta, but they certainly generate very different management and working styles.

At the extreme end of the spectrum, the portrayal of the Alpha woman we're used to in popular culture is not positive: it's the classic bitch or manipulator, from Cruella de Vil to Sigourney Weaver's Katharine Parker in *Working Girl*.

The reality is obviously more nuanced. Eddie Erlandson, co-author of *Alpha Male Syndrome*, characterises the Alpha woman as 'the velvet hammer . . . they maybe have a little higher EQ (Emotional Quotient, or Emotional Intelligence) [than Alpha males] . . . but they can be equally as urgent, assertive and aggressive as men are'. So, the

Alpha female could be less obviously identifiable than her male counterpart, because she will be more inclined to wind in her Alpha-ness when the situation requires, but still possesses the same drive and assertiveness.

And, of course, there are many examples of the classic Alpha woman in popular culture and current affairs – it makes sense that Alpha women will, by definition, be the ones we all know about. Think Beyoncé, Hillary Clinton and Madonna.

So what's the difference between an Alpha and a Beta woman? A Beta woman is 'more likely to be the one who isn't taking accolades,' explains Nicole Williams, careers expert at Works. 'Instead she's saying, "Look at what my colleagues did . . ." The Beta is more receptive. They aren't dogmatic.' Or as *The Urban Dictionary* puts it: 'The Beta female will be called upon to voice her opinions, and her evaluations will most times be valued by the Alpha female. She also knows when to keep silent and when to talk. She is second in command.'

It's harder to find IRL examples of Beta women in popular culture – Beta women's tendency to work for the group rather than personal glory will put paid to that. (Jennifer Aniston's name is often bandied around as the celebrity example of choice, pitted against Angelina Jolie's Alpha, but I'm not buying it.) Then there are the *faux*-Betas, whose #relatable 'real' persona no doubt hides an Alpha-worthy hide of steel (Taylor Swift, I'm looking at you). But more on *faux*-Betas later.

Even when it comes to fictional female characters, the Beta is rarely at the forefront. One exception that springs to mind is Helen Fielding's Bridget Jones. The nineties poster girl for 'normal women' is about as Beta as they come, but maybe that's because her life is presented to us in diary format – we get to read every thought she has. Every insecurity, moment of self-doubt, loneliness or fear is laid out in full for us. Maybe we're all a Beta in the pages of our diaries.

We're told – in a nutshell – that being Beta is all about being a professional sidekick. The perpetual Robin to an Alpha's Batman. Betas are often perceived as weak, embodying the female traits we don't consider to be powerful or valuable in the workplace: empathy, collaboration, the ability to listen. But does being a woman mean that you're statistically more likely to be Beta? Sort of. Ish.

Research by Erlandson and his wife and co-author, Kate Ludeman, found that men are more socially conditioned to embody Alpha traits than women, and Alpha women are likely to possess fewer 'Alpha risk factors' than men. HR consultant Tanya Hummel agrees: 'We're talking about Alpha versus Beta but it could just as well be men versus women, because as much as you do get the Queen Bee who pulls the rungs up behind her, you also find that [women leaders] tend to be good coaches and that everyone wants to work with them because they're collaborative, they're accommodating. They allow creativity because they're less aggressively competitive than if you were in an all-male environment.'

Hummel also explained that about two-thirds of those identified in personality tests as being people-focused and -oriented (a classic Beta trait I have in spades) will be women. Meanwhile, two-thirds of those who are much more outcome-focused (a more classic Alpha trait) tend to be men. Not all men or women fall into either category, but there is a gender bias.

And although Alpha women like to win, most experts agree that they tend (on the whole) to be less belligerent and authoritarian than their male counterparts. And if you believe that Alpha or Beta is about learned behaviour as much as about genetics, then few would argue against the premise that women are still taught to embody more classically Beta behaviour than men.

Dr Marianne Cooper, sociologist at the Clayman Institute for Gender Research and lead researcher for *Lean In* by Sheryl Sandberg, prefers to think about personality types in terms of agentic versus communal ('agentic' being direct, ambitious, self-starter, forceful, and 'communal' as, her words, 'nice and warm and friendly'). 'With these two different sets of behaviours, the agentic are strongly associated with men, and what culturally we think men are like, and the communal are the same but in women, so this is the root of stereotypes about men and women. And as there's so much belief and understanding that you really have to be type A in order to be a leader, that's where we arrive at this place where leadership is seen as a better match for men.

'So the problem for women is, if they engage in these sort of alpha or agentic behaviours, they're violating expectations about how women are supposed to behave and they get pushed back for it. And then women who exhibit the marking in all characteristics – the ones we expect and associate with women – they're often not taken seriously and they're seen to be less competent.'

It's a double bind.

And here's why this book is about Beta women and not Beta men. Those same traits that women are taught and conditioned to embody, from being accommodating and flexible, to being nurturing and pragmatic, are often the same traits that are dismissed in the workplace as a sign that one is not 'serious' or 'competitive' enough or 'doesn't have the edge'.

'There's a very narrow framework through which we allow people to be leaders and display their sense of leadership, and I think it narrows even more for women and people of colour,' says Dr Cooper.

The traits that are found more often in women than in men (and before a squillion Alpha women write to me in outrage, I appreciate that this won't apply to everyone) aren't those that are considered traditional makers of success.

There's a simple reason why our view of success is so bizarrely narrow. Men have always dominated the workplace – and still do. Of course we automatically – wrongly – use traditionally male traits as markers for professional success and rarely question it. That's how it's always been.

But it's plain wrong. The markers of success, of a good boss, of a productive employee or a successful entrepreneur, are far more complex than how Alpha you are. Otherwise this would be a very short book indeed.

For starters, according to Nicole Williams, being a Beta can make you a better leader than an Alpha. 'As a manager, it's your role to make other people shine,' she explains. 'And one of the great boss-like characteristics of Betas is that they bring out the best in others.'

I asked dozens of women of different ages, working in

different industries, to tell me about the characteristics they most admired in their past bosses and managers and to describe some of their key traits. Their responses were strikingly similar. Almost everyone talked of people who gave them clear objectives and tracked their progress, but didn't micromanage them. And almost everyone mentioned a boss who was smart and inspiring. The more important traits were almost always empathy and the ability to be inspired by their team; the great boss didn't harbour unrealistic expectations or make hardcore demands.

People remember the bosses who gave them the direction and freedom to do the best job they could and encouraged their personal development. You know, the team players, the nurturers. The Betas.

At the moment we're seeing, more than ever, how dynamic Alpha leadership doesn't always translate into a good management style. In early 2017, Uber's CEO Travis Kalanick was forced to apologise after he was caught on camera having a heated exchange with a driver during a night out. The driver complains about the company's pay rates and business model, to which Kalanick can be heard saying, 'Some people don't like to take responsibility for their own shit. They blame everything in their life on somebody else. Good luck!'

The company has since been plagued with numerous claims of sexual harassment and dodgy HR practices, so this incident is potentially a drop in an ocean of toxic behaviour. Kalanick comes across as the worst type of Silicon Valley bro, but when the video came out he was contrite: 'By now I'm sure you've seen the video where I treated an Uber driver disrespectfully. To say that I am ashamed is an extreme understatement. My job as your leader is to lead, and that starts with behaving in a way that makes us all proud. That is not what I did, and it cannot be explained away.'

Kalanick went on to say that he'd realised he needed to change as a leader and receive help. We have no way of knowing how sincere he was in his apology, but it's interesting that he knew he needed to make it, that his brash, arrogant (and extreme Alpha) leadership model wasn't impressing anyone even if it worked for him (and his investors) in Uber's fast-moving, fast-growing early years.

Similarly, Miki Agrawal, the dynamic female founder of Thinx, an online female-hygiene company, faced accusations of sexual harassment from staff in early 2017. Aside from the allegations, it was noted that as the company quickly grew Agrawal failed to employ any HR staff or implement HR policy. She later stood down as CEO, to focus on promoting the brand, saying, 'I'm *not* the best suited for the operational CEO duties, nor was it my passion to be so.'

Tinder, Airbnb, Snapchat – the small, agile tech start-ups of yore, where big ideas, even bigger vision and brash arrogance ruled the day – are now fully fledged businesses, with HR practices, shareholders and customer expectations to adhere to. And what we're seeing is that some of the big Alpha bosses who got the businesses off the ground aren't necessarily the right people to see them through the next ten, twenty, thirty years.

It's not just about the tech industry either. I heard a story about a creative, dynamic, energetic and Alpha CEO, who had the vision, drive and energy to transform a large publishing house's fortunes when they needed a total change of direction. Later, when the company was in 'business as usual' mode, she was let go, and replaced with a much more process-driven, quieter Beta leader. The reason? She was amazing when huge, disruptive changes had to happen, but couldn't manage people properly or keep things ticking over on a day-to-day basis.

You want someone to steady the ship? Get a Beta in.

But Betas are timid, shy and introverted, right? How can they ever be leaders? After the publication of Susan Cain's brilliant *Quiet: The Power of Introverts in a World That Can't Stop Talking*, much was made of how overlooked the introvert has become in the workplace. But it's wrong to say that an extrovert is always an Alpha and a Beta the opposite, although there are some big areas of crossover. Nicole Williams agrees: 'What makes people extroverted doesn't always make them a leader and vice versa, and charisma and magnetism can be taught and learned,' she explains.

But there is a difference. While your Alpha or Beta-ness is to do with your position within a group, your work team or a friendship circle, your response to being around other people depends on your extroversion or introversion. Simply put, extroverts gain energy from being around other people, and introverts find it drains them.

Many of the characteristics found in introverts may also be found in Beta women, but equally they may not. As it happens, I'm an introvert, but a fairly outgoing one. I find it intensely draining to spend all my time around other people, and although being in a room full of people I don't know isn't my favourite thing, I can handle it. To some

Alphas, though, a party where they know just one person is a source of extreme anxiety.

And, as I can't emphasise enough, when it comes to personality types, few of us sit on either extreme end of the scale and most of the women I know who are characteristically Alpha have the emotional intelligence to switch between the two as necessary: they can read a room. But none of this explains why we persist with the myth that Alpha is better.

It's important because if – like me – you don't fall into that tiny subset of people who are Alpha all the time, you'll never feel you're doing enough or good enough. We all have the persistent inner voice that tells us we're not good enough – and when you're constantly being told that your personality fundamentally doesn't fit the job you're doing, that voice can be impossible to ignore. Your self-worth at work becomes about who you are, not about what you're doing.

I hate conflict, but for years my inner voice would tell me that I wasn't passionate enough because I didn't get into screaming rows with my editorial team over every feature. Striving for consensus meant I was putting people-pleasing above doing my job, and being nice meant I was a pushover. For ages I couldn't get past the idea that to be a good leader – someone people look up to and trust – you have to be at the front, shouting the loudest, and possibly throwing a desk lamp out of the window when things don't go your way.

This has always been rubbish, but never more so than now. Times are changing: we live in a world where the hard skills we learnt just ten or even five years ago at university or in training are fast becoming obsolete. In a world where the pace of technology makes the concept of a job for life laughable. Right now, I'm thirty-four, and Facebook didn't exist when I was at university. Social media (or, indeed, digital content) didn't feature when I did my journalism training. Now if a lecturer in journalism didn't encourage their students to understand and be fully prepared for a digital world, it would be neglectful, never mind remiss.

Similarly, setting up your own business without a website, or without understanding social media as a vital tool in reaching your customers, is now unthinkable. Fifteen years ago, an online presence was an afterthought. Fifteen years is no time at all, when you consider that we'll all be working until we're seventy.

So, yes, being 'really good at shouting' is great, but to survive the twenty-first-century workplace you need to be flexible and you need to be able to face change head on. Which is why the so-called 'soft skills' found in women (specifically Beta women) – emotional intelligence, the ability to work with people, pragmatism – are becoming increasingly prized.

In fact, the World Economic Forum's 2016 job report highlighted emotional intelligence as one of the top ten skills required in the workplace by 2020, alongside persuasion and teaching others – all strong Beta skills.

With all of this in mind, why do we insist upon such a narrow portrayal of success and successful women in popular culture, in the media and even in how we present ourselves to others via social media? It's because we still accept as fact several untruths about workplace culture, which cloud everything that comes after.

When I was a child, my mother (who was very good at her job) used to work long hours – often leaving before we woke up in the morning and not returning until long after we'd gone to bed. She was company secretary to an engineering firm. She was lucky in that she was well rewarded for her hard work with a career that paid well and offered clear progression – plenty of people work just as hard without anything like the benefits.

But despite spending most of her career in environments where gruelling long hours were the norm, her takeaway to me when I first started working was 'There's no glory in working late.' She certainly wasn't saying sack off work at five on the dot, irrespective of what else is going on. What she meant was, no one notices or cares if you're working late (or, to put it another way, a good boss shouldn't be mentally totting up team Brownie points based on how late it is when you get all your work done: they should be querying why you have so much to do that you can't get it done in a working day). And we automatically assume that if other people are staying late, it must be because they're incredibly busy or working so much harder than we are. But maybe they're staying behind to work on another project, or spent half their day watching reality TV and need to stay late to catch up on their work.

But the basic message is simple: attribute working long to working hard at your peril.

There are numerous studies into the link between productivity and hours worked, and the correlation is clear: the fewer hours someone works, the more productive they are in that time. In an experiment conducted by Gothenburg City Council over two years, nurses at the Svartedalen retirement home in the city switched from an eight-hour to a six-hour working day for the same wage to see if a six-hour working day would boost productivity. It concluded that fewer hours' work led to more productive staff (and that the staff working six hours a day were far less likely to take sick days than those working the standard eight – although the scheme was later scrapped when the council concluded that the associated costs of hiring seventeen extra staff for the duration of the experiment outweighed the benefits). Meanwhile a survey in the UK revealed that six out of ten British bosses believed that cutting the working day from eight to six hours would be beneficial for productivity.

But if you've just come back to work feeling refreshed after a long weekend, taken a sneaky afternoon off work because you can't bear to look at your screen any more, or noticed how much of a zombie you now are on a Friday afternoon, you knew that already, didn't you?

Rob Yeung, an organisational psychologist at consultancy Talentspace, agrees: 'Particularly for people who think it's very important to go home and spend time with their family and friends, or do things other than their nine-to-five jobs, then, yes, the longer you need to stay the more you may resent it and you may feel less productive. You can feel anxious, and even experience burnout.'

All excellent reasons why sticking around at work until stupid o'clock is rubbish for productivity, and why, as a boss, terrorising your team into staying late is a Bad Idea.

Yeung adds, 'In an ideal world, yes, your boss should care if they have an employee who's regularly having to stay late at work – and there's good research showing that bosses who have greater empathy and provide greater support tend to get more productivity and hard work out of their employees. But there are many organisations in which staying late seems stitched into the fabric of the culture. I know that many people, particularly in professional service industries such as finance, law, and management consultancy, feel compelled to stay late because everyone else seems to be doing it. In those cases, trying to get away early has to be a careful balancing act.

'Yes, by all means leave early if you are certain that your performance is above average. But if you have been told that your performance is somewhat lacking, or you're at all unsure how you're perceived in the workplace, it may not be a good idea to leave earlier than your colleagues.'

Numerous productivity studies over the years have shown that it's the people with less time to spend in the office (such as mothers working part time or rushing to leave at five on the dot so they can do the nursery pick-up) who use it most productively. (And a 2010 study in the *European Heart Journal* found that if you spend more than ten hours a day in the office, you're 60 per cent more likely to have a heart attack. Argh.) Being able to delegate, to make thoughtful decisions quickly, to prioritise work for yourself and your team are all signs that you're a banging boss. And yet . . . and yet . . . Starting work at 7 a.m. is still seen as a badge of honour, especially if you've managed to get in an Instagram of that networking event you made it to the night before. Because . . . hardcore.

And the really stupid thing is, all those productivity studies are looking at whether we should be working fewer than the standard eight hours, while actually we're working far more than that already. From the extra hour or so you habitually clock up in the office, to the constant checking of emails in the evening, or logging on to finish a few things off, we're always on, and we're always expected to be on, and it's frying out brains.

I made Alyss, who works for me, switch off the emails on her phone when she was on holiday because she kept replying to things and checking them. 'It's not that there was anything in particular I'd left undone, or that I needed to do. It's just that other people were emailing me in the expectation that I'd reply, so I felt like I had to.'

It's not necessarily that we all have so much work to do that we can't get it done in any given forty-hour week. It's that when everyone else is plugged in, constantly emailing and constantly on, your opting out marks you as less than committed – especially when your boss or direct line manager is always on and expects the same from you.

Getting tired, needing a day away from our desks and demonstrating anything less than slavish enthusiasm for our jobs are all frowned upon. Not because that's real life, but because we have such a narrow spectrum for what success looks like.

MYTH 2. SHE (OR HE) WHO SHOUTS LOUDEST PROBABLY KNOWS WHAT THEY'RE TALKING ABOUT

Ever noticed that if no one in the room really knows what they're talking about, they instantly defer to the one person who's talking loudly and authoritatively about the matter at hand? Whether there's any value in what they're saying

26

is irrelevant. It's far better to have an instant, definitive opinion on everything than to say nothing at all. The result? People with loud voices, who tend not to think before they speak, often assume positions of power or authority.

It's often why people clamour to criticise an idea, pitch or project they don't really understand: it's better to get in there first and say something than to keep schtum. I've certainly done it myself. I can think of more than one occasion when an external person has pitched or presented to me and I've responded by listing all the things I didn't like about it. On one occasion, I'm ashamed to say, I made the presenter so nervous that she fluffed the meeting. I could just as easily have started with the good stuff in a constructive conversation rather than a barrage of negativity. But what if you don't have a chance to get your criticism in and people subsequently think you're too nice or a pushover? We can't have that, can we, ladies?

It's something I'm hyper-aware of, and I still find myself doing it on occasion. And the end result is that we mistake the volume of someone's voice, and the frequency with which they speak up in meetings, as competence. We also end up assuming that people who are particularly extroverted, outspoken by nature, good at public speaking, or who are just really chatty, are the ones who know what they're doing. Of course one can be all of these things *and* incredibly competent, it's just that they're not mutually inclusive traits. Being outgoing or even a loudmouth is a personality trait, not a mark of intelligence or judgement (the flipside, of course, is that being quiet or shy doesn't make you an idiot or an automatic genius: the two just aren't linked).

MYTH 3. GOOD MANAGERS NEVER GET EMOTIONAL, AND KEEP THEMSELVES AT ARM'S LENGTH FROM THEIR TEAM. THIS IS ESPECIALLY TRUE FOR WOMEN

To be authoritative as a woman, you have to be something of a cold fish, right? This is why so many famously powerful and authoritative (fictional) women are depicted as such – and why so many prominent, successful IRL women are portrayed in such a cartoonish way by the media. If you show an interest in your team's life outside work, engage with them on a personal level, or show any other evidence of caring about the people who work for or with you, you're in danger of giving in to your almost uncontrollable maternal instincts. Next thing you know, you'll be handing out pay rises to female members of staff for being really stoic during their periods and rewarding male members of your team with a special bonus if they get in before midday when they've got a really bad hangover. Because you're a woman, you're either a bleeding-heart walkover or an ice queen.

To demonstrate authority, to be a 'good' boss, to be 'good' at your job in general, you must, supposedly, be the latter. Ruling through fear is how proper (Alpha) career women do business: if you're genuinely busy and important, you won't have time for the niceties, or to consider other people's feelings. Being nice, saying 'please' and persuading rather than telling people to do what you need are signs you've got too much time on your hands. After all, getting your subordinates (or colleagues) to do something for you because they like you and you've asked nicely is a total cop-out – right?

*

Now I've obviously signposted that these myths aren't true (for starters, I've called them myths, which should be your first clue) because they're so ridiculous. But in the real world, with all its unspoken rules and social nuances, they're not. I bet if you're a woman who has been at work at some point, you'll recognise at least a grain of truth among the silliness. It's so insidious we barely notice it's happening, but among all the progress ostensibly being made in the workplace, it's still there. The way women are viewed (and the way we view other women) at work is still binary. You're Alpha or Beta. You're good at your job or bad at it, and never the twain shall meet.

You see, you have to be one of those two broad personality types, just like you have to be either the loudmouth or the mouse, the hardcore workaholic or the flake – because how else will people make snap judgements about whether you're good at your job or not, based on no firm evidence?

But the thing is, Alpha and Beta behaviour, in its modern form, is learnt behaviour: it's not hardwired into our DNA (apart from anything else, all typical Alpha traits that would have been useful to caveman Alpha, like 'being really good at hunting bison', have limited practical application in, say, a career in the City).

In fact, Eddie Erlandson believes that our Alpha and Beta traits are all part of different personas that people develop in childhood. Women are more likely to develop Beta traits than men, in behaviour learnt from childhood, and are capable of switching it on or off. 'I think you can see Alpha traits by age three,' he explains. 'Now you could say, if you see them that clearly, they must somehow be

29

communicated through the genetic pathways. On the other hand, remember that people are learning all their key styles around security, approval and safety before the age of six, so they are picking up a tremendous amount from the environment around them, whether that be parents or uncles or siblings or whatever.'

Erlandson found that explaining this to Alpha clients actually had a liberating effect – 'It helps them see their behaviour as a collection of habits that were formed early in their lives rather than as an unchangeable genetic trait.'

I like this theory: it feels far more attuned to how we actually live our lives than the idea that women are constantly having to fake professionalism to fight their almost overpowering maternal instinct.

The fact is, we're all capable of operating on a broad spectrum of Alpha and Beta behaviour, and doing so is a far better representation of our true personalities than the one-note parody of the classic Alpha or Beta.

And, of course, most people are more complex than one of the two broad, lazy categories all women are assigned to, but that's how we're assigned nonetheless. Alpha or Beta, workaholic or work-shy, good or bad.

It means that we're supposedly failing if we're not the most accomplished woman in the room. It means that succeeding on our own terms doesn't count: we're only winning if we've beaten everyone else. Picture the classic Alpha woman. It's such a narrow definition that it can't possibly represent more than 5 per cent of the population (mostly white, professional, middle-class Western women). I keep hearing about this woman and her many achievements because versions of her probably take up a disproportionate amount of space on my social-media newsfeeds (and the rest of us are emulating this behaviour because we feel we should), but does she represent all women? Of course not.

And, in fact, when I remember the dozens of supremely talented, inspiring, successful women I've worked with over the last decade, I can think of only a couple who come close to the classic Alpha role. Now, they are great bosses and great people. But so are all the others. And yet we're told if we're not one of the 5 per cent, we're not doing enough, and we're not good enough.

So this is for the other 95 per cent of us. Because there's more than one way to absolutely boss it at work, and I'm going to prove it.

2.

Who's your Beta role model? Hillary Clinton? Oh, come on, she's the most famous Alpha on the planet. Taylor Swift? She's such an Alpha that she can lord it over her own squad – although she can switch to Beta-ness which can actually bolster her personal image. Or maybe it's Emma Watson. You know, Hermione. She's pretty Beta, right? Well, I think she demonstrates a laser-like focus that implies an Alpha personality. We just assume she's 'quiet' (Beta) because she doesn't give many interviews.

Alpha women are all we see, not that you'd always know it. There's a weird disconnect between women on television, in films or in politics and the personas they use. Because relatability – the ability to appear 'normal' and 'just like the rest of us' – has become like fairy dust for anyone with a public persona, from politicians to celebrities. Hillary Clinton was lampooned before the 2016 election for not being relatable enough. (Incidentally, would a male politician have had to go so far to prove they were 'real'? Probably not: no one worried about that picture of Donald Trump posing outside his gold lift after winning an election campaign he fought on the basis that he wasn't part of the 'elite'.

Similarly, actresses like Jennifer Lawrence, and comedians and writers like Tina Fey and Amy Schumer saw their careers skyrocket because, apart from being supremely talented, they were also seen as 'real' and 'fallible' and crucially 'normal'.

And 'normal', of course, is lazy shorthand for what we'd probably imagine a Beta woman to be. It's the quirky hot mess, the pizza-eating Oscar fall-overer (Jennifer Lawrence, I'm looking at you). Even Taylor Swift, whose micro-managed personal image, prodigious output and schedule are the very definition of Alpha, still wants us to know how cute and normal she is. Because Alpha means you're trying hard, Alpha means you want it too much, and no one's going to admit to that. Similarly, Alpha means you're not relatable: you're not like the people you're selling your wares to – you don't get them, so they won't get you.

It's like that age-old question (age-old if you're me, anyway). Why do people love Jennifer Lawrence but dislike Anne Hathaway? J-Law can do no wrong, whether she's papped enjoying what appears to be a large spliff and an even larger glass of wine on a hotel balcony, or face-planting at yet another awards do, she's the ultimate woman of the people. Yes, she's a preternaturally beautiful, Oscar-worthy actress, but she also has the same foibles as the rest of us (the same photogenic foibles anyway: we're still waiting for the leaked video of her picking her nose or squeezing her blackheads). Yet when Anne Hathaway, another incredibly beautiful, talented and indeed Oscar-worthy actress, revealed that she'd practised her Oscars acceptance speech in 2013 to make herself seem more likeable, it turned people off her: that wasn't 'real', it was 'try hard'.

Journalist Ann Friedman discussed this phenomenon in a 2013 article she wrote for the *Cut*:

When she [Jennifer Lawrence] jokes about sucking in her stomach on the red carpet or her publicist hating her for eating a Philly cheesesteak ('There's only so much Spanx can cover up!'), it feels real, not designed to fool her fans into thinking she's not one of those salad-but-hold-the-dressing girls. Lawrence said she ordered a McDonald's on the red carpet at the Oscars.

Hathaway is a vegan.

The problem, Friedman opines, is that we just don't find seemingly perfect, successful women particularly likeable:

Hathaway, who has been acting for a decade and was a clear favorite for the Best Supporting Actress award, seems to fit the broader cultural pattern (I've called it the Hillary Catch-22) in which we simply don't find successful, 'perfect' women very likable. Lawrence is well aware that it serves her well to stay the underdog.

When a celebrity stops being relatable, we fall out of love with them. When their life becomes too perfect, they start to sound too media-trained. When they become too slick, we no longer compare ourselves to them in a favourable way – they start to make us feel bad about ourselves. And then they get the Anne Hathaway treatment.

So Beta equals relatable, relatable equals popular, and the more popular you are as a woman in the limelight, the more bankable you are as a star. Pitch it right, and being a Beta is big business.

But let's be real. Jennifer Lawrence is surviving and thriving in the cut-throat world of Hollywood. Amy

Schumer and Tina Fey cut their teeth in the male-dominated writers' room at *Saturday Night Live* before joining the boys on stage. Is an actress, writer or comedian who's especially Beta capable of doing all those things? Of course. Do we live in a culture where a Beta woman would be given the time and space to thrive in those environments? I really don't think so.

Because here's the paradox. To make it as a female actress, writer, comedian or musician, you need to have the sort of tunnel-vision determination and penchant for self-publicity that you'll almost only ever see in an Alpha woman. We live in a world where celebrity is cherished above all else – and the noise from people trying to reach the top is deafening. It's not an environment where a self-effacing, polite, think-before-they-speak Beta is likely to lead the way.

There are plenty of industries full of Beta women who are totally bossing it, but are they bossing it in the limelight? Probably not. And if they do happen to find themselves in the limelight, chances are they have . . . Never. Been. So. Uncomfortable. In. Their. Life.

Of course this doesn't mean there aren't any Betas in popular culture – there are plenty. It's just that they're fictional. Despite the apparent lack of Beta women in the upper echelons of Hollywood, all female-focused films will have at least one token Beta (as opposed to all other films, which don't feature women in a meaningful way at all), whether she's the female lead's kooky sidekick friend or, more notably, the female romantic lead (who will invariably be Beta, lest she try to wear the Alpha male lead's testicles as earrings at some point – that doesn't make for great cinema, apparently). And in the unlikely event that she starts off the film Alpha, we'll watch the male lead break down her Alpha-ness until she's a quivering Beta ball of lust and love. By breaking down her defences (also known as her very reasonable reservations about dating such an aggressively arrogant narcissist) and convincing her that there's more to life than her career (convincing her to ditch her appearance in a massive human-rights case to go on a mini-break with him to the Cotswolds), he's revealed her true Beta self. And now she can be the passive Beta she'd always secretly desired to be. She can be happy.

Journalist Caitlin Moran points this out in her column for *The Times Magazine*:

> The parameters of jobs for women on film are pretty consistent: they should allow her to wear whatever she wants, so she can express her personality through her wacky/hot outfits (that's half of a woman's entire personality, amirite?). They should be flexible enough for the woman to sack off her duties to take part in other more romantic scenes involving her male co-star. They should allow her to be her crazy, winsome, possibly problematic-drinking self – able to blurt out whatever's on her mind, which confirms what an untameable maverick she is.

And you can't have verbal diarrhoea when you're running a large multinational, can you?

Even in films where a woman's job might actually be a plot point, it's often just that – a plot point. Her looks and romantic vulnerabilities are of far more interest to the average casting director.

There's a great Twitter account, @femscriptintros, which tweets the intros written for female characters in film scripts. Choice samples include:

> JANE (late 20s) sits hunched over a microscope. She's attractive, but too much of a professional to care about her appearance.

> JANE stands next to it (30s), dressed in a paramedic's uniform – blonde, fit, smokin' hot.

> The next candidate is JANE. She has her hair pinned back and wears glasses. In her late 20s, she's attractive in a reserved kind of way.

And we wonder why there's confusion over how women should or shouldn't behave in the workplace.

This is also borne out in the statistics. According to the Geena Davies Institute on Gender in Media, when you look at every general-audience film released in cinemas between September 2006 and September 2009, 57.8 per cent of the male characters are depicted with an occupation, compared to 31.6 per cent of the females. And although 24.6 per cent of the females held professional roles compared to 20.9 per cent of the males, the types of roles depicted are woefully narrow. Across more than three hundred speaking characters, not one female is depicted in the medical sciences (a doctor or a vet), in the top levels of senior management (CEO, CFO), in the legal world or the political arena.

The report also notes that female characters are noticeably absent from the upper echelons of power across multiple industries. Not one woman is present at the top of the business/financial sector, the legal arena or journalism. Among the fifty-eight top executives portrayed in the corporate world (CEOs, CFOs, presidents, vice presidents, general managers), only two are female (and in case you're curious as to which two female characters they're referring to, as I was, they keep the specific films anonymous to avoid shaming specific actors – soz).

Similarly, in their 2015–16 report *Boxed In*, the Centre for the Study of Women in Television and Film at San Diego State University revealed that 'Regardless of platform, gender stereotypes on television programs abound. Female characters were younger than their male counterparts, more likely than men to be identified by their marital status, and less likely than men to be seen at work and actually working.'

The report also stated that 'Overall, male characters were almost twice as likely as females to be portrayed as leaders.' Nine per cent of males but only five per cent of females were portrayed as leaders, and 'Female characters were more likely than males to have personal life-oriented goals, such as caring for others or being in a romantic relationship. In contrast men were more likely than females to have work-oriented goals.'

So what does this tell us? First, that according to Those Guys in Charge of Cinema, Alpha women are fundamentally less lovable than Beta women, and will end up all alone (not in a good way) if they carry on down this path. Second, if you are a Beta woman, your career will be a filler that will serve only to make you more attractive to the man who will become your husband because, let's face it, ending up Not Alone is your primary goal, unlike your Alpha sisters, who are too scary for love.

It's obvious that the ways in which female Alpha and Beta personalities are conveyed to us by popular culture fall far short of reality, and when you place those female characters in a working environment, the total lack of nuance is thrown into sharp relief. Apart from the fact that marked success at work in a female lead is seen as an obstacle for the male lead to overcome, there's an edict that says any female character who is, say, a bit messy, can never remember which bag she put her keys in, dresses in loud prints and favours a biker boot over a pair of massive heels will have a 'soft' job (librarian, dog groomer – although, to be fair, both of those sound like cracking jobs to me) or a job that has no reasonable chance of adequate financial compensation or promotion because it serves as an outlet for her creative frivolities (and she's going to end up with the male lead who owns a darling little flat in Putney that's simply crying out for a woman's touch so she doesn't need a job that pays her rent). The woman wearing a suit, shouting at people and adjusting her monstrous shoulder pads? She's good at her job, for sure. But she's probably miserable and lonely – how else could one introduce a ham-fisted element of personal growth into her storyline?

But does this matter? Films aren't real life, and we all know that. They're not *really* going to change how we behave in the workplace, are they?

According to the guys at the Geena Davies Institute, it

matters a lot. In their report, which focuses on gender bias in family or children's entertainment, they explain,

> Failing to represent females on screen may affect viewers in at least two different ways. For one thing, young children grow up consuming biased media messages. With time and repeated exposure, some children may come to normalize inequality in storytelling.
>
> This normalization process may 'spill over' to other arenas, where girls/young women and boys/young men fail to question or even perceive gender bias in a variety of academic, athletic, social or even occupational contexts. For another thing, the lack of gender balance on screen, if noticed, may communicate to girls that they are of less value than boys.

The same thing happens when you only ever see women in charge, or successful women behaving in a homogeneous way.

'You can't be what you can't see,' is a catch-all phrase that explains the lack of gender-diverse roles at senior level in most industries. I think it gets used a bit too simplistically to explain a complex problem, but the nub of the point definitely stands. Once something becomes accepted in popular culture, it becomes an idea that's addressed in soaps, covered in the mainstream press and your nan is talking about it. Then it becomes far easier to translate into, say, legislation, or a new HR code of conduct in your workplace, or in breaking down those unconscious biases that impact on every job interview you have, every male-dominated meeting you attend, or every time you put in for promotion.

The way we talk about actresses, the number of diverse (in every sense) female leads that make it into mainstream films, the more often women in films and on television present more than a one-dimensional version of what we think a woman in the workplace should look like, the less likely we are to treat women who work, who are your bosses and who succeed, like women.

The Miss Representation Project was set up off the back of a film of the same name that tackles this very issue. The project identifies the issue as the fact that 'The media are selling young people the idea that girls' and women's value lies in their youth, beauty and sexuality and not in their capacity as leaders. Boys learn that their success is tied to dominance, power and aggression. We must value people as whole human beings, not gendered stereotypes.'

But what happens, in reality, when those gendered stereotypes are all we see? Dr Caroline Heldman is an associate professor of politics at Occidental College, Los Angeles, and is also research director at the Geena Davies Institute. She points out that, although it's harder to measure the negative impacts of gender stereotypes in popular culture (that is, it's harder to gauge what young women are not becoming because of what they don't see on television), the positive effects are easier to measure. In this instance, the number of young women taking up archery: 'So there's been a boom in archery, female archers since 2012,' she explains. 'And it can be traced back to *Brave* [the Disney film] and Katniss [Everdeen, Jennifer Lawrence's character] in *The Hunger Games*. So we know for sure that it had a direct and immediate effect on the lives of hundreds of thousands of young girls.'

In short, how film and TV represent women is crucial in how young women's ambitions and aspirations are formed. It matters. A lot. 'Entertainment media is the largest, the biggest influencer in how we shape our lives. Entertainment global media really gets under the radar. I think that really gets into our subconscious and produces implicit gender bias and implicit racial bias. But also it tells us who the good people are, who the bad people are, it tells us who we should respect and deify and it tells us who we should villainise.'

I never saw myself becoming an editor when, in my teens and early twenties, I was envisaging what my career would look like, I always saw myself as a cog in a machine. I pictured myself working on a magazine, doing what I was told, sticking to deadlines and producing decent copy. The idea that I'd be the one setting the deadlines didn't occur to me, because I couldn't picture someone like me in that role. I'd always grown up in an environment where I was told I could achieve whatever I wanted – and I believed that, in the broad sense. I knew I was bright enough and capable enough to do most things (or, more accurately, I knew there were a lot of morons out there who had very important jobs, and I was possibly less of an idiot than some of them). But I didn't believe I was the right 'type' of person to be an editor. The only editors I came across were of the pseudo-fictional sort (ranging from the Paul Dacres and Rebekah Brookses of this world on one side of the spectrum and Anna Wintour on the other) or the actually fictional Miranda Priestly. The mythology surrounding these terrifying figures was so great that I could never equate my own future with that sort of job.

Had I read an interview in which a passionate editor waxed lyrical about the amazing feeling when you really connect with your audience on an issue you really care about, or how fantastic it is when a new writer files their copy and it's the best thing you've read all week, I might have reconsidered. But as far as I was concerned then, the job wasn't about the job, it was about the personality, and I didn't have the right one.

Of course, a more bullish Alpha woman might have thought differently: the idea of thriving in such a macho environment might have excited her and convinced her to pursue an editorship doggedly. She's probably my boss's boss's boss now. But the problem then is that you retain the homogeneity in senior positions that I've been talking about – it becomes an endless cycle. A job's probably not for you because you've never seen anyone like you doing it . . .

Jemma used to work for me. She's someone I'd massively characterise as Alpha. (I've always assumed she must have found it intensely frustrating to work for me because her boundless energy and enthusiasm was sometimes met head on by my desire to do 'one thing at a time' and 'wait and see what happens'.) She is fantastic at her job, works incredibly hard and never runs out of steam, but when I asked her how she'd define herself, she was far from emphatic.

'I spent a lot of my twenties aspiring to be an Alpha, and it probably wasn't sitting very comfortably with me because I felt that was probably going to be the only way I'd be successful. The women I saw that I aspired to be – all the women I was surrounded by in my first jobs, and probably the women that my parents were surrounded by

– were these big-personality eighties power-shouldered kind of women, so I was like "Okay, I definitely want to be like that." But it never sat that comfortably with me because I'm really awkward in situations of conflict – I just really hate it, and then I'm very bad at competition, like I have no desire to win really.'

Then she says something that really resonates with me: 'I spent a lot of that time in my early twenties lying in bed with my heart beating fast and analysing what had happened that day and thinking, Oh, fuck it, because I thought I hadn't dealt with a situation hard enough, or pushed it, or worked hard enough. I also think I definitely defined a lot of my life around work.' I did this too – for years. And I can pretty much guarantee that Jemma was not, by any stretch of the imagination, underperforming at work while she was worrying so much about it. But what she was worrying about – and what I worried about so much – wasn't about performance or achievement: it was about not being the right 'type' of person. Because we're taught that success is a personality type, not a mark of achievement.

And it's not just about how women deal with their own aspirations. The sort of job a female lead in a major block-buster or soap holds matters because the men we work with also see these films, watch those soaps and have to adhere to the same HR codes of conduct that we do. If your male colleague, employee or boss believes that you're only demonstrating your authority when you're shouting at someone and you don't enjoy shouting at people, how will you ever exert your authority?

It matters because women's voices simply aren't being

heard on their own terms. Numerous studies have shown that women are interrupted far more in meetings than men, as well as in the classroom and the doctor's surgery – as a 2004 study from Harvard Law School and a 1998 study by the University of California Santa Cruz demonstrated respectively. And, according to a study by Princeton and Brigham Young University, if women talk 25–50 per cent of the time in a professional meeting, they are seen as 'dominating the conversation'. A 2014 study at George Washington University found that when men were talking with women, they interrupted 33 per cent more often than when they were talking with men. The men interrupted their female conversational partners 2.1 times during a three-minute conversation. That dropped to 1.8 when they spoke to other men.

Similarly, studies show that while men in leadership positions are seen in a positive light when they demonstrate traditionally Alpha leadership traits (so, being decisive, dominating the conversation, being dogged and dogmatic in the pursuit of goals), women who demonstrate traditional Alpha leadership traits are viewed negatively by both men and women. And while men who have a more relaxed or Beta style of management are still seen in a positive light, female Beta managers aren't considered at all – because Beta women can't be managers. But why are we so unwilling to compare the relative merits of different personality types in female managers?

It's simple. It's because until comparatively recently female managers were a rarity (or an oddity, depending on how you want to define it). Relatively speaking, women's mainstream presence in the workplace, particularly our existence in white-collar management positions, is in its infancy. Our fascination with what makes our male boss tick and with how to get the most out of our male employees is long-standing.

If we want to move things on and make proper progress, popular culture is key. The homogeneous nature of female personalities in film and television – especially how they're depicted in the workplace – has a huge impact on how we view women at work.

It's not just about women believing they can do those senior roles that we're always told require a sharp suit and a sharp tongue. It's about our colleagues, bosses and employees, male or female, believing we can too.

Kesstan Blandin is the director of research at the Centre for Applications of Psychology Type, which uses the Myers Briggs Type Indicator (MBTI) as a tool to further our understanding of different personality types. (You know those personality tests you sometimes have to take as part of a job interview? You might well be taking the MBTI.) She agrees that our view of what a good leader looks like is limited, which can leave women feeling boxed in. 'It's true that women [in leadership positions] may be seen more as nasty women, a bitch, that type of thing, and not seen as strong but seen as shrill. And it's both men and women who will judge women like that, so it's a double hit.'

She also explains that our view of an archetypal leader is still severely limited to the Alpha male model. 'The cultural type ideal in America is ESTJ – so an extroverted, sensing, thinking, judging type – and . . . the stereotype or the archetype, is the military general, you know, someone who gets things done, and that's very masculine, very male.'

Blandin goes on to explain that a 'lopsided majority' of leaders in American organisations will have a combination of TJ (thinking, judging) in their personality type – so that's someone who is 'objective and rational in their decision-making. TJ is typically a very decisive style and that's what we like. We like leaders who are very sure of themselves, who are very decisive and very tough and impervious to emotional pleading, because that gets in the way.'

The result is that women are typically viewed as a sidekick to an Alpha male leader – or, as Blandin puts it, 'Women are left in the position of being the type that flatters and supports the leading man.' I interviewed her before the 2016 American election, and she mused on the possibility that those hegemonic views of men and women in leadership positions might shift. If the subsequent results are any sort of bellwether for this (and whether they are or not is subject for debate) then they're not shifting particularly quickly.

But what is it really like to work where there are few other women – and none in a senior position?

Yasmin, twenty-nine, is an engineer, operating in the energy industry. She's worked in power stations, offshore at times, and is currently managing a team of six – five of whom are men, who are older than she is.

'For my entire career I've always been the only or one of the only women sitting in a meeting, or in any situation – so for my trips offshore, I was the only woman there. I make a point of counting how many people are in the room and what the percentage of women is.' One thing that Yasmin notices when she's in a male-dominated environment is the type of language that's used. 'It's very macho and it makes me laugh because I can't take it seriously when people are going "Oh, we've got to put pressure on them," and "We've got to deliver," rather than "What's our aim and how do we help each other get there?"' Yasmin's talking specifically about gender here, but to me she's perfectly described the difference between an Alpha and a Beta in the workplace.

But how much does language matter? Yes, it sounds pretty stupid to talk like you're on Wall Street when you're heading up the accounts department of a paper manufacturer in Kettering, but words are just words, aren't they?

Yasmin thinks it goes far deeper than this: 'When I look at businesses that maybe fail, I blame egos, because you'll have a manager who'll just come out with "We're going to make X amount of money in the next five years," and they'll stick to that because that's what they've said. Then they can't see the truth and back down.'

An environment that's about 'do or die' – even in terms of the language used – quickly becomes one in which mistakes aren't tolerated and lessons aren't learnt. And anyone who's worked in that sort of environment knows how dangerous it can become. 'It makes people not admit that they don't know something,' explains Yasmin. 'And it's a culture of pretending you know what's going on when you might not – and, in fact, a lot of those around you don't know what's going on either. And I don't like that.'

Introducing more women into senior roles doesn't instantly mean that you get a more Beta environment (and plenty of women I've spoken to who work on all-female, but very Alpha, teams admit that this has challenges that aren't dissimilar to the ones Yasmin faces on a male team) but having a more diverse leadership team naturally means you're balancing out dominant personality traits and creating a more balanced environment. Few people would disagree with the idea that collaboration and teamwork are key to a team's or a project's success, yet we're never going to create environments where those two things flourish until we change the template for what strong leadership looks like.

And this stuff will stick eventually. Trying to change the ingrained beliefs of a white, middle-aged, middle-class man who has always done things in a certain way and has no interest in having his worldview challenged may get you nowhere. But what about the guy in his thirties who's got a couple of young daughters and a pretty egalitarian set-up at home?

More nuance around what women in work, women in leadership and good leadership models across both genders look like will benefit everyone – whether you're a Beta bloke who's bored with all the willy-waving you have to do just to get a project signed off, or a young female graduate, who wishes the phrase 'willy-waving' had never been coined.

The vast majority of young men I have worked with, and are friends with, would hate to be accused of being a sexist dinosaur. Admittedly I work in a particularly liberal profession where being right-on is akin to godliness, but how many blokes in their twenties or thirties want to be That Guy at work? The guy female colleagues will avoid in the pub because he's said a few things that make you suspect he doesn't like women. The guy who can't work out why he's the only person on the team who's been sent to 'diversity training' three times in one year.

No one wants to be that guy. He's a throwback that shouldn't exist any more. And when we reach the point where more young men are being managed by smart, capable women and are just as in touch with their Beta side as their female colleagues, That Guy will become extinct. Which means we can all get on with our jobs, minus the pointless noise.

3.

SHOULDER PADS ARE BULLSHIT: ISN'T IT TIME WE
REDEFINED WHAT A SUCCESSFUL WOMAN LOOKS
LIKE?

When I was in my mid-twenties, I was offered a job I was potentially unqualified for. (At the time I assumed I was offered it because of some administrative error and decided to go along with it because I didn't want to stay where I was and . . . why not? Even now I'm not sure why I got it.) Not only did I not know what I was doing, I didn't even really want to be there. I think I thought that accepting the job would force me to become a different type of person – more professional and together. But, as I came to realise, there's nothing about having a panic attack in the second-floor loos on your first day to make you feel the opposite of professional and together.

Almost everyone on the team was older than me and, from what I could tell, a couple had turned my new job down because it was probably going to be a poisoned chalice – or, to use the vernacular, a total ball-ache. I had my first big team meeting about forty-eight hours after I'd started. It was the first time I'd had a team to manage, and I'd been told several times what an unenviable task I had on my hands. Budgets had been slashed, redundancies had been made, audience levels were sinking and several editors had been and gone in quick succession.

My team were crying out for a strong leader who'd turn them into a successful, motivated team working towards a coherent strategy and vision. And in the short term? They probably wanted a desk-thumping, shouty speech from me about how I was going to lead them to victory. And maybe the spectacle of me firing someone on the spot, just to show HOW VERY SERIOUS I was.

I knew I had to knock it out of the park. I had to make them realise I was the boss, that I was going to be their fearless leader, that I was going to take charge and sort stuff out and that I was to be obeyed at all times. In short, it was the most important meeting of my career to date. So I . . . fluffed it.

'This is a new start for everyone,' I began (for fun, I like to imagine that I sound exactly like the Queen at Christmas when I look back now and picture myself giving this speech). 'I know there's been a lot of upheaval in the last year but that's all about to change. [Sound of me unable to catch my breath.] I . . . uh . . . [face goes pink] . . . um . . . [tempo of foot-tapping increases dramatically] . . . aaaaand that's all. Thanks.'

My new team blinked in what certainly felt like total unison, then carried on as though it was a normal meeting, discussing their plans for that week's content (ostensibly pitching ideas to me, but in reality politely informing me of their plans, while I nodded and grinned manically).

I hadn't said anything horrendous, I hadn't lied, over-promised or misled them. I hadn't given away confidential information, pooed myself in fear or cried. I just hadn't done anything else either. And what they wanted from me was something. They wanted me to take the initiative. Or, at the very least, talk about how I was going to take the initiative at some point in the future.

As that meeting drew to a close, my team appeared to assume they were the victims of a cruel practical joke, but they weren't. They were stuck with me and, based on a one-hour meeting with absolutely no self-aggrandising speech, I wasn't up to the job. Because as much as I was confused about what success and successful looked like at that time, my team weren't. I wasn't it.

Because this was real life and not a film, there was no massive resolution. It kind of worked out okay in the end because some people left, and were replaced with a younger team I recruited, who saw me as the boss for that very reason. And I was older and more experienced than them, so of course I was making the decisions – authority is a pretty relative thing, as it turns out.

And when I stopped feeling as if my every move was being second-guessed, I relaxed into the job. I knew the answers to more questions than I didn't, and I stopped being the new girl. But that whole process would have happened in a third of the time if the expectation (mine and the team's) of what a boss should look like had been less rigid. As far as I and they were concerned, I was too young, too nice, too nervous, and I said, 'I don't know' seventy-five times a day. Therefore I was doomed to fail.

Success no longer means following a linear career path. It can be measured by Instagram followers, a banging Etsy store, or the blog you set up on your lunch breaks winning a bunch of awards. Yet our view of what a successful woman looks like remains incredibly rigid. We still expect successful women to dominate the room, the conversation, the meeting. We assume that the women we're hearing about bossing it in all industries must be Alpha because that's the way they're presented to us. Self-promotion comes far less easily to Beta women because we're not hardwired to push ourselves above everyone else, but even the most Beta entrepreneur will know how to compose the perfect rousing Instagram post about living her brand 24/7 or whatever, even if she cringes as she presses send. Because social media, the internet and the technology that have made it possible for us to follow such diverse and individual paths to success have removed so much of the nuance around how we're allowed to present ourselves. Even the most Beta woman can shout about herself in the most Alpha way when she's doing it from behind a screen. The result? The way success is viewed is becoming narrower, more homogeneous, not broader.

We tell young women that they need to become their own personal brands to succeed, to find their niche and learn how to market themselves. But are we teaching them how to lead for the future? How to collaborate, work with others and motivate people? (That is, how to be a good Beta boss.) Everyone is told to be disruptive, to tear up the norm and to lead from the front. But what if that model for success is at odds with your personality? What if disruption makes you anxious? What if you find leading from the front emotionally exhausting? How are you ever supposed to be the best version of yourself? And, crucially, why do we assume that disruption is always the best route to success?

Many of the accepted wisdoms I came out of school with – that vocational degrees aren't as valuable as humanities degrees, that three years at a Russell Group university will set you up with a job for life, that the internet is just a distraction – don't apply any more. So what skills do young women need to make it in the workplace now? And are they being taught them?

There's some pretty compelling evidence to suggest that careers advice to young women (and young people in general) is falling far short of where it needs to be. The 2015 *Scarred For Life?* report for the Young Women's Trust looked at, among other things, young people's experience of careers advice, and found that many of the young women and the organisations they spoke to were 'critical of the advice offered to those under sixteen, and consider that schools have been given an unrealistic challenge'. One government agency was cited in the report as observing, 'In schools we have found that the focus is on moving them [young women] onto anything rather than what they will do as a career.'

Similarly, the think-tank Fabian Society's 2014 report *Out of Sight* looked at what has happened to the fifty thousand or so NEET (Not in Education, Employment or Training) young people who have fallen out of the system. It found that careers advice is now the statutory responsibility of schools, and 'Unfortunately the careers advice in schools is systemically weak.' It points to Ofsted's 2013 report, which stated that just one in five secondary schools were giving their students effective careers advice. The report suggested that young people need careers advice that looks 'further ahead than the next course or year of learning. It is not enough for a young person to be participating in "something" between the ages of 16 and 18; even something for which they have a weak preference or interest. They must be working towards the time when they need to succeed in the competitive jobs market.'

The focus of these reports is young people who aren't necessarily going to university, but with the cost of tuition fees far outstripping what graduates can expect to earn, more young people will flounder for their next move once they've left full-time education. And when the focus seems to be to get young people onto a course – any course – where will they learn what it really takes to succeed in an ever-changing job market?

'The things young people have been told for the past twenty years or so are "Follow your dream, follow your passions. If you don't follow your passions you'll have an unhappy life,"' explains Tania Hummel, the HR consultant and executive coach we met earlier. 'So most of the things people have been told have turned out not to be true – "Go to university, get a degree, get a doctorate, get a great job." It's not happening. The world is changing too fast and the promises that were made are not being fulfilled.'

I take Tania's point – I left full-time education at the beginning of 2005, and everything I learnt seems hilariously obsolete now. But Tania believes that the uncertain nature of the world we're in may work in the Beta's favour. 'When the World Economic Forum wrote about the skills that people will need in the workplace in 2020 compared to 2015, they talked about critical thinking and emotional intelligence, and emotional intelligence was a totally new addition to that list.

'Because, actually, if you're looking at this volatile, complex, ambiguous world, where everything is so unpredictable, the only thing you can do is work on yourself and your own resilience to be able to cope and keep up and roll with the punches.'

Sociologist Dr Pamela Stone agrees that there's a generational shift in our attitudes towards success. 'When you swing away from the baby-boomer generation down through the millennials you do see a gradual moving away from a purely monetary, classic sense of achievement as being status and power and high salaries. You still have those old models in big hierarchical organisations employing lots of people – the IBMs, the big banks and so on. But that's all breaking up as we move to a gig economy [one where people are temporarily contracted to work for organisations for a short period, so essentially self-employed rather than in full-time work]. So when you move to an economy where you don't get jobs for life, there's no track, there's no ladder to climb, there's no natural hierarchy. So it's not surprising to me as a sociologist that millennials are modifying what they call success, because there's no way for them of achieving success according to the old model.'

Writing for Fast Company, LinkedIn's Eddie Vivas believes that the so-called gig economy will soon become . . . life. 'We're about to see more power shift away from companies and into job seekers' hands as technology makes it easier than ever to find or change jobs,' he explains. 'The rise of gig-economy players, like Uber, Lyft and Upwork, is just the latest evidence of a trend that's set to continue, with technology empowering people to take more direct control of their careers and livelihoods – even if the world that it ultimately creates isn't something we'll still call the "gig economy", as though it's something distinct from the job market overall. Because, increasingly, it won't be.'

The Deloitte Global Human Capital Trends report for

2016 found that 42 per cent of US executives expected to use more contingent workers (freelancers, or giggers, if you will) in the next three to five years, and that a third of American workers are freelancers, with that set to increase to 40 per cent by 2020.

The report pointed out that many companies are moving away from a hierarchical organisational structure towards a model where teams come together to tackle a specific project before disbanding again. Which means employers are increasingly looking for freelancers who can demonstrate strong project management and team-working skills.

Plenty of the skill associated with this evolving economy will make easy reading for most Betas – emotional intelligence, the ability to work with different types of people, and to be flexible and pragmatic are classic Beta traits. But in an economy where we're increasingly likely to be working for ourselves and placing increasing value on our personal brand and our ability to self-promote, are we going to become a world of Betas in Alpha clothing?

Maybe so. The report also – unsurprisingly – identifies networking as a key skill to embrace in the gig economy. And Susan Chritton, an executive career coach, also identifies development of your personal brand as one of the key and unavoidable skills required to thrive in the gig economy. 'Having a strong personal brand will serve you well in the gig economy,' she explains, in *Personal Branding for Dummies*. 'Instead of hoping that someone notices you and offers you steady, long-term employment, you must be prepared to take your personal brand on the road and leverage your skills.'

Now, I know plenty of Betas who are also excellent

networkers, but I'm not sure I'd count myself among them. I can do it if I have to, but I have to psych myself up and pretty much pretend to be a different person to resist the almost overwhelming urge to stand in the corner and shove canapés into my mouth until I'm allowed to go home. Basically, I have to be a Beta in Alpha clothing. How very gig economy of me.

But the 'in Alpha clothing' bit is crucial – I still have to play dress up because success still only looks one way. Our world is constantly and quickly changing, yet certain values remain at a premium. And most of us learn that quickly – which is why the way people use social media has almost instinctively shifted in line with this new economy.

Have a quick flick through your Instagram and check out #buildingmyempire: apart from all the motivational memes, it's filled with snapshots of people's lives that demonstrate just how much they're 'bossing it', 'smashing it' or 'nailing it' (pick your favourite). Not shown: when they spent a week staring at a wall because they couldn't work out what to do next, or took on some personal brand unfriendly data-entry work to pay that month's rent, or how much of their new business venture is being funded by their parents. Why don't we see those bits too? Because they don't fit with the tale we're trying to tell.

We're increasingly taught to create a narrative around our careers and our (back to that phrase again) personal brands. You know the adversity-story thing they always do on *The X Factor*? In the last few weeks of the competition, as things start to hot up, they'll introduce a narrative around each of the remaining contestants. The detail is always slightly different, but the gist is the same: something bad happened to them in the past that makes this particular contestant's Personal Journey to the finals more poignant than those of the others. Then they'll talk about How Far They've Come, before cutting to a family member, who confirms that said contestant has indeed Come Far. Finally, the video will cut back to the contestant, who will say, 'This has been a dream come true for me. It's been the journey of a lifetime. I don't know what I'll do if I go home tonight,' before bursting into tears. Rinse and repeat.

There's little variation on this theme, although I remember one year watching a grown man sobbing to camera because he couldn't bear the thought of going back to putting up wedding marquees for a living.

So why do it?

Because we root for people who have a clear story – beat the odds, fight against adversity and win – whether that's presented in a video clip before one goes on stage to belt out a cover version of 'If I Can Turn Back Time', or through a series of motivational Instagram memes. Whether your business is building or blogging, if people root for you and relate to you, they're more likely to support your endeavour.

And all this might feel inauthentic, or like a distraction from the bigger picture or a bit . . . boasty? Immodest? . . . but there's no escaping it. And when everyone else is shouting loudly about their achievements, keeping quiet about yours doesn't make you modest or discreet. It means no one will ever hear about them.

But how do you have any semblance of work/life balance when your work revolves around your personal brand? Emma Gannon has made a career out of her personal brand – and with a blog, book (*Ctrl Alt Delete: How I*

Grew Up Online) and podcast of the same name, she's a poster-child for how success can look in the Noughties. I'd say she was Alpha because her career is so closely tied to who she is. And, given that her personal brand is her career, I'd say, based on what I see on social media, she's never not working. But is that an illusion?

'It definitely looks like I do more work than I am doing in the evenings, because it comes very easily to me now,' she admits. 'I'll do a blog page in half an hour and spend the rest of the evening with my boyfriend. But it probably looks like I've spent the whole night doing something.'

And it's that filter through which we view other people's lives that can alter our perception of what success looks like. Emma certainly works hard, but is the sixteen-year-old girl who follows her and dreams of a similar career getting a true version of her life?

'It's curated. You're not lying but you are leaving stuff out. So you're always telling the truth. I'm presenting the truth at all times, but it's like a sliver of everything. And I do genuinely believe that we have an offline and an online identity now.'

I'm not a sixteen-year-old girl and I should certainly know better, but the issue I've had when comparing myself to colleagues and other women in my industry is that I take the filtered snapshots of their lives as a statement of fact – which means my own work ethic, enthusiasm and, indeed, life come up wanting (and again, yes, I should know better). It makes me feel inadequate and it makes my life seem banal and suburban by comparison. Far from inspiring me, it leaves me feeling that I'm not living my life in the right way. Because, for me, that's another element of what being a successful Alpha woman looks like: being always on, always focused, always thinking about work, 24/7. In my head, this (fictional) success story never wastes twenty minutes gazing out of the window, daydreaming about what she'd wear to collect her Oscar for best screenplay. Ahem.

It takes Emma to remind me that no one's living their role 24/7, even if it appears they are. 'How can you be Alpha and be a human being? Because you can't be Alpha all the time. We're all vulnerable. Like I'm not going to be an Alpha if I go to a grandparent's funeral. You just can't be.'

Emma thinks those days of presenting ourselves as always-on superwomen are over and we're looking for more authenticity in our role models. 'I don't think we respond to Alpha women as much as we used to, maybe. I don't know. I just know that, as a twenty-something, I don't look up to and idolise a career woman who shuts herself off from being authentic. We're used to bloggers and YouTubers and the like who are talking about their depression, or what medication they're on, or how they feel when someone they know has died. We're used to seeing human beings 360, so when you're presented with a 2-D cut-out of someone who's really successful it's like "Well, I can't connect with you."'

'Authenticity' is a word I've been hearing a lot – authenticity is apparently why some YouTube vloggers have reached the stratospheric levels of fame among teenage audiences previously only enjoyed by boy bands. And lack of authenticity is a charge that gets levelled at any person, or brand, who can't connect with their audience. When then Labour leader Ed Miliband was lampooned after being photographed eating a bacon sandwich in the run-up to the 2015 election, it was because no one believed he really *meant* to eat it. Eating a sandwich was seen as a cynical (and failed) stunt and became an emblem of his failure to connect with voters. You may have thought it was impossible to eat a bacon sandwich inauthentically, but you'd be wrong.

Yet when Ed Balls – another Labour politician who inauspiciously lost his job at the 2015 election – agreed to be a contestant on *Strictly Come Dancing*, a gig with arguably more potential for public humiliation than eating a pork-based breakfast staple when there are cameras around, he went from unpopular ex-politician to national treasure. Why? Because he came across as completely authentic. He was a middle-aged man in the aftermath of an enforced career change, trying something new, often failing, but trying nonetheless.

Politicians, individuals and brands know that they need to appear authentic to connect with their audiences, but what they are slower to realise is that you can't stage-manage human connection. 'Being yourself' only works as a selling point if you're not trying. The minute it becomes a conscious effort, you're putting on an act. And people aren't stupid: they notice.

It's the same when you're leading a team. 'Your greatest impact as a person and as a leader is authenticity,' agrees Eddie Erlandson. 'You can't fake it, and if you're a non-Alpha, and you're working around Alphas you may need to adapt your style at times to be effective with Alphas, but it doesn't mean you change.'

Erlandson believes that good leadership is less about Alpha and Beta, and more about specific personality traits – some people are more fine-tuned for it than others. 'I think the good leader is the one that people will follow. If people are not following, and you are not able to generate productivity and output and creativity then you are missing the mark on leadership. The really good leader, in my opinion, is the conscious leader, the one who is self-aware, who is aware of other people, who can basically adapt on the fly to have healthy influence and create healthy account-ability.'

Take this description of working for Jeff Bezos, chairman and CEO of Amazon by Manfred Kets de Vries, a clinical professor of leadership development and organisational change at INSEAD, writing on the INSEAD website: 'Working for Bezos is quite a challenge. He is a typical Alpha male: hardheaded, task-oriented and extremely opin-ionated. He is known to get very upset when things do not go his way, and living up to his excessively high standards can feel like a mission impossible.

'The more pressure Bezos feels to perform, the more his leadership style transforms from being constructive and challenging to intimidating and even abusive. He is known for outbursts of anger when things don't go his way – a consequence of his total commitment to customer service – and for making demoralising statements like, "Why are you wasting my life?", "I'm sorry, did I take my stupid pills today?" or "This document was clearly written by the B team. Can someone get me the A team document?"

'In his dynamic, metrics-driven corporate culture, there is little time for soft talk. He is even known to walk away from meetings if people do not get to the point quickly. Faced with this Alpha-male behaviour, people who work for him do so in constant fear. While this Darwinian-like, performance-based culture reaps benefits for Amazon's customers, it comes at the price of a devalued and demoralised workforce.'

Kets de Vries points out that although Alpha leaders often possess a huge amount of drive and passion, it can be accompanied by a fatal flaw – narcissism means they are often unable to recognise their own limits, so when the pressure on them increases, their leadership style can go from constructive and challenging to intimidating and even abusive. 'Not surprisingly given their dysfunctional behaviour,' he concludes, 'companies run by destructive Alphas can easily go down the drain.'

And when it does go wrong? It's time for a change of management style, as Tania Hummel explains: 'For some reason it would appear that most companies hire women when things are going wrong and they hire men when things are going right. I would speculate that this is because women would be more likely to bring people together, to be a reassuring presence and to be more cautious when times are difficult.'

Actual success is far more difficult to quantify than we pretend, but if you're looking for it from a bloke in a suit shouting in a boardroom, you might be looking in the wrong place.

In the Introduction, I described what I imagine when I think about Alpha Woman as a person – she's successful and perhaps a little intimidating, yes, but she's still human. We can all identify her because we've all worked with someone like her.

But imagine if you had to personify female success itself: what would that look like? Again, she's probably tall, white, middle class, university-educated, perfectly dressed, well-groomed and articulate. She's also decisive, focused and driven. Are her team scared of her and her peers in awe of her? Is she always prepared, never caught out, unafraid of confrontation and never without her blow-dry?

Of course she is. She's Alpha Woman, and she's nowhere near as much fun at parties as the Cool Girl identified by Gillian Flynn's *Gone Girl*, described perfectly by protagonist Amy:

> Men always say that as the defining compliment, don't they? She's a cool girl. Being the Cool Girl means I am a hot, brilliant, funny woman who adores football, poker, dirty jokes, and burping, who plays video games, drinks cheap beer, loves threesomes and anal sex, and jams hot dogs and hamburgers into her mouth like she's hosting the world's biggest culinary gang bang while somehow maintaining a size 2, because Cool Girls are above all hot. Hot and understanding. Cool Girls never get angry; they only smile in a chagrined, loving manner and let their men do whatever they want. Go ahead, shit on me, I don't mind, I'm the Cool Girl.

But the point is, Cool Girl isn't real, as Amy explains: 'Men actually think this girl exists. Maybe they're fooled because so many women are willing to pretend to be this girl.'

And it's the same thing here: Alpha Woman – as in the embodiment of what we see female success to be – is just as much a work of fiction. Most of us could pretend to be her if we really wanted to – a shameless deployment of Instagram, a healthy dose of narcissism and a little creative licence will do it. But it isn't real and it isn't what success is. Success is whatever gets you out of bed and into work in the morning – whether that's a creative passion, the desire to see the job through or just the knowledge that you'll pay your rent this month. You haven't failed if you haven't met a series of arbitrary requirements that have no bearing on your actual life, and the very fact that we're telling ourselves that we have, day in day out, is total nonsense.

So let's lift the curtain and start giving ourselves a pat on the back for our actual success and stop thinking about our perceived failures. (Got that very boring PowerPoint done for your boss? Hurrah, give yourself a pat on the back and bask in the warm glow you get only when you complete a task well and on deadline. Exceeded expectations in all sections of your annual review this year? Make yourself a cup of tea and text your mum to celebrate! You deserve it!)

Success is about what we have done and what we can do. It's about achievements. It's not about image and it's not about how many things you can cram into every given day. If you want to see what successful looks like, get off social media and look in the mirror.

4.

FAKE IT TILL YOU MAKE IT? WHY YOUR ONLINE
SELF IS TROLLING YOUR IRL SELF

I remember the first time I was interviewed for a Saturday job. I was sixteen and had seen an advert in the paper that said the picture-framers around the corner from my parents' house in Harrow wanted someone who could help out on a Saturday. I assumed it would involve ringing stuff up on the cash register, finding people's orders, that sort of thing. It quickly transpired that they were after something a bit more involved – someone who could advise clients on mountings and frames for their pictures. They'd need to demonstrate that they had 'an eye'. Suffice to say, I don't. I harbour no secret desire to become an artist. Nor do I believe I'd make a great interior designer in another life. I could work out a 20 per cent sale discount on a watercolour from a local artist and ring it through the till, no problem. But advise on the best border to go with a specific frame? Absolutely not.

So, over the course of a twenty-minute interview, the job went from something I could do in a heartbeat to wildly out of my comfort zone. For the first time I experienced what's now an all too familiar feeling: that I was a fraud who really shouldn't be there. Or, at least, I'd become a fraud if I were to maintain the fiction that I was a competent person who knew what they were doing (albeit within the very specific realms of framing mediocre watercolours for the residents of Harrow).

I said as much to the manager of the shop. (Actually, I whispered it, complete with a stutter and a red-hot face, and I didn't mention the mediocre part.) He looked a little confused, then disappointed, and said, 'I really don't understand you. You've instantly gone from seeming incredibly confident and competent to really nervous and young.' I think what he was getting at was . . . Couldn't I have just faked it? I didn't know what I was doing, but I'd have worked it out eventually, and I certainly wouldn't have done an absolutely horrible job. But, actually, at that first interview I developed a pattern that has followed me round for most of my working life. When I know that I know something, I'm fine. But the minute I'm unsure, or I think someone else knows more than I do, I'm plagued with self-doubt. With that Saturday job, the minute I realised there would be someone else out there who would do a better job than me, I didn't want it. Because what I hadn't worked out, aged sixteen, is that most people are faking it a lot of the time – and some people are faking it all of the time. No one is the perfect fit for the job they're in, knows what they're doing all of the time, or feels comfortable in every situation. The difference between an Alpha and a Beta is that an Alpha would never not fake it.

But working that one out – and this is no exaggeration – has been one of the most important lessons of my career to date. For one thing, it meant I stopped looking like a terrified teenager every time I was asked something I didn't understand. 'Fake it till you make it' is the philosophy of one of my favourite ever bosses (a true Alpha, in case you're wondering). And although I still think pretending to be someone you're not for great swathes of time is the stuff of nightmares, there's something strangely liberating about the discovery that everyone is putting it on, and that you're basically operating in a carefully constructed skit. It's like imagining the audience members of your public-speaking engagement are all naked – but for life.

There are two dangers. The first, of course, comes when we forget that everyone else is faking it, and when we start to take all the posturing seriously and try to match up to it. Second, faking self-confidence in a meeting when you're nervous is a very different proposition from being totally inauthentic all of the time. The latter – I believe – can make us really very unhappy. But more on that later.

While I may have failed in my first attempt at faking it, back in 1999, I'm a veritable pro now, in that, like most of you, I'll probably fake it several times a week. With a lightly filtered Instagram post cropping out the dirty plates or pile of boxes in the background. Or a tweet about a huge work achievement without mentioning that getting said work achievement out of the door nearly made me cry from tiredness and anxiety. Life is never easy or effort-less, and it's probably not meant to be, so why do we continue to propagate the myth that we're having a great time, even when we've got period pains, a cold and we're four days late paying our rent?

The self-discrepancy theory was developed by E. Tory Higgins in 1987 (before Instagram was barely a glimmer in someone's eye), and it looks at the discrepancy between our different selves. Our actual self – who we actually are, our ideal self – the person we want to be, and our ought self, which is our understanding of what others want us to be. The self-discrepancy theory looks at what happens when our ideal and ought selves don't match up with our actual self. In short, it results in psychological and emotional turmoil. When we don't match up with our ideal self we feel disappointed, sad or despondent because we aren't the version of our self we want to be. When we don't match up with our ought self we feel agitated, guilty, distressed and anxious because we feel as if we have violated some perceived standard we should be living up to.

So, my ideal self may be a version of me who organises my outfits for the week and makes lunches on a Sunday night (instead of spending all my money in Pret), and has a handbag that isn't covered with ink and full of fluff-covered cashew nuts. I'd probably go to the gym more often, have shinier hair and drink less too. These are all achievable things that I feel better about when I achieve them but don't cause me particular levels of anxiety when I can't.

My ought self is someone who shows impeccable judgement, makes decisions quickly and brilliantly, is slightly scary but also well respected. She is fine with confrontation and happy to tell people what they don't want to hear. She never puts being liked above getting the job done. These are all things I think I should do, and ways I think I should be, and I feel guilty and anxious when I don't live up to them. And, of course, I don't live up to them because they're not who I actually am. They're benchmarks of a standard I feel I should live up to.

Social psychologist Ben Voyer also believes we use social media to try to reconcile these different senses of self – further complicating what actually makes it onto our social-media output: 'Individuals are consistently torn between their actual, desired and ought selves, and use social media to try to reconcile these – or sometimes to construct what they think would be the best possible "ideal self".'

And let's not forget that we're naturally performative creatures – the act of playing a part is one that comes naturally to us, and long predates Twitter and Facebook. 'The American sociologist Erving Goffman introduced in the 1950s a difference between what he called a "public self" and a "private self",' explains Professor Voyer. 'The private self is a self that we keep for ourselves, and maybe close others and relatives. The public self is a self that we manage and shape so that it conforms to what we want others to think we are. Goffman's approach is known as a "dramaturgical approach," meaning that he suggests that individuals are "actors" of their own lives. We now increasingly "stage" our lives online.'

But what happens when we're constantly playing a role in our own lives? Social media is regularly blamed for rising levels of anxiety and depression – and maybe this is why. We exist in a world where we're trying to live up to a perceived standard set by whomever we happen to follow on social media. Meanwhile we're constantly pushing an 'ideal' version of ourselves out there, which means that, at the same time, we're probably distorting the standard by which other people feel they should be living their lives.

If you've ever felt a twinge of jealousy, FOMO, or indeed guilt at someone else's perfectly curated Instagram post, a bit sad about your jacket-potato dinner because it looks like crap, even with the Clarendon filter, or faked an early-morning gym-class post (disclaimer: I've done all of the above), you'll know what I'm talking about.

Writer Daisy Buchanan agrees that the way we communicate on social media is fuelling a pursuit of perfection we'll never live up to. 'We cannot underestimate how much social media has changed things and how the meaning of perfect has changed, and perfect has become impossible; but we're still doing it, we're still flinging ourselves into the fray. "Goals" has become the hashtag of the decade; and it's become meaningless because we never stop to celebrate, it's always – what's the next goal?'

Ah #goals. Work #goals, life #goals, friendship #goals – all new arbitrary benchmarks to set ourselves based on someone else's (probably fairly inaccurate) social-media output to make ourselves feel guilty about something else we haven't done.

And it's making us feel bad. Anxiety and depression among young women are on the rise: a 2016 NHS study found that 12.6 per cent of women aged 16–24 screen positive for post-traumatic stress disorder; 26 per cent of women of the same age had anxiety, depression, panic disorders, phobias or obsessive compulsive disorder. Sally McManus, the lead researcher on the survey, said at the time that social media was a likely factor: 'This is the age of social-media ubiquity. This is the context that young women are coming into and it warrants further research.'

Another study by the University of Copenhagen suggests that too much Facebook browsing at Christmas specifically can make you miserable – because seeing other people's apparently perfect families can have that effect. Researchers warn of a 'deterioration of mood' from spending too long looking at other people's social-media stories, sparked by 'unrealistic social expectations'.

And the more our working lives become intertwined with the rest of our lives, the harder it is to resist the feeling that we're not quite nailing it at work. That we're not pulling enough late nights, not networking right, that our desks don't pass the Instagram test. (Incidentally, mine very much does not. Last year I discovered a mouse colony living in the empty cardboard boxes, with the bag of sunflower seeds and old gym towel under my desk. Turns out that the strange smell that had been emanating from my corner of the office was mouse urine. I did not put *this* on social media.)

I only realised how much I marked my own success by external factors rather than what I'm actually achieving at work when I was bemoaning my relative lack of success to my boyfriend. He asked me how my success was measured by my boss, and by the company I work for. By any measure I was achieving what I needed to, but because I didn't think I 'looked' or 'acted' like the right sort of success, I felt a failure.

Ironically, the bigger the gap between our actual self and our ought self, the less likely we are to achieve anything. Studies show that those with high levels of actual–ought discrepancy show the highest levels of procrastination.

When you think about it, that makes sense. Our ideal self is focused on achievement and successful goal pursuit; our ought self is about avoiding harm and not doing something bad. When our attitude to other people's social-media output starts to feed into our ought self, the entire interaction becomes negative, based on guilt and anxiety.

'The way we are is influenced by millions of other fake selves that we interact with constantly,' agrees Daisy. 'Sometimes I think I can type faster than I can articulate something. I never say, "Um, well, you know . . ." on Twitter whereas that makes up most of my actual conversation.'

So what's the answer? And if the life advice to live by is always to present a true version of yourself on social media, is that even possible?

For writer Laura Jane Williams, who wrote a personal memoir called *Becoming*, authenticity in her social-media output is important. 'The biggest compliment someone can pay me is when they say, "I follow you on Instagram and you're exactly how I thought you'd be in real life. I pride myself on that. I feel like a very responsible social-media user."'

But when Laura was diagnosed with depression and anxiety, shortly before the release of her second book, she discovered just how quickly and easily people make assumptions about you based on your output at any given moment: 'I'd released an e-book the year before last called *The Book of the Brave* . . . and this person said to me, "I just never thought you'd get depression after writing something like that."

'I thought, Oh, my God, this person thinks I sold a mistruth when I wrote this book about being brave and bold. And actually that was so, so true in that moment, and now my moment is raw and sad and blue and I'm documenting that in a different way and it's all about who I am, but you can't communicate those things all at once in what is essentially a two-dimensional medium.'

Because human beings are complex and complicated, when we present ourselves as one thing (Happy! Successful! Bored! Lonely!), which may be completely true in that moment, we forget that although we may have moved on to something else in the next instant, the snapshot we presented is what other people will see and remember. People – naturally – make assumptions about each other based on the information they have and, with the best will in the world, a ten-minute conversation face-to-face still reveals more about our true selves than a social-media post ever could. It's not that we're faking it or being fake online, it's just that it's only part of the story. Yet it's often the only part of the story we see.

Blogger and writer Emma Gannon believes that you can't fake the authenticity of someone who is truly happy in their skin, no matter how many filters you use. 'I believe in faking it until you're making it. I think when you get more relaxed, genuinely happy in yourself and in your career, there's no need to fake it any more. I've seen that in myself, and I've seen it in people I admire.'

But I still feel there are huge, crashing limits to how authentic anyone can be online because it's still a controlled image. It's who we want to be in that moment, not who we are.

And we can't even necessarily make the distinction ourselves. Studies show that we don't always have the self-awareness to know when we're posting a photo for validation rather than just for fun (although, seriously, when was the last time you posted anything and could convince yourself it was 'just for fun' and not for the associated validation?). Which makes it difficult to gauge how much we rely on the validation we receive from likes, retweets, comments and posts to give us a sense of self. How often do you stop to consider your motivation before posting a picture on Instagram or sending a Snapchat?

Take, for example, the evolution of the selfie. I've never liked photos of myself because, apart from anything else, they don't represent how I see myself in the mirror. A static image is obviously different from a moving one, and in the mirror my face is reversed. But this is how I see myself, and when I discover that other people see me differently, it makes me uncomfortable. But I'm much happier with a picture I've taken on my phone into a mirror. Why? Because it comes closer to representing how I think I look (never mind that this is further away from how I actually look – 'actually' isn't the point). Selfies give us a unique opportunity to control our image – and if these heavily edited, flatteringly posed, lit and filtered pictures are the only version of ourselves that people see, then that becomes what we look like. To our followers, that is reality.

Which actually feeds into another school of thought: maybe the idea that the people who appear the most successful, who have the most perfectly created lives *are* the most successful, is an illusion. Maybe it's the exact opposite: that those who are shouting the loudest may be faking it most. I asked Daisy Buchanan what she thought of people who posted about their early-morning gym classes before heading off to their high-powered jobs. (For some reason, it's this particular combination that really gets to me – I could probably, at a push, get up and go to the gym super-early if I had to. I could do a full day in the office, then an event in the evening, but I've never been together enough to do all three in one day. Apart from anything else, I wouldn't remember to pack enough pairs of pants.)

As Daisy points out, intention with that sort of online posturing is crucial. 'So much depends on attitude. If I got up at 4 a.m. to go to the gym, but did so because I was sad and I felt insecure about my body, and I found it a very difficult experience, then that would feel like quite a Beta thing to do.'

And, of course, we can never know someone's true intention or the full story behind how someone chooses to present themselves online. And, as we've already seen, the reasons behind why someone chooses to behave in a certain way on social media are far too complex to second-guess. The early-morning spinning-class picture could represent a massive sense of achievement, a massive feeling of stress, or a torn hamstring, we just don't know.

A friend and I were recently discussing a party she had gone to and I had skipped in favour of a night in the local pub. The party looked insanely cool and hipstery on Instagram, and played a massive part in my Sunday morning, guilty-hung-over FOMO. ('What's the point of getting trashed and having a hangover if you're not at a party like that?' was my general thinking.)

It turned out the party was horrible: the drinks were too expensive, everyone was really obnoxious, and they all fell out, which meant groups of people were huddled in various corners of the room, crying or throwing vitriolic glances at each other. Of course, I wouldn't have known this because, to give the impression that they were HAVING A GREAT TIME, everyone came together for the obligatory group selfies halfway through the night, then skulked back to their respective corners. I know, mental.

Basically, the only authenticity or truth you can get from

most people's social-media output is how much time and energy they're willing to put into curating it.

But what if you have no social-media output? Is that the mark of an ultimate Alpha?

Or put it this way: a lot of what I imagine to be my most Beta traits probably stem from my adjusting my behaviour or decision-making to keep other people happy – to ensure they like me. So: what's the difference between me taking on work that probably isn't mine to keep the peace and avoid confrontation, and sharing or liking a cringy aphorism on Instagram posted by someone you admire? And what's the difference between a self-deprecating 'Aren't I scatty?' Facebook post and me telling a self-deprecating 'Aren't I scatty?' story in real life – when I'll probably exaggerate my own stupidity and ignore the fact that 80 per cent of the time I'm not particularly scatty at all?

I always think a true Alpha IRL is someone who ploughs their own furrow, irrespective of other people's opinions (they rarely ask for them). Surely in Social Media Land, this becomes someone who doesn't think twice about retweets, comments or their social reach. Perhaps opting out of all media where you're expected to project a version of yourself to other people for scrutiny, judgement and approval (because, at its heart, that's what the majority of social-media interaction is) is the truest sign there is of someone who is genuinely comfortable in their own skin and totally self-possessed. Actually, that's a level of high Alpha-ness I could genuinely aspire to.

'I've definitely become more independent in how I think about things and how I conduct myself, which was kind of the point,' explains Rachel, a thirty-four-year-old teacher, who deleted her Instagram, Facebook and Twitter accounts when she realised just how much they were impacting on her decisions and thought patterns. 'Instagram was the worst, because it was affecting what I wore, the decisions I made about which parties to go to, the kind of friends I hung out with.

'I've always prided myself on being a really independent thinker, but there's such a sheep-like quality to how we behave on social media that even when someone is posting something that's meant to demonstrate how quirky or individual they are, it's really just a reflection of what they think other quirky or individual people are doing.'

And now she's gone social-media cold turkey? 'It's that massive cliché but I definitely feel more present in the moment. I hadn't realised how much I'd stopped making decisions about what I wanted based on what was happening in my actual life as opposed to my virtual world. I'm sure some people can separate out the two consciously, but I don't think I'm one of them.'

The focus might be on Facebook when it comes to how we disseminate and share news, and distinguish fact from fiction, but I really believe that the insidious ways in which Instagram now influences our behaviour are becoming far more ingrained – and sinister because we don't realise it's happening.

Look at the beauty industry: sales for contouring kits, foundations and illuminators designed to give you the perfect selfie-ready face have shot up in the last few years, and while it was estimated that in the UK we took 1.2 billion selfies in 2014, the earned media value (EMV) for brands and influencers across different platforms found the EMV for Instagram had increased more than nine-fold from 2014 to 2015, according to digital marketers Tribe Dynamics. This is compared to 26 per cent for blogs.

I think the specific problem with Instagram is that compared to, say, Facebook, which your mum is on, posting twenty-three pictures from your nan's seventy-fifth birthday party, it is designed to promote a snapshot or a single moment. Even if that moment is true for just the next thirty seconds, it quickly becomes part of your past – but for the person looking at it, liking it, chewing their lip in anxiety because they're not having as much fun or aren't as thin, it's the present.

When Essena O'Neill, an Australian teenager with half a million Instagram followers, loudly announced in 2015 that she was quitting Instagram, she described the platform as 'contrived perfection made to get attention'. 'I remember I obsessively checked the like count for a full week since uploading it,' she wrote at the time, on her first ever post. 'It got five likes. This was when I was so hungry for social-media validation . . . Now marks the day I quit all social media and focus on real-life projects.'

But it's not just teenagers, it's all of us. It's lawyers, doctors, engineers in their twenties, thirties, forties and beyond. We're all buying into it and we're all left wanting. And how we are at work – how successful, organised, passionate – has become as big a part of that fiction as how we look in a bikini or how many squats we managed that day.

I mean, I'm not sure if, in the twenty-first century Western world, being truly comfortable with your sense of self, relationships and environment is even possible. But if it is, isn't that a true Alpha Nirvana we could all work towards? And if that is the case, surely any concern about how you're projecting yourself to others (which is 95 per cent of most people's social-media output) is a total anathema.

Working out that everyone is faking it was one of the best things I've ever done. Learning to stop faking it is something I'm still working on. Authenticity – the buzzword *du jour* – should be easy. Just be yourself, right? But the reality is, it's harder than ever.

I wrote this book to try to work out if and articulate how you can be just as successful in the workplace if you're a Beta woman as you could be as an Alpha woman. And to do that we have to look at the bars against which we all measure ourselves. Some are the standards set by our employers or potential employers, but many are the standards we set for ourselves and others. And as much as social media is, on the face of it, a place to celebrate individuality, most of us are still marching to a fairly homogeneous tune in terms of how we measure and celebrate female success.

And that is why Betas need to write their own tune. We could all spend years on Instagram, ruminating on other people's apparent success and how we fall short in comparison. But focusing on what success looks like for us IRL, and striving for it, sounds far more satisfying and fruitful to me.

5.

BETA OR LAZY? UNRAVELLING MY IMPOSTOR SYNDROME

Every negative moment in my career has one common thread: an overriding belief that I don't belong in that role, that I'm not good enough and never should have been given the job in the first place. As part of my first job, for that small agency in south London, I ended up covering a maternity leave after someone else had dropped out suddenly. It was a big promotion to editor, but in reality I'd been doing the job unofficially for months without a problem. But that was because I knew I was helping out as a favour, rather than doing the job for real, which meant I was happy and confident that I was doing well. The minute I was given the editing job that changed.

It was a tricky gig, involving lots of late nights, constant pressure and difficult clients, who wanted constant assurance that they were getting value for money. They wanted to know they were getting a proper editor, not an editorial assistant who'd been given a new job title.

And that was the problem. The more the pressure was piled on, and the harder it got, the more I started to agree with their assessment that I was absolutely useless. Producing the magazine was the easy part – we had a fantastic team and everyone knew what they were doing – but dealing with the client was a whole other ball game.

Yes, they were demanding, but so were most clients, and

they were by no means impossible. And, anyway, I'd worked with them for years before that without incident. But I became so convinced of and consumed by my own ineptitude that every change they wanted to make felt like a criticism of me personally. And every time they challenged me (in hindsight they were trying to get the measure of me) I crumbled. It wasn't that I couldn't do or wasn't doing the job, it was that my belief that I was the wrong person to be there became so overwhelming that it was all I let other people see.

It was almost like the opposite of 'Fake it till you make it.' I couldn't project any measure of confidence or competence lest people get the wrong impression of me. If I acted like I didn't know what I was doing, at least people would be pleasantly surprised if I came good. And if I messed up? At least I could say, 'I told you so.'

I've made a conscious effort to change how I project myself as I've got older. (I don't think I've got it nailed: I still frequently feel like the least competent, least serious and least grown-up person in the room, and it probably shows.) And it's not necessarily that I've got better at hiding it when I'm terrified or out of my depth. It's more that I've realised that messing up, getting things wrong and not knowing the answers are a fact of life, not a mark of incompetence. I've become less scared of failure, which has made the thought of failing less scary. And, crucially, I've stopped thinking that making a mistake or not knowing something automatically means I shouldn't be doing my job or that I'm a fraud. It's called Impostor Syndrome and we all get it (although the jury is out on whether women get it more than men). If you're a Beta woman in the workplace, I'm guessing it has had a marked impact on your career.

Impostor Syndrome was first recognised in 1978 by Georgia State University when academics realised that successful women had high levels of self-doubt. It can be defined as 'a psychological phenomenon in which people are unable to internalise their accomplishments. Despite external evidence of their competence, those with the syndrome remain convinced that they are frauds and do not deserve the success they have achieved.' So that'll be me, then.

Naomi, thirty-three, is a project manager in the construction industry. In her experience, Impostor Syndrome is a uniquely female phenomenon, which she particularly noted working in her male-dominated industry. 'I have rarely met a man at work who struggles with confidence or a sense of belonging, but I have met a lot of women who do. We feel out of place in an environment that is not designed for us, or led by us. Having worked in construction for six years I have seen how intimidating male-dominated environments can be. Men and women are also motivated differently, and I think we seek external praise more often than men do.'

It's certainly something she's experienced: 'Despite years of project-management experience, and proven delivery, I struggle to believe that I am the right person for a job. I often fear that I'm about to be tapped on the shoulder and told, "it's okay. We know you don't know anything. You can go home now!" And this is despite getting nothing but positive feedback in every job I've ever had.'

Now, I'm not a perfectionist in the classic sense. My

approach to most projects could charitably be described as having a 'helicopter view' – I'm great with big ideas, but get a little bored when it comes to the detail and final execution. I'm also generally happy to let smaller stuff go, even if it's not quite right – I'd always rather get it done than get it perfect. But that's okay – I try to work with people who are more detail-oriented and, between us, we tend to get the job done. But I do set insanely high demands on my own time – the number of things I want to get done in any given day is always a stretch target, and I always feel like I'm a disaster when, inevitably, I don't get through everything on my to-do list. I feel that, if I'm not constantly busy and constantly productive, I'm failing. I only have two settings: total success or total failure. Which means, if I'm not 100 per cent nailing it (and, let's face it, who's doing that all of the time?), I feel as if I shouldn't be there.

I'm not alone: Sheryl Sandberg, Facebook's COO, has said, 'There are still days when I wake up feeling like a fraud, not sure I should be where I am.' Actress and UN ambassador Emma Watson and actress Kate Winslet have admitted to suffering from Impostor Syndrome, while writer Maya Angelou once said, 'I have written eleven books, but each time I think, Uh-oh, they're going to find out now.' If those women are getting Impostor Syndrome, then it's probably okay if you or I are too.

The problem with Impostor Syndrome is that it doesn't push us to be better. Instead it makes us crave anonymity. A study by Ghent University has found that, rather than working harder to prove their abilities, sufferers bury themselves in their tasks and avoid extra responsibilities, becoming trapped in an 'impostor cycle'.

When I look back to that job where I was suddenly made editor, this resonates. It wasn't that I simply felt I didn't deserve to be there, it was that the Impostor Syndrome fed on itself, making me smaller, more cautious and more timid. Every day became about survival, not getting found out, rather than doing more, or doing things better. It wasn't about winning praise, accolades or awards or doing a good job. It was about keeping my head down and not being found out for the fraud I felt like.

Some studies demonstrate that Impostor Syndrome increases when women begin comparing themselves to their high-achieving female colleagues. In a 2013 study US sociologists Jessica Collett and Jade Avelis investigated why so many female academics ended up 'downshifting' – switching path from a high-status tenured post to something less ambitious. Impostorism was to blame, but studies also revealed that when institutions match younger women with high-ranking female academics to try to counter this, it had the opposite effect. Those high-ranking academics made the younger women feel like impostors, who would always fall short in comparison to such superwomen.

The irony here is that those superwomen probably experienced plenty of their own impostorism, but because we can only ever compare our own inner world with other people's outer world, we never get the inside track on their insecurities. The reality is, only absolute idiots never feel like an impostor or a fraud, but because Impostor Syndrome is insidious and generates such introversion ('I'm not meant to be here, but the worst thing would be if anyone found out. Therefore the most important thing is to keep my head down and hope no one does' no one ever talks about it. So our 'superwoman' boss or colleague, who appears super-competent, organised and collected may be making us feel like a fraud, but she's probably battling all of the same thoughts and feelings (irony of ironies, maybe about you) and doesn't feel she can talk about it.

I can see why this is: the idea of the career superwoman is still so prized that when she appears before us ticking all those boxes (efficient, decisive, composed, stylish, swishy hair), she takes on a deity-like status – something 'other' that we mere mortals could never live up to. Until you find out she's no more of a deity than Beyoncé, and thinks the same about you.

Perspective helps a little – some of the women I thought were the very epitome of unattainable collected profession-alism at the start of my career have since shared stories of the chaos that surrounded their personal and professional lives in their twenties and thirties. Stories that I never would have guessed at when I was starting out – they were my scary boss-ladies, who never made mistakes. Until they did.

I'm pretty sure that to some of the women (and men) who worked for my mum, she was the scary boss-lady. Apart from everything I've heard anecdotally (including several of her former colleagues and employees saying she was 'amazing but intimidating'), I can imagine how her prodigious work ethic and insane levels of organisation would have made me feel as a young woman working for her. Like a massive impostor.

But, in reality, no one I've spoken to has been able to describe having Impostor Syndrome as well as my mum could because, over the course of her forty-year career, she had it in spades.

'Throughout my career, I often had the sense of being an impostor, who was not good enough for the job, and that one day I would be "found out",' she told me. 'At one point in my career, I was working as head of investor relations for a major utility company and this lack of belief in my credentials for the role led me to undertake a master's degree in finance, to better equip me for the job.'

And does she believe it's a uniquely female trait?

She's not so sure. 'I've always worked in male-dominated sectors, but the women I've worked alongside – particularly those in senior roles – seemed comfortable in their roles, with good self-esteem. If anything, I felt like the exception. I think class can play a role. I suspect that Impostor Syndrome doesn't affect too many privately educated middle-class men or women, in whom a particular sense of entitlement and self-confidence has been instilled from an early age.'

I suspect she's right. But also my mum's assessment that most of her colleagues seemed comfortable in their roles highlights just how insidious Impostor Syndrome is: how could she have known? After all, I'm sure my mother will have projected an air of total confidence to her colleagues, so who knows how many of them also secretly felt they were winging it?

As I've already said, the only people who never feel impostorism are probably total idiots and, to an extent, I can see how a modicum of it could be a good thing. It's certainly kept me on my toes and stopped me getting complacent about my job. But it's also held me back because it's encouraged me to spend more time comparing myself to other people than focusing on the task at hand.

There's nothing like a good dose of Impostor Syndrome to stifle productivity and creativity. Time spent in a meeting sulkily contemplating how Susan from Marketing had that really great idea that you really should have come up with isn't time well spent. It's also held me back in all the projects or jobs I haven't gone for. All the times I haven't put myself forward for a promotion and all the times I've procrastinated so long about deciding on a job that I've taken myself out of the running. To some people, feeling out of your depth is a challenge to be grasped with both hands. To me, it's the worst feeling in the world and something to be avoided.

The link between my Impostor Syndrome and my Beta-ness is complex. On one hand, many of the Alpha women I spoke to talked about feeling like a fraud if they didn't meet the impossibly high standards they'd set themselves – the fact that they were Alpha didn't stop them having Impostor Syndrome. It fuelled it.

But if Impostor Syndrome has held me back, how much has being a Beta done so? What if I'm worse at my job in some ways because of certain aspects of my personality?

I've talked about the positive traits of being a Beta boss, but what about the toxic elements of Beta-ness? Does my laid-back attitude equal sloppiness? I don't enjoy confrontation, but does this mean I don't push my team enough to do the best job they can, or that I don't stand up for myself enough? I've certainly been told that I need to be 'more of a diva' to fight for what my team and I need from other departments, and I'm sure that's just one of many ways that my turning on more Alpha would make me better at my job.

Just as not all bosses have to be Alpha, Beta doesn't automatically mean better. It's about balance, and I can't say I always get there.

For example, I very much believe that a role will shrink or expand to fit the person inhabiting it. Injecting a certain amount of ego into your interactions, pushing boundaries and taking on more work, you can make your role and yourself far more significant than someone who does the job asked of them but doesn't look beyond it. This is especially so when you work in an industry with ill-defined job titles or boundaries.

I sometimes wonder if the role I'm in becomes smaller for having me in it. An element of that is probably because my ego doesn't get too involved. Maybe you need ego, drive and single-minded determination to move things along. That doesn't mean we all have to be like that all of the time, but surely if embracing a more Alpha outlook from time to time will help me see a project through to its final conclusion, or deal with a difficult team member, then I should do it. As for shouting louder, getting noticed, making things all about me, it might make me cringe, I might be at odds with my very Beta sensibility that you shouldn't make a fuss or shout about your achievements or take credit for anything you ever do . . . but it's just good PR, isn't it?

We can get bogged down with all the things that may be wrong with an Alpha boss. The dogmatism, the temper tantrums, the penchant for self-promotion above all else can be a nightmare when you're working for a nightmare. But the right Alpha, who is emotionally intelligent and mindful, can be a spectacular and inspiring boss. In fact, as a Beta who is incredibly comfortable with being told what to do, I've loved working for Alpha women because I've always felt they inspire and drive people in a way that I may not always manage.

Eddie Erlandson agrees that it's important to get out of the mindset that an Alpha boss is automatically a 'bad boss'. 'These are people who get things done, they have many, many, many strengths and they have a few "underbellies", as we say – a few weaknesses.' And, crucially, Alphas have a dynamism that, if channelled in the right way, can be really powerful. 'One thing I love about Alphas is, if they want to change, they can do it overnight,' Erlandson goes on. 'They can be stubborn and they can be difficult to work with, but when they decide they're going to shift something, either in themselves or in their behaviour, they do it, whether they're male or female. That's what I love about working with them.'

Maybe it is a fundamental personality trait – I always feel that being constantly Alpha would involve a huge reserve of energy that I don't have. And maybe if it feels exhausting and like an act I shouldn't be doing it. But what if that's a cop-out? What if my Impostor Syndrome is actually the impostor here?

And rather than dressing it up as a cute or endearing character trait, or a blueprint for great future leaders, is it possible that Beta-ness (specifically my Beta-ness) comes from laziness? What if my desire to be liked is greater than my desire to do my job to the best of my abilities? What if I'm opting out just because I can?

I don't *think* I am, but it's something worth considering

– not least because the amount of privilege attached to my potential professional laziness is huge.

Maybe being 'not Alpha' is a choice – it's me opting out of the hard stuff other people have to do every day at work. The difficult decisions, difficult conversations, working ultra-hard and risking being disliked because it's the right thing to do. Maybe I prize too much being liked above being right.

And that applies to all life, not just work. 'But don't you ever just want to stay in bed?' I asked Jemma, who used to work for me, when we were talking about her seemingly endless energy, her desire to do and see everything.

Her answer cut short my certainty that a four-hour lie-in is the best place to be on a Saturday morning. 'We're in such a place of privilege and I have so much life for the taking that why would I not go and take it?' she asked. 'So, I could stay in bed until eleven a.m., or I could get up at seven and go to some incredible spinning class and an amazing brunch with interesting people.

'I love bed, but I feel that bed is an opportunity that everyone has, whereas I have the privilege that I have access to these other things, which I feel very lucky that I do, so I try to take them by the balls.'

By opting out of stuff, am I exercising my right to be who I want to be in the workplace, or am I too lazy to make the most of opportunities that I'm lucky enough to have?

There's no way of dressing it up: I'm a white, cis-gender, university-educated, middle-class woman, who works in a female-dominated industry. I've got privilege coming out of my ears. I work hard, yes, but lots of people work hard.

I'm good at my job, but so are lots of people. But also I've been lucky, and I exist in a structure that naturally works in favour of people like me. And I love my job, but do I love it enough? Do I approach it with enough gusto? Is 'good enough' adequate when I know, in my heart of hearts, that talent and hard work has only got me so far?

Maybe I'd be more of an Alpha if I'd had a harder time starting out. If I'd had to graft a bit more at the beginning, elbow a few more people out of the way, I might have developed a few more edges. Or I might have given up completely, and moved into a less competitive profession. Maybe the reason so many female editors are Alphas, or at least appear to be, is because if you don't learn how to assert yourself, and how to shout the loudest, you don't get very far. What if I'm the anomaly because I got lucky?

Or, as I said earlier, perhaps the reason I've done okay, and survived in a fairly turbulent industry, is because of my innate Beta-ness, not in spite of it. I took on work that other people might have turned up their noses at because I've never been particularly snobby or ego-driven about the type of work I do. Or, to be fair, very focused on my career path. But, as it happened, it made my experience far more diverse and future-proofed my career in a way that evaded some of my colleagues. My pragmatism worked in my favour but that was through chance rather than design – which sounds like a very Beta path to success, if you ask me.

I suppose what it comes down to is how much my, or anyone else's, Beta-ness is a fundamental personality trait, and how much you can change it. If I demonstrated greater willpower, could I force myself to become an Alpha boss?

Would that make me better at my job or would I – would most people – eventually crack under the pressure?

And say I could fight it, say I got souped up on Berocca and started tackling each day like a true Alpha, would that make me better at work? At life? I suspect the answer would be sort of yes, sort of no. I'd get used to some aspects of it, I'm sure, but maybe the pressure of constantly being on would make me a total misery to be around. And, yes, I could start pushing my team harder, but in the process I would become totally unapproachable. It's a trade-off, and I'm not sure that anyone ever gets the balance right. And I believe balance is all we should be aiming for. I should always try my hardest, I should always push things, and push myself a little harder than I'm comfortable with – because otherwise what's the point? I should always remember how lucky I am to be in the position I'm in, and I should do everything I can to bring as many women up with me. But should I stop being true to myself and who I am? Should I lose all sense of authenticity? I suspect the answer is no.

And that's why we're here. We (women) feel like impostors because there are so few working environments, particularly in the corporate world, where we feel we automatically or instantly fit. We either change to fit in and feel like an impostor or we stay true to ourselves and feel like an outsider because we just don't fit. So where's the middle ground? I can't imagine a man having the same internal dialogue about staying true to himself versus fitting into a working environment, but maybe I'm wrong.

So when – and how – will it change? If Impostor Syndrome is a symptom of so many of us working in environments where we feel we don't fit, do we need to stop trying? Is it time we stopped trying to squeeze into the spaces we're given, and let the spaces expand or contract to fit us instead?

'Authenticity' is a buzzword, but it's vital if we want to retain our sense of self in a world that rewards homogeneity. Alpha or Beta, the only way we'll stop feeling like impostors is if we start being honest about who we are and what we bring to the table, rather than trying to fit into a one-size-fits-all template of a working woman. Easier said than done? Of course. But if we took all the energy we put into questioning ourselves and used it elsewhere, think what we could achieve.

6.

I think, if pressed (or if I had to find a good way of opening a chapter), I'd call myself a girl's girl, or a woman's woman, depending on where you fall on that particular debate. Not because I don't have any male friends, or because I particularly enjoy walking down the street arm in arm with my three besties while the Sugababes blasts out from a giant speaker in the sky, but because I like other women, I 'get' most women and, with a few exceptions, I can normally find a way to get on with them when I meet them. I certainly don't subscribe to the belief that women are 'too bitchy' or 'two-faced' or 'not as straightforward as men'. Obviously some women are some of these things but so are some men. I've never found female friendship difficult to negotiate, or that working primarily for or with other women for the majority of my career has ever been an issue. Quite the opposite. I thrive in all-female environments.

This is partly because I've worked mostly with brilliant, original, passionate, smart women, and have found it a pleasure to collaborate with them on a project. But it's not just about the work we do: the atmosphere a female team engenders (in my experience) can be supportive, fun, empathetic and nurturing. And, if I'm honest, I also love those little things that happen in a team of women who truly feel they're able to be themselves in the office. Like when the makeup-remover wipes that someone bought when she was going to the gym at lunchtime magically spawn toothpaste, a tinted moisturiser, a pair of straighteners and some mascara that turn into a communal emergency going out/ walk of shame kit without anyone saying anything (and everyone on the team takes turns to replace things quietly when they run out). Or when new team members shyly become friends at the work Christmas party, or Friday-night drinks, then start hanging out together at weekends or become flatmates. Female office relationships can be fraught and tricky, but they can also be essential to surviving life at work.

My innate Beta-ness definitely helps here: my instinct is to fit in with other people, not to make a fuss and go where I'm needed. With every new job I've ever had, my desire to find a common ground with the team and just get on with it has overridden any shyness.

But it's more complicated now that I'm a boss. It becomes far more obvious how Beta I am when you see me interact with Alpha women. I have plenty of traits that could be considered Alpha, and there are plenty of scenarios throughout the working day to back that up – when I'm running our morning news conference and deciding which stories we're going to cover that day, or making a call on how we spend our budget. I know they're part of my job, I know how to deal with them, and I can do them well because I've done these things before. But put me in a room with a group of Alpha women and it quickly becomes obvious just how Beta I am. I can't compete and I simply don't want to.

My natural role is conflict negotiator. When I'm in a

room full of Alpha women, I am more about managing their egos and respective agendas than pushing my own. The downside of this is obvious – I don't always get to push my own agenda, and this is to my detriment. But the upside is that people generally like working and dealing with me – they know I won't be a pain in the bottom and that, generally, stuff will get done. This means that, in turn, they're more likely to do me a favour when I ask for it. So, sometimes my agenda still gets pushed, just in a more roundabout way.

The first time I realised there was power to be had in being, essentially, the pushover of the team (as I was seen at the time) occurred when I was still very junior, an editorial assistant, and I found myself dealing with a particularly tricky client who had fallen out with my (Alpha) boss and my boss's boss. But she'd still deal with me. From her point of view this was because she believed I was so junior that she'd get her own way. But the more I dealt with her, occasionally cajoling her into doing things our way, working out which stuff we could push back on and which we could use as a bargaining chip on other matters, I realised she was basically happy to defer to our judgement on any number of things. There were a few issues she wouldn't move on, but otherwise she just wanted to be asked. She wanted to feel that the end result was down to her work, her ideas and her judgement as much as ours.

It took me ages, but eventually we got a final product signed off that everyone was happy with. You could argue that I got there by being a creep, but I like to think I did it by being nice (and protecting my client's ego by putting mine to one side). It earned me a small promotion (and the dubious honour of dealing with the aforementioned tricky client going forward).

You'll notice that I've only talked about Alpha women here. And that's because I've found that I operate differently when I'm dealing with Alpha men. I don't know the rules as well, I don't get them, and I'm not sure where I exist in the hierarchy (if at all). It's probably because I've almost always worked with other women, but when I have to operate in an environment with primarily brash Alpha men, I find myself disengaging completely. Would I operate differently among men if I were more Alpha? Almost certainly.

I suppose the part of this that intrigues me most is how we treat female relationships in the workplace: I feel I instinctively know the rules when I'm dealing with most women, but I couldn't tell you where I learnt them. Popular culture has about as much to say on female working relationships as it does on how women behave in the workplace (not much, applied with broad brushstrokes). With a few notable exceptions (*Working Girl*, *The Devil Wears Prada*), they don't get a look-in at all. And when they do, two women are generally pitted against each other, one good, one evil (and, more often than not, the good Beta versus the evil Alpha). But there's certainly no room for nuance, or real life.

It's another symptom of the wider issue we discussed earlier: the narrow way in which women are depicted in popular culture, and how that impacts on our IRL expectations of women at work. 'It's almost as though if you are a powerful woman in a Hollywood film you basically are going to be either the evil Maleficent or you're going to be presented as very unhappy. So you're either really nasty or really unhappy or you're both,' agrees Caroline Hedleman, research director for the Geena Davies Institute.

And when we do study all-female teams, or female working relationships, the focus is on the supposed negatives – none of which has anything to do with work or a workplace. Here's a sample from a first-person interview given to the *Daily Mail* in 2009 by Samantha Brick. 'I was often out trying to win contracts, but back at the office, work was an afterthought. It came second to conversations about shopping, boyfriends and diets – oh, and spiteful comments from my two research assistants who were sharpening their claws against another staff member, Natasha.'

Brick then goes on to describe how one of said research assistants went on to terrorise poor Natasha, while the (also female) general manager refused to step in for fear of being the 'bad cop'. Brick also mentions that the atmosphere improved measurably every time a couple of freelance men were introduced into the office, and that, overall, the team became more productive with that crucial injection of testosterone into the mix. (She supposes this was because her employees 'were too busy flirting'.)

Obviously I have no idea what went on in that company, but Brick's implication – that the women's sex lives, love of fashion and diets ruled the office, and they behaved like that only because there were no men around to temper their behaviour – is bizarre, reductive and unhelpful (and, obviously, what Brick was doing to manage this team is never mentioned). But the most troubling part of the article is that those women, and this torrid, barely believable tale, are obviously meant to be a proxy for all women in the workplace. It feeds into a dangerous wider narrative that women can only exist at work in the context of men. Without that all-important injection of testosterone, an office becomes a coven.

And this ties into a wider point as to why there's so little conversation in the media, in popular culture, about female-dominated teams or offices: we simply don't see women collectively as protagonists in an office environment. There may be a boss-lady, but if she were in a film, she'd be a plot point all on her own. Individuals learning how to thrive in a male-dominated environment is one thing, but women existing as a professional team with its own internal hierarchies and politics, getting a job done with no male input? Nah. No one will watch that.

There's also a mistaken and rarely questioned assumption that the only women inhabiting senior roles in most workplaces will be quite Alpha. I say 'mistaken assumption' because I think that, whatever her personality type, for a woman to thrive in an almost entirely male environment, she would feel the need to adopt as Alpha a persona as she could.

Look at it this way. According to the FTSE Woman Leaders Review 2016, twelve FTSE 100 companies still have all-male executive committees, and while the number of women on boards for FTSE companies is on the rise, the numbers are still woefully low – ranging from 21.1 per cent to 26.6 per cent – and almost all non-executive directors are men. The glass ceiling is still very much a reality, and it creates an environment in which women are allowed to behave in only one way – as close to adopting as masculine a persona as possible.

But there is huge value in understanding inter-female

relationships in the workplace, not least because women interact and operate with each other differently from men, and sometimes with levels of nuance and subtlety that can't be found in male relationships.

'Working on an all-female team has been a dream – this sounds like hyperbole but it's true,' says Danielle, twenty-eight. 'Everyone is supportive of one another and problems are discussed, which means they are resolved quickly. On a mostly male team I felt frustrated often and as though my voice was stifled. There was a combative and competitive atmosphere, which, in the end, exhausted me.'

Naomi, the thirty-three-year-old project manager I mentioned earlier, also feels it was easier to get stuff done on an all-female team. 'In the construction industry for six years, I have worked with mainly male teams for the entirety of this time. It's an aggressive atmosphere – competitive and process-driven rather than with any personal goals or connections. I had previously worked in an all-female team in aviation and found it to be a much more supportive and encouraging environment.'

There have been lots of studies into the relative productivity and harmony of all-male or all-female teams versus mixed-gender groups. A study by the Massachusetts Institute of Technology (MIT) and George Washington University published in 2014 found, for example, that employee morale and satisfaction were higher on single-sex teams, but groups that had a more diverse gender spread were more productive and produced higher revenues. The reason for the higher satisfaction levels in single-gender teams is simple – and explains why I find female colleagues easier to deal with than men. In the words of the study's co-author, Sara Fisher Ellison, speaking to the *Wall Street Journal*, 'People are more comfortable around people who are like them.' She also speculated that single-sex teams 'socialise more and work less', hence the dip in productivity.

In another study – also by George Washington University – more than three hundred management students were randomly assigned teams, some predominately male or female and others gender-balanced. The study found that men in teams with a balanced gender mix had a more positive experience than those in teams dominated by men. The study also found that the mixed-gender teams tended to out-perform the predominately single-sex teams.

'We examined the impact of team gender on several variables important to team success, including trust, cohesion, inclusion and task/relationship conflict,' said Kaitlin Thomas, a doctoral candidate in industrial-organisational psychology at George Washington. One reason for this, she suggests, is that women tend to be more relationship-oriented than men so place more focus on collaboration within the team.

Whatever the gender mix of the offices I've been in, one thing has consistently got me through the day when things have been hard: my work friendships. And although these are often the women we see more than anyone else, those work friendships aren't explored or celebrated enough. They can be crucially important when it comes to looking at how women progress in a workplace that is still in many ways pitched against them.

We haven't worked together for almost a decade, but Christina was my first – and best – work wife. She picked me up when I fell backwards off the stage at the office Christmas party, and let me crash on her sofa the following year when I lost all my possessions and couldn't get into my flat. We've travelled from Caracas to Kiev together and still go on holiday when we can, children and partners allowing. When she got married I was her bridesmaid.

But the defining moment when I realised she was my work wife happened eight years ago when I was made redundant from the company we worked at together. It was my first job, and I'd been there almost four years. I kind of knew it was time to leave, and it wasn't the biggest shock in the world but, still, no one *really* expects that conversation on a Monday afternoon. I wouldn't have bought all my lunches for the week from the supermarket next door an hour earlier if I had.

After being told I was probably losing my job, I went straight to the pub and called Christina, who came straight away with my handbag, which I'd left behind. She stayed all evening, and took me for dinner in an attempt to sober me up, offering me a space in her bed if I didn't want to go home on my own. She said she'd clear my desk for me, too, so I wouldn't have to go back to the office if I didn't want to.

And that's why a work wife is brilliant: she's somewhere between your colleague, who totally gets why you hate Claire, the office manager, with a passion, and your best friend, who gets you, but rolled into one person.

Having a 'work wife' is good for your career. According to a 2016 study by the guys at CV-library, 47.2 per cent of UK professionals either have or wish they had a 'work spouse'. Respondents cited the benefits as 'offering support and mentorship, providing advice and guidance and offering friendship and companionship'.

Another study shows that 50 per cent of those with a best friend at work feel they have a strong connection with the company, and 70 per cent of employees say having friends at work is the most crucial part of a happy working life.

I keep referring to a 'work wife' – because who doesn't love alliteration? – and we are looking at female friendships, but I am, of course, referring to a work spouse. They are your work 'person', someone who has your back in any situation, will give you proper good advice, and will never stab you in the back just to get in there with Geoff from Procurement.

She (or he) is the person you make a pact with before the Christmas party to whisk you away when you start to get 'boozy melted face', which means you're about to do something bad, because you know she'll be keeping an eye out and will move heaven and earth to ensure you don't get caught feeling up that new guy from Finance in the disabled toilets. She's the person you can complain to about your boss without fear of reprisals. She's also the person who will give you proper objective career advice when you're not sure what your next move should be, if you messed up that presentation, or whether you should be going for that promotion. It also means you've always got someone to go to lunch with.

A good work wife is – or should be – the absolute opposite of Samantha Brick's deranged depiction of an all-female working environment. It should be the epitome, the absolute pinnacle, of female colleague-dom. It's not the same as a mentor, or a boss who really cares about your personal development, or even that fun colleague with great gossip about the team on the third floor. It's someone who understands you and the job you do better than anyone else in the world. They know why you care because they care too. They aren't going to roll their eyes when you mention for the fourteenth time how annoying you find Claire because they 100 per cent feel your pain. And they can also tell you, better than anyone else in the world, when it's time for you to go. If your work wife tells you you're wasted where you are, or that it's time to move on, that's excellent advice, worth taking into serious consideration. Because no one cuts their work wife loose – and potentially loses the only person in the office up for a hung-over Nando's at lunchtime – unless they really mean it.

'I think, when you're in a very male environment, a lot of it is about having that constant ally,' explains Sara, who works in the science department of a university. 'My best friend and I worked together for four years, and having that person who totally had my back was amazing. It meant I was able to relax into the job more than I probably do now we're not working together.'

But, as with all human interactions, it's complicated, as Sara explains: 'I tend to gravitate towards other women when we work together, but some women are really anti that and push you away a bit – I think they see it as a sign of weakness. But everyone's different, I guess.'

For Cara, forty, who has worked in marketing in London and Canada (so has had to find her feet in new office environments and a new country), work wives have punctuated some of the most important moments of her career.

'Over the years I've had several work wives (and even a work husband!) and I can honestly say these women have helped me get through some of the most challenging moments of my career. It's just so nice to have someone "human" to connect with at work and look forward to seeing every day. The ability to sneak away for a quick chat and ask for helpful advice from someone you trust is a huge perk of having a work wife. You never have to worry about eating lunch alone, and she is always up for a cheeky coffee run to Starbucks or a little nip outside to get air.'

And, as Cara learnt, a good work wife should enhance the rest of your life: 'I recently celebrated a milestone birthday and had an afternoon-tea party with a number of friends who didn't know each other. As the ladies chatted and established how they knew me, it quickly became apparent that 90 per cent of the guests were women I had worked with over the years. That bit was amazing – my work wives were meeting each other and sharing funny stories about our escapades together. It really made me realise how blessed I've been to have worked with such awesome females and I'm so glad that I've maintained the relationships even after moving on to different roles.'

I totally agree. When I was organising my hen do, I wanted it to be fairly small, so I invited only the women I'm closest to. Two-thirds of the guest list was comprised of women I had worked with in some capacity over the last decade.

In a 2016 study by the University of Pennsylvania and Arizona State University of the relationships between female baboons (stick with me here), they discovered that, although the males leave the group once they've grown up and go to join another group (where they have to fight their way to the top hierarchy), females stay with the same group from birth. They inherit their position within it (Alpha, Beta, Gamma and so on) from their mothers. Scientists also discovered that these hierarchies remained stable with almost no change for fifteen, twenty or thirty years.

It was assumed that evolution dictates that those baboons with the most Alpha-like traits are most likely to survive and pass them on to their daughters. In fact, it turns out that the baboons that did best were those that had the strongest relationships with other females in the group – the same females, year after year. This was so for groups thousands of miles apart, and feels strangely reminiscent of numerous studies that have found our relationships with other people are the key to our happiness.

In the case of the baboons, scientists found that those who were the most closely bonded with other females in their group had the lowest levels of stress hormones. This makes sense: they supported each other in disputes, their friendship generated fewer disputes over food, and they'd groom each other a lot, which everyone knows is the best stress-buster there is. They're each other's work wives, and they're happier, less stressed, and thrive as a result.

With good reason, I've banged on at length about the virtues of working with women and having fantastic female working relationships. It's my friendships at work that have made terrible jobs bearable, and great jobs out-of-this-world amazing. I've worked with women far more than I have with men, so it's those relationships that stand out for me. I stay in touch with most of my old female work friends far more than I do with male former colleagues. This means plenty of opportunity to rehash funny or scandalous work stories. Our friendships and our time at work together develop a mythical status with each retelling to a new boyfriend or friend-of-a-friend who joins the group. Even the most dull, banal or depressing jobs take on a rosy glow when revisited with my work wives.

But what if female friendships don't work for you? Or if they do, but you don't like, or get, your female colleagues? Not every all-female team is a pulsating mass of oestrogen ready to explode at any moment, but neither is every experience of an all-female working environment going to be positive.

Take Natalie, thirty-four, whose experience of an all-female PR team in her early twenties made her avoid them thereafter: 'The senior managers, who were all at least a decade older than us juniors, bitched about us in private and openly. It was different if you were one of their chosen ones whom they'd support blindly – the office was incredibly cliquey – but if they took against you that was it.'

And, of course, sometimes it's a mixed bag – just like working in an all-male team. 'It has been both,' says Sue, a fifty-seven-year-old management trainer. 'The male environment was straightforward, hard-working, focused on achieving goals, but lacked heart and the desire to do the right thing by people. The female environment felt more complicated – lots of decision-makers, creative, a bit catty, but good fun and value-based.'

Obviously it depends on the job, on the team, on the boss and the mix of people. Gender is an element, but it's one of many. For me, it almost always works and I see working in a female-dominated environment as a privilege.

But either way you cut it, it's clear – and shouldn't even need noting – that how women deal with each other at work is just as complex and deserves just as much airtime as how we deal with men, how they deal with us, and how men in the workplace interact with each other. Yet unless it's to highlight some extremely unpleasant behaviour or to muse on how pregnancy affects a woman's ability to behave rationally in a professional setting, the inner workings and dynamics of a female team are rarely considered in popular culture or the media.

How we are perceived as individual women in the workplace is the thin end of the wedge – it's indicative of the wider picture around how women are viewed in the workplace. And equally, how we are perceived as a group, or how women are perceived within a team, is crucially important. The collective noun for a group of female colleagues working together towards a common goal should be 'team', not 'coven' – the actual term used to describe one of my all-female teams. By a bloke, of course. You can be as Alpha or as Beta as you like, but if you're not allowed to exist in relation to other women in a professional sense in the workplace, that all becomes pretty academic.

7.

When someone says, writes or indeed tweets something stupid, offensive or in some cases downright dangerous, the race to call them out for it on social media is a reflection of what goes on in meeting rooms around the country every day but on a more terrifying scale. There's a certain weird kudos in being the one who spotted it first. In having that thing to say that everyone is agreeing with. Opinion – especially negative opinion – is currency and everyone wants to record the best opinion first.

The mundane IRL version of that? A regional sales meeting in which someone gives a perfectly adequate presentation that one of his bosses criticises as 'just not what I had in mind' and . . . leaving it at that. Which is basically shorthand for 'I dislike your ideas for non-specific reasons, but I want to get my bit in before anyone else and I haven't had time to form a proper opinion.'

Because Boss Number One has said something, the race is on for everyone else to get in with their feedback before someone else says it first. Everyone's attempting to make that one, incisive, cutting observation that nails what the problem is with Gareth's (let's call him Gareth) presentation. In the end, Boss Number Six, panicked at having said nothing so far, pointedly remarks that Gareth neglected to use the company colours on slide seventeen. Everyone else nods thoughtfully. The next day Gareth is signed off work with stress.

How do you show the world how Alpha you are? You talk a lot and slag everyone else off. It's a ruse as old as time (probably) and, often, it works. Most people are busy dealing with their own stuff, so they tend to assume that if someone is vocal, self-assured and sounds knowledgeable (read: has a loud voice), they must know what they're talking about.

And the best way to really nail your Alpha-ness? By saying, repeatedly, how useless everyone else is. Of course, a true Alpha, who was confident of his or her place in the Alpha food chain, would never bother with that sort of rubbish. They're too busy building empires to keep talking about the time Mhairi in Accounts messed up the projections for Q4. But an insecure person trying to assert themselves as head honcho? They're slagging off Mhairi's rudimentary grasp of Excel to everyone who will listen.

Whether you're Alpha or Beta, being on the receiving end of spurious criticism happens to us all. And neither Alphas nor Betas will do it more: it's about competence, not personality types. If you're good at your job you won't need to. But the difference is in how we respond – and that's why we're talking about it here. While an Alpha woman may instantly question or confront criticism, a Beta woman may internalise it – and start to believe it (as I certainly have done). But understanding what motivates others, and learning how to negotiate tricky and toxic working environments without compromising our sense of self, is vital for any Beta in the workplace.

My friend Alice works in the civil service, and recalls

dealing with a notoriously incompetent senior manager, who has the added delightful reputation for being really difficult. 'She's rude, aggressive and dismissive,' Alice explains, after yet another run-in with said manager. (Incidentally, Alice is very good at her job. You know how with some people you just know?) 'Her first response to any question or proposal is always "No." I've seen her make some truly terrible judgement calls as a result. She obviously knows she's got a rubbish reputation and this is her way of reminding everyone that she's the boss. In reality people are just less forgiving when she messes up, because no one likes her.'

Alice doesn't necessarily think she is the worst manager she deals with – but she's the one who sticks in her mind because this woman has invested so much time in making life difficult for everyone else.

I ask Alice if she thinks her boss would get away with that sort of behaviour if she were a man. 'Probably,' she concedes. 'If she was a man people would still note how incompetent she is, but I don't think her overall attitude would have been mentioned in the same way because the expectation would have been different. If a male manager is rude, that's just the way it is. If a woman is rude, it's a conversation topic for everyone else.'

In Alice's boss, her rudeness, her refusal to agree to anything may be a defence mechanism born of insecurity and what sounds like incompetence. And I understand how being critical or negative can be seen as shorthand for being good at your job. After all, according to Conservative MP Kenneth Clarke, Theresa May is a 'bloody difficult woman', the implication being that, like her predecessor Margaret

Thatcher, she is competent (although 'difficult' is an interesting choice of word, did he mean that she may be competent but she's still a pain because she's making life harder for men like Clarke)?

But saying no all the time means you have a critical mind, you're an analytical genius who can get straight to the heart of the problem. It never occurs to anyone that saying no all the time could be as much a sign of indecisiveness as it is in the person who says, 'I don't know' sixteen times a day. At the other end of the spectrum is the person who says 'Yes' all the time. She's a pushover: who would want to be her?

So saying 'no', always finding fault, jumping in with your criticism before anyone else does is a defensive move, designed to shine a light on other people's shortcomings and blind people to your own.

But the inner politics of the AGM at a plastic-bottle manufacturer in the Home Counties is one thing. What about when criticism one-upmanship takes place on a macro level? What happens when you're Twitter-shamed?

You may be familiar with the story of Justine Sacco. In 2013, she was senior director of Corporate Communications for IAC, an American media and internet company. She made the news when she travelled from New York to South Africa to visit family, tweeting during a stopover: *Going to Africa. Hope I don't get AIDs. Just kidding. I'm white!*

She switched her phone off, spent the next eleven hours on a plane to Cape Town and landed to discover that her tweet had been retweeted three thousand times and she had been fired. Not only were people outraged, the public shaming of Sacco quickly became a form of fun – as Jon

Ronson notes when he interviews her in his book *So You've Been Publicly Shamed*:

> The furor over Sacco's tweet had become not just an ideological crusade against her perceived bigotry, but also a form of idle entertainment. Her complete ignorance of her predicament for those eleven hours lent the episode both dramatic irony and a pleasing narrative arc. As Sacco's flight traversed the length of Africa, a hashtag started to trend worldwide #HasJustineLandedYet.

One Twitter user went to the airport to tweet her arrival, taking her photo and posting it on the internet.

In the same book, Ronson has talked about the pleasure and satisfaction he has taken in the past from joining in with the public shaming of someone who has said or done something deemed offensive or distasteful. 'In the early days of Twitter I was a keen shamer. When newspaper columnists made racist or homophobic statements, I joined the pile-on. Sometimes I led it.'

He recalls the satisfaction he took from being one of the first people to alert social media to the story the late A. A. Gill wrote about shooting a baboon on safari, partly because 'Gill always gave my television documentaries bad reviews, so I always keep a vigilant eye on things he could be got for.' Ronson's tweet did the trick: 'Within minutes it was everywhere. Amid the hundreds of congratulatory messages, one stuck out: "Were you a bully at school?"'

Where did the satisfaction come from? Was it in spotting it first? In being the person who made it go viral? Or is the value, when you're highlighting someone's offensiveness on social media, in being able to dish out the most incisive criticism? The most acerbic? In being the one person who can best explain What Is Wrong With the World in 140 characters?

When Polly Vernon released her book *Hot Feminist* in 2015, she expected it to cause controversy. The reviews were mixed – and a couple were particularly damning. She wasn't expecting the subsequent barrage of abuse she received from hundreds of women who were, in her words, 'all keen to tell me how stupid my book and I were'. She later wrote about the experience in the *Guardian*: 'I'd been destabilised by Twitter's rush to shame me. Shame: such a distinct, old-fashioned – old – feeling. Exactly the sort of thing you might feel, if hundreds of disembodied voices turned on you, denounced you, shunned you.'

Now Polly tells me, 'I think that we are operating in a time when it does inform reviews and critics in that if you want to cause a big old fuss and get retweeted hugely then to really take issue with something is one easy way to do that. A really brilliant woman told me that she was approached by someone for a negative quote for my book, and she said, "I haven't read it," and they said, "That doesn't matter."' She adds, 'It would have been horrible but I would have dealt with it, if it hadn't provoked this onslaught on Twitter – if I hadn't been the subject of this lampooning. It was a whole thing to prove you're a good feminist. It was not only okay to slag me off as a woman and a feminist, it made you look like a better feminist.'

Criticism had become currency: bad reviews drove traffic and online chat, and that online chat became a game of one-upmanship, with each user looking to out-damn the previous one.

And it happens every single day. Why do we do it?

Dr Bernie Hogan, of the Oxford Internet Institute, believes that social media simply mimic our real-life behaviour in this respect: 'There are a lot of cases where mob rule is the rule of the day – crowds and mobs have been a feature of human society for a very long time.

'Boundaries are really important for one's identity – and not just about being able to say, "I'm part of this group." It's about policing boundaries and saying who's in and who's out.'

Essentially, in a world where we're constantly looking for belonging or acceptance, we demonstrate who we're with and what we stand for in as broad a brushstroke as possible. But does Twitter make this worse?

'It doesn't necessarily amplify this process,' explains Dr Hogan, 'but it might make this process more likely because of the real lack of cues on Twitter. It's really hard to know which side someone is on. Furthermore, having a "side" will probably get you more retweets.'

Ah, yes, because opinion is currency.

People's desire to be on the 'right side' but also first can be seen when Ronson talks about Justine Sacco's story: 'I think self-righteous people who piled onto Justine Sacco, robbing her joke of its nuance and just trying to destroy her because they wanted to be seen as a kind of Rosa Parks – but of course they weren't, because there was nothing brave about it – they're more frightening, actually, than trolls.'

So, back to poor old Gareth and his mediocre presentation. He's not having to deal with hundreds of people telling him how lacklustre his PowerPoint game is, but he is the unwitting victim of six people vying for top-dog status, and there's no better way to prove you're right than to demonstrate that someone else is wrong.

And there's the classic not-wanting-to-admit-to-having-the-'wrong'-opinion – that is, one that's diametrically opposed to someone more senior – so you get in your criticism at the outset just to be on the safe side. I've definitely been guilty of this one. There have been points in my career where I've worked on hierarchical teams where (and this is crucial) I haven't been able to get to grips with what my editor wanted, what they did and didn't like from a writer, or why. Maybe it was my fault, maybe it was theirs but, for whatever reason, something was not clicking.

Part of my job was to take in copy from writers, give them initial feedback and make edits before passing to my boss. I later realised that I responded with some vague criticism to almost every piece I received – even when I was perfectly happy with it – getting the writer to make a few cursory (and probably pointless) amendments. I was essentially hedging my bets in case my editor didn't like the piece, in which case I could say, 'I don't like it either – I've already given them a load of amends, and it *still* isn't right.' If I'd had a better idea of what my boss was after, I'd have been able to give the writer a better brief in the first place, or gone back with the right sort of amendments. And if I'd had a bit more confidence I'd have stood up for a piece I loved and explained why I thought it was fine as it was, or asked the right sort of questions to get a better idea of what my editor actually wanted. But I didn't do either of those things. Instead I used criticism of someone else as a shield to disguise the fact that there were some bits of my job that I wasn't getting. I passed negative feedback uselessly up and down the food chain, without ever resolving what the problem was – because if it was someone else's fault, and someone else was being told they weren't getting it, no one was looking at me. And that, above all, was the main thing.

It was about me and it was about my boss. The only person it was never about was the writer.

It's hard to realise when you're in an office environment that has a steep, sometimes toxic hierarchy how much time people spend trying to shore up their own positions, rather than focusing on the task at hand. When you grasp that the vast majority of office interactions are nothing to do with you, it can feel incredibly freeing.

And it turns out we all remember that bad boss – the hyper-negative, overly critical one who made life a misery for everyone. And I have never heard a story like that where the team ended up being more productive as a result.

'I have experienced bosses who seemed to believe, mistakenly, that a negative managerial style would motivate their team to do better work,' explains Annie, who is a copywriter for a large retail brand, and has worked for retail or media brands throughout her career. 'Instead it just demoralised people, leaving them feeling that nothing they did could ever be good enough. In every instance it led to burnout and a culture of presenteeism. The best bosses lead by example and leave work on time and encourage their team to have a good work–life balance.'

Maybe I'm being a little hard on myself when I talk

about my own history of being overly and pointlessly critical. After all, I can remember that specific example so well because, for the most part, I hate giving people negative feedback and rarely do it. So when I do, I try hard to make the criticism as constructive as possible.

It's a rule I've stuck to fairly consistently ever since I got myself into that negative-feedback loop between my editor and the writers – I don't criticise people's work unless I can say what I don't like about it, or what I'd prefer instead. I see the dishing out of negative feedback as a tool that should be used sparingly and with care. It's my job to give my team feedback they can interpret properly to produce what I need. It's not their job to read my mind.

There's also a dangerous misconception that saying, 'I'm not sure,' or 'Can I just go away and think about it?' or keeping your mouth shut because you genuinely don't have a strong opinion on whatever's in front of you means you're indecisive and don't know what you want. Which is nonsense, because very few of the best decisions are made on a whim or a gut feeling, with little thought or consideration. 'Can I just go away and think about it?' should be the slogan of smart bosses everywhere, not a sign of weakness.

But it's not. Knowing what you want and what you think at all times are the hallmarks of a good boss. No one mentions what happens when the thing you want is the wrong thing and culminates in you sending your team down a rabbit hole of three months' pointless work. Thinking your opinions through before you share them never seems to be as valuable as just having an opinion.

We've all seen the statistic that men dominate 75 per

cent of the conversation on average in most meetings, and we all know, as we step into another meeting, whose voices we'll be hearing most for the next hour. They're not necessarily those of the smartest people in the room, but they're the loudest. And don't get me wrong: in a meeting full of women a couple of people will always emerge as the most outspoken in the same way. And when you don't have anything useful to say, what do you do? You complain about someone else.

But there's plenty of evidence to suggest that brevity is far more productive than talking just to fill the silence, as Joseph McCormack, author of *BRIEF: Making a Bigger Impact by Saying Less*, discovered. 'Brevity is an essential skill that can propel people's career in an age where the people that they're talking to are overwhelmed.' His point is that people tend to switch off after a certain point, and in many circumstances – a job interview, for example – rambling on makes you appear unprepared. He also believes we're conditioned to believe that when we over-explain something we demonstrate how smart we are – at school and university, essays are all about reaching the hallowed word count rather than what we have to say, and that attitude carries through into our adult lives.

But back to criticism. Obviously, not all criticism is created equal. Constructive criticism can be incredibly useful. (How individuals deal with constructive criticism is a whole other matter.) And critical thinking is vital in any business. My boss, for example, is far more likely to question what's in front of her than I am, and will robustly test the value of any new project or idea we have. But this stops me going off on a tangent every time I get enthused about an idea that doesn't necessarily have legs, or that I want to take up for no other reason than to keep someone else happy. My willingness to say yes can sometimes be a great thing, but you need someone else around to play a more questioning role.

Critical thinking isn't the same as toxic or hostile criticism, which can inhibit us from changing our behaviour or performance at work or school. Bad criticism is bad for everyone.

'You've got to start off by thinking about whether there's any truth in what this person is saying,' suggests Corinne Mills, a careers coach. 'Is it discomfiting because there's an element of truth or value in there? You have to consider whether this person is just being honest and start off with that position, but if you really feel like this isn't fair, and there's another agenda going on, then you'll know about it – you'll get a strong sense of being undermined.' And in those instances, Corinne says, it's rarely about you. 'Perhaps they don't realise they're doing it, there could be no agenda there at all. It could just be that they're not very soft-skilled. It's their style. There's no edge to it – they're just no good at dressing it up.'

But, of course, there may be another reason: 'Maybe they feel threatened by you, and keeping you down is a reflection of their insecurity and desire to keep you at bay. Or it could be transference, which is where you, for whatever reason, remind them of someone from their past or their family life – it could be an overbearing father or mother, an ex-husband – and they have a totally disproportionate reaction to you.'

'It's not you, it's me,' is never more true than when

looking at why you're getting unwarranted or constant criticism from your boss, or from a group of senior people in your organisation. For starters, the nine most common defence mechanisms, as defined by Anna Freud (her dad was a big deal) in her book *The Ego and the Mechanisms of Defence*, include displacement. Simply put, it's when someone is criticised by their boss or superior but is unable to display their anger or frustration with that person. Instead they take it out on an easier target: you. Basically, your boss has shifted their frustration away from the source of their anxiety to someone who will do them less harm.

And then there's the dynamic I mentioned above. The one where putting your head above the parapet and saying yes, or saying you like something, feels like a huge risk – and it's a risk your boss doesn't want to take. Maybe you work for a large organisation that's ruled by inertia and bureaucracy. Or maybe your boss's boss says 'No' all of the time, and that's the behaviour they've learnt. Or maybe they simply don't know what their superiors want from them so they're hedging their bets, as I did.

But what about when you work somewhere where saying 'No' and criticising other people is a power play? Not necessarily because it's intended to get someone else into trouble, but because, like Twitter, everyone is clamouring to get their really insightful piece of criticism in first to prove how invaluable they are to the process and the organisation? ('You couldn't possibly fire me, or not have me in this meeting,' they're trying to say. 'Look at all the costly embarrassing mistakes you'd end up making if I wasn't here to tell you all where you're going wrong!')

The irony is that constant negativity for the sake of it,

or criticising other people to shore up your own status, is something a true Alpha, who's confident in their position, would never do. They wouldn't have to.

Sir Richard Branson (the billionaire? Founder of the Virgin group? Yep, that guy) has said in the past that he was raised never to be nasty or negative about anyone, and claims it's a mantra he still lives by today. 'If I ever hear people gossiping about people I'll walk away. As a leader, you've just got to get out there and look for the best in people, and that's really, really important. Let them get on with it, not criticise them when they make mistakes, and praise them when they do good things.'

If you're someone who knows what you're doing and isn't afraid of being wrong, it costs a lot less to be nice. Certainly criticising people for the sake of it or as a reflex isn't the thing. But knowing when to give your team space to work things out for themselves, and letting them become okay with making mistakes and learning from them, is crucial.

As a freelancer I once did some work for a large retail brand and worked with two people in particular, a man and a woman. He was her boss, and it was pretty obvious he wasn't particularly good at his job. His instincts weren't great, and he seemed jealous of anyone who had the creative skills he clearly lacked. I think she was far more competent than he was – and when I had to deal with her directly, she was straightforward, positive and demonstrated decent instincts. But the minute he became involved in a meeting, the whole tone changed. My work – and other people's – would be criticised for reasons as broad and varied as 'I'm just not really feeling it' and 'This feels flat . . . I'm not sure why. Were you tired when you did this?'

Constructive criticism was not deemed necessary – in no small part because he didn't know how to give it. Which meant his weird, meaningless and always negative feedback became the benchmark against which everything was judged. And because he constantly used criticism of other people to shore up his own position ('If I know what you're doing wrong, when no one else can see it, then I must know what I'm doing'), his colleague started to do it too. I'd see her nervously glancing at him when they looked at a new piece of work, trying to gauge what he thought before stating her opinion (which was always negative).

I could even tell if he was standing next to her when she was on the phone to me, so different was the tone of the conversation. As far as he was concerned, she wasn't doing her job properly if she wasn't saying she hated something, so she complied. And she was stuck in that weird holding pattern where she had to keep him happy to avoid becoming the subject of his ire. It meant she couldn't do her job properly. What I've never been able to work out is the extent to which she thought he was right. Did she trust his instincts or just not trust her own? Did she believe his assertions that he was a creative genius and no one else was getting it, or did she know exactly what was going on, but was clinging grimly to her job for dear life? Probably a bit of everything.

When you create a situation where only negativity and criticism count, you end up existing in an environment where the only way people learn to assert themselves is by being critical and negative about others' work and behaviour. Social media can generate the same response, on a much larger scale, in which having an opinion first is the most important thing, and disagreeing with someone, or disputing their version of events, has far more currency than positive feedback. And not saying anything at all? Keeping your thoughts to yourself till you've really considered your response, or deciding that your opinion isn't needed in this instance? That's not an option. If you're not *seen* to be doing something, if you don't have an opinion, any opinion, you don't count. Because in a world where 140 characters can make you famous, it's what you say, not what you do, that counts.

It's hard to identify when you're on the receiving end of spurious criticism because it feels so personal: it's a direct attack on your work at best, or your character at worst. When I'm in a meeting where the tone is overly negative, and I can't work out if it's about the work at hand, or just the general vibe that's developed (on account of all the criticism one-upmanship), I like to imagine the whole thing is a race-to-the-finish computer game in which each player has to throw out as much criticism as they can before the timer goes so they can make it to the next round and face the evil boss. (See? It works on several levels.) Once you look at it in that way, you start to see how much it's about other people and not about you, which instantly makes it easier to deal with.

Another tactic? Criticise the criticism. If the feedback is unclear, or you're not sure what conclusions to draw from it, say so. If people are giving you conflicting criticism, or no way forward, say so. If the criticism directly contradicts what you were originally asked to do, and no one has acknowledged this, say so. Nothing will catch someone out in the act of lazy criticism like asking them to explain themselves.

And always remember the golden rule of office politics, which will stand you in good stead through most work crises: it's not you, it's them.

*

8.

BURNOUT: A MODERN MALAISE FOR MODERN LADIES

You know how some people never get knackered, never run out of steam and never lose enthusiasm for a project? Yeah, I'm not that guy. I love my job, but when I'm tired, or stressed out, or doing something I don't want to do, I have to remind myself that I love it. That I'm lucky to be there. And that my job can be as enjoyable as I make it.

But I've had to learn these things the hard way. It took me a decade to realise that the more you put in, the more you get out – but that sometimes you simply can't put in any more without facing diminishing returns. And that's okay too.

In my twenties I constantly felt knackered and stressed, as if I never had enough headspace. Remember the story about the migraine tablets? This happened – as you can probably imagine – when I was going through a tricky work period with a boss I didn't really get (and who, no doubt, didn't really get me either) and very little support. I started getting migraines three or four times a week. They weren't particularly severe but they knocked me out for half a day at a time, putting me further and further behind in a job I already felt as if I couldn't cope with. After a month or so I was spending any time when I didn't have a migraine staring at a computer screen trying to catch up – which gave me more migraines.

In the end I stopped. I went to see a Reiki healer and life coach (don't laugh: it was the best money I've ever spent) who got all Captain Obvious about it and suggested that I made an appointment with my GP, another with an optician, and strongly suggested that I find a way to Chill Out. In the end, I discovered that the migraines were a direct result of too much screen time and not enough sleep (because I was averaging about four hours a night, and spending the rest gazing at a wall, my body coursing with adrenaline and nervous energy).

There were any number of problems with my job scenario, some of which I could control, others that I couldn't. The main one was that I was working in an environment where I could not get the headspace I needed. It was an American company where it was perfectly acceptable to come in at eleven a.m. or not at all (working from home was encouraged and regular hours weren't monitored). However, taking a couple of days off sick and being completely offline or (the horror) going on holiday was completely at odds with the culture. I almost cancelled a two-week holiday to Asia I'd booked before accepting the job because they were so baffled by the concept of twenty days' guaranteed annual leave: in the States there's no minimum statutory paid vacation and, according to the Bureau of Labor Statistics, 77 per cent of private employers offer paid vacation to their employees of ten days per year, on average, after one year of service. In that instance, wiser counsel – my furious travelling companions – prevailed. But I never lost the sense that taking my holiday was the first black mark against my name. An early sign of my lack of commitment to the job, which they were constantly seeking to reaffirm every time I didn't reply to an email quickly enough, or appeared to be thinking about anything that wasn't work.

This creates a culture in which taking time out is frowned upon (American friends frequently talk about not taking their full annual-leave entitlement lest they earn the side eye from their harder working colleagues), and you're expected to be 'always on', no matter how this impacts on your productivity. It was exhausting. The result: I became panicky, dull and uncreative. More concerned with getting through the day and ticking all the 'bare minimum' boxes than doing anything truly great.

But would a few proper days off sick, away from my laptop and my phone, have fixed anything other than my tired eyes? I'm not sure. Part of the problem was that, yet again, I felt a total fraud and completely out of my depth. Now I don't think I was out of my depth: I knew what needed doing – but I was so convinced I shouldn't be there that I couldn't bring myself to do it.

And it turns out that when you feel like that, your body responds in kind. I felt constantly tired, my limbs seemed heavy and cumbersome, and I couldn't think straight enough to make a decision about anything. I can't remember much about huge chunks of that period in my life – which I've since found out is a classic symptom of anxiety.

There are so many reasons why people – women in particular – suffer from anxiety. I don't have an anxiety disorder and I can't imagine how it must feel. But have I been anxious? And has it impacted on how I've felt and behaved in a significant way? Certainly – on numerous occasions.

And for me, it's always come down to one thing: feeling that I'm not a good fit at work. And that I'm not the best possible person on the planet to do that job – which (a) I may or may not be, and (b) what a ridiculous standard to set yourself. It's the doom-laden certainty that I'll mess up monstrously at any moment and my whole life is going to crash around me.

It's moments when I know with absolute certainty (or think I know) that to survive I need to be at the absolute top of my game, defy all expectations (especially my own) and be the best possible version of myself at all times. That's when my body rigs the game against me. And every time I've crashed and burnt, it's because my brain has decided I'm not good enough for the job I'm in, and the rest of me has set out to prove it right.

I'm tempted, for the sake of ease, to describe this as burnout. But I don't think that does justice to the full physical and emotional breakdowns others have gone through at times of emotional strain and crisis. For me a culmination of a couple of months of full-pelt anxiety will be a (sometimes alcohol-fuelled) meltdown and an inability to get out of bed for a couple of days. Or, at worst, a couple of weeks' inertia while I get my head straight and decide what I want to do next. I like to see it as my brain resetting itself, a survival mechanism, so that I don't, in fact, burn out. It's probably best phrased as 'brownout' – an internet-friendly term that, as well as describing a drop in voltage in an electrical supply, can refer to the low-level lethargy and discontent that may come when you're just not feeling it at work. According to some studies, it's on the rise for any number of reasons – from technology (reading your emails in bed is bad, guys) to a reduction in roles with incremental career progress.

Ironically, I get like this when I'm particularly anxious: symptoms of inertia and exhaustion mask the huge levels of anxiety I'm feeling. But, as I've said, there's normally a way out of this. I've worked out the biting point where I need to stop, have a rest, reset my mind and carry on.

But true burnout is more insidious. The phrase was coined in the 1970s to describe the psychological effects of work stress, and is now used to describe everything from a full physical breakdown to that slightly insane feeling you get 2.5 days before you're due to go on holiday and your boss asks you to write a nineteen-page report. But feeling depressed, cynical about a job you used to love, constantly exhausted and falling ill all the time are signs that you could be about to crash.

Author and blogger Laura Jane Williams found this happening to her just as her book, *Becoming*, was published. 'I wasn't myself. I wasn't engaging with books and movies and TV shows – nothing brought me joy or any kind of reaction,' she tells me. 'I was very irritable. Everyone wanted too much of me, whether that was a sixth-former reaching out because they wanted to interview me for their sociology coursework or a friend asking if I wanted to go for drinks tomorrow night. Everything was an inconvenience to me. There was no joy – I had used up all the serotonin in my body. There was none left.'

Laura thinks the pressure of writing such a personal and heartfelt book – and doing it so quickly – contributed to her burning out, as well as a desire to 'appear' successful. 'I think I probably felt a lot of pressure that to do something well is to always be on. I've had to learn to switch off. I think it's a millennium of being scrutinised as a woman. When everything you do is scrutinised how can you not become performative? How can you not pretend to be Someone Who Has It All Together?'

And she's right. The organised, together, quirky, funny, sexy, clever, popular woman we're all meant to be is the vision we're supposed to be presenting to the world, but the pressure of trying to realise that fantasy can be overwhelming.

'It took burning out for me to realise that sometimes I have it together, sometimes I don't, and I'm still worthy. I don't have to perform this role. I feel like I've taken the mask off a bit,' Laura concludes.

But what if you're in that environment all the time? Charlotte, who works in a very Alpha female (and competitive) magazine environment, spoke of the exhaustion of just trying to keep up. 'I find it really tiring. It can make you feel a bit fucking rubbish, like you're not good enough. It can make you feel like you're in competition with each other. Someone will be like "Have you read this article?" and someone else will respond with "No, but have you read this one, or seen this TV show?" And then someone else chips in with "Have you heard this album, or this album, or this album?"'

Assigning Alpha or Beta status to whether we've watched enough of the right box sets, or listened to the right album, sounds ridiculous. Yet we've all done it. I'm constantly feeling disorganised and out of the loop because my film and television consumption are not what they should be. I feel anxious and guilty if I don't read the Sunday papers and an utterly pointless sense of achievement when I manage to get through them. Every time I see someone I know Instagramming from an exhibition I sort-of know I *should* go and see at the weekend (note 'should'), I feel bad. I feel bad that they're sufficiently organised to go out and do stuff at weekends while I'm desperately trying to wash my pants and catch up with work, and then I feel bad because I know that when I do get some down time, I'll probably spend it in the bath, or mindlessly scrolling through my phone, or gazing out of the window.

It's a failure on all fronts for me. Why? Because I haven't sufficiently maximised my leisure time in a way that conforms with a standard absolutely no one, apart from myself, has set for me. Who cares? Why do I care?

And this is why we're all knackered.

Have you noticed that when Barack Obama was president he only ever wore blue or grey suits? No? Well, he did. He explained this choice in an interview with *Vanity Fair* magazine. 'I'm trying to pare down decisions. I don't want to make decisions about what I'm eating or wearing because I have too many other decisions to make.'

Famously, Steve Jobs, the late co-founder and CEO of Apple, always wore a black turtleneck and jeans, while Mark Zuckerberg, owner of Facebook, is rarely seen in anything other than a black hoodie with a grey T-shirt and jeans. Why? Because, like Obama, they want to focus their decision-making energies on the important stuff, not the minutiae of day-to-day living. Decision fatigue exists: studies show that making lots of decisions has a detrimental impact on our willpower. The more decisions we have to make, say, before going out for a drink with a friend after work, the less likely it is that our willpower will hold out: you will make a bad decision (three large glasses of red wine, a packet of salt and vinegar crisps and a box of chicken on the way home). The other way people respond to decision fatigue? They preserve the energy that making another decision would use up by making no decision at all. A study by Jonathan Levav of Stanford and Shai Danziger of Ben-Gurion University, cited in a 2011 article about decision fatigue by John Tierney in the *New York Times*, found that the parole board of an Israeli prison, comprising a judge, a criminologist and a social worker, paroled offenders they saw first thing in the morning 70 per cent of the time, compared with 10 per cent of the offenders they met at the end of the day.

Offenders were much more likely to be paroled in the morning because the board members' minds were fresh and incisive. By the end of the day, when they had used most of their energy, they would deny parole rather than make a bad decision – thereby making none at all. The prisoners hadn't been released, which would have risked them going on a crime spree, but there was still the possibility that they would be paroled at a later date.

Decisiveness is a trait commonly associated with Alphas and strong leaders. I am not very decisive. Or, more accurately, I can be incredibly decisive in the right circumstances, but those circumstances don't come along very often. When I'm feeling low-level harassed (that is, most of the time), I put off making even small decisions, until those small issues become huge, almost insurmountable problems that require much more mental energy to tackle. I'm good at making a decision when I absolutely have to, such as when the now almost insurmountable problem absolutely has to be tackled or when I'm about to go on holiday and stuff just 'needs sorting', or when I have a completely clear head and desk, with no big problems hanging over me. Between those two extremes, when my head is full of the fug of everyday life? I'll put off making a decision and look to maintain the status quo wherever possible.

The female leaders who – outwardly at least – appear the most Alpha to me (and they are often some of the women I admire most) are able to make thoughtful decisions quickly, seemingly without becoming weighed down by them. They don't attribute emotion to decision-making or, indeed, to the decision itself in the way that I do. How do they cut out the crap and focus on the important stuff?

A few years ago, journalist and writer Anna Hart realised she had made her life so busy that she never had time to enjoy any of it. 'I spent my early twenties after I first moved to London accumulating stuff. Clothes and DVDs, yes, but also friends and acquaintances, hobbies, habits like yoga and zumba and other things to occupy my time. This was probably right for me for a time, but one day it hit me that all these things I'd used to build my life were actually holding me back from doing what I wanted to do. This sounds dickish, but I had too many friends – I couldn't see them all and felt like a crap friend to everyone. I spent my nights dashing to two or three drinking sessions, spending way too much time on the tube and not really enjoying any of it. It was the same story with my stuff – my wardrobe was so full I couldn't see those amazing dresses at the back of it. And by trying to cram in yoga, climbing, running, swimming and zumba classes, I never really got good at any of it.

'So I made a decision to simplify my life: I went freelance, immediately cutting out at least three hours of travel every day. My productivity immediately soared, and by biking everywhere rather than taking public transport, travelling was no longer a waste of time, it was exercise and pretty enjoyable.

'I became super-strict about the work events I would go to – I used to force myself to attend them all in case I missed a networking opportunity or whatever. But it took its toll on my energy levels and productivity. Ultimately being pickier about what I attend has definitely improved my career rather than harming it.

'I'm not completely closed to new people, activities and things – that would be a recipe for a joyless life – but I've learnt to accept that time is finite. And doing something new means less time for what you've already got in your life. So it needs to really, really be worth it.'

I love this story because it's a great reminder that our time is precious, and it's our own, yet so many of us give it away to other people without a second thought out of . . . guilt? Obligation?

Anna is a great example of someone who has managed to cut the minutiae out of her day . . . but did you notice that the three other examples I've cited, who have done that with their wardrobes, are men? Because a lot of the crap, whether that's deciding what to wear, working out who can pick up the children from school or finding a meeting room for the client who's coming in, naturally falls on women's shoulders. It's harder to make that big strategic decision about the future of your department if you've already made thirty smaller decisions that day and it's only eleven a.m.

Barack Obama's suit story is a good one: compare that (and that no one had particularly noticed that he only ever wore two suits until he pointed it out) with the scrutiny of his wife, Michelle, as First Lady, particularly her clothes. Arguably the First Lady role, as Michelle Obama understood it, is to be more than a clothes-horse. In her eight years she tackled childhood obesity with her Let's Move initiative, became an advocate for military families, joined the campaign to bring back the Chibok schoolgirls, who were kidnapped in Nigeria, and was a vocal supporter for same-sex marriage. She probably had to make more decisions in any day than most chief executives, and had more important things to think about than whether she was wearing Jason Wu or J. Crew today, but those were still the decisions we judged her on.

Or let's look at the British Prime Minister Theresa May. From the Vivienne Westwood coat she wore to meet the queen when she took office, to her infamous leopard print kitten heels (yes, a pair of kitten heels can be infamous) her clothing choices are scrutinised in a way that her colleagues or rivals rarely are (Jeremy Corbyn's anoraks and Boris Johnson's bicycle clips get noted, yes, but they don't get anything like the same sort of air time). Yes, Theresa May and Michelle Obama have big teams around them, but that doesn't change the fact that they are still, as individuals, expected to make hundreds of decisions every single day. And, unlike the Mark Zuckerbergs and the Steve Jobses of the world, they can't opt out of deciding what they wear, because how they present themselves is a big part of how we judge them.

Obviously, Michelle Obama's Jason Wu dress is the thin end of the wedge. The point is, we all know what happens when you have to make too many decisions each day – your ability to make the big ones becomes impeded. You burn out. And the playing field isn't level: women are expected to make dozens of micro-decisions each day that simply don't trouble most men. And that will impact on our ability to be decisive and thoughtful when we need to be.

And my decision-making, like most people's, is certainly worse when I'm plagued by self-doubt. If I don't believe I'm in the right role, if I don't believe I'm doing a good job, or if I think someone else could be doing it better, then I become much more indecisive because I'm constantly second-guessing myself and trying to work out what a better, more Alpha woman would do in my shoes. The mental energy used up by each decision is equivalent to that which would normally be spent on three. When I feel like that, every decision becomes a series of trade-offs – further zapping my willpower and leaving me feeling stressed and knackered.

A series of fairly heartbreaking studies shows that people living in poverty demonstrate less willpower over time because they constantly have to perform small trade-offs to make their income meet their needs. This constant decision-making makes it harder for them to reserve energy for less important stuff. It's been found that low self-control and low income are linked, but the concept of decision fatigue changes the narrative around this at a fundamental level: it suggests that low self-control is born of circumstance, rather than being its cause.

This also matters in a workplace context: if you're over-burdened with decisions, constantly making trade-offs – even if they're just with yourself – and second-guessing everything, your willpower and energy levels will become more depleted. The seeds of self-doubt that have been planted in your brain will flourish, and the more you question yourself, the harder you will find it to be effective.

Writer Daisy Buchanan discovered this when she took on a new role at a magazine she had always adored. She quickly realised it wasn't for her – but couldn't bring herself to make an active decision to quit. 'I felt like I was being crap at work because I was a bad person, and leaving would make me even more of a bad person. By staying I was not making a decision to do anything, and it meant I was in stasis – it was like I'd gone into hibernation and couldn't make a decision about anything.

'It was like every decision I made felt like the wrong one, so I'd try and do the opposite, but that felt wrong too. I was like a tyre that had lost its tread, and not just at work. I got really scared about getting dressed in the morning and deciding what to wear to work, I wasn't sure if I was allowed to leave in the evenings, and there would be meetings where I was never sure if I was supposed to be there or not – and I'd always get it wrong.'

I've definitely experienced this at work too: the worse things get, the harder it is to pull yourself out of that spiral of self-doubt. It becomes utterly exhausting.

Daisy continued: 'My friends said that in this period I seemed really far away, almost like I was medicated – but once I'd handed in my notice, and made the decision to leave, I wrote the freelance piece I'm most proud of. Once I'd done that everything lifted and it was like I was myself again.'

It's hard to discuss burnout, or the modern definition of burnout, without looking at social media a bit more. Not just the expectations it places on us to be perfect and present a certain image, but the impact the very act of being plugged in all the time has on our brain, our cognitive function and our ability to make decisions and implement them effectively (the very definition of productivity at work, surely).

Let's revisit the fictional archetypal successful woman, shall we? Because how she is outside work is as intimidating as her professional life. Yes, she's constantly connected (although she doesn't give the impression that she's a slave to social media, she's far too in control for that) and can demonstrate laser-like focus and an effortless ability to dart from one topic to another, solving problems quickly and incisively, and always able to recall the most obscure but useful statistic or make the most salient argument for her case. But when she's with her friends she's fun and attentive, and when she's with her colleagues, she's absorbed in the task at hand. And she can also explain the story behind every trending topic on Twitter, her every social-media account is updated at entirely appropriate intervals, she's watched every important box set on Netflix, is horrified that you still haven't finished season one of *House of Cards*, and confesses to watching old episodes of *The Hills* as a guilty pleasure when she's hung-over. There's no podcast she hasn't listened to, no album she hasn't heard, no gig she hasn't been to, and no book she hasn't read. Opting out isn't an option.

Has anyone wondered why this woman's brain hasn't short-circuited?

Phrases like 'social-media burnout' and 'information overload' are frequently bandied about to describe what can happen when we're constantly assaulted with information and distractions on social media. But what we're really talking about here is good old-fashioned multitasking on an industrial scale. We absorb so much information on an hourly or even minute-by-minute basis, yet studies have shown that if we don't use it almost immediately, we lose up to 75 per cent from our brains, rendering useless most of the stuff we're bombarded with.

Constant distractions by social media, beeping phones and computers, and colleagues asking you questions are all impeding your ability to get the job done. Glenn Wilson, visiting professor of psychology at Gresham College, London, found that people's problem-solving performance dropped by the equivalent of ten IQ points when they multitasked – and crucially discovered that their stress levels also rose.

Earl Miller, a neuroscientist at MIT and one of the world experts on divided attention, agrees that multitasking isn't the ideal state for the human brain because we're 'not wired to multitask well . . . When people think they're multitasking, they're actually just switching from one task to another very rapidly. And every time they do, there's a cognitive cost.'

So, a lot of the hallmarks of a busy, obviously successful person you see – constantly moving from task to task with seeming ease and unbroken focus – are probably a myth. And the busy Alpha woman who is able perfectly to curate and update her social-media feeds while managing a team of twenty with an iron fist, and nailing her passion project on the side, may be better at creating the impression that she's multitasking than actually doing it (or maybe not doing everything properly).

The problem, according to Dave Crenshaw, author of *The Myth of Multitasking*, is the 'switching cost' – the time taken to switch from one task and refocus on another. 'You take much longer to accomplish things, make more mistakes and increase your stress.'

Professor Wilson also noted that while women were better multitaskers than men, their stress levels rose more significantly than men's when they were forced to multitask – and, of course, multitasking requires constant decision-making, and we all know what that can do. Which begs the further question: if multitasking isn't any good for our brains, what is it doing to our souls?

Here is the headline from one article on the subject from Motherboard, Vice's technology website: 'All of Your Devices Are Bumming You Out'. They were referring to a Michigan State University study, which found that higher media multitasking was associated with higher depression and social-anxiety symptoms, and that 'The unique association between media multitasking and these measures of psychosocial dysfunction suggests that the growing trend of multitasking with media may represent a unique risk factor for mental health problems related to mood and anxiety.' Meanwhile a newer study by the University of Sussex found that social-media multitasking can change the structure of our brains, shrinking the part that processes emotion.

That's why the link between the way we make decisions, our attitudes towards multitasking and the use of social media are all so important in how we measure success. Alpha or Beta, we're setting the bar too high for ourselves in pursuit of a level of perfection it's impossible to emulate. Our brains are capable of amazing things, but when we're constantly trying to work the angle, multitask and make hundreds of decisions each day, all focused around how we're perceived by the wider world, our brains are liable to short-circuit. It's time we gave them – and ourselves – a break and took life one step at a time. That might be the most Beta sentence ever written: after all, stopping, taking a step back and doing nothing is rarely cited as the secret to anyone's success. But it may stop us having a massive meltdown.

Because this culture of competitive perfection and nailing everything doesn't make us the best at what we do. It doesn't make us fulfil our full potential, or be our most creative or our happiest. It dulls sharp minds. It means we spread ourselves too thinly. *And*, despite all of the work, stress and effort, we *still* think everyone else is doing more than us.

And that is the biggest myth of all.

9.

IT'S WHAT'S ON THE OUTSIDE THAT COUNTS (AND WHY EVERYONE'S JUDGING YOU)

'You just know as a black girl that you're not allowed to be outspoken, you just know. When I had my first job I worked for a TV magazine and I learnt very quickly that the girls that were my age who were white were allowed to speak out. But when I did the same, there would be a throwaway comment like "You don't need to have that attitude." That was when I was twenty-one and I just learnt very quickly that I'm not allowed to have the same sort of opinion as my white female counterparts.'

I don't have a silly anecdote about a mishap at work to start this chapter because my experience here isn't that relevant. If we're looking at how race, sexuality, body size, disability or even the way you speak impact on how you're treated in the workplace, then all the cards are in my favour. Anything that's holding me back is internal. It's stuff that's going on in my head. Fear, anxiety or lack of confidence – the things people can't see.

But what if the thing that affects people's perception of you is external? What if it's something you have no control over that impacts on how people perceive you at every level? What do you do then?

'I'm very aware of how much I speak,' says Tobi, in her twenties, the journalist who opened the chapter. 'I am very aware that if I'm in a group setting and it's quite mixed . . .

Let's be real, if I'm in a group setting and it's very white and I'm the only black woman in the room, I don't want to be the woman about whom they say, "Oh, yes, she speaks a lot, she's really loud." I just don't want to be that person, I don't want people to have that memory of me.'

Beverly, fifty-four, works for a large international leisure brand. She's African American and characterises herself as 'driven, determined, very aggressive, focused, data-driven, very intense'.

So, Alpha. Beverly isn't particularly concerned about being considered a tough boss. 'I'm older, I'm African American, I'm female, tall, intense. I'm aggressive, assertive, very direct and specific with my language, I'm experienced, I know what I'm doing, so not only do I have that personality, I have the experience to back it up. So, yeah, it's intense. I imagine working for me is hard.

'One of the things I think I compensate with is that I smile a lot. I'm very happy and tell lots of jokes. I'm always in a good mood for the most part – and even if I'm not actually in a good mood, I'm always "spectacular". I think that people expect me to be angry based on how intense I am so it throws them off when I'm not. Also, I've found that humour and smiles disarm people because the stereotypes of being an angry black female in American culture are very intense.'

Although a classic Alpha, Beverly is aware that for Beta women of colour the challenges are myriad. 'I have a couple of young women who work on my team – they're more Beta than Alpha without question. One of the things I've tried to teach them is to avoid using colloquialisms in their conversations. They're the digital generation and they tend to bring memes to life in their conversation . . . One of them will become very exaggerated with her language, she'll say things like "*Girrrrl*" or "No, ma'am," and I've told her that her personality isn't strong enough to combat the unconscious bias that is associated with her playing that caricature.'

This works on two levels, part of which I can relate to. A trait I see in myself, which feels very Beta, is that I'll sell myself short, or tell a silly joke or story against myself to make other people feel comfortable – even though I might be setting myself up as a buffoon. I undermine myself when I do it. Beverly's employee might be doing the same thing to make other people feel more comfortable, but she is also playing into people's unconscious bias about her. And that's something Beverly feels you need a very strong (Alpha) personality to overcome. 'It's one thing to do that sort of thing in the context of your friends and the people who know you and what you're capable of, but it's another to do that in the workplace, because for women of colour, and women of colour who are Beta, that can torpedo your career. It allows people to paint you into a box and they then begin to have ideas about where you can and cannot excel. If your personality is not strong enough to combat this narrative, then you are limited.'

Beverly's story really does highlight how my agonising over whether I'm Alpha or Beta enough at any given time is very much a white-girl problem. Because although I believe my white male colleagues have more autonomy than I do to be themselves in the workplace, every woman of colour I've spoken to has talked of having far less latitude in the workplace than I do.

148

In America, the Center for Women Policy Studies found 21 per cent of women of colour surveyed did not feel they were free to be 'themselves at work'. The study also found that more than a third of women of colour – ranging from 28 per cent to 44 per cent – believed that they must 'play down' their race or ethnicity to succeed.

Also in the States, a 2015 study by Catalyst, *Women in S&P 500 Companies by Race/Ethnicity*, found that women of colour make up 0.4 per cent of S&P 500 (Standard & Poors 500: an American stock market index) CEOs, and that only 4.6 per cent of S&P 500 CEOs are women at all. Catalyst also talks about women of colour facing a concrete ceiling rather than the glass one their white female colleagues have to contend with. The difference? It's virtually impossible to smash through, and you can't even see through it.

The issues around gender, race and office politics are complex and myriad. 'When you're in it, it just becomes a case of "How do you survive?"' explains Nicky, who eventually left her job in advertising after she found herself listening to daily instances of casual racism from the rest of the team she was in (which was all white, all male), and felt unable to speak out. 'I did not have the perspective to find the right thing to do. Even when I spoke to my friends about it outside work and they were like "Are you kidding me?"

'But the point when I decided I was not doing this any more was when I thought, If my dad were a fly on the wall of this conversation in this room, and saw me not saying anything he'd be so ashamed. But I felt like I couldn't flag it up because it would be seen as me playing the race card.

It's a ridiculous thing to say because, realistically, there are very, very few instances in which a person of colour would play the race card. It's just not something that you're comfortable doing, it's not an easy go-to option. In the end, I just left.'

Part of the trouble, she feels, is that a lot of the tiny acts of racism she encounters as a woman of colour at work are so insidious – micro-aggressions she's expected to deal with constantly on top of her actual job. 'That's the thing, you never know. But it's like a sixth sense you have in your back, when you can't quite point to what it is but you just know. So that's the thing, you can't quantify it and you can't say what it is.'

Bridget is a freelance writer in her twenties. The prospect of untangling the gender and race politics of an office environment have put her off applying for permanent jobs, even though having a regular job and a steady income appealed to her. 'The friends that I have, women of colour, have all had a lot of issues,' she explains. 'It only really works if you're in a very female-oriented workplace, which is a real privilege. Generally my friends who work in mixed environments find it very, very difficult. Whether they're at the bottom of the ladder and people think they're the cleaning ladies, or if they're somewhere in the middle and they get treated like someone who is brand new.

'My friend said, "I feel like I have to work so hard to prove myself to people who are junior to me." She looks very young – she's thirty-one but could pass for twenty-four – and she's black but didn't go to uni. She said she feels like she has to prove herself so she puts on this aggressive

Alpha role. She's not like that but it's the only way she gets their respect.'

And it's not a trade-off Bridget wants to make. She's also aware that even in the media or the theatre, where people are aware that they should be more diverse, actually putting it into practice is another matter. 'In a space that is very white, like the arts and journalism, people are aware of race problems and, with a few notable exceptions, they broadly want change. So when you're already there, people naturally want to stay in that realm because it makes them feel better. But, if there were ten people on a team then two people would have to leave in order for more diverse people to arrive.'

And the nuances of race and gender in the workplace are intensely complex. Laura, thirty-four, works in tech. She is Chinese, and she feels that, much of the time, this works to her advantage as it plays up to the stereotype that if she's Chinese she must be good with numbers and data: in that context, her face fits. 'I feel like on very rare occasions that I'm just different – but for the last ten years I've managed to embrace it and use it to my advantage.

'When I'm in a room with a group of Caucasian middle-aged men, they don't know what to do with me. I'm "the other". But, on the whole, my experience has been that if you're a woman in tech you're protected, but if you're in an area that's less data- or tech-oriented, if you're in the service industry, for example, then it doesn't work the same way.'

This is what Nikki, a Chinese English woman aged thirty-seven discovered after several years in a customer-service role: 'There was a big difference in my work ethic from that of my white colleagues. I was working silly hours, which they rarely did. People who were less capable than me were promoted above me, and you're not meant to talk about your pay, but I found out they were earning more than me too. One of my friends at work – who was white – kept saying it was a race issue, but I only fully realised it once we got a new CEO in. He was Asian, and all of a sudden I started being invited to more senior strategy meetings, and my hard work started to be recognised. Eventually all those tiny things – being looked over for promotions, other people being promoted above me – clicked. It was a race issue – my face just didn't fit.'

The thing is, everyone should get to say how they're defined in the workplace, not other people, no matter how unconsciously they're doing it. No one's card should be marked the minute they walk through the door. You need to be able to do your job, to speak up in a meeting, to defend yourself and show passion if you want, without someone making a value judgement about you in the process.

For Tobi, her hair is a big part of this – case in point, changing attitudes to women of colour with natural hair. 'At the moment I have quite curly big hair and it's quite a statement, an unapologetic statement. And for a while, I would never have had curly hair like that, I would always have it straight, because it's this whole thing about [how] our hair is politicised, like I'm trying to make this massive statement about being black – it couldn't just be hair. But things have moved on so that now, like if I got a job tomorrow in a mainstream office, I think I could have natural hair, especially in journalism. I think people are over it now. I think people get it more. But rewind four years ago, I was definitely less comfortable having it.'

There's a long and depressing history of black women being disciplined, sent home from work or even losing their jobs over their hair – from the Zara employee in Toronto who was told her box braids were 'unprofessional' to the woman who was told by her London employer to wear a weave because her natural hair was . . . unprofessional. This happens time and time again in office environments, restaurants and even schools. And the word 'unprofessional' is so loaded, isn't it? It implies you're sloppy or lax. Like you just couldn't be bothered to make that bit of extra effort to get your hair all slick and shiny and straight.

But what it really means is 'You don't look the way I think someone who works for me should look.' And how women 'should' look appears to be as Caucasian as possible. This is so far removed from any given person's ability to do their job it's laughable, and yet it persists.

And then there's the clothes we wear, the makeup we may or may not put on our faces, the amount we weigh. Ninety per cent of the time they have no relationship to how we do our job, yet everyone has an opinion on them – and is keen to dish it out like the sagest careers advice you've ever heard.

Bridget used to wear her hair in braids, before deciding to shave her head completely. She said the act itself was freeing – 'It feels liberating. I hated doing my hair. It feels so much nicer not to spend a fortune on getting my hair braided every month.' But it has also had an impact on how she is viewed, and the unconscious bias people have towards her. 'I [now] feel like I'm allowed to wear big bold hoops from my youth again, whereas when I had big hair, words like "ghetto" and "hood" would come to mind. But the image of a woman with their head shaved is more middle class. It's different.'

I've worked at casual, laid-back agencies where I've been told my jeans and trainers weren't appropriate, just as a more senior male colleague emerged from a meeting room with a client in jeans and trainers. I've been told I dress too 'young'. I've been told I look too 'corporate', and I've been told I look 'tired' almost every time I don't wear makeup to work. In fact, I once stopped wearing makeup to work for about three months because I was very busy and tired, and several people asked me if I was 'coping'.

On the other hand, when I 'get it right' that's noted too – and not in the 'women admiring other women's clothes' way. It's more 'I see you've stepped up your game/started wearing mascara again/finally bought a new dress. Got your eye on that promotion, have you?' from a smarmy (male) manager, who tries to read you via your wardrobe choices so he doesn't have to make the effort of actually finding anything out about you.

I do it too. The women I most admire in the office always look fantastic – smart and cool, not too corporate, just the perfect version of who they're trying to be. It's part of why I admire them because to me it's a sign that they've got themselves together, that in the long list of things they've had to remember to do that day, they also pulled out the perfect outfit from their perfectly curated wardrobes. They've done the one last thing, that cherry on top, that screams, 'I'm really professional,' or 'I've got it together,' or 'I make loads of money and am really successful.'

But what I've done – and what we all do to some extent – is go from admiring these women because they have a good eye for nice clothes, great personal style and make an effort to thinking that their appearance is the reason they're great at their jobs.

My boss is pretty kick-ass in most scenarios, and is also very stylish. The two aren't mutually inclusive, but I always secretly think that if I were as good at wearing a blouse as she was, I'd be a bit more kick-ass too.

But what about the guys? Everyone wears clothes, so they have the same problem too, right? Sorry, I'm not buying it. When it comes to men and clothes, there are fewer rules, there's less ambiguity, and less consequence when they get it wrong. If it's a formal working environment they wear a suit, or an open shirt and a jacket, while women periodically grapple with whether or not a trousersuit is a thing. And if it's a casual office . . . Well, I've only ever worked in offices with no formal workwear policy, and while my outfits – and the outfits of my female colleagues – have been commented on or noted on numerous occasions, I've never seen or heard it happen to a man, including the guy who wore flip-flops and shorts to work every day of the year.

As if further proof was needed, a 2017 report by the parliamentary Petitions Committee and the Women and Equalities Committee reveals just how archaic our generalised attitude to what women wear in the workplace still is. As part of the report, MPs spoke to women who had been sent home from work for not wearing heels, told to dye their hair blonde for their jobs, and wear more makeup or more revealing clothes. And, of course, the report unearthed more stories of black women being told to remove their braids or get their hair chemically relaxed, lest they look . . . unprofessional. That word again.

You could argue that women have more choice in terms of what to wear – which in turn gives women more opportunity to get it 'wrong', whatever that means. But, fundamentally, women are judged far more for their appearance than men ever are – from politicians to pop stars.

A 2016 study by the University of the West of Scotland found that when employers look at the social-media profiles of prospective candidates, they're more likely to judge women on appearances and men on content. Researchers asked a group of men and women to look at a series of Facebook profiles and judge each person as a potential candidate for a job.

Dr Graham Scott, who helped to conduct the study, explains, 'When it comes to assessing female candidates, there is a lot of reliance on photographs to judge the qualities of the candidate – this is true regardless of whether it's a man or a woman reviewing the profile. Name is looked at first, then images. Finally, recent posts and friends are looked at. When it comes to assessing a male candidate, both men and women focus on name, profile information, recent posts, and friends.'

And women are more concerned with their external appearance than men because, simply, we are judged far more on how we look than men are. How we look is part of how we're evaluated.

It's like a code we have to unpick: what sort of person does my boss/employer want me to appear to be? How much of my own character or personality can I afford to include before they start to feel uncomfortable? How do I translate this into an affordable, flattering, comfortable wardrobe of clothes I don't hate?

And even if you're willing to go along with it and to play the game, you can't ask. You can't say to your boss, '*Soooo*, Kevin, if I were to dress like a real-life avatar of the woman you imagine is the perfect employee, so as to ensure that you feel comfortable and reassured in my presence, what would that look like?'

That would be a very strange conversation indeed, and would probably result in HR taking you to one side to reiterate that Kevin has never said, on any occasion, that he'd like to conduct an extramarital affair with you. Nonetheless, most of us dress to please our boss, our colleagues, our clients. We dress to make them think we're a safe pair of hands but not too safe, that we get them, but we're also injecting something new into the mix. That we're original, passionate and creative, but not so much as to become a liability.

If I'm being honest, sometimes I enjoy it. If I've got the right thing to wear, that I know I look good in and doesn't give me sweat patches, it boosts my confidence, makes me feel I look the part, as if – for once – I've got the whole package right. I look the part, therefore I am the part. It must be true. I've nailed the cherry on the top.

But I'd say it makes me 2 per cent better at my job. Possibly 5 per cent at an absolute max if I have to do something particularly scary that day.

And this is all great . . . but what if you don't want to wear what other people deem 'stylish', or 'professional', or 'appropriate'?

A few years ago I put on a bit of weight – a couple of stone, so not loads in the grand scheme of things, but enough to take me from averagely slim through to 'Wow, your boobs have got big,' and 'Getting a bit matronly . . .' Before that, I'd considered what I wore in a professional capacity to an extent, but I'd never worried about what I could 'get away with' or 'dressing for my age'. Suddenly these were primary concerns. I felt as if putting on weight was a sign I was getting a bit slobby and lazy (in reality it was mainly a sign that I rarely left my desk), and if I didn't wear the right clothes, people would think I hadn't noticed, or didn't realise, or wasn't trying to do anything about it. Having more flesh on display than usual no longer felt fun or risqué, it felt like an undignified move that would embarrass my colleagues as much as it would embarrass me. People only want to see flesh when it's young and nubile and, well, not very fleshy, you see.

Fashion was out, obviously – I wasn't allowed to do fashion until I bucked up my ideas and trimmed down – so I started wearing 'classic' clothes in muted colours, ostensibly in an attempt to look 'more professional' and 'my age'. In reality, I was making a transition to the person I thought I was about to become: 'the slightly bigger girl who dresses well for her size'.

Just to reiterate, it was two stone. I'm not even that short. It was not a big deal. I wasn't even really overweight on the BMI chart. No one gave a damn except me. Yet something I'd never once considered, my weight, suddenly became of crucial importance at work: it meant I was out of a club I never knew I was a member of – The People Who Just Fit In.

And then there's our voices. We think about what we're saying all the time, but have you ever considered how you're saying it? As much as I hate the way my voice sounds in recordings, I always kind of assume that when I'm talking to someone face-to-face they're more concerned with what I'm saying than how I'm saying it.

But I could be wrong.

There are some aspects of how we speak and how we're judged by it that cut across gender lines (although I still maintain that, as with most things, men have more latitude than women) – the use of slang, swear words or regional accents, for example. How much of an impact these things have is up for debate. A 2013 ITV/Comres study found that eight out of ten employers admitted making discriminating decisions based on regional accents, while 28 per cent of British people feel discriminated against because of how they speak.

Meanwhile a 2015 report from the Social Mobility and Child Poverty Commission found that recruiters favoured people with certain accents over others, regardless of academic merit. Speaking with a Birmingham accent is considered less intelligent and attractive than not opening your mouth.

Dr Alex Baratta from Manchester Institute of Education believes that, while in America regional accents tend to be indicators of race, in the UK it's all about class. In one small study he conducted with trainee teachers, he found that those from the north or Midlands were told to modify their accents far more than those from the south. He also noted that women were asked to modify their accents more than male trainees. Posher accents weren't necessarily a bonus: 'RP [received pronunciation] can be seen as authoritative, posh, educated, but it can also come across as arrogant and stuck-up. It's all about the perception people take from it.'

He's right – although a posh accent still works in your favour in some areas – acting as a signifier of a private school, then an Oxbridge education (the City, the upper echelons of the Tory Party), in other areas, a regional accent might actually work for you.

Louise, thirty-two, flattened her Yorkshire accent when we were at university together in London. She then went to work in PR before becoming a researcher for a Conservative MP. 'I affected my accent a lot at university because most of the people I knew had been privately educated and were really well spoken – I just assumed that's what you were expected to do. It certainly was in PR – even though my accent had all but disappeared by then, the fact that I was "northern" was still commented on.'

Later, when she was working for the MP, she realised that her gender and Bradford background were a bonus: they made her stand out from a sea of posh white men in similar roles. It made her interesting in a world of dull people.

Conversely, my friend Alice, the civil servant I mentioned earlier, was privately educated and thinks her relatively posh accent sometimes works against her in an environment that's (ostensibly) committed to egalitarianism.

But there's one aspect of the voice that is still, for the most part, a female problem: pitch. While Louise spent years thinking about her regional accent and what that would mean for her career, she never considered that the pitch of her voice might cause her a problem. 'I've got a high-pitched voice in a company where only 13 per cent of employees are women – it's definitely noted,' she says. 'I'm fine when people get to know me, but I think it really impacts on how people see me at first – I've caught someone almost unthinkingly going to mimic me on more than one occasion. It's definitely been noticed in the business – I'm being sent on a Speaking With Impact course soon, not something any of my male colleagues have ever been asked to do.'

Scientists reckon that the pitch, timbre, volume, speed and cadence of your voice have a massive impact on how convincing you are and how people judge your character. And if you're high-pitched, or even sound 'too feminine', you're judged more harshly. A study by scientists from Northwestern University, the University of Colorado and Tilburg University in the Netherlands found that a more feminine voice is perceived to be 'less competent' than a male voice, while research suggests that both men and women prefer people with masculine voices in leadership roles.

And let's not forget vocal fry.

You'll have heard vocal fry, even if you don't realise it. Vocal fry is 'the lowest vocal and is produced through a loose glottal closure which will permit air to bubble through slowly with a popping or rattling sound of a very low frequency'. It's that low, slightly growly affectation that you'll sometimes hear in American women (the Kardashians are prime offenders, if that's the right word). In 2011, a group of scientists at New York's Long Island University recorded thirty-four different women speaking. Two speech pathologists listened to the recordings in search of instances of vocal fry, which featured in two-thirds of them. Hardly a rigorous study, but it spawned a series of articles reporting that vocal fry was (a) really annoying, and (b) on the rise among young women.

The perceived problem with it seems to be that it has Valley Girl-esque connotations, making the speaker sound less bright than she would otherwise, and that it's seen as very much an affectation – something women put on to sound more attractive? Less decisive? Certainly more Beta.

On an episode of the podcast *This American Life*, presenter Ira Glass discusses the issue, noting that while listeners used to write in to radio shows to complain about female presenters using the word 'like', and up-speak (ending a sentence so that it sounds like a question), they now complain about vocal fry. But it's totally gendered: no one is complaining about any of the affectations found in male voices in the same way.

Incidentally, as an article in website Mental Floss points out, linguist and philosopher Noam Chomsky has a pretty bad case of vocal fry, and no one's moaning about that because he's Noam Chomsky.

It's also an age thing. Glass spoke to linguist Penny Eckert, who had conducted a study in which she asked people to rate a radio presenter with vocal fry on how authoritative they sounded. Those under forty thought the presenter sounded authoritative; those over forty did not.

The Society of Teachers of Speech and Drama even describes vocal fry as a speech impediment, with their chairperson saying, 'It seems extraordinary that, having fought hard for the right to be heard, women risk not being listened to, or taken seriously, by adopting a speech impediment – one that is at best laughable, at worst vocally damaging.' It doesn't seem to have occurred to them that if young women aren't being heard it's because people aren't listening properly.

It should go without saying that there's far more value in what people say than how they say it, just as there's far more value in the work you produce than the colour of your skin or your skirt. Yet it all adds up. It all counts towards that one big impression you're making in the workplace so that people can mentally place you in the most convenient box without the effort of having to get to know you. 'Ball-breaker', 'pushover', 'maternal', 'aggressive', 'difficult', 'emotional', 'bitch'.

You can control what you do or say, but how you present yourself, the impressions people are gaining of you day in, day out, are less easy to get a handle on. Everyone wants to belong in the place where they work, and fit. But what if the only way you can fit is to be less weird? Less passionate? Or to stop wearing bright colours, lose weight or wear a weave?

'Fit in or fuck off,' as one of my old bosses used to say, about anyone who didn't really 'get' our company's ethos or culture. He wanted to work with people who thought

like him, had the same values as him – and looked like
him.

But if fitting in is all about looking and sounding like
everyone else, then, as I get older, I know which option
I'm going to take.

10.

Q: WHAT HAPPENS WHEN YOU PUT A BETA PEG IN
AN ALPHA HOLE?

A: CRIPPLING ANXIETY

The first time I had to chair an event in front of a room of people (probably no more than fifty, so relatively small) should have been easy. It was an 'in conversation' session with a highly experienced, professional woman, who's widely respected across the industry. I also know her personally. True to form, she was fantastic, self-assured, and completely knew what she was doing. I, on the other hand, was a complete mess. I was stuttery, rambling and a little bit drunk (it was an evening event and they'd been serving wine for a couple of hours). It was like that first team meeting when I became an editor all over again. I lost my train of thought, trailed off mid-sentence, and had absolutely no connection with the audience (who were all rooting for me to succeed, which made the whole thing worse). I was so panicked that I lost all sense of why I was there and the story I was trying to tell. My fight-or-flight instinct had kicked in and I just wanted to get off the stage as quickly as possible.

My friend was fantastic. Sensing my discomfort, she launched into a series of juicy anecdotes, which required very little prompting from me, and everyone in the room lapped it up (apart from me: I was desperately trying to pretend I was on Mars).

My friend was born to be on that stage. She was relaxed, funny and self-deprecating. She was confident, had presence and instinctively knew how to connect with the audience. She could talk in detail about her area of expertise without notes or losing track of what she was saying. I looked like I'd rented the stage via a dodgy sublet that I couldn't get out of.

Nothing terrible happened – it was only a small event, no one was filming it and we certainly weren't saving lives, but I was rubbish and came away from the whole thing feeling bruised. Even worse, to anyone watching, I was wildly unconvincing as an editor – a role in which I'm meant to demonstrate authority and confidence, connect with people and tell a compelling story. And I had failed on every front.

A year ago, I had to do a talk. This time I had to present to several hundred people for twenty minutes. I was nervous beforehand, sure (full disclosure: I got total tunnel vision thirty seconds before going on stage), but I got through it, and a few people even came up to me at the end and told me how much they'd enjoyed it. I'm not saying people are now queuing round the block to hear my *bons mots*, but I'm basically fine. That's for two reasons. First, I've made myself stand on stages and talk to people far more frequently than I'd like to – I've taken myself out of my comfort zone on purpose because I know it's the only way I'm going to get better at something that I have to be decent at for my job. But I've also learnt to be honest about my strengths and weaknesses, and thought a bit more creatively about how they can work for me.

I'm far better when someone else is asking the questions,

and tapping out a rhythm in my head keeps my breathing regular and me focused on what I'm trying to say. And memorising what I want to say so that it's imprinted on my brain is crucial, because if I only half know something, or if I have to search around for a piece of information when I'm already feeling panicked, I can guarantee that my mind will go blank.

So, I've learnt how to fake it, but I'll never be a natural public speaker, and it used to go wrong when I pretended otherwise, tried to wing it, didn't prepare properly, or give myself enough time to calm down beforehand.

My point is, you may be able to fake some Alpha behaviour for a twenty-minute slot on stage, for a few hours or days or, in some cases, months, but it all unravels eventually. 'Fake it till you make it' is great advice for when you've got to suck it up and do something that terrifies you – and pushing ourselves out of our comfort zone can sometimes be as rewarding as it is challenging. But what if the role you're in requires you to fake who you are just to get through the day? You've either got to change how the role works for you or find a new one.

When Mary joined the civil service's Fast Stream programme in the 1960s, she had to learn pretty quickly how to fake it. 'I was put in charge of a team of middle-aged men when I was in my mid-twenties – all old suits. Even though I was terrified inside, I told them all, in no uncertain terms, that I was in charge. I've always been able to front it out when I've had to.' Mary had quickly realised that in such a highly dogmatic, masculine world, the only way to get the job done was – in her words – to 'front it out'.

But even though she became adept at exerting her authority when necessary, she discovered that 'faking it' as a matter of course had its limitations when she took over the administrative management of a hospital for a short period: 'The twenty or so consultants were some of the most difficult people I've ever had to deal with – they all behaved like they were God. The whole time I was there, I had to be as difficult as they were in order to get anything done. I could do it, but I hated it – it made me miserable.'

Everyone I've spoken to believes that too much 'faking it' is bad for you – it's bad for your mental health and general sense of wellbeing, and it also makes it impossible for you to demonstrate any semblance of authenticity, which, as we're always being told, is everything.

But what if being authentic means revealing to the world that you're terrified? Or wildly out of your depth? Won't that just lose you credibility? Or is our professed attraction to authenticity simply a way of keeping ourselves in our comfort zones?

There are different views on the psychological impact of constantly being inauthentic. One 2015 study by psychological scientists at Northwestern University, Harvard Business School and Columbia Business School suggested that inauthenticity doesn't just make us feel uncomfortable but as if we've been morally compromised – 'Feeling inauthentic is not a fleeting or cursory phenomenon – it cuts to the very essence of what it means to be a moral person,' explains Maryam Kouchaki, of Northwestern. The scientists speculated that being inauthentic may have similar psychological consequences to overtly lying or cheating.

Faking it all day is said to be more stressful than we

realise. LinkedIn influencer Annie Murphy Paul writes on the site:

> This kind of faking it is hard work – sociologists call it 'emotional labour'. It's psychologically and even physically draining; it can lead to lowered motivation and engagement with work, and ultimately job burnout.
>
> Having to act in a way that's at odds with how one really feels, eight hours a day, five days a week (or longer), violates the human need for a sense of authenticity. We all want to feel that we're the same person on the outside as we are on the inside, and when we can't achieve that congruence, we feel alienated and depersonalised.

Similarly, a study by Alex Baratta from the Manchester Institute of Education found that when people modify their accent, which Baratta feels is common practice in the UK due to 'negative class-based assumptions regarding regional accents in particular', this is not a neutral act. Instead, he found that a third of those studied felt that in modifying their accent – and, as a consequence, their fundamental identity – they were 'selling out'. Faking it didn't sit all that comfortably with them.

So, being inauthentic isn't necessarily great for your brain, or your happiness levels – although let's not discount the serious satisfaction that can be gained from totally fronting something out and it actually working. I still give myself a mental high five when I think about that talk I did. But if I'd been my most authentic self I'd have either stuttered my way through the whole thing or hidden in the toilets. Putting on a face got me through it and allowed me to communicate a big idea to an audience of people I wanted to hear about it. So there's that.

In a 2013 *Harvard Business Review* article, Professors Rob Goffee and Gareth Jones explain why they think authenticity is one of the most important traits for a good leader to have: 'Simply put, people will not follow a leader they feel is inauthentic.' But, more than that, they discovered that the key to happier, more productive staff was an organisation that was authentic in terms of how it was run, and allowed its employees to be true to themselves. They cite research which found that those who feel able to express their authentic selves at work exhibit higher levels of organisational commitment, individual performance and the propensity to help others.

However, as Goffee and Jones point out, very few organisations are able to do this effectively, because other things, like offering people clear career paths, traditional hierarchies or appraisal systems, get in the way. Basically, all the stuff that keeps companies ticking along from a human-resources perspective is at odds with the laudable aim of promoting individual authenticity.

Nonetheless, large organisations, from Waitrose to Apple, still aim to promote individualism because that's where the good ideas come from. Whether it's a data analyst who can number-crunch like no one else, a genius news reporter who can sniff out a great story first, or a visionary creative director who puts the competition in the shade, our talents are part of who we are. The stuff we're good at – really good at – is in our DNA. 'Authenticity' as a buzzword is in danger of being overused to death (certainly in this chapter) but the idea of doing what you're best at, in a way that makes you happy, for an organisation you believe in and whose success is linked to yours is simply the recipe for happiness at work, isn't it?

And it sells. The term 'post-fact world' is more overused now than 'authenticity' but it describes a world in which politicians, news outlets, a blogger or a member of the public can present their version of the truth as fact, and people will be influenced – whether they believe the 'facts' presented to them or not. In a mid-year report in the run-up to the 2016 US presidential election, PolitiFact, a fact-checking outlet in Florida, estimated that 78 per cent of Donald Trump's claims were 'mostly false' or worse. Yet that wasn't enough to stop people voting for him – because what he was saying was less important than the general sense voters got that he was authentic, unvarnished, real.

And it didn't end there. When Trump's press secretary, Sean Spicer, claimed that the president's inauguration drew in the 'largest audience to ever witness an inauguration', a claim that was demonstrably false, all of these discrepancies were explained away by the president's counsellor Kellyanne Conway as 'alternative facts'.

Basically they were lies, but we now exist in a world where the president's press secretary telling outright falsehoods in a press briefing is acceptable, because the broader idea, that Trump and his team are 'authentic' and 'say it like it is' (or, in this case, isn't), counts for more.

At the other end of the spectrum, you have only to look at the stratospheric rise of the vlogger industry. Beauty vlogger Zoella is said to be worth £3 million net, and in 2016 YouTube was estimated to be worth $86.22 billion.

Many of the most prominent – and profitable – bloggers are young people who started making videos at home, from home beauty tutorials to general updates about their lives and lifestyles. It's simple and it sells.

So what's the appeal? It's the A word again – authenticity. Zoella talking about how she struggled with panic attacks seems far more compelling, and real, to young people than Gwyneth Paltrow explaining why she steams her vagina. 'Realness' sells, especially for millennials. If you're discussing every aspect of your life with your mates, blogging about your anxiety to your followers or Snapchatting while you floss your teeth, why wouldn't you expect to be yourself in the workplace?

Goffee and Jones's article on authenticity was written in 2013 and was noteworthy at the time. But that was before 'authenticity' became a buzzword used to describe everyone from Adele to Nigel Farage. But has it been overused to the point at which it's lost all meaning?

Because that's what we do, isn't it? We take a concept or an idea, and we flog it to death until it ceases to mean anything, or until it starts to mean the opposite of what we originally intended. Is that what we've done here? Is authenticity at all costs just another dogmatism to be avoided? Or a cop-out for people looking for a reason not to push themselves?

In January 2015, the *Harvard Business Review*'s cover feature for that issue was 'The Paradox of Authenticity'. The author, economist and leadership guru Herminia Ibarra re-examines whether authenticity really is all, particularly where leadership positions are concerned. She points out that those in leadership positions have to move out of their comfort zones and push themselves. During those transition periods, being authentic isn't always the smartest move, yet when we're uncertain, we often retreat to what's familiar in order to protect our identities. 'Because going against our natural inclinations can make us feel like impostors, we tend to latch on to authenticity as an excuse for sticking with what's comfortable,' she explains. 'But few jobs allow us to do that for long, and that's doubly true when we advance in our careers or when demands or expectations change.'

Ibarra identifies several key reasons why authenticity isn't always the best route to take. Apart from anything else, our authentic self is constantly evolving and changing. And pushing ourselves out of our comfort zones is part of this. Despite all natural inclinations to the contrary, I'm certainly less wary of confrontation than I was, say, three years ago. Circumstances have changed and I've had new challenges to respond to so I've learnt different skills, but also it can be easier and more effective to change your style to get things done than to expect people, or the task you're facing, to mould around you. So, because I'd always hated and feared confrontation, I avoided it like the plague until I realised I'd wasted time and energy in not confronting problems that wouldn't go away – and were getting bigger. Confronting issues as soon as they arise takes a lot of effort on my part – my natural inclination is to ignore or smooth over the bad stuff – but it's sometimes the right thing to do, so I try to make myself do it.

But the idea that your authentic self changes over time is interesting. I would always have characterised my friend Catherine, a former colleague, as an Alpha. And until recently she would have agreed with me. So what's changed?

Motherhood. Or, to be more specific, it was what happened when she went back to work. 'I work part time now and can't – don't want to – put in the hours some of my colleagues do. As a result I've had to become more Beta, let stuff go and take a step back, because it would drive me mad otherwise.'

We'd all like to think that who we are is who we are, and that's that. But external circumstances change our attitudes and our approach to life, and we change too. We aren't one person all of the time, for all of our lives, and by sticking too dogmatically to who our authentic self is, and by staying in our comfort zone, we risk stunting our development.

Another issue with true authenticity lies with our private sense of self: we still need to have one, and throwing ourselves completely open to our colleagues is probably as dangerous as behaving like a completely fictionalised version of ourselves when we're with our colleagues. 'Being utterly transparent,' Ibarra notes, 'disclosing every thought and feeling, is both unrealistic and risky.'

She also points out that cultural norms change from country to country, so if your authentic self is bold and brash, and you find yourself doing business in, say, Asia, where modesty is favoured, it would make sense to adjust your approach accordingly.

Then there's the issue of selling yourself within your organisation. If you're the sort of person who feels your work should speak for itself, you may find doing the jazz-hands aren't-I-great dance to your boss's boss's boss distasteful and inauthentic. But if that's the only way to get your new project signed off, or to get the extra funding you require, surely a bit of inauthentic jazz-handing is worth it.

It's about pay-off, really, isn't it? If you know who you are, what your limits are, and what you want to get out of a role, then inauthentic schmoozing is fine: chances are, you'll emerge with your morality intact.

But no one wants to spend eight hours a day playing a part, and no one wants to think that their partner or best friend wouldn't recognise them if they saw them in the office. I've touched on social media a lot, and that's not really what this chapter is about, but I've always been struck by the contrast between some of the intimidating (read: focused and scarily efficient) work people I know in a professional setting and their social-media personas. They might be known for making four interns cry, but they have friends, and a partner, and children, none of whom appear to be particularly wary of them. Obviously they're just very good at coming to the office with their work head on and leaving it at the door when they go home. But isn't that, in itself, a bit knackering?

I guess it depends on what's required of you. I spoke to Suzanne, a female barrister in her thirties who, at home, 'defers to the needs of the household' but simply has to be more assertive at work to get the job done. 'I'm decisive and a "leader" at work because that is the nature of the job. At work I often think I'm the best qualified to answer. At home I think my view is just one view.'

That's something I hadn't considered until she said it. For me, authenticity is easier to find because I work in an environment that is relatively relaxed, not massively corporate, and broadly encourages creativity and individualism. When your working environment is either a courtroom or legal chambers, of course you're going to be different from how you are at home – they might as well be different worlds.

And then there's the stuff you don't want anyone to know about at work because you think it will change how they see you. When I asked female friends what they like to keep separate from work, some people mentioned their spirituality or religion; others talked about their relationships, their sexual orientation, their financial status or their children. Everyone had different reasons for doing so, but broadly it always boiled down to the same thing: not everything is for public consumption.

Eddie Erlandson, co-author of *Alpha Male Syndrome*, believes that faking an Alpha personality in the workplace is a mistake, but that there are benefits to developing 'alpha personas' where necessary. 'Your greatest impact as a person and as a leader is authenticity and I have what I call "alpha personas" – some of those people who can take on an acting role, and some of them can do it quite well.'

Eddie talks about how his wife and co-author, Kate Ludenham, was able to do this: 'Kate is an Alpha, she is a very evolved one, but when she was head of HR she had a huge male alpha team and she decided that if she was going to be heard in senior leadership meetings, she would have to raise her voice, lean forward, and occasionally slap her hand on the table. So she practised it. It didn't change her but it did allow her to get to the table and in the conversation.'

You don't have to become a parody of yourself, but if you're going to do that scary meeting, or give that presentation, and you can tweak your delivery style to make you feel better about the whole thing, or more in control, why wouldn't you? This isn't about ensuring you fit in by behaving in a certain way, or about making other people feel comfortable by adjusting your behaviour. It's about doing what you need to do to get through something that makes you uncomfortable.

But is it harder for women in the workplace to be authentic than men?

There is some evidence to suggest that women are better suited to adopting an authentic leadership style than men because they tend to be more collegiate and empathetic. However, psychologists Margaret M. Hopkins and Deborah O'Neil believe that it's harder for women to be authentic, particularly in masculine corporate environments. In their 2015 article 'Authentic Leadership: Application to Women Leaders', they identified three reasons why the concept of authentic leadership, as it's currently understood, is gendered, and therefore harder for women to achieve. First, 'masculine leadership behaviours such as assertiveness and competitiveness remain the norm', so women are either expected to behave in as masculine a way as possible or go against leadership norms. Second, and as I've already said, most companies have an organisational structure that is designed for men. When we talk about authenticity at work, we're often talking about authenticity in a male structure, as Hopkins and O'Neil go on to explain:

Even the most progressive modern organizations have been created by and for men, and thus tend to have systems, policies, norms, and structures that favour the male life experience. Behaviours and values regarded as the norm at work tend to favour traits and characteristics traditionally associated with maleness and to undervalue traits and characteristics traditionally associated with femininity.

And, finally, discussion of authentic leadership assumes that the influence an authentic leader has is a one-way street. But you can't adopt an authentic leadership style if the people who work for you simply refuse to respond.

For Naomi, the thirty-three-year-old project manager who works in construction, it's hard to make her desire to be authentic at work into a reality. 'I am a lot more reserved at work than I am at home. I try to control my emotions, including my reactions and facial expressions, as I find being vulnerable in the office is looked down on rather than respected. I have been working on closing the gap to try and be my more authentic self at work, but it is difficult.'

But is authenticity always better? Another woman I spoke to said she embraced the separation between her home and work life. 'They need to be separate to keep things in perspective and alive in both worlds.'

Careers coach Corinne Mills agrees that our authenticity shouldn't compromise our professionalism, although she also feels that it still needs to exist in some form. 'You're a version of your authentic self at work – you don't want to bring all sides of yourself to work because that's not appropriate. The difference in a work scenario is you're expected to have emotional control, at home not so much.'

But although she advocates a decent amount of professional distance from your work colleagues, to ensure professionalism when you're in charge, she thinks being fundamentally authentic in terms of your values is crucial. Because doing what we perceive to be the right thing and doing what's right for our employers isn't always the same. 'If your authenticity is stretched so tight it's going to snap at any moment then it's not the right job for you.'

So where does that leave us? Facing emotional ruin as we try to negotiate a working world that would really rather we were a slightly different type of person? Constantly seeking and failing to find a modicum of that all-important authenticity lest we come across as too soft or too much of a bitch, too sappy or too cold?

I believe it's about self-protection – in every sense. Protect who you are and what you cherish, and don't let what you do for a living eat away at those things. Do what you have to do to protect yourself, even when you have to do things that make you feel tense, nervous or wildly out of your comfort zone (because we all do: it doesn't mean you're bad at your job, it means you're being brave and taking on something new. So give yourself a little high-five for that).

And protect what you do for a living, and what you love about it. Everyone I spoke to who truly felt they had found a way to be authentic at work had done so because they loved most of their job, if not every element of it. And they were committed to the end goal, whatever that was. Because if you truly believe in making something happen, it becomes that little bit easier to be true to yourself in the process.

11.

BE THE ROBIN TO HER BATMAN: HOW TO DEAL WITH YOUR ALPHA BOSS

I've realised that during some of the happiest points in my career I've had an Alpha (female) boss: I'm always happiest when someone else is taking control of the situation while I do what I'm told. I was also an insanely obedient child – make of that what you will.

When I described in the Introduction what I would view as a classic Beta, I was almost entirely describing myself. And this has always seemed to make me good at dealing with Alpha women. I'm a good sidekick: I'll always help to realise someone else's ambition even if it's at odds with my own – if that's what it takes to keep the peace (this isn't necessarily a good thing) – and I find relinquishing control and ultimate responsibility to someone else ultimately quite freeing. It makes me more creative, gives me more headspace.

There aren't many things in life I'd actively boast about (classic Beta there, y'all), but that's one of them. I don't feel threatened by Alpha women because it's like comparing apples and oranges – we're operating on totally different planes, and unless they're just wrong about something, I'm generally happy to buy into someone else's vision of how stuff should be done and fit in to make that work. Cog in the machine, that's me.

But what if your Alpha boss is a total nightmare? What

if your innate Beta-ness is overridden by your desire for control, or your fear that a certain idea or project is going in totally the wrong direction? What if you unwittingly find yourself in a weird power battle with your Alpha boss and don't want to be, but she's really into it so you'll have to continue to glare at each other across meeting rooms and say things like 'Yes, Pamela, I see your point, but strictly speaking I'm not sure if this issue is in your jurisdiction,' until she gets bored and goes off to terrorise someone else?

When one of my friends, Harriet, got her first proper job, in PR, after uni, I didn't see her for a couple of months. When we finally got together for a drink, she was a shadow of her former self. She'd dropped a dress size, had dark circles under her eyes and could barely speak because her mouth was covered with ulcers. The problem? Her new boss was an unreasonable lunatic (I'm paraphrasing) and despite my friend's best efforts (she's a natural people-pleaser), nothing she did was ever right for the woman, who sent her on pointless errands across London at five minutes to six on a Friday evening, gave her piles of work she had no idea how to do (or any time to do it in) and constantly told her she was useless. My friend responded by doing everything she could think of to make her happy. She tried to make herself as likeable as possible so her boss could have no reason to be affronted by her very presence. She did everything that was chucked at her, plus more, and it didn't work – in fact it enraged her boss. In the end she realised she was about to have a nervous breakdown and quit.

I wonder if another tactic would have worked better.

When you're a Beta woman, with an apparently Alpha boss, your first instinct might be to give them exactly what they say they want (mine certainly is). But this woman wasn't an Alpha boss who knew what she wanted, and demanded a lot from her team. She was newly promoted from her own graduate job, on a power trip, and took far more pleasure in terrorizing the intern than any sane person would. In fact, looking back ten years on, she probably should have been sacked for her behaviour. But if you're a Beta, especially when you're new to the working world, everyone with a loud voice and decisive manner can come across like an Alpha boss who knows what they're talking about. But working out the difference between a bully and an Alpha is the key to being a successful Beta. Had my friend seen her boss for what she was – a bully – she might have responded differently. Or maybe not: standing up to bullies isn't easy.

But just because you're not thumping your fist on the table, speaking up the loudest in meetings or kicking off every time you get your own way, it doesn't mean you're a pushover. One of the most important parts of being a successful Beta is knowing when you're being taken for a ride and having the confidence to speak up and do something about it – even when that goes against every grain in your body.

According to careers coach Corinne Mills, the relationship between your Beta personality and your Alpha boss should be harmonious – that's why you're there. 'In some respects, they've probably chosen you because you're Beta and because they think you're going to be complementary to them.' But, obviously, there are pitfalls, especially when you're a people-pleaser with a demanding boss. 'You just have to be careful if they become unreasonable – we've all had Alpha bosses where there's some power play going on for the sake of it. You have to find a way to let them know you're not in competition with them, to let them know you're there to support them, that you're not there to oust them from their job and you want them to be successful.'

This chapter is looking at how to deal with your female Alpha boss, who may or may not be lovely: it isn't about pitting women against each other. Equally, if you're Beta, this isn't about suppressing your own hopes, desires and ambitions for your job in favour of someone else's. But we all do things differently, and work towards success differently, and we need to get better at acknowledging that: it will make us all enjoy our jobs and careers a lot more in the long run.

We're not very good at talking about women in charge without resorting to broad-brush caricatures. Advice on how to deal with an Alpha female boss often won't tell you how to cope with a powerful and decisive woman, who knows what she wants. Instead, it will – unhelpfully and reductively – be about how to deal with your 'bitch boss' or lament that she's allowed to be your boss at all.

The reality, of course, is far more nuanced and, regardless of whether we're an Alpha or a Beta woman, we all want to do a job that we're fulfilled by and care about. And if you're anything like me, you still want your thoughts and ideas considered properly. You just don't want to have to shout to get them across. How do you do that when your boss is a through-and-through Alpha whose default position is to steam forward with her own ideas, much in the same way as it's your default position to do what you're told? You need to understand what motivates her.

Executive coach and HR consultant Tania Hummel once worked with a chief executive and an MD, whose wildly different approaches to management meant they kept clashing. This is about a man and a woman, not two women, but I love this story because it demonstrates just how different Alphas and Betas can be. It also shows how a Beta isn't always the pushover sidekick and the Alpha isn't always the shouty bitch. They are literally just two different ways of working.

'She had been mentored by a boss who was very like her,' explains Tania of the chief executive. 'She was all about the vision and so was her old boss. But her new MD was very down to earth.

'When she'd worked with her old boss she could bound into his office with all of her ideas and say, "Let's do this," and he would say, "Yeah, let's do this," and they would bounce the ball around. Nothing needed to come of it, but they'd both be satisfied that they'd had that exploratory need fulfilled.

'But when she tried to do the same with this new MD, who was reporting in to her, she would bound into his office with her latest idea, he'd be surrounded by stuff to do and he would go, "Why are you here? We're supposed to meet next Tuesday. Can't you see I'm busy? Do you want me to drop everything to follow this?"'

You can see where the clash lay – but it came from a failure to understand each other's approach rather than a fundamental difference in opinion. 'It's, like, she'd come to him with her ball to play with him [her MD],' Tania continues, 'and he'd say, "What are the rules of the game? This is not scheduled," put the ball down and walk off the pitch until she'd met his requirements.'

Obviously this was a problem because (a) she was his boss, and (b) he failed to realise that she needed to discuss her ideas and have them acknowledged. Bringing them to fruition was the next step – which was what he was preoccupied with. But she was far more concerned with having her ideas discussed in that moment.

Once the pair understood where each other were coming from, their working relationship became much easier. And that is why finding a way to understand your boss's perspective and approach is crucial – even if it varies wildly from yours.

I think, in many ways, Alpha women are easier bosses than Alpha men because they *tend* to be more evolved and more emotionally intelligent than their male counterparts, which makes sense – Eddie Erlandson, co-author of *Alpha Male Syndrome*, described (most) Alpha women's approach to management as akin to a 'velvet glove', and they are said to be less likely to indulge in 'risky' behaviour (as in risky to the business) than their male counterparts. This means that most of the Alpha women I've dealt with have at least attempted to see things from my perspective as much as I've tried to see things from theirs. It doesn't matter how different you are, as long as you both understand your respective roles in the skit.

But what about Queen Bee Syndrome? That's a thing, right? People are always banging on about it as the reason why there are still, relatively speaking, so few women in senior business roles.

The theory, developed in 1973 by three (male) researchers, G. L. Staines, T. E. Jayaratne and C. Tavris, hypothesises that so few women exist in senior positions because those who do make it to the top pull the ladder up with them – thus making it harder for others to succeed. Obviously it's all our fault. Women, eh? A Canadian study from 2008, which found that women with female supervisors had more depression, headaches, heartburn and insomnia than those with male bosses, seems to back this up.

But the reality, of course, is a little more complicated than that.

Yet another study from 2015 suggested that Queen Bee Syndrome as a phenomenon doesn't exist. Research by Columbia Business School found that companies with a female chief executive were more likely to have women in senior management roles. However, in those cases women were facing an unofficial quota: once a woman reached a senior management position (not chief executive), it became 51 per cent less likely that another woman would follow. The implication is that the one woman who makes it to the top is seen as legitimising the business's attempts at diversity, and that's that.

The research team explained: 'Women face an implicit quota, whereby firms seek to maintain a small number of women on their top management team, usually only one. While firms gain legitimacy from having women in top management, the value of this legitimacy declines with each woman.'

The problem isn't other women, it's men (or, at least,

the institutional misogyny that still pervades in plenty of large organisations). But another study also suggests that something more complex is going on: when women with low levels of gender identification – who feel their gender is irrelevant to their role – face gender bias, they attempt to get over this obstacle by setting themselves apart from other women. This may be by displaying typically masculine behaviour or putting down other women.

But the point – and this is crucial – isn't that this is inherently female catty behaviour: it's that this is how some women end up responding to a masculine environment that devalues women. It's the system that's the problem. When there's only one seat at the table for All Women, and you've got it, you want to protect it. You can't have a system that allows one woman at a time to succeed, then act surprised when women start vying to be that One Woman.

Pamela Stone, professor of sociology at Hunter College, New York, agrees that Queen Bee Syndrome is a symptom of a certain workplace culture: 'In the old days, when we used to talk about the Queen Bee Phenomenon, the sense was that the women who made it to the top were basically men, in that they were male identified: they weren't changing culture because it worked for them – their attitude to other women was "If I can do it, why can't you?"

'There was this notion that women in this position would see other women as competition so they wouldn't necessarily be helpful. The chance of any women making progress was so low that it created a hyper-competitive environment among women.'

But as the culture around the workplace (slowly) changes,

Professor Stone believes that the Queen Bee is becoming even less relevant as a cultural phenomenon. 'Now, as we see progress and we see more and more women [in senior positions], it's still competitive as you get higher up, but it's a little bit less sharp-elbowed. We're starting to get research that says the more women you get in leadership positions, it does appear that these organisations create cultures that are a little bit more family-friendly, for example. So you hope that we are in a different era now and women can be a bit more assertive about creating a culture that reflects women's values – not just the Alpha values.'

'Queen Bee Syndrome' is a horrible term for a phenomenon that's been woefully misunderstood. But is it surprising? What do you think would happen if the tables were turned and blokes were given one opportunity in twenty to sit on the board or get the corner office? Within hours it'd be a cut-price version of *Gladiator*. Although the mental image of a bunch of middle-aged wannabe chief executives battling it out in the amphitheatres of Surrey in their vests isn't, admittedly, a great one.

But that's not really the point, is it? The point is, when women are given the latitude to do so, studies suggest that they are active and successful mentors for other women. One survey of high-potential leaders showed that 73 per cent of the women who are developing new talent are mentoring women, compared with 30 per cent of men who are developing talent. When women work with a higher proportion of women they experience lower levels of gender discrimination, and when they have female managers they report having more family and organisational support than when they have male supervisors. And as any number of different studies demonstrate, the more women in management positions, the smaller the gender pay gap.

The Queen Bee Syndrome, as it's described to us, is a myth, a damaging one as it feeds into any number of assumptions we make about female interaction in the workplace.

A study from the *Academy of Management Journal* asked people to read about conflict between two male co-workers, two female co-workers and one male and one female co-worker. The results found that conflict between two female co-workers was viewed as a problem far more than conflict between two male co-workers or a man and a woman. The women were seen as far more likely to quit as a result. (I can only imagine that the study's participants assumed that the women were plotting each other's deaths with a letter-opener while the men were simply 'hashing out some ideas' and 'letting off steam'.) Similarly, a 2009 poll carried out by OnePoll revealed that men gossip more in the office than women – an average of seventy-six minutes per day, compared with fifty-two for women – yet the myth still remains that this is a uniquely female trait.

But if every conflict between two women is a cat fight that must be picked over for days, and if every time you haul your team over the coals for messing up, you're a Queen Bee, trying to hold other women back, how is anyone ever meant to get anything done? As much as I prefer to avoid confrontation when I can, sometimes it happens, and sometimes it's even necessary. And some people, male or female, absolutely thrive on that sort of conflict. The frustration if you're an Alpha woman who finds herself stymied far more often than her male colleagues must be immense.

'I'm quite direct and tend to ask for exactly what I want without couching it in niceties,' explains Jackie, in her twenties, who works in advertising, and has been reprimanded at work for being too 'direct' with colleagues and clients. 'When I first started work, straight from university, I thought that was just what you did, and I think to an extent people were impressed with how assertive I was. It was only after a year or so, when I had my twelve-month review, that I found out how many people had complained about me being rude, or aggressive. There was no way that was my intention, I just didn't bother trying to qualify everything I said, or make every request sound like a question.'

She says she's softened herself a bit now, just because it's easier, but that it doesn't always sit comfortably with her. 'If I'm asking someone to do something, and it's part of their job, why do I have to make it sound like they're doing me a massive favour?'

I've worked with plenty of direct women, and I quite like it. As I've said, one of the reasons I've always enjoyed working for and with women is that I can normally work out where each one is coming from – even when I don't agree with her. I can normally work out what motivates her, why she's made the decision she has. But knowing what makes someone tick, and responding in a logical, non-emotional and fearless way, are two different things. And being a Beta to an Alpha boss can certainly have its pitfalls. How do you get your point across, and your own way on something you feel strongly about, when your superior's natural inclination is to pursue their own agenda rather than stop and consider yours?

'The risk is that you comply rather than hold your ground,' explains Eddie Erlandson. 'You hold your ground, you summarise, you state your view, rather than going into compliance and then resentment. So the risk of being a non-Alpha with an Alpha manager is that you end up wasting some of your great psychic energy in resentment and frustration and feeling controlled.'

The word 'control' is quite interesting. I used to work with a woman called Leanne, a senior female manager who was pretty Alpha, and was also very good at her job – very knowledgeable. A male colleague, who was junior to Leanne, was underperforming, and she got involved in trying to improve his performance. She was also one of the few people in the business who knew as much about his specialist subject as he did, if not more.

He totally refused to engage with her, resisted any attempts she made to manage him. And when he was asked, by a senior (male) colleague what he was playing at – he was in danger of losing his job – his response was, 'I don't like being controlled.'

I'm convinced he wouldn't have felt 'controlled' by a male colleague, he would have felt he was being 'managed'. But Alpha men are labelled 'decisive' where Alpha women are 'controlling' – like your nagging wife, or your mother-in-law.

And let's be clear. Assuming your boss isn't a tyrant or a bully, and assuming you're able to stand up for yourself when required, being a Beta sidekick to an Alpha boss can be wonderful and inspiring. The best kind of Alpha boss will bring out the best in you, will stop you quitting because something is hard, and will inject passion and energy into the most mundane project. When I talk to some of the Alpha women I know about their workloads and general life loads, I feel exhausted on their behalf, but they never look or sound it.

What about the dynamic in your friendship circle? When you think of all the Alpha women you know outside the workplace (and I believe that someone who's particularly Beta at work can still be very Alpha in their personal life and vice versa), they're the ones remembering to book tickets to the amazing exhibition that's opened, or the only person in your friendship group who will organise a villa for twenty people and dozens of budget airline flights so you all get to go on an amazing holiday together (she's already booked you into the best restaurant in town for your last night, bonus). In our personal lives, we need the Alphas: they're the doers, the make-things-happen guys, the leaders of men (women). And, in the same way, working for and with Alpha women can be crucial in injecting that all-important motivation and energy into our professional lives when we need it most.

They can be difficult, stubborn and sometimes pig-headed, sure. But they can also be insanely creative because their uncompromising worldview can create a truly original way of thinking. They care about their work, their people and their lives and, if you're lucky, a bit of that magic dust may rub off on you.

So never be put off a job because you've heard your new boss will be difficult, or high maintenance, or exacting. If you've also heard that they're great at what they do, that they inspire incredible loyalty in their team, if they're respected by everyone they know, then, chances are, it'll be totally worth it. You've just got to understand what motivates her, be honest about what motivates you, understand the parts you play and give it your all.

12.

BEING BATMAN WHEN YOU FEEL LIKE ROBIN
INSIDE: HOW TO DEAL WITH YOUR ALPHA TEAM
WHEN YOU'RE THE BETA BOSS

Despite spending most of my career trying to avoid being put in charge of everything, I've ended up as the boss several times, with varying degrees of success. Weirdly, I think it's because I'm such a classic Beta – it means I'm an excellent deputy: competent, confident and focused. So when the main role comes up, people naturally assume I'll be just as good stepping up. And I can do it. But it's been hard work getting there.

Being in charge has certainly never come naturally. I've had to feel my way around the role of boss, test my limits, work out how to make it fit me. And for great swathes of time, it's made me feel ill at ease. I certainly don't sit in the captain's seat, shift around a bit, think, This is nice, and start planning how to redecorate the office (this is a metaphor: obviously no one has an office of their own any more).

When I was younger it worked out fine because I ended up in charge of people I was already friends with. We had a decent enough personal relationship, and they were good enough at their jobs that everything just sort of worked out – although I suspect they didn't always love having an apparent 'boss' who turned to them for advice far more often than she dished it out.

Then there have been the occasions when it hasn't

worked. *At all*. I've found myself playing the role of subordinate to someone who sat below me on the team organogram. I've shied away from dealing with bad behaviour on my team until small issues have become massive problems, and there have been plenty of occasions when I've lacked the authority I needed. As a general rule, I'd always be fine if there was a big issue or crisis to deal with there and then. One quick burst of energy, knowing exactly what was needed, and I could deliver. But the minute the crisis was over, I'd lapse into my usual Beta self.

I don't do this too much any more – mainly because I've reached the point at work where I'm older and more experienced than my team. It means I have a certain level of authority that I can't shake off, no matter how many times I catch my shoelaces in the wheel of my chair and have to be rescued by the intern.

Kerry is thirty-eight and works in the media. Her early career was spent in all-male teams, and she would characterise as Alpha at work. She's now on a female-heavy team, under a woman she feels is extremely Beta – and it's not without its challenges. 'My boss is super-empathetic,' she explains. 'So gentle, really sweet and kind, but also incredibly passive-aggressive.

'If I do something wrong, or not the way she likes things done, she'll always say, "Don't worry, I probably didn't explain properly, or I may not even have told you," even though we both know she has. She can never just be straight and say, "Kerry, can you perhaps do it this way?" She dithers, and there always seems to be a worry about causing offence.'

I'm wary of conflating negative leadership traits with

being Beta, but I also recognise some of this in my own behaviour – apologising when you're asking for stuff to be done, for example. But Kerry, who's straightforward and straight-talking, just wants to be told when she's done something wrong. So her boss's behaviour leaves her feeling frustrated.

Another, very Alpha, woman I spoke to mentioned how frustrating she found her boss's desire to avoid confrontation. 'I see confrontation as part of communication and relationship building. They see it as scary and aggressive. But without that, how am I ever going to understand their point of view?'

I'm still very much a Beta, but the difference now is that I don't let my Beta traits morph into something more sinister. I embrace the Beta characteristics that make me good at my job, and I keep an eye on the ones that are less helpful. For example, I can be indecisive when I panic about doing the right thing and don't have all the information. So I've had to get better at asking more questions, and demanding more information from other people. In the past, I'd have panicked and put off making the decision until it had become a crisis that needed to be managed.

But when I look back to when I've been at my most Toxically Beta (indecisive, low energy, consumed by Impostor Syndrome), it strikes me that these were points when I was least happy and focused at work for a whole raft of reasons, very few of them to do with the job. I was emotionally overextended and it had a massive impact on my ability to manage a team or do my job.

I now know that my mind is on my job, and I have the time and the headspace to make thoughtful decisions

I'm happy to stand by, and be strategic so I know I'm not wasting my energy in the wrong places. Then everything tends to fall into place. Being busy is fine – in fact, it's preferable to the alternative – but it has to be my decision.

On the other hand, the minute my back is against the wall or I'm playing catch-up to everyone else, or I'm being pressured into doing things I don't think I've got the time, information or knowledge to make an informed decision about, I revert back to the most Beta version of myself possible.

And that's why having Alpha team members can unnerve me more than having an Alpha boss. When you have a passionate, hard-working, talented Alpha woman working for you, they want to move things on, make things better, keep pushing everything, which is great. But they want to do it at their pace. And their pace might not be right for me. Instead of telling them to slow down and taking control of the situation, I tend to shut down, frustrating myself, and frustrating them even more.

Which is a problem that spirals into lunacy if you're like me, and your natural instinct is to give your team what you think they want above what you want. The danger is you end up negating what you need from them (which is why they're there in the first place). And, trust me, nothing can make you feel more Beta than the realisation that your entire focus is around meeting your team's needs, whims and timelines rather than your own.

So what's to be done?

You can fight it, try to be more Alpha than the Alphas, but that really isn't sustainable. Put all your energy into trying to be something you're not, and that's all your energy gone.

What if you don't have time on your side to gain authority over your team through age alone? What if you're younger and less experienced than some of your colleagues and need to fake authority? Or what if you're older and more experienced but they're just really, really Alpha?

How do you do it without compromising your sense of self and who you are? How do you find your inner bad-ass boss without becoming a shoulder-padded caricature of what you imagine she should be like?

Embrace your Beta to unlock your Alpha.

I suspect that none of us is quite as Beta (or, indeed, Alpha) as we think we are. I say this because we're all so complex: our emotions, experiences, reactions and triggers all vary wildly, yet we rarely consider the facets of our personalities, especially in the workplace, where everyone's behaviour is so loaded and layered with meaning. But imagine what would happen if we were able to unlock these dormant, hitherto undiscovered elements of our personality and deploy them as and when required, just to get the job done. It's not about changing who we are to fit in better, it's about making better use of the tool we already have at our disposal – our massive, amazing, brilliant brains.

For example, although I identify as Beta, and no one who knows me has ever really questioned that, I've always suspected that I may have a few dormant Alpha traits, which are far more likely to emerge when I'm confident, or fired up, or excited about a project.

I want to find out a bit more about myself and why I

respond as I do to different work situations. Tania Hummel, the executive coach and HR consultant, suggests I try a couple of psychometric tests by a company called Lumina, which she uses with her clients. 'They tell you what your strengths are, but also your weaknesses, outline areas of development for you and advise on how to deal with people who are different from you.' Which is exactly what I'm after. But the tests also look at and compare our natural self, our everyday self and the type of person we are when we're overextended, which means stressed out or over-whelmed. (Again, exactly what I'm after: I've always suspected that long periods of stress exacerbate my most negative Beta tendencies.)

I complete two tests, called Spark and Emotion, and each questionnaire takes fifteen to twenty minutes to do online. They're both multiple choice, asking me how I respond to certain scenarios, and how certain scenarios make me feel.

Lumina doesn't use words like Alpha and Beta to describe people: they prefer to refer to 'traits' rather than types. But when Tania looks at my profile, she immediately tells me I am 'people-focused, inspiration-driven, and big-picture thinking'. This is all stuff I know, but it's nice to have it confirmed. Tania also says that I have a lot of 'green' traits (traits are divided into four main groups, red, green, yellow and blue). I'm sure you can see where I'm going with this: green is the most Beta group of traits, red is the most Alpha. 'So you're hugely accommodating,' Tania explains. 'Hugely intimate, very empathetic, very adaptable. You're imaginative, sociable, conceptual.' And my least preferred traits? 'Tough, competitive, takes charge, purposeful, but still quite logical.' Ah.

Talking through all of this confirms that I'm as Beta as I thought I was. But how does the information help me deal with an Alpha team?

For starters, the tests explore how my behaviour or traits change when I get stressed or emotionally overextended. For example, they highlight that I'm a good listener in everyday life, but when I'm overextended I become more so and this becomes a negative trait. I become passive. Also, I have a strong collaborative streak that becomes more prominent when I'm overextended, at which point I become obsessed with everyone else's happiness beyond the task at hand.

These are both true, and tap into what I view as my negative Beta qualities. But by pinpointing exactly what they are, and when they occur, I can work on them specifically (by making a concerted effort to become more decisive and vocal when I'm under stress). I can be more effective without fundamentally changing who I am.

So if I can switch on more of my Alpha side when I need to, giving someone a stern telling-off or confronting them a difficult situation straight away becomes less of a slog.

I already know that I'm more Beta when I'm under pressure and when I have less time to make decisions (or when other people are pushing me to make decisions I haven't had a chance to get my head around), but I've also grasped that I become my most Beta self when I'm bored, or when I'm not interested in what's going on around me. And I've always struggled with that feeling of inertia and low energy when nothing exciting is going on.

I guess it's efficiency – if my brain doesn't feel the need to engage in what's going on around me then it just doesn't.

When I'm busy and focused, with deadlines, challenges and projects I'm interested in, my brain responds in kind. I'm high energy and efficient. I'm decisive and cut to the chase – I simply have to. In the immediate aftermath I continue to be efficient, organised and decisive until I reach a point where I don't have to any more. Then I get bored and I switch off.

Working this out was fantastic because it made me realise that Beta-ness isn't about me being lazy, or a pathological people-pleaser. It's about what motivates me.

For example, how I manage my day and my time is key. When I first started working in magazines, we had a monthly schedule we had to stick to like clockwork – we had a final deadline we were all working towards, which was characterised by late nights and an intense flurry of work. After that we were all working towards the next deadline. It suited me really well, but working on a website is a different kettle of fish. Our deadlines are hourly, not monthly, which can be very intense when you're not used to it, but becomes less of an event over time. And that's when I get bored.

So, once I cottoned on to how my time and energy levels were linked to my inherent Beta-ness, I changed things. I've started imposing hard deadlines on myself to get certain things done to ensure that I'm busier for the first four days of the week, then give myself Fridays for admin and implementation, so I don't burn out. Admin can become an endless, ever-expanding act of procrastination if I start the week with it, so forcing myself to crack on with the big stuff straight away means it actually gets done. If I find myself doing too many dull or routine jobs in one week, I make sure I have some harder or more engaging work to do too, just to keep my brain switched on.

All of this makes me a more engaged boss. It makes me more alert and decisive and means I tend to have more energy. In short, I've found out how to borrow a bit of Alpha without changing who I am or how I behave.

The thing with psychometric tests or personality tests, or those quizzes at the back of a magazine, is that they tell you a tiny bit more about yourself. They won't necessarily give you the vital piece of information that makes everything in your life fall into place, but they might offer a snippet of insight into why you do and say things in a certain way, and how you can change those things without compromising who you are. For me, it was about seeing my personality traits – negative and positive – as small parts of a bigger picture that can be controlled and tweaked by me as required, rather than a stick with which to beat myself up.

Beta women aren't fundamentally 'lazy' or 'pushovers' and Alpha women aren't essentially 'bitches' or 'control freaks': we're just motivated by different things.

And that's at the heart of any careers manual you'll read, including this one. It's about finding out who you are and what you need, then working out how to get what you need to be the version of yourself you want to be in the workplace. It's never about faking it or being someone you're not. It's about embracing your own traits and quirks, and reminding everyone else how wonderful they are.

13.

HOW TO DEAL WITH SEXISM IN THE WORKPLACE WHEN YOU'RE BETA, ALPHA OR JUST A WOMAN

I've never been confronted with the overt, inherent sexism you read about in the papers, where women are fired from their high-powered City jobs for refusing to get their tits out or get off with a lap dancer at their office summer party at Stringfellows (I'm paraphrasing, but you get the gist).

In fact, ask me at twenty-three, twenty-six or twenty-eight about examples of sexism I'd faced at work and I'd have struggled to come up with any. Because often (but not always) when you work in a female-dominated industry, like I do, sexism comes in subtler, more insidious forms, plenty of which have only been revealed to me as I've got older. Apart from anything else, if you've got your head down and are desperately trying to do your job without messing up anything too drastically (which basically defined my working life in my twenties), it's easy to miss what's going on around you. Also, as you get older you gain a bit of perspective on how other people work. Getting your backside grabbed by a much older male colleague in the pub isn't about sex it's about power. The guy you work with who makes a not-that-quiet comment about your breasts to his mates when you're getting a mug out of the dishwasher isn't trying to make them laugh: he's exerting his authority. Actually . . . maybe I've witnessed more sexism at work than I first thought.

It's only now that I see how often women get boxed in as 'easy-going' or a 'bitch' (potentially any woman who disagrees with the general male consensus).

I've definitely found myself in situations in my career where my opinion hasn't been sought on something I know more about than anyone else in the building. I've also overheard (male) colleagues agreeing to keep 'tricky' (argumentative, probably Alpha) women out of the loop because they didn't want them to 'complicate issues' round specific projects (the same projects that would later go tits up because no one was asking the right questions from the outset). One woman I know, who works for a male-dominated tech company (in a non-technical role) has been told that there's no point in her coming to meetings because the team 'will just be talking tech-speak the whole time, so I won't understand it'. She was then told it was actually because her habit of asking difficult questions was 'making the project lose focus'.

The result is that in some of the (fairly evenly gendered) offices I've worked in everything seemed to descend into boys' and girls' clubs with men disappearing for secret meetings that female team members were either too unimportant or too 'difficult' to consult on, while said women huddled together to complain about all the projects they were being phased out of.

It's not the case everywhere I've worked, but the formation of boys' clubs, even in an industry as dominated by women as mine, doesn't seem to be anything new or surprising. I canvassed Alpha and Beta friends in similar jobs to mine, and they've all seen similar things.

The only way around it? 'Be the *über*-bitch,' suggests

a former colleague, who, although quite Alpha by my standards, is in awe of her high Alpha boss, who gets her own way (and sets her own agenda) by making it clear, in no uncertain terms, that she's the Alpha in any room she walks into – whatever the room's gender mix. 'She [her boss] screams so loud and makes such a fuss that she always gets what she wants done,' my friend explains. 'It must be exhausting being like that all the time, though.'

But when you're a Beta woman, like me, when you aren't naturally loud, pushy or outspoken, how do you navigate sexism in the workplace when it exists to keep you quiet, keep you small, and keep you in your place?

Christine, thirty, works in the property industry. Her experience at her first job reads like the sort of cautionary tale HR executives would share on a training day. It ticks virtually every imaginable box for sexism in the workplace. A full house in the game of sexual-harassment bingo, if you will.

'It was an all-male team,' she tells me. 'I was one of only two women there. The entire team were straight white men, with the exception of one gay man.

'Over the four years I was there, my boss would constantly share his theories on male/female dynamics, his favourite being the "thirty power switch" – the idea that when women reach thirty they lose all their sexual power and men gain it, and therefore want to date twenty-two-year-olds. I was repeatedly told that I didn't need a pay rise because I would just get married and my future husband would give me money. I was repeatedly told, "I can't wait until you come in here and tell me you need nine months off because you're going to have a baby. Women are all the same." I was twenty-two and single.

'Oh, and he would call me into his office for some spurious reason, then tell me to hang on because he had to reply to an email – he didn't realise that I could see the reflection of his computer in the window behind him. He was watching porn every time.'

Christine stuck it out because she needed the work, and left as soon as she got a better job offer. But in an all-male company where this culture was rife, she simply didn't believe there was any way she could speak out. And as much as I'd love the story to end with Christine righteously taking her old boss down (he was eventually fired for a series of other misdemeanours when he sufficiently creeped-out a more senior female member of staff and HR started digging around), I would never suggest that she should have been the one to stick her neck out and make a fuss. And, frankly, I have no idea what I would have done differently in that scenario.

The problem is, it's tough to give advice on how to deal with sexism, or even sexual harassment, in the workplace without putting the onus on women to sort it out. When someone develops coping mechanisms in the workplace to get their voice heard, or just to get through the day, they might not be that helpful to the wider workplace culture, but sometimes just getting to the end of the day, or getting that project out of the door, is all you can think of, and that's okay.

'I've totally done it,' admits my friend Rachel, who's in her late thirties and works for the HR department of a bank in the City. 'I've let gross comments slide, because

I'd spend my life in confrontation with people otherwise. On the other hand, it's not a great example to set to anyone. I'm fully aware that if I don't do something about it it'll never stop, but it's also exhausting and only ever seems to make my working day harder.'

Equally, if you quit a working environment because the casual sexism, outright misogyny or full-on sexual harassment is too much to deal with, should you feel guilty about letting down the sisterhood? Of course not. But we all internalise these things, make them about ourselves and our behaviour, when really they're about the system we're living in.

If your boss is sexist, it's because he's a sexist person, not because you don't know how to charm him. He is in the wrong, not you. If one of your male colleagues speaks over you in a meeting, takes your suggestion as his own, and everyone else lets him have the credit, the culture of your workplace needs serious work. But is it your fault for not screaming him down in public until he conceded that it was originally your idea? Of course not. Very few people would feel comfortable demonstrating that sort of behaviour in the workplace and you shouldn't have to do so because one of your colleagues can't be trusted to act courteously and professionally.

If you're being sexually harassed at work, or if you've been sexually assaulted by one of your colleagues, it doesn't matter what you wore. It doesn't matter how many drinks you had in the pub after work. It doesn't matter if you were the only person who laughed at their bad jokes. Not only were they in the wrong, they were also breaking the law. You weren't responsible for any one of those tiny decisions they made in the run-up to their one big decision to feel you up in the smoking area at the back of the office, or take you back to theirs for sex after the work Christmas party when you were semi-conscious.

I have to say that now, explicitly and clearly, because we (women) are very good at blaming ourselves for behaviour that isn't our fault. We internalise the sexism we're faced with. We allow someone to write off sexual harassment as 'a bit of fun' because we feel inexplicably guilty about it when someone else has committed an actual crime against us.

Whether it's thinking we need to be the last in the bar at night and the first up for breakfast the next day at a conference filled with male colleagues, or laughing off office banter that's (a) not funny, and (b) an HR nightmare in the making, for fear of getting a reputation for being a misery, we become adept at moulding ourselves to fit the environment we're in – even if that environment is hostile. It's a great life skill when you're shipwrecked on a deserted island, but knackering the rest of the time.

And that's why any advice I give you here on how to get through the day is just advice on how to get through the day, how to get that project out of the door and how to achieve the things at work that are actually important to you. I'd love to tell you these things will smash the patriarchy and change the world, but if I knew how to do that, this would be a very different book.

However, every time I find myself laughing at a faintly gross joke in the office because I 'don't want to cause a fuss' or 'be *that* person' (full disclosure: I've done it lots, and I've done it recently), I think about a woman I used to work with. She was really great at her job and made a massive impact on the brand she worked on. The (all-male) tech team had a couple of running jokes about her. Nothing major or particularly cruel in the grand scheme of things (and, honestly, these were pretty nice blokes for the most part). It was a couple of little cues that one of them would pick up whenever her name was mentioned, causing the others to snigger and join in. Childish stuff, and she may have known about it. I'm not convinced she'd have cared either way. But why did they do it?

Because they were, collectively, a lazy, apathetic and poorly run team. They weren't untalented, but getting them to inject a bit of drive or passion into a project was almost impossible. And she was the only person who called them out on it. She'd go down there and demand a response. She'd tell them off when stuff wasn't delivered on time and, in no uncertain terms, when their work wasn't good enough.

Basically, she showed them up, and rather than considering that there might be something in it, they took the piss, just a little, just among themselves, to undermine her. Because she was very, very good at her job, and they just weren't as good at theirs.

So now every time I worry about being the butt of a male team's jokes or dubbed 'the boring one', 'the shouty one' or, *eye-roll*, 'the feminist one', I remember her, how good she was at her job, and resolve to be more like her, and less like them.

The problem I've always had is that most of the advice knocking around on how to deal with men in the workplace always seems to revolve around beating them at their own game (earlier Eddie Erlandson described how his wife adopted specific physical traits, leaning forward, banging her hand on the table, to deal with her Alpha male colleagues). An Alpha woman could do this but a Beta?

I used to work with Sian, who was, by her own admission, an Alpha with Beta tendencies. She could be very chilled out and easy-going, yet she was also capable of switching on the Alpha when required. And I only saw her do so with one guy. In meetings he would constantly talk over her, cut her off, interrupt and misinterpret what she was trying to say. 'The stupid thing is, he was my friend,' she told me recently, when I asked her about those meetings. 'I go round to his house, I hang out with him and his wife, but in those work scenarios, he was a total nightmare.'

Her response was to confront it head on: she told him, in no uncertain terms, to stop interrupting her, and she did it every time until he gave in. But you've got to have guts to do that. I'm sure my response would have been just to stop talking in those meetings.

So what do you do?

I've only ever worked on an all-male team once, for a relatively short period. I enjoyed it for lots of reasons – it was fun, social, and everyone was clever and creative. But it was also far more testosterone-fuelled than anything I've experienced before or since. The veneer of politeness that characterises so many of our interactions in the workplace just wasn't there – and without it I floundered.

If someone thought a piece of work was rubbish, they'd loudly ask, 'Who did this shit?' and whoever had produced it would say, 'That was me – what's wrong with it?' And they'd have a bit of a shout, then eventually reach some sort of consensus on what needed to be done to improve it. Then everyone went back to work, no one took offence, and it was never mentioned again. There was no negative atmosphere; nothing was ever left to fester. All great.

Except when I was the culprit. Then, when someone shouted, 'Who wrote this feature? It's total crap,' I'd sit silently, wide-eyed and pale, staring at my screen, totally at a loss as to how to respond. Eventually I'd put my hand up and whisper, 'It was me . . . but what's wrong with it? I thought it was okay.' I sounded whiny and unsure, and I certainly wasn't taking the opportunity to robustly defend my work. Because if someone else is kicking off, my default position is to shut down. I can't help it, it's instinctive, and I'm certainly not the only one who does it.

And if I don't like environments where people are talking over me, you can imagine how I felt in meetings when everyone was yelling at each other – which happened a lot. I should probably have adopted a 'when in Rome' approach and joined in. But for all my desire to dial up my latent Alpha, that sort of direct confrontation fills me with fear and dread. And it also comes back to style over substance: slamming your hand on the desk and shouting is all well and good when you've got an important point to make, but if you're arguing over the exact wording of a picture caption? Is it worth it? Shouting for the sake of shouting, fighting for no discernible purpose, seems pointless to me – which is probably what marks me out as Beta.

But that's why I like a working environment in which everyone is polite to each other. Yes, politeness can sometimes mean you don't get your point across. And, yes, there is a fine line between pursed-lipped politeness and passive-aggression, which we've all crossed, but I'd take that over an environment in which everyone's constantly shouting about how terrible everyone else is at their job.

And for all the talk about female-only environments being hotbeds of bitchiness and simmering resentment, almost all the women I have worked with have been huge champions of each other's work, loudly praising each other when they've done something brilliantly, talking openly and admiringly about women whose work they love. Maybe I've been lucky, but anyone who says you can't have a creative, dynamic, positive environment without the shouting is just plain wrong.

The other thing I found tricky was the bantz, the constant piss-taking. In normal, day-to-day life, I'm relatively thick skinned – probably more so than some of the blokes I was working with. But I can only presume that they have a banter switch somewhere in their brains that I don't know about, allowing them to absorb every lolz that was chucked their way, process whether or not they could be bothered to take offence, then lob something just as 'hilarious' back. I found it exhausting. It meant I could never relax, or just focus on the task at hand. A bit of my brain constantly had to be focused elsewhere on the Top Chat, which was basically verbal willy-waving, to make sure I didn't miss the joke or become the butt of it.

Although admittedly the time I snuck in early and moved the keys about on everyone's keyboards was pretty funny.

Maybe once you've stripped out the overt sexism, the sexual harassment, the gender pay gap, all the big, loud stuff that we know is Really Bad and needs dealing with, working in an environment that's overtly and specifically geared towards men comes down to one thing for me: it's exhausting. It's exhausting having to pretend. Having to try to fit into something that's just wrong for you. (I certainly can't speak for everyone here – maybe you work in an all-male environment and love it.)

Remember, the working world is set up for men to succeed in: we're still interlopers, and we're not allowed to forget it.

Whether you're Alpha or Beta, negotiating a workplace that's inherently male, as so many are, is so hard because most workplaces – and the very institution of work – are not designed for women's progress or comfort. They've evolved over history with a very different purpose in mind. We talk about the big stuff all the time because it's news-worthy, it's noteworthy. But the daily grind of just finding a way to fit in, not falling off the banter bus, not being so po-faced that you stop being a laugh, that's not noteworthy: that's just life.

SEXISM AT WORK

Being mistaken for the secretary; being asked to take notes in a meeting, even though you've already explained that you're not the secretary; being asked when you're planning to have children in a job interview, even though that's totally illegal; being asked to fetch drinks for a meeting even though you're the third most senior person in the room; being expected to order the team's stationery even though you're the second most senior person on the team and the

214

busiest. These are all punchlines to a bad joke about sexism in the office and all happen to actual women every day.

And the sliding scale from a bit creepy to sexual harassment gets blurred with paternalism and ownership. I questioned a lot of women about their experiences of dealing with male bosses and male teams, without specifically asking them about sexual harassment or assault. And that's when the in-between stories emerged. The ones women didn't necessarily want to describe as sexual harassment, because what had happened didn't seem to go far enough. The stories of male bosses who were too married, too proper or too scared of getting caught to sexually harass a female member of their team but felt they had a proprietary relationship, nonetheless.

One woman I spoke to, who worked in a very male-dominated industry, found her older male boss particularly tricky to negotiate. 'He insisted on a very close relationship. He needed to know everything about what I was doing, including my personal life, and he took offence when I started dating someone at work – but only because I hadn't asked his permission first! Even though I was under no obligation to do so. He also took offence when I became more confident working for another boss.'

Another woman told me how, when she was just starting out in tech, she took on some contract work for a guy who promised to 'show her the ropes'. The role turned out to be that of a glorified PA. A few weeks in, they were scouting venues for an event. In one restaurant he burst into tears and said he was getting a divorce. 'I've always known, don't go anywhere near the guy who starts saying that his wife doesn't understand him,' she told me. 'I was really young, but even then, there was no way I was falling for that. So I picked up some serviettes from the side, gave them to him and left the venue.'

She was confident she'd done the right thing, the smart thing. A few days later, he told her that the project was over and her services were no longer required.

SEXUAL HARASSMENT AND SEXUAL ASSAULT

The big stuff is unfortunately all too common. A 2016 TUC study found that 52 per cent of women have experienced sexual harassment at work – this goes up to 63 per cent of women aged between eighteen and twenty-four. The debate around whether women could or should be more Alpha or Beta in the workplace carries little worth when you consider that it doesn't matter what personality type you are, how you do your job, or the role you have, at least half of all women will face sexual harassment or assault just for doing their job. It has nothing to do with women's behaviour or performance at work, but it is a reality many have to negotiate every day.

Sexual harassment and assault in the workplace are a power play. They're a short hop, skip and a jump from the 'joke' comment about your ovaries in that board meeting, which was your colleague's way of reminding everyone else in the room that you had no right to be there. It's a sliding scale from the bloke who whispers 'I would' to your boss as you bend over to try to fix the printer (because none of them is even attempting it) and the guy who thinks it's okay to grab your breasts when you're alone in a meeting room because 'they're there'. And it's not about your breasts or your ovaries. It's about reminding you who's in control, whose house you're in and who's the interloper.

If you want to know just how sinister those power plays can be, we should return to Christine. When she was explaining why she didn't report her old boss, she said a bit more about the complexities of their relationship. 'It was my first job so I didn't realise how abnormal it was. And he'd always tell me how HR wasn't my friend and how I should never report anything to them because they'd always report it back to the person you were complaining about.

'I grew up with abusive parents, and had abusive partners from the age of sixteen. My boss told me this was what the workplace was like, and I believed him. He cried when I left, and we stayed in touch for a bit afterwards – it was only once I'd been away for a few months that I realised how weird the whole thing had been.'

I could give you some tips on how to deal with being sexually harassed or sexually assaulted in the workplace, but I won't because there are so many variables at play there. Not everyone can stand up for themselves in the workplace, or has someone to do it for them. Maybe the fear of being fired and the need to pay your rent is too real. Maybe your boss, the HR director or the chief executive was the person who attacked you. Maybe you just cannot bring yourself to talk about it. But if you're working somewhere you really feel you won't be backed up, believed and supported, then you have to make it your priority to remove yourself from that environment. Leaving doesn't make you weak, or a failure, and it certainly doesn't make it your fault.

And obviously if you can, report it, shout it from the rooftops, make it a problem for the person who attacked you – make it a problem for your boss, the head of HR or the chief executive. Make it anyone's problem but yours to deal with.

To an extent Alpha or Beta doesn't really matter when it comes down to stuff like this. Stuff that reminds us how relatively recent women's mainstream acceptance in the workplace is, and how tenuous our place at the table as equals. Many women won't be sexually harassed or assaulted at work, but plenty will. Too many. Most women, though, will have to find coping tools to deal with sexism in the workplace – whether it's overt or insidious. Acts of sexism chip away at our right to be there at all.

And let's not forget that sexism in all its guises is designed to shut us up. Anyone trying to shut me up at the earliest points in my career would have had a devastating impact on my later success. As a Beta woman, I've needed to be coaxed into making my voice heard, and twenty-two-year-old me would have become quieter, smaller, less significant, with a boss like Christine's. And maybe that's why, in many industries, only the women who shout the loudest make it to the top. Because, as it stands, that's the only way to front down the breast-grabbers, the banter machines and the office chair sexists. By being more Alpha. And that has to change.

But it's not all bad and it's not hopeless. We don't need to shut up and put up with it, but we do need to do our bit to be bigger and louder wherever we can, so we can make things better for the women who can't make a noise or kick up a fuss.

All of us – Alpha, Beta, women or men – need to change the shape of the table so that it's the right fit for everyone. So that it doesn't turn half its occupants into victims.

14.

ALPHA OR BETA, IS ONE EVER BETTER THAN THE OTHER?

So the big question is here. Alpha or Beta women: which is better? Only kidding – I'm not here to pit women against each other. We have the internet, popular culture and certain sections of the media to do that for us.

Because, actually, it doesn't matter whether we're Alpha or Beta – they're just new ways to put us in a box and keep us in our place. What does matter is that we get to understand who we are and how we tick and be that person in the work-place without being told we're 'unprofessional', 'too aggressive' or 'overly emotional' (or whatever particular crime you or I have committed against the Gods of Office Politics this time).

And that in itself is why there's never been a more impor-tant time to discuss these issues. One of the words used to describe Alpha women in a derogatory way is 'nasty' – Alpha women are bossy, bitchy, controlling and nasty.

Nasty Woman was famously co-opted by women all over the world after Donald Trump referred to Hillary Clinton as such during the 2016 presidential election debates. He claimed she was 'such a nasty woman' when she made a dig at him during the debate over Medicare (this from the man who had repeatedly attacked her during the campaign, leading chants to 'lock her up' at his rallies).

By calling her 'nasty', he was attempting to denigrate her, to dismiss what she was saying as the words of a bitchy woman with an axe to grind. Instead it became a rallying cry for women who were willing to stand up and be counted to have their say and to stand up for what they believed in, in a world where being a woman who's too loud, too opinionated, too much is harder than ever.

Equally, it's as important for me to know, as a Beta woman, how I can turn my natural strengths into personally fulfilling and successful career opportunities, without wasting my time and energy trying to be something I'm not, as it is for an Alpha woman to find out how she can harness her drive and passion and turn it into something that showcases her talents and means she's not constantly banging her head against a brick wall.

Because OF COURSE you can be a good leader if you aren't Alpha. It's about what you do, not who you are. Believing that we can't is holding us back. And substitute 'Alpha' for 'masculine' and what do you get? Forty-seven per cent of the workforce believing that to succeed they need to change who they are and how they work.

It matters, because our whole attitude to work can shift on it. Believing that I wasn't 'the right sort of editor' held me back. It took me a decade to realise that even though I had none of the obvious personality traits that I imagined were needed in my role, I'm good at my job. But, really, I became a good editor when I stopped questioning whether I was the right person to do the job and started focusing on my strengths – which, incidentally, are all Beta traits. I'm collaborative, good with people, happy to get my hands dirty and work hard. I also faced my Beta weaknesses and considered how to be more Alpha in those areas.

What I realised, in the end, is that no one is all good

or all bad at their job: we all have strengths and weaknesses. And I may sound like Captain Obvious, but that gets lost in all the noise, the endless posturing and constant comparisons we make with each other. And even if it is obvious, I only got there in the most roundabout way, and perhaps never would have done so at all if I hadn't started examining properly who I was and how I worked.

The idea for *Beta* came about after I wrote an article about being a Beta boss with an Alpha team. It started off as a lament, because I felt you couldn't do it and I couldn't do it. But speaking to careers experts and psychologists when I was researching the piece forced me to think about what I was good at for the first time in ages. It also offered me a bit of perspective on the things I wasn't so great at: they weren't that bad, they weren't deal-breakers, and they were things that I could probably work on, if I was willing to embrace them head on rather than shy away from them. It also reminded me – sharply – that I'd spent all this time worrying about how bad I was at my job, panicking, making myself and the role smaller than they could be, and all the while I was doing the job, and doing it well. I was succeeding – but I worried so much that my personality didn't fit that I barely noticed.

The difference was almost instantaneous. Suddenly I looked forward to going into work every day. Sunday-night fear was almost eradicated, and challenges became something to embrace. I remembered that I loved my job, and I cared about it, and that I needed to nurture it more, rather than treating it like an unexploded bomb that might go off at any moment. I stopped treating work as something to be fearful of lest the bomb exploded and everyone saw me for a fraud who should never have been given the job in the first place.

The amount of headspace my own personal brand of Impostor Syndrome must have taken up was incredible: suddenly I could engage my brain again. I had time to think, consider things, take a decision without freaking out that it was going to be the wrong one. I'm not constantly exhausted (feeling like you're wearing the wrong boots all the time is exhausting), which means I can take on more, be more dynamic and passionate. I can be a bit more Alpha when I want or need to be.

If this all sounds a bit too vague, here are some of the things I have always dismissed as 'not the sort of thing I do' that I now do. Not because I'm always great at them but because my fear of doing them wrongly doesn't paralyse me any more.

PUBLIC SPEAKING

I'm still terrified of this one, but I make a point of doing it every time I'm asked. Sometimes it goes well, sometimes not, but I'm trying to train myself to see the occasions where it goes badly as progress in their own way. (Full disclosure: last time I had to speak in front of twenty people I had to lock myself into a toilet cubicle for half an hour afterwards to calm myself down. I'm really not as chilled out and Zen as I'm making it sound.)

RADIO OR TV

See above. I get massive tunnel vision about thirty seconds beforehand, but I'll always take the opportunity if I get it. And I have even been known to enjoy myself.

I always told myself that my talent was in enabling other people to do a great job, and that, although I could be creative, I wasn't the sort of person who could generate lots of good ideas. I also told myself I wasn't commercial, wasn't good in front of clients. I told myself that I was good at the housekeeping stuff – keeping everything ticking over, making sure everyone else was happy. It's all hard work, but it's not difficult – it's also sometimes thankless and dull. But that's who I thought I was, the safe pair of hands who wouldn't do anything stupid, but certainly not someone with huge amounts of creative flair or enough charisma to sell an idea.

Once I learnt to relax and embrace my strengths, I remembered that, actually, I'm good with ideas. I'm creative and I'm good with people. In fact, those were some of the reasons why I became a journalist, and why I was given my job. But I got so used to trying to keep my head down, not make too many big mistakes, not draw too much attention to myself, that I went for the lowest risk strategy possible. I became dull but reliable at my job, when what was really needed was someone who wasn't scared of making a mistake occasionally.

None of these things changed because I changed as a person, but because I stopped thinking I needed to change as a person.

So why is this a women's problem, not a people's problem? To an extent, I'm sure, it is also a problem for men, but then again, almost every single woman I spoke to said she had suffered from Impostor Syndrome in her career, and I've never come across a man who feels that way. (There's no real consensus on whether this is more of a female issue:

some studies suggest that men and women get Impostor Syndrome in equal measure, others that men are less affected by it as they are raised to bluff and exaggerate.)

One woman I spoke to told me that her old boss used to turn down her requests for pay rises (while awarding them to male members of the team) because 'she was lucky to be there in the first place'. That he felt he could say that out loud demonstrates just what a dinosaur he was, but workplace sexism is still depressingly rife – and Impostor Syndrome still depressingly potent – because plenty of people are still thinking it. And while some people still believe women are lucky to be allowed to participate in the workplace at all, women will only succeed by shouting the loudest, by being the most Alpha of the Alpha. And the rest of us? We will become smaller, quieter and less significant. Not because we can't succeed, but because the world doesn't want to make room for us.

So what do we do? How do we change the script, and the accepted expectations for what a successful woman looks like? I can't tell you what will change the world, and I can't tell you what to do, but I can tell you what worked for me, and I can tell you what I wished I'd known when I was twenty-one.

1. WORK OUT WHAT MOTIVATES YOU

I'm serious. Before you start worrying about what your boss and your company want, think about what *you* want, and why you're there. No one loves their job all day every day. But even if you clock in for eight hours a day just to fund your secret passion for making terrariums, that's still eight hours a day, five days a week. It's a long time to spend doing something that doesn't motivate you in any way. Whether it's the satisfaction you get from completing a task, the colleague who has become a best friend, or even being able to go for a pint on a Friday night and feeling like you've earned it, work out what presses your buttons and how you can do more of the same. Any opportunity you get to make your job more fun or engaging, take it. Work won't always be fun, but it doesn't necessarily have to be miserable either.

2. YOUR JOB SHOULD WORK FOR YOU AS MUCH AS YOU WORK FOR IT

Is your job giving you the opportunities you were told about when you interviewed for it? Do you still get to travel as much as you'd like? Are you being given new challenges? Are you being properly compensated for the work you do? We all get stuck in work ruts, and I always feel like they happen to me more when I feel I have no choice other than to turn up each day and get on with the grind, no escape plan. But, actually, we do have options and we do have power. If you want more out of your job, say so. Fight for it. There's a reason why you took that job, and you sometimes need to remind yourself of what it is. And if that reason no longer applies, or your boss can't or won't give you what you want, then it's time to look elsewhere.

3. DON'T TURN DOWN THE HARD STUFF

Take on the challenges, and embrace them. Finding them difficult, and not getting things right first time, doesn't mean you've failed: it means you're working stuff out. I try to alternate every three or six months now – I push myself, try new stuff, do things that are hard, then ease off for a while. I actually learn from it, and am not just in a constant state of panic or stress when I'm continuously out of my comfort zone and never have time to think about what I'm doing or why.

4. REMEMBER THAT THE WORST-CASE SCENARIO IS NEVER THAT BAD

What's your worst-case scenario at work? Mine is always being fired in a way that results in public shaming within my industry. People would *know*, I'd think. They'd *talk* about it.

And, yes, were I to be fired publicly from my job (which seems unlikely), I'm sure it would garner a bit of gossip. But that would be it. Nothing bad would happen, really. People would forget about it eventually. And being the topic of gossip isn't necessarily that bad – most people are too polite to come up and talk to you about your very public firing. Unless you do an important job – you're a police officer or a doctor, for instance – then the worst-case scenario is rarely that bad.

5. DON'T ASSUME EVERYONE ELSE IS BEING POLITE – IF YOU'RE DOING A POOR JOB, SOMEONE *WILL* TELL YOU

This is crucial. Is your boss an idiot? Okay, maybe, but is their boss an idiot? Or their boss? At least one person you work for will have their head screwed on, and they won't be paying you to come in every day and do a bad job. No one is that nice. If you're messing stuff up, someone will tell you. If you're constantly messing things up, they will have a slightly more formal word with you about it. If you absolutely cannot do anything right, well, yes, you might get fired, but by that time you'll know all about it. People won't pay you to be bad at your job. They won't spare your blushes and let you mess up over and over again just because they feel sorry for you. And you did not get that promotion because you once complimented your boss's tie: you got it because you earned it. You deserve your job and you're great at it. If that wasn't true you just wouldn't be there.

6. BUT ONE LAST THING . . .

Not everyone is great at their job all day every day. We all have off days, or afternoons when we just can't concentrate, or make a decision, or get something off the ground as quickly as we'd like. If that happens once a week, and it's usually on a Wednesday after you had a jacket potato at lunch, well, put it down to a Hump-day carb overload and don't worry about it too much. Do your expenses, sort out your email inbox and put that big creative project off until tomorrow. Everyone does it, even the people who are pretending otherwise on Instagram.

But if you feel like that most days, or most afternoons, then you need to think about that too. Because you shouldn't. Are you depressed? Unmotivated? Knackered? Bored? Because you can do something about all of those things. It doesn't mean you're lazy or useless. It just means something isn't connecting right now. So stop beating yourself up, take a deep breath and reset.

But mainly what I wish I'd been told at twenty-one is this: you have to work at your job if you want it to make you happy. You have to give it time and love in the same way as you have to give a relationship some love if you want it to work. But in the same way as a relationship should give you more than it takes, your job shouldn't suck out your soul. It should give you more than it takes. Because you're great and you deserve to spend forty hours a week doing something you like, in a way that feels true to you.

If you can give yourself the opportunity and the headspace to focus on the job at hand, and what you bring to the table (rather than what you don't), it can be transformative to the point of being life-changing. It spells the end of Sunday-night doom, Monday-morning blues and Hump-day. It's time for the scales to fall from our eyes and for us to remember that our jobs should work for us, not the other way round.

ACKNOWLEDGEMENTS

An extra special thank you to two people – my husband Bear who provided the catering for this whole endeavour, and put up with endless tantrums, freak-outs and melt-downs along the way, and my mum Jackie, who's first job after retirement was part-time research assistant, part-time sub editor, part-time transcription service, and full-time cheerleader for BETA.

I also need to thank my amazing agent Bryony who hand-held me through the entire process and shaped my book proposal into something great, Charlotte and the team at Coronet who have been absolutely fantastic. And, of course, the dozens of women who gave up their precious time to tell me about their experiences in the workplace.

Finally, all the great women I've worked with who've been Alpha, Beta and everything in between. I literally couldn't have done it without you.

THE GUIDE TO
THE FUTURE
OF
MEDICINE

Technology AND The Human Touch

Bertalan Meskó

Publisher: Webicina Kft.
The Guide to the Future of Medicine: Technology AND the Human Touch
Bertalan Mesko

Editor: Dr. Richard E. Cytowic
Cover Design: Szilvia Kora
Interior Design: Roland Rekeczki

ISBN 978-963-08-9802-7

Printed by CreateSpace, An Amazon.com Company.
Printed in the United States of America.

References and illustration sources are provided.

Table of contents

About the Author

Bertalan Mesko, MD, PhD is a medical futurist who graduated from the University of Debrecen Medical School and Health Science Center. He received the Weszprémy Award as a medical doctor and finished his PhD summa cum laude in the field of clinical genomics.

As a medical futurist, he envisions the next steps to be taken and the trends happening now in order to have a mutually positive relationship between the human touch and the innovative technologies that await us in the future of healthcare.

Dr. Mesko is the managing director and founder of Webicina. com, the first service that curates medical and health-related social media resources for patients and medical professionals. He has given over 500 presentations at institutions ranging from Yale, Stanford, and Harvard to the World Health Organization and the Futuremed course organized by the Singularity University. He is also a consultant for pharma and medical technology companies.

He is the author of the Social Media in Clinical Practice handbook, as well as the multiple award-winning medical blog, Scienceroll.com. He is the founder of and lecturer at the Social Media in Medicine online-and-offline university course, which is the first of its kind worldwide.

Dr. Mesko's work has been cited by CNN, the World Health Organization, Nature Medicine, The New York Times, Al Jazeera, the British Medical Journal, and Wired Science, among others.

He is a member of the World Future Society.

Foreword by Lucien Engelen

In fifty years from now, I expect more than 50% of the revenue in healthcare will come from companies that do not exist, or do not have any business in healthcare today.

Technological developments as well as changes in society will create the 5th democratization. After music, travel, retail and media; healthcare is next to be disrupted. Adding to that, the increasing patient empowerment brings in "the perfect storm" for health(care). In my keynotes I often use the 4D anagram: Delocalization, Digitalization, Dollars and Democratization. Because they are all tied together and starting to peak at somewhat the same time, it creates the ideal eco–system for autonomous change.

Change that will hit health(care) for a lot of people ‚overnight', not that this wasn't foreseeable, but the signs have been neglected over and over again. Medicine is starting to adopt new treatments, medications and protocols but is lacking far behind where it goes on reflecting on the model of health(care). We basically deliver healthcare the same way it was done a hundred years ago. Now due to the exponentially growing possibilities technology is bringing to the table, we, for instance, will start bringing back health(care) into the homes of people. This also brings the need of new payment models, changes in curriculum for medical students like the one that we've crafted at Radboud University Medical Center, or even new legislation.

For these kinds of transformational processes, we need people who can address these changes and paint a picture of the world of tomorrow. In my work of changing healthcare through innovations, conferences (TEDxMaastricht 2011, 2012) and lectures, I sometimes meet people who have the ability to bridge the world of medicine and the one of technology on a high and, most of all, broad level. One of those was a young medical student who was running a medical blog (Scienceroll), at that time already the best read blog in this area. Sharing the same vision with a different approach we got connected through the Internet in 2009 and I asked him to speak at our REshape conferences in Nijmegen.

Berci is one of the few people who have the insight, the feeling, the expertise, the tone of voice and the network to guide medicine through this era of change. He's crafted himself a way through huge challenges, carefully choosing his options, staying authentic to changing medicine. Being faculty at Singularity's University in the Exponential Medicine track (formerly known as FutureMed), I asked Daniel Kraft who is running the track, if I could donate half of my lecture time to Berci in 2013. What better place than NASA's Moffet Field campus to show this guy's great competence that equals the levels most of us have at the end of our career; and as expected he absolutely rocked the place. Over time, his opening sentence in his keynotes changed from „I'm a medical geek" to „I'm a medical futurist" and that is spot-on. The question only was how and when he would set the next step. His latest endeavor is the book you are holding right now.

An exciting journey and guide through developments, paradigm shifts, hurdles and opportunities. Although the model of writing a book might become obsolete in the future, it nowadays still is a great form factor to spread knowledge. This book should be added to every curriculum's mandatory reading list in the medical as in the nursing field, but also to every Health MBA program out there. I'm also looking forward to the online course version of this book that he hopefully will create.

In here you'll find a lot of very interesting topics assembled into one place to guide you through your own journey. Since that is Berci's biggest suggestion to you: start NOW exploring the world around you from an innovation perspective, find your own way, and choose your own battle.

My 'prescription' to you would be to read a chapter a day, digest it for another day, explore that area yourself for the day after, and then execute on it the next. But the chances you'll read this book in one take are actually much higher, and that's fine too.

Next to this incredibly well written and overarching book, he's also created a virtual landing space for the discussion on **www.medicalfuturist.com.** I really do hope to meet you there.

To Berci: congratulations my friend, you've done it again! You never stop amazing me and many others with the thorough steps you take. I would like to advise you with an adapted quote of the great Steve Jobs „...keep the courage to follow your heart and intuition... Stay hungry, and be a bit more foolish sometimes..."

Lucien Engelen
@lucienengelen
Director REshape & Innovation Center, Radboud University Medical Center
Chief Imagineer Dutch National IT Institute for Healthcare
Faculty Exponential Medicine, Singularity University, Silicon Valley

Preface

We are facing major changes as medicine and healthcare now produce more developments than in any other era. Key announcements in technology happen several times a year, showcasing gadgets that can revolutionize our lives and our work. Only five or six years ago it would have been hard to imagine today's ever increasing billions of social media users; smartphone and tablet medical applications; the augmented world visible through Google Glass; IBM's supercomputer Watson used in medical decision making; exoskeletons that allow paralyzed people to walk again; or printing out medical equipment and biomaterials in three dimensions. It would have sounded like science fiction. Sooner or later such announcements will go from multiple times a year to several times a month, making it hard to stay informed about the most recent developments. This is the challenge facing all of us.

At the same time, ever–improving technologies threaten to obscure the human touch, the doctor–patient relationship, and the very delivery of healthcare. Traditional structures of medicine are about to change dramatically with the appearance of telemedicine, the Internet full of misleading information and quacks offering hypnosis consultation through Skype; surgical robots; nanotechnology; and home diagnostic devices that measure almost anything from blood pressure to blood glucose levels and genetic data.

People are generally afraid of change even though there are good changes that bring value to all of us. The challenge we are facing now can lead to the best outcomes ever for the medical profession and for patients as well. My optimism though is not based on today's trends and the state of worldwide healthcare. If you read this book you will realize, as I did, how useful technology can be if we anticipate for the future and consider all the potential risks.

Many of us have already witnessed signs of these. Patients, for example, use online networks to find kindred individuals dealing with similar problems. Doctors can now prescribe mobile applications and information in addition to conventional treatment. Given what I have seen over the last few years as a medical futurist, no stakeholder of healthcare—from policy maker, researcher, patient, to doctor—is ready for what is coming. I see enormous technological changes heading our way. If they hit us unprepared, which we are now, they will wash away the medical system we know and leave it a purely technology–based service without personal interaction. Such a complicated system should not be washed away. Rather, it should be consciously and purposefully redesigned piece by piece. If we are unprepared for the future, then we lose this opportunity.

According to "Digital Life in 2025" published by the Pew Research Internet Project in 2014, information sharing through the Internet will be so effortlessly interwoven into our daily lives that it will flow like electricity; the spread of the Internet will enhance global connectivity, fostering more worldwide relationships and less ignorance. These are going to be the driving forces of the next years. But without looking into the details, the upcoming dangers will outweigh the potentially amazing advantages.

My background as a medical doctor, researcher, and geek gives me a unique perspective about medicine's future. My doctor self thinks that the rapidly advancing changes to healthcare pose a serious threat to the human touch, the so-called art of medicine. This we cannot let happen. People have an innate propensity to interact with one another; therefore we need empathy and intimate words from our caregivers when we're ill and vulnerable.

The medical futurist in me cannot wait to see how the traditional model of medicine can be improved upon by innovative and disruptive technologies. People usually think that technology and the human touch are incompatible. My mission is to prove them wrong. The examples and stories in this book attempt to show that the relationship is mutual. While we can successfully keep the doctor-patient personal relationship based on trust, it is also possible to employ increasingly safe technologies in medicine, and accept that their use is crucial to provide a good care for patients. This mutual relationship and well-designed balance between the art of medicine and the use of innovations will shape the future of medicine.

This book tries to prepare readers for the coming waves of change, to be a guide for the future of medicine that anyone can use. No one can say what exactly is going to happen and how healthcare will be redesigned, although it is possible to paint a picture of the key directions we are headed in, and act as a "tourist guide" for what kind of skills and knowledge will be necessary to make informed decisions.

I have spoken with global experts about the role that artificial intelligence can play in medical decision making; how surgical robots can assist surgeons; how genomics can make primary care uniquely personalized, and how wearable devices can eliminate the need to go to a clinical laboratory. I have conducted nearly seventy interviews with these experts to augment my own analyses. Through online networks I leveraged the power of crowdsourcing by giving other experts a chance to inform me of trends they find interesting. Experts in medical ethics, for example, helped ensure that individuals for or against extensive technological use find the information and perspectives they are looking for.

Through its stories, descriptions, and suggestions, I hope this guide will fulfill its mission and prepare you for the future of medicine.

Part I. Introduction

"Prediction is very difficult, especially if it's about the future."
-Niels Bohr

In the early 1990s when I was about 10 years–old, I volunteered in computer shops in order to learn about the hardware behind the software. I learned how to construct a personal computer (PC) myself, something I still do these days. As a kid I enjoyed getting access to the newest gadgets and witnessing the continual improvement of computing power.

One day a man in his forties came into the shop and asked about the largest hard drive available that time. When we told him its capacity was 40 megabytes, he asked what he would do with so many megabytes. His operating system, programs, and files would not fill up that much space back then. Today, home computers have terabyte–sized hard drives. As of 2014, the Internet holds approximately 2 zettabytes of information (about ten thousand billion times larger than that man's hard drive). This improvement occurred in just over a decade.

I am lucky to live in an era when technologies are improving at an incredible pace. I remember exactly when I first went online, and know that most of my own students have no idea when they did. On November 21, 1996 at exactly 2 a.m. my computer's modem squealed and as if by magic I was online. I could browse the web if I knew the addresses by heart. Mostly that was it, the whole experience of using the Internet. Eighteen years later I work and sometimes seem to live online in order to experience a world seemingly without limitations. Now smartphones track health parameters and record electrocardiograms (ECG). Artificial intelligence is getting better at diagnosing complicated cases; and augmented reality could let us see more of the online world in real life. I managed to crowdsource a rare diagnosis by having hand–picked experts to follow on Twitter for years. I see how technology can improve the quality of life. Yet new technologies have not really changed the way we organize healthcare.

Even though I passionately love technology as a geek, I know it will certainly not solve the problems that healthcare is facing now. It can facilitate healthcare renovation by providing powerful tools, data, and solutions, but patients need emotional attention and empathy from their caregivers. The lack of connectivity among people and healthcare institutions is a basic problem we struggle with worldwide. I think I might tell my children in 10 years that the early 2010s was a barbaric era because neither physicians nor patients had access to the data they truly needed.

The exponential amount of medical information makes it impossible to be up to date and doctors burn out. Instead of reading a few articles that might be of interest to a particular doctor, let's curate and crowdsource the very best of medical research in a customized way for them. Instead of manually typing data via keyboard, let's speed up the process and make it more interactive through augmented reality. Doing that, the doctor can look the patient in the eye and engage their problems in a conversational manner. There is no smartphone application for empathy and offering emotional care.

Let stakeholders access whatever information they need about a medical condition or its treatment. Let them access public health data that can monitor one's health status and automatically send out customized alerts about advisable changes in lifestyle. Let doctors use this information and devices to provide better care, and let patients use home monitoring services to take better care of themselves. Everyone will benefit.

New technologies will finally help medical professionals focus more on the patient as a human being instead of spending time hunting down pertinent information. They will be able to do what they do best: provide care with expertise. In turn, patients will get the chance to be equal partners in this process taking matters into their own hands.

Let's prepare for what is coming next

I give a lot of presentations every year traveling to many countries. Everywhere I have seen the same kind of system shaped like a pyramid. The base features health insurers, governments, and pharmaceutical companies depending on the country. In the middle of the pyramid are medical professionals bearing almost all the responsibility. These stakeholders sometimes mention patients in the smallest segment at the top of the pyramid. This system has been dramatically changing for years to move the patient to the center and break the pyramid down. The patient will soon be able to measure any health parameter about themselves at home; tell what exactly they eat; record blood pressure, ECG, and other basic data almost constantly.

These patients, now called e–patients, who are ready to hack and disrupt healthcare need to be educated about the use of the digital world as some of them cannot find what they need online, and thus become frustrated, frustrating their doctors in turn; while others face the problem of too many choices. Moreover, without proper health management taking care of their own health, not only disease; it is going to be impossible to change the structure of practicing medicine as the activity and participation of patients are required for that too.

With a few exceptions medical education has not trained medical professionals for this world full of technological advances. They are trained for today's trends and technologies, while computational power has been increasing at an exponential pace. As futurist Ray Kurzweil has pointed out, these exponentially fast developments might lead to a point where we will not be able to embrace the next logical step. We might create an artificial intelligence that can design algorithms and robots we can no longer understand. I think such changes will lead to even bigger concerns in medicine due to their sensitive nature. Fully automated surgical robots; microchips modeling human physiology, or nanorobots living in our bloodstream all will provide incredible opportunities as well as pose threats.

Evidence based medicine is meant to ensure that quality treatment options are chosen and diagnosis is based on empirical evidence rather than personal assumptions. But this area adapts to changes more slowly than other industries do. For example, after the driverless car developed by Google ran for 1 million miles without incident, car manufacturers such as Volvo announced the inclusion of such algorithms in its future models. For obvious reasons things are a bit slower in healthcare. But soon an ever–increasing gap is going to be too big to cope with.

The most tech–savvy people would agree that the human touch should not be eliminated from practicing medicine; and those who are against technologies must agree that without technology it is impossible to provide healthcare today.

The solution is to prepare patients, doctors, nurses, policy makers, and other stakeholders for the waves of change coming toward us. I remain confident that it is still possible and that we still have time. The goal is to initiate public discussions about the potential advantages and risks we will face.

The role of a medical futurist

In 2012, at the age of 27, I fulfilled my childhood dream by becoming a medical doctor and finishing my PhD in genomics. I was ready to live my entire life as a researcher. But to be honest I was not completely satisfied, and felt unable to leverage the power of my geek self and the technical experience I had gathered. I had to create a new profession in which I could use my different backgrounds and points of views. This is how I became a medical futurist.

The role of a medical futurist is not that of a trend watcher. My interest lies in the intersection of improving healthcare with technology and being a doctor trained for the art of medicine. This gives me both the chance and responsibility to offer my analyses of the future of care.

Early on I received an exciting challenge from a medical journal to summarize the future of healthcare in 2050—and to do so in one Twitter message, in 140 characters. I preferred to write essays, but came up with this: "In 2050, transparent healthcare, decision trees, curated online content, e–patients, web–savvy doctors, and no collaborative barriers."

I'm certain we are heading towards that direction, although without a public discussion initiated now, the chance for establishing a mutual relationship between technologies and the human touch is getting smaller every day.

Part II. Trends That Are Shaping the Future of Medicine

"Don't follow trends, start trends."
–Frank Capra

The hardest part of the job of any futurist, particularly a medical futurist, is picking up the trends, technologies and concepts that seem to play a major role in the future of medicine and healthcare as extrapolations for the next years based on today's trends. What makes it truly complicated is the fact that many of these technologies and concepts intertwine and mix together from many perspectives. The use of artificial intelligence is imminent in the world of electronic medical records, as well as advanced robotics or portable diagnostics.

I chose the topics that appear in the next chapters because they demonstrate the most potential to illustrate what I see as future trends. The goal of these chapters is to give you a clear picture about the key steps being taken in technology by keeping the future of medicine in mind.

The anatomy of a trend description

Each trend's sub–chapter contains basic descriptions about the technology, real–life stories, practical examples, the concepts that determine its use in medicine and healthcare; and possible future directions. Regarding the twenty–two trends, we will move from concepts that are currently available to technologies that are way off in the future.

At the end of each section are scores that meant to give a better understanding of a particular technology's usefulness:

- **A score of availability** between 1 and 10, where 1 is currently too futuristic a concept while 10 means it is already available.
- **Focus of attention** that describes which stakeholder can best take advantage of the trend.
- **Websites & other online resources** that keep you in the information loop by following them.
- **Companies or start–ups** working on the particular trend and being in the forefront.
- **Books and Movies** describing the advantages and disadvantages of the trend or technology.

Trend 1. Empowered Patients

In November in 2013, I was waiting at the airport in Budapest for e–Patient Dave deBronkart. I had invited him to speak at Semmelweis Medical School. Years ago he decided to empower patients worldwide through advocacy, books, and speeches. His experience in tackling kidney and then skin cancer drove him to seek new approaches and solutions.

In January 2007, he was diagnosed with late–stage kidney cancer after a routine shoulder X–ray showed a spot in his lung. It turned out to be one of many kidney cancer metastases all over his body. The median survival time at diagnosis was 24 weeks. Surgeons at Boston's Beth Israel Deaconess Medical Center removed the extensive mess, and gave him a chance to participate in a clinical trial for the powerful interleukin–2 he also read about in online patient forums. By September he had beaten the disease. During his treatment he was in constant contact with his physician, Dr. Danny Sands, one of the earliest proponents of e–patients.

Healthcare cannot really advance without physicians letting their patients help themselves and be a full partner in making the decisions that affect them. This is the key message of deBronkart's book, *Let Patients Help*. After reading it, and reading it again, I sent him a Twitter message that his book should be available to every medical student in the world. He accepted my invitation and flew to Hungary, explaining what he saw as the key problems we have to face during the drive to the medical school.

"A century ago, a patient with diabetes could not know their status without going to the doctor. Today we have home test strips, and sometimes we even have continuous glucose monitors. This has not put endocrinologists out of business; instead, it means we can spend clinic time discussing what to do with the situation, instead of giving part of the time to understanding what the situation is.

You could say that a doctor has many skills: knowledge, diagnosis, prescribing, caring, monitoring, on and on. It is inevitable that some of them will be automated. This is no insult to the physician unless the physician feels they are sacred because "Only I have this magic skill." To me, when some tasks get automated, it creates more space for the skills that remain."

E–Patient Dave deBronkart with his physician Dr. Danny Sands.

He thinks it is possible to make medicine truly patient–focused by ensuring its scientific background while encouraging patient empowerment at the same time. He valued having doctors and nurses who *cared* about him when he was dying and in need of surgery. He now cannot imagine why a smart, caring, and scientifically–minded doctor would not also be able to do the same with a patient who is empowered.

"The only problem I've seen is the rare case where a doctor has been taught to think that the only reason they're valuable is because they know something other people don't know. If that's your self–image, then indeed it's a threat when somebody else knows something. To that, all I can say is that my doctors know thousands of times more than I do, and I love them for it, and I still want to be the best partner I can for them."

He has come across many examples of medical professionals' adoption of digital communication. His doctor, Dr. Sands, is a great and positive example of a physician who wants to be equal partner with his/her patients. deBronkart explained their relationship with a recent story.

"A year ago I had just arrived in Switzerland, and I had a worrying symptom in my leg. Did I get a deep vein thrombosis on the flight? We fired up Skype and I used the webcam to show him the ripples on my leg. Boom: he was much better able to assess my situation. He said "Yes, find a clinic," and I did."

In medicine as in other fields, the ability to do our best depends on awareness of the situation, which technology makes infinitely easier from afar. That, in turn, makes it infinitely easier for patients to access care. This is transformational for the provider, whether they want to sell more services or to reach more souls in need.

As deBronkart described, no medical school 10 or 20 years ago was teaching doctors that in their professional lifetimes they would be expected to adapt repeatedly to completely new tools that were unforeseeable. Now that is reality. In his 1987 book, The Media Lab, visionary Stewart Brand spoke of how people would ponder questions like "What could we do if we had unlimited free bandwidth?" This seemed insane in the days of old modems, but today we can see how valid that question was. deBronkart shared with me the three things he looks forward to in the future.

1. Instant dissemination of information where it is needed. That could be by push or by pull (e.g., RSS subscriptions), and includes medical literature and data about any patient's status.
2. A demand for that information, because if people do not know about an opportunity and do not ask for it, then nothing good will come of it.
3. Finally, a layer of analytics that will analyze the data flood and draw our attention to it only in situations that require it.

Dr. Bob Wachter at UCSF Medical Center pointed out that in commercial aviation it became necessary to display less as more and more data poured into the cockpit. In such a world, scarce commodity is not the issue; the viewer's attention is. If that resource is squandered on a flood of mixed-value data, nothing can be optimized. The filter, the analytics, becomes the gate.

New online communities

If healthcare already served the absolute needs and rights of patients, there would be no reason for the empowered patient movement to be born. But obviously it is not the case. Patients need to step up in order to reach a relationship with their doctor that is more of a partnership than the traditional hierarchy. Patients in the early 2000s started to take matters into their own hands; launching movements that promote healthy lifestyle and information management; looking for details about their condition to be able to better manage it; and using digital channels and devices to acquire data about their body.

First they started to look for information they had not had access to before. It used to be a privilege of medical professionals. Then they brought the data and information found online to their caregivers, but not all professionals were glad about this. I personally witnessed such cases when the professor left the examination room saying "Well, then you do not need me here" after the patient told him she found information about her symptoms online. This is certainly not the way of assisting patients who want to check online resources. Instead, doctors now need to acquire skills related to digital literacy making them able to assess the quality of a medical website and help their patients in this way too.

Gradually, e–patients have been transforming this approach. They have formed communities sharing insights and details about living with their conditions. I have been in touch with e–patient leaders for many years who have proved that a fellow patient can understand their problems better than any medical professional.

PatientsLikeMe.com was the first widely popular site. It was only open to patients who could log a lot of data about their condition and everyday life. The results of the first research using data obtained through such online communities were published in Nature Biotechnology in 2011 and in the open access paper PLoS Medicine in 2012. In 2014, PatientsLikeMe announced a five–year agreement with Genentech, a pharmaceutical company, to use PatientsLikeMe's global online network to develop innovative ways of researching patients' real–world experience with disease and treatment.

Frustrated patients tend to turn to the Internet for help. Instead of seeking a formal second opinion they try to crowdsource the diagnosis behind their symptoms. CrowdMed.com was designed to serve this special need.

Users can create a case by describing the symptoms and relevant details. For cash rewards medical detectives suggest potential solutions and then collectively vote on the most likely ones. Then CrowdMed's patented prediction market technology aggregates this knowledge to assign a consensus–based probability to each.

There is a personal story behind any true innovation. Carly Heyman, the sister of Crowdmed founder Jared Heyman, was desperately seeking help for a serious condition after contacting nearly two dozen doctors and spending over $100,000 in medical bills. Jared founded CrowdMed to harness the wisdom of crowds to help solve difficult medical cases. Carly's medical case was ultimately solved by collaboration among an interdisciplinary team of medical experts.

Another innovator, Gilles Frydman, played a crucial role in patient empowerment by launching mailing groups for cancer patients and founding the Association of Cancer Online Resources (ACOR) in 1995. These e–mail groups provided patients with a chance to interact with others dealing with the same condition and facing similar issues. ACOR grew to become the largest cancer mailing list ever, and Frydman continued innovating to help cancer patients globally.

I met him several times in locations from California to Paris. He always amazed me with his vision about how we should assist patients in finding the information they need and connecting them to one another. I was not surprised to hear about his new venture, Smart Patients, an online community site that shares details about treatments, clinical trials, the latest science, and how it all fits into the context of an individual's experience.

As a result of these, a new movement was born. The mission statement behind the movement known as Participatory Medicine states:

"Participatory Medicine is a model of cooperative health care that seeks to achieve active involvement by patients, professionals, caregivers, and others across the continuum of care on all issues related to an individual's health. Participatory medicine is an ethical approach to care that also holds promise to improve outcomes, reduce medical errors, increase patient satisfaction and improve the cost of care."

It has its own peer–reviewed journal, provides a forum for collaborative research exchange, educational resources, and advocacy.

E-patients are the hackers of healthcare

The term e-patient is derived from attributes such as empowered, engaged, equipped, enabled, equal, or expert. All of these represent the way e-patients disrupt healthcare.

Kathy McCurdy, a designer in her professional life, has been dealing with a neurological disorder for many years. When she had to visit a new doctor she decided to help him by creating an infographic containing years of details about her medications, treatments, operations, and other elements. It gave her new doctor a clear picture and facilitated their working together.

Salvatore Iaconesi from Italy launched a crowdsourcing effort when he found out he had brain cancer. Being a good coder, he cracked the code of his medical records and made the data open source that anyone could analyze. He encourages people to create a video, an artwork, a map, a text, a poem, or a game from the data to help find a solution for his health issue.

In another case, a mother suddenly developed malignant high blood pressure and complex partial seizures after giving birth to her third child. She was treated at Stanford, but received no final diagnosis. Her husband launched a Facebook page to solicit suggestions. He also created a wiki page for listing potential hypotheses so that anyone could easily leave comments. Later they published the graphs of seizure activities and noticed strong and consistent intervals. So many ideas were submitted in their crowdsourcing campaign, that they had to launch another one for finding a method by which this huge amount of data could be analyzed.

Such examples highlight ways patients can obtain a second opinion or assist their own caregivers in solving a complicated issue. As a consequence, more and more start-ups are focusing on this area. Developing services for e-patients, however, is not as simple as it may sound.

I met Jason Berek-Lewis, social media consultant at Healthy Startups, in Melbourne, Australia because I wanted to hear his thoughts about social media and the world of start-ups in healthcare. He has extensive experience working with digital health innovators. We talked about driving forces that shape innovation for start-ups focusing on healthcare.

"You can boil most of the factors driving innovation in healthcare into two categories: money/cost/affordability and improving access to healthcare. With Western governments facing major financial challenges together with increasing health costs (driven by technology inflation and aging populations), start–ups and innovators will play a critical role in creating faster, cheaper, better and more accessible ways to deliver essential healthcare services."

Healthcare start–up clones will probably arise, meaning that cost pressures in Western health systems will lead to innovators to look toward other countries' start–ups and adapt their innovations in their local health system.

Berek–Lewis has firm views on what trends seem to be truly disruptive in medicine. One is crowdfunding for healthcare. Some patients will look to crowdfunding to help them to afford access to care and new technologies. Another is increasingly cheaper smartphones and tablets. Asian and African phone manufacturers will continue to drive down the cost of Android–based phones, and the ability of the Android operating system to run on lower specced processors coupled with a backlash against Apple's rumored HealthBook will drive more developers to build for Android first. He also described how hospitals could become the new health start–up incubators. Doctors, nurses, medical specialists, and administrators will continue to push the "bring your own device" boundaries and will work with others to build mobile tech solutions that get around outdated technologies used in hospitals.

With respect to the obstacles that health–related start–ups face in promoting more access for patients, he thinks the Western model is broken.

"The stakes are obviously very high in healthcare; you are potentially 'playing' with people's lives when utilizing new technologies. But trying to reform and change healthcare by doing exactly what we are already doing, and trying to jam this reform into existing and broken models of delivering care, and expecting better health outcomes and more efficiencies is the epitome of insanity. We have to accept that the prevailing Western model of delivering healthcare is broken and free up the regulatory framework (while protecting physician/patient safety) to unleash new opportunities for innovation."

According to Pew Internet Research 72% of Internet users say they looked online for health information within the past year. It is partially the responsibility of medical professionals now to assist their patients in learning the meaningful use of social media and the Internet in general. Doctors should acquire the required skills for this. In order to deal with the huge amount of false information online, dynamic resources should be curated by medical professionals and expert patients. On Webicina.com, which I founded, such resources curated by experts are available for free either for patients or their caregivers in over twenty languages. This is the only way to assist all stakeholders.

Today's hierarchy of the patient–physician relationship will dramatically change to create a system in which the patient is in the center of attention. They can measure anything about themselves; access information and resources without limitations, manage their health or disease, and take equal part in making medical decisions with their caregivers. Examples of how healthcare is being transformed include patients buying companies that go bankrupt conducting clinical trials so that they can continue the trials themselves; and patients launching their own companies to help others. The movement is still only taking baby steps. It is just the beginning.

Score of availability: 10

Focus of attention: Patients

Websites & other online resources: E–Patients (http://e–patients.net), Patient Opinion (https://www.patientopinion.org.uk)

Companies & start–ups: SmartPatients (https://www.smartpatients.com), CrowdMed (https://www.crowdmed.com), ACOR (http://www.acor.org), Patientslikeme (http://www.patientslikeme.com), Webicina (http://www.webicina.com)

Books: Let Patients Help by E–Patient Dave deBronkart; The Complete Guide to Managing Health Care Using Technology by Nancy B Finn

Movies: Extraordinary Measures (2010)

Trend 2. Gamifying Health

Do we currently have health care or sick care? Do we care more about disease or health? All of us know how hard it is to keep ourselves in shape, have a healthy diet, and live a healthy life. Gamification seems to be the key in persuading people to live such lifestyles or stick to the therapy they have been prescribed to. Over 63% of American adults agree that making everyday activities more like a game would make them more fun and rewarding. Wearable gadgets, online services, games, and mobile health solutions can lead to better results if gamification with the right design is included. Improving our health or making our job more efficient can and therefore should be fun.

Since the age of 14, I have been logging details of my life every single day. It means not one day is missing from my digital diary which now consists of over 6,600 days with data. I have logged how much I slept; the major things I worked on; and a physical, mental, and emotional score from 1 to 10. Based on that, I have been able to make significant decisions about my lifestyle as I could always check my health data when I changed an element in my diet, habits, or exercises. It has been a tremendous help. I use Withings Pulse, a small tracker, to measure my daily physical activities and the quality of sleep; and I play on Lumosity.com for 5 minutes every day to constantly improve cognitive skills that I use in my personal and professional lives.

The grandmother of Mike Scanlon, Co-Founder of Lumosity, was diagnosed with Alzheimer's disease, and he saw how devastating it was. While a neuroscience PhD candidate at Stanford University, he came across advancements in brain research that never made it out of academic settings. He wanted to make those results and methods available for the general public. That was when Lumosity was born. By playing games online every single day, our short- and long-term memory, flexibility, attention, and focus can be improved.

A study conducted by the University of Washington found that performance on Lumosity games can distinguish between patients with cirrhosis of the liver, pre-cirrhotic patients, and healthy controls. In that study Lumosity games were used as psychometric tests to detect subtle cognitive impairments. Such gaming solutions will be immensely implemented in future research and even clinical trials.

The movement of making lifestyle-related decisions based on everyday measurements of health parameters is called "Quantified Self".

Patients facing the same medical problem such as sleep issues gather around a table and discuss the potential underlying reasons, bad health habits, and ways to improve their sleep. Then they measure the outcomes, collect as much data as possible, and then assess the success of the methods they agreed upon. By incorporating technology into data acquisition about aspects of a person's daily life from mood and diet to physical activity it has been leading the way for gamified solutions in healthcare. People everywhere can now easily measure health habits and parameters every day, compare data, share it with others and make informed choices.

Gadgets and devices that can measure fitness, sleep, and even blood glucose levels have started to flood the market. It is becoming hard to choose the right one. Amazon.com has recently launched its wearable technology marketplace where different tools can be compared to each other based on several parameters.

By making more social applications, the Quantified Self has recently started to transform into the "Quantified Us" movement. Imagine that with the right data, anyone could tell why they had an awful sleep last night, or what the reason was behind the last seizure for a patient with epilepsy. The opportunities are endless and there are only a handful of obstacles to overcome such as the quality of the logged data, or the potential overuse of these gadgets.

Persuading people to follow therapy

WellaPets is a smartphone application that can be downloaded for free on the App Store, Google Play or Amazon Appstore. The child adopts, customizes and begins caring for his or her own Wellapet. By regularly visiting their pet, kids are able to play games with them, collect items for their pet's home, and care for their pet's asthma. Developers have worked with pediatricians to ensure that Wellapets teaches kids what they need to know if they, their friend or their sibling has asthma.

I discussed the use of gamified applications with Alexander Ryu, the Co–Founder and CEO of LifeGuard Games, Inc. who took leave from Harvard Medical School to launch his company.

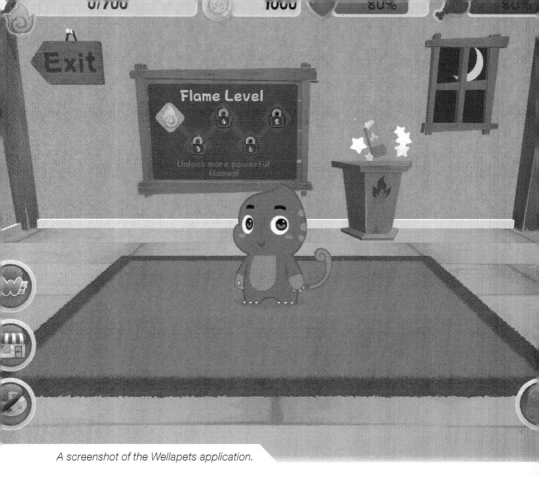

A screenshot of the Wellapets application.

"We have seen Wellapets improve the way clinicians connect with children by helping clinicians speak kids' native language, through games. Wellapets helps clinicians replace jargon and often-somber topics with a more playful and understandable medium for teaching kids how to stay well. We have also seen that the social nature of games helps foster dialogue between kids, talking about health and wellness in a way that feels normal and free of stigma."

Although he thinks that gamification is not the right term for what they actually do. Fun and good game design should be consistently prioritized over educational objectives or behavior change strategies, because perfect educational content serves little purpose when a game is not fun enough to hold a user's attention. Speaking from experience regarding early prototypes of Wellapets, Ryu describes that gamification unfortunately implies taking a concept that is not a game and applying some magic treatment that turns it into a game which is fundamentally the wrong approach to designing quality games.

The ultimate goal according to Ryu is healthcare payers accepting such technological alternatives at least as much as traditional medical services given the fact that these can improve health outcomes in a significant way.

Gamification expert and author of *The Gamification Revolution*, Gabe Zichermann, said that fundamentally people are bad at deferring pleasure now for future gain and avoidance of pain. Games are designed to help raise people's engagement in a way that is more powerful than what we have seen before.

Even, companies tend to realize the power of gamification and use it in keeping their employees healthy. According to Gartner, an information technology research and advisory company, more than 70% of the world's largest 2,000 companies are expected to have deployed at least one gamified application by the end of 2014. Keas, an employee health and wellness program in the United States, integrates gamification with biometrics devices to motivate employees at large enterprises to engage in health and wellness activities. Moreover, using personal health data, it can identify risks and suggests actions that can be taken to manage those risks. In the near future, being a good worker might not be a good enough reason to be kept in your job, but being healthy will be an additional requirement.

An example of health–related gamification is "stick" developed by Yale University economists. Users create so–called commitment contracts that bind them to a specific goal. Users define goals such as losing weight or learning new languages. They can add incentives such as putting money at stake. They can designate a referee to act as a third party and they can add supporters to help them reach their goals.

"MySugr Companion Diabetes Management App" works as a diabetes logbook providing immediate feedback and rewarding users with points which can be used to tame their "diabetes monster". The goal is to tame the user's monster every day, thus keeping track of their medical condition.

A New York–based company, Kognito, developed "Start the Talk", an educational, role–playing game to help parents talk about underage drinking with their kids. Players develop conversational strategies to approach, educate, and build trust with their kids about drinking.

"Run an Empire" typifies the group of apps that use alternate reality. It challenges users to conquer territory and defend it from rivals through actual physical activity. "My ASICS" is a smartphone app serving as a mobile monitor that personalizes running based on current stamina. The smartphone application "Zombies, Run!" requires the runner to pick up virtual supplies and escape from virtual zombie hordes. It is an ultra–immersive running game and audio adventure, delivering the details of zombies attacking the city into the user's headphones. By using augmented–reality devices such as Google Glass, runners can actually see the virtual zombie hordes added to the real life scenario.

Video games and platforms in the hospital

Years ago, I had a chance to receive a few copies of the "Re–Mission" video game and distribute it to local pediatric clinics. Children fighting cancer loved the 3D shooter game. They could play through 20 levels that took a character on a journey through the bodies of young patients with different kinds of cancer while shooting at cancer cells and bacteria with an arsenal of weapons and super–powers: chemotherapy, antibiotics, and the body's natural defenses. The color of the pills they shot at the cancer cells could actually resemble the ones they took in real life. A study of 375 cancer patients concluded that playing "Re–Mission" led to more consistent treatment adherence, faster rate of increase in cancer knowledge, and a faster rate of increase in self–efficacy in young cancer patients.

Other video gaming platforms offer different opportunities. The controller of Nintendo Wii is different from the controllers of other video game consoles as it can be held with one hand and uses technology that senses the player's movements. The Wii has been used in studies to measure its effectiveness in neurocognitive rehabilitation or in the treatment of Parkinson's disease. Retirement and nursing homes use Wii to motivate their residents to be more active by imitating the movements of bowling or tennis with the controller.

The Microsoft Kinect 3D sensor is able to monitor and analyze performance in real time, giving patients feedback as they exercise and complete assignments. By playing interactive games that use motion–reading sensors, doctors can track up to 24 points on a patient's body. The Kinect is used to promote healthy lifestyle and fitness; manage physical therapy and rehabilitation, facilitate virtual visits by medical professionals, and even screen young children for autism spectrum disorders. An Israeli company called BioGaming developed a cloud–based platform that lets physical therapists and trainers create personalized exercise routines that are automatically transformed into interactive, engaging games.

Skills acquired while playing video games have been proven useful in training surgeons, because using new surgical instruments requires similar skills. Laparoscopic or minimally invasive surgery that lets surgeons perform operations in the abdomen through small incisions demands fine movements, while surgeons watch the camera's view on screen instead of looking at their own hands. In one experiment surgeons who had a history of playing video games for more than three hours a week made 37 percent fewer mistakes and completed tasks 27 percent faster than the surgeons who had no history of playing video games. Several medical schools such as the University of Washington now advocate teaching surgeons these skills through similar games in clinical settings.

Sticking to a therapy is hard

Adherence or compliance, the degree to which a patient correctly follows medical advice, raises crucial issues in improving health and decreasing the cost of healthcare. An estimated 50% of patients with chronic diseases do not follow the prescribed treatment. The economic burden of this is evident.

Several start–ups have targeted this issue with different solutions such as a pill bottle that glows blue when a medication should be taken, and red when a dose is missed while alerting family members at the same time. In another example, tiny digestible sensors can be placed in pills and transmit pill digestion data to physicians and family members. Proteus Health develops such digestible sensors which transmit the pill's identifying signal with the exact time of detection to a smartphone or other Bluetooth–enabled device. It even includes an accelerometer. Don Cowling, the company's senior vice president, told about a man in California who can track whether his father with Alzheimer's disease, who lives in a nursing home in the United Kingdom, has taken his medication. He can also see how his father sleeps at night. Online health tracking has gone to a new level.

In the future, it is going to be extremely difficult not to fully comply with the prescribed therapy patients agreed upon. Moreover, compliance with medication should be as simple and comfortable for patients as possible. The real goal is to be able to measure health parameters, monitor them and engage when needed. As it is nearly impossible to get everyone motivated about their own health, let's find solutions that trick them into that by implementing methods of gamification seamlessly into their lives.

What if it became common to track our health parameters and get alerts when something goes wrong? People could get rewarded for living a truly healthy lifestyle by getting access to premium services or wellness facilities for lower fees. Gamifying our health could facilitate compliance and teach children how to cope with a chronic condition. Gamification might be the key for a broad range of issues for which we currently have no good solutions.

Score of availability: 6

Focus of attention: Patients more than medical professionals

Websites & other online resources: Amazon's Wearable Technology database (http://www.amazon.com/b?node=9013937011), Games for Health (http://gamesforhealth.org/ and http://www.gamesforhealtheurope.org/)

Companies & start-ups: AdhereTech (http://www.adheretech.com/), Proteus Digital Health (http://www.proteusdigitalhealth.com/), Wellapets (http://www.wellapets.com/), My ASICS (http://my.asics.co.uk/), Re-Mission (http://www.re-mission2.org)

Books: The Gamification Revolution by Gabe Zichermann

Movies: Believe in Gamification! (Short Film – http://youtu.be/ziHCvpikLh8)

Trend 3. Eating in the future

Many of the innovative technologies presented in this book will fundamentally change not only the way we consume food but also food itself. Today, getting access to clean water and basic nutrients is a constant battle in several parts of the world; while obesity and non–healthy diets place an economic burden on the society in developed regions.

The world population is expected to surpass the 9 billion milestone by 2050. Estimates by the Food and Agricultural Organization suggest that demand for meat will more than double over the next 40 years. Traditional livestock methods will struggle or fail to meet this demand, and the challenge to keep people healthy will get more complicated. The culture of eating and producing food therefore must change.

As a potential solution for global food shortages, companies have been experimenting with 3D printing, although most 3D food printers can only print basic foodstuffs that require only one to six ingredients. The ultimate goal is to print out complete customized meals on demand. In the movies "Back to the Future II" and "The Fifth Element," delicious dishes were constructed in seconds by putting the ingredients into a special oven. Today Foodini, a project introduced on the crowdfunding site Kickstarter, aims at printing out food using fresh ingredients. It can make ravioli, cookies, or crackers. The instrument's food capsule must be filled with fresh ingredients, and the recipe has to be inputted. In caseds where the ingredients are pre–cooked, the food is ready in a few minutes' time.

Jeff Lipton, a researcher who develops 3D printed food at the Cornell Creative Machines Lab, in Ithaca, NY, said that most innovation is aimed at overturning the status quo, with the focus on either making food production more efficient or more customized. This is the direction the food industry is about to look at.

Another example of how 3D printed food could ease our lives is the use of 3D printers in nursing homes. Plenty of nursing home residents suffer from dysphagia characterized by the inability of the larynx to close properly while swallowing, causing renal failure, pneumonia and even death. Purified food could be a solution. Because meals are important social events in nursing homes, and it can be frustrating to look at the delicious plates of other residents, the smoothfood concept was born. It is about deconstructing and reconstructing fresh food to smoothfood which looks equal to the original.

In a new project to be finished in 2015, 3D printers will help create food that can be easily swallowed and looks great at the same time. According to Matthias Kück, chief executive of Biozoon, when residents bite on the reconstructed food, it is very soft, and practically melts in their mouth.

Stem cell burgers and the world's healthiest food

A few years ago, growing hamburger meat from the muscle tissue of a cow would have been the perfect basic story for a documentary about the future, but now it is possible to do so. It started nearly 20 years ago when NASA got approval from the United States' Food and Drug Administration (FDA) to begin developing meat for use during long–term space missions. In 2008, People for the Ethical Treatment of Animals (PETA) announced a prize of $1 million to anyone who could create stem–cell derived chicken meat. To date there is still no winner of the prize. For years, environmentalists and animal

Jellified chicken wing with carrots and potato mash printed out by Biozoon.

rights activists, among others, have been awaiting a commercially–viable alternative to conventional meat using stem cells. The final product is referred to as "schmeat" because it grows in sheets and the cells remain flat while differentiating into muscle tissue.

The Cultured Beef project aims to make commercially available meat created by harvesting muscle cells from a living cow. It is incredibly efficient as it uses 99% less space than modern livestock farming; moreover, cells from a single cow could produce 175 million quarter–pounders while traditional farming methods would need 440,000 cows for that. Raising livestock takes a tremendous amount of food, water, and energy; additionally, the methane produced in the gastrointestinal system of the animals is adding to greenhouse gas emissions. According to a recent estimate, lab–grown or "in vitro" meat has the potential to reduce energy consumption by 45%, greenhouse gas emissions by 96%, and land use by 99%. Imagine the economic and logistic advantages of switching to this new method. Of course, the technique is not ready for mass production, and the taste is still an issue.

The taste of "stem cell burgers" is not like what we prefer today, but it will likely improve at the same exponential rate as computing power did over time. Currently, the lack of naturally–occurring fat in schmeat requires that fillers and substitutes be used. By 2020, though, we might not be able to differentiate burgers made by traditional means and those created by this new method. In 2013, Mark Post of the University of Maastricht in the Netherlands hosted probably the world's most expensive barbecue in London, inviting two food critics and one chef to try the schmeat burger. Each serving cost about $385,000. The test–tasters concluded that the burger's texture was good, but the patty was not really juicy.

Lab–grown meat does not benefit from the animal's natural immune system that keeps harmful micro organisms away; therefore the use of antibiotics in the production process of the schmeat is another issue that needs to be addressed. Conventional livestock consumes 80% of all antibiotics sold in the United States and this should not be an example to follow.

The 1968 movie "2001: A Space Odyssey" showed astronauts consuming very simple–looking food that contained all the ingredients the body needs on a long space mission. Recently, Rob Rhinehart invented Soylent to make this concept real and widely available. He looks forward to the point where instead of being an obligatory function to stay alive, eating food can be art.

Soylent is a beige-colored beverage that Rhinehart claims contains every nutrient the body needs. It was named after the ubiquitous food substitute in the dystopian science fiction movie, "Soylent Green." After raising $3 million from investors, and testing the product on himself and a few volunteers, Rhinehart believes it is ready to be commercially available. Soylent ingredients are open-sourced and classified by the FDA as "generally recognized as safe."

For months Rhinehard has consumed nothing but Soylent every day. He plans to get the cost down to $5 per day for a diet yielding 11,000 kilojoules or 2,600 kcal. Some newspapers such as The Telegraph sought comment from academics about Soylent, but they were so skeptical about it that they declined to be interviewed. Other experts expressed surprise that anyone would want to replace real food with a synthetic mixture. They also underlined the importance of the many micronutrients in fruits and vegetables that cannot be exactly replicated in a formula. Even if Soylent were formulated properly and individuals could live on it, these nutritional experts doubted they would experience optimal health.

While it not might be the ultimate solution for hunger globally, it shows the way where researchers are heading.

Do you know what you eat?

It might surprise you that right now we can only assume to know food ingredients based on the short descriptions printed on food cans and packages.

One solution might be provided by TellSpec, a hand-held device designed to determine what macronutrients or specific ingredients the food contains using spectroscopy which is the study of how wavelengths of light change when reflecting from various surfaces. Isabel Hoffmann, founder and CEO of TellSpec, ran a successful Indiegogo campaign that raised $386,392 in 2013. I asked about her personal views and vision. As usual, there was a personal story behind this novel idea.

Hoffmann, a serial entrepreneur, started several software, Internet, and healthcare companies before moving to Canada in 2011. Only three months after arriving in Toronto, her 13 year-old daughter became really sick. She experienced a series of allergies, angioedema (swelling of the subcutaneus tissue), and anemia (a decrease in the amount of oxygen-carrying hemoglobin in the blood). Medical professionals thought it was a viral infection that would get better on its own. But it did not. She dropped out of school. Hoffmann stayed at home taking care of her daughter. At times the girl's blood pressure became so low that she couldn't walk to the bathroom. Hoffmann happened to come came across a book by Dr. Neil Nathan in which he offered hope to those whom the medical system had been unable to help. She took her daughter to Dr. Nathan who diagnosed the girl with severe penicillin allergy and an array of food allergies. As a result of this episode Hoffmann began to meet other people suffering from similar problems.

Her goal then became to help people who must avoid toxic foods, and those who have to watch their diets closely but cannot be sure of what they are actually eating ingredient by ingredient, allergen by allergen. She found the right people, created a concept, and finished the crowdfunding campaign in 2013. She shared with me what happened after the campaign.

"A group in Brazil tries to deal with the epidemics of obesity among Brazilian Indians due to the fact that now they have access to processed food. There are challenges related to obesity and famine we have to face now. We don't really know what we eat. Regarding environmental diseases, the number one exposure is the skin; while the number two is the gastrointestinal system therefore what we eat is crucial. Technology finally got to a stage where people can really benefit from that. Between October and November in 2013, we received 20 000 e–mails."

The two directions TellSpec is heading in at the moment are genomics; and establishing a spectrome, a database of how the wavelength of reflected light changes depending on the surface characteristics of the object illuminated. The direction she wants to head in is truly personalized medicine.

Hoffmann, a TED Global speaker in 2014, envisions a bright future of portable diagnostics. She described, for instance, a wristwatch device that would integrate TellSpec data with that from the genome and the microbiome (the genetic fingerprint of the microbe colonies that live in our gut). With such a device people could make decisions based on real–life data. They could know what breakfast should be on a given day based on these data. They would have power, knowledge, and information that we are missing now in our society.

New devices are meant to make sure we eat the right food with enough nutrients and in the right way. Examples include HapiFork, an electronic fork that vibrates when the user eats too fast. It also helps monitor

The TellSpec device.

and track eating habits. For example, it tracks how long it takes to eat a meal, the amount of "fork servings" per minute, and how long the intervals are between fork servings. Like many others I cannot find enough time to eat. The HapiFork taught me how to slow down, although it is embarrassing to know how fast and how incorrectly I used to eat every day.

Other ideas with the potential to transform the way we eat could include smart knives. Besides measuring the levels of nutrients such as sugar, vitamins, protein and fat in the food that it cuts, such a smart knife could also check levels of harmful bacteria and pesticides. It might emit negative ions to help keep the food fresh. A Spanish company has invented food tattoos: a laser can safely etch logos and even QR codes onto fruits and vegetables.

Amazon's new smartphone can scan and recognize almost any product, including food items, and direct users immediately to the relevant website. Augmented reality can help people stick to a diet: researchers in Tokyo used a visual headset to make food look one–and–a–half times bigger, which led to a 10% decrease in consumption.

For many decades human populations around the globe have not been able to deal with the nutritional opposites of obesity and famine even though our knowledge about the optimal diet has dramatically increased over the same time. Futurist Ray Kurzweil and nutritionist Dr. Terry Grossman described a futuristic concept in their popular book, *Fantastic Voyage: Live Long Enough to Live Forever*. They would eliminate the need to actually eat food by using nanorobots that would transmit the right amounts and types of nutrients to each of our cells. Future people would wear a "nutrient belt" loaded with billions of nutrient–laden nanobots that would enter and leave the body through the skin as needed.

A thorough review recently concluded that technology will increasingly change the way we interact with food and drink. It will facilitate our interaction with and knowledge of what we consume by enhancing entertainment value, providing diners with targeted multisensory interventions, and providing alerts or nudges to those who may wish to eat in a more healthy way. There is a risk of technology becoming a distraction to diners, possibly resulting in an unwanted increase in food intake or the emergence of bad habits. It depends on us.

slo contro! HAPI.com

The HapiFork device, application and web portal.

Score of availability: 3

Focus of attention: Consumers

Websites & other online resources: The Future of Food (http://food.nationalgeographic.com), European Learning Partnership About The Future of Food (http://fof.galaysofia.com), Personal Blog of Bill Gates (http://billgates.com/about–bill–gates/future–of–food).

Companies & start–ups: Soylent (http://www.soylent.me/), Hapi (http://www.hapi.com/), Tellspec (http://tellspec.com/)

Books: The Prince's Speech: On the Future of Food by Prince Charles; Can We Feed the World? by Conway

Movies: Soylent Green (1973)

Trend 4. Augmented Reality and Virtual Reality

Augmented reality (AR) is a real–time view of a real–world environment that is enhanced by computer–generated sound, video, graphics, GPS data, or inputs we may not have thought about yet. Imagine wearing an AR device while you are walking, and receiving promotional offers from shops you pass. Simultaneously you see the real and online worlds superimposed. A company called Metaio, for instance, provides an AR application for technicians to service and repair the Volkswagen XLI without any prior training. Instructions are projected on top of what they are looking at in the auto shop. Getting information via a Google Glass or digital contact lenses could greatly augment the practice of medicine.

Google Glass, a wearable computer with an optical head–mounted display, was made available to testers and developers in 2013. As of July, 2014, it is not yet commercially available, although Google did sell it publicly for one day in April, 2014. Google Glass has a touchpad on the temple piece, a camera, and an optical display. It works like a smartphone by letting users take photos and videos, browse the web, take notes, and make calls. Wearers access the Internet via natural language voice commands such as "OK, Glass, do a search for diabetes".

Dr. Rafael Grossmann, a Venezuelan surgeon living in the US and also a good friend of mine, woke me up late at night in June 2013. He was about to become the first surgeon to demonstrate the use of Google Glass during a live surgical procedure. I got out of bed and followed his operation sitting at my computer. It was a fantastic proof that AR is advancing, and that one of the areas most likely to benefit from it is medicine.

Dr. Grossmann noted that students used to learn while looking over the surgeon's shoulder. Now he can demonstrate what he is doing much better, and to hundreds of students at a time because his point of view can be projected onto huge screens. Stanford medical doctor, Dr. Abraham Verghese, started using Google Glass because he can make videos of patient examination for medical students to watch from his own point of view.

Dr. Grossmann gave a presentation at one of the most beautiful places in Central Europe, Lake Balaton, at a congress organized for young surgeons. He described how difficult it has been to maintain eye contact with the patient during an office visit when he had to repeatedly turn to his computer and input data. Even with the subsequent spread of tablets, he

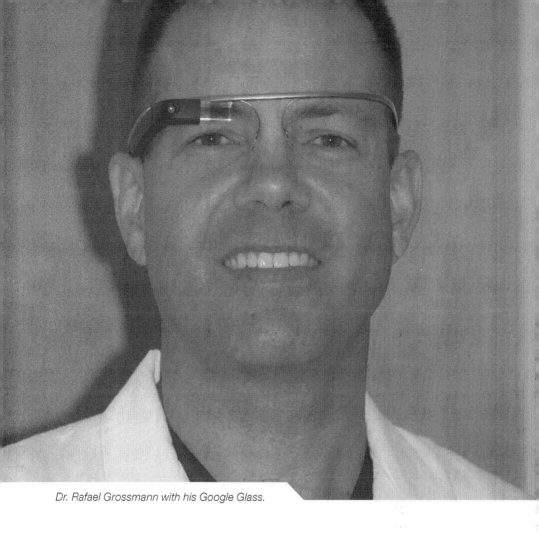

Dr. Rafael Grossmann with his Google Glass.

still had to look down at a screen. With Google Glass, eye contact is steady. Being able to always face the patient creates a much better ambiance and doctor–patient relation.

Lucien Engelen, director of the ReShape Innovation Center at Radboud University Medical Center, The Netherlands has studied using Google Glass in clinical settings since 2013. His focus has been the quality of pictures and videos, the opportunities for remote consultation, how checklists can be displayed to the treating physician, and even the device's battery life. While there are many potential benefits in a healthcare setting, Engelen concluded that technical issues currently make using the device complicated and limited.

In the near future laypersons could save lives if the basics of cardiopulmonary resuscitation were displayed on the Glass. The app could be launched with the simple voice command "OK, Glass, CPR." An algorithm developed by Hao–Yu Wu and colleagues at the Massachusetts Institute of Technology (MIT) demonstrated that an ordinary cell phone camera can detect a person's pulse with accuracy. Building on this, Glass might be able to tell if an individual who has collapsed has regained a pulse or not. Imagine a case where it detects no pulse: the Bee Gees' "Staying Alive" starts up and guides the user to perform chest compressions at a 100 beats per minute. The motion tracker embedded in the Glass could determine if the compressions are adequate, and the accumulated number of compressions would be tracked. At the same time the device summons an ambulance to the exact GPS coordinates and sends send text messages to the nearest hospitals with information about the situation so they can prepare.

With Google Glass, a clinician could look at the lines on a test strip used with blood or urine, and receive back the correct yes/no results as well as quantitative measurements—all within seconds. In the future, the strips are marked with individual QR codes to make this possible in everyday clinical settings.

Glass could let patients quickly get in touch with a medical professional who would see what the patient is seeing from their point of view. In Melbourne, Australia a company called Small World teams up Google Glass with the Australian Breastfeeding Association. It allowed their telephone counselors to see through the eyes of new mothers as they struggled to breastfeed at home.

Another project initiated at the Rhode Island Hospital in the US used Google Glass in the Emergency Room to remotely connect with a dermatologist whenever their expertise was needed.

Since December 2013, doctors used Google Glass at Boston's Beth Israel Deaconness Medical Center to see whether it can facilitate either doctor–patient interactions or the input of data. Huge QR codes hang on the walls and doors of patient rooms. These can be scanned when the doctor steps into the room, and Glass transmits the relevant patient records and information. Doctors can keep eye contact with the patient while receiving pertinent information right away. In April 2014 Google Glass scanned through the entire history of a patient and revealed that that person had given incorrect information. As a result the doctors could save his life.

In another case an Emergency Room doctor was dealing with a patient with a massive brain bleed. Google Glass automatically pushed the patient's allergy history and current medical regimen into the doctor's field of vision. It gave him critical extra time to reverse, time he might otherwise have spent turning away to a laptop or notepad.

I had a chance to see a Google Glass AR application called MedicAR in action. Looking at a specified image through the camera of Glass, a 3D anatomical model appeared just like in real life.

Dr. Christian Assad–Kottner and colleagues published the first paper on using Google Glass in medical education. It concluded that wearable technology has the potential to enhance medical education and patient safety once widely available. The authors recommended that medical institutions should develop policies that address patient privacy when using technologies to enhance medical care.

In a parallel development, the Alvin J. Siteman Cancer Center announced the development of high–tech glasses to help surgeons visualize cancer cells. Live ones glow blue when viewed through the eyewear. First used during surgery in February 2014, the device helps distinguish cancer cells from healthy ones and also lessens the number of stray tumor cells left behind. While the technology is certainly not a 100% accurate at detecting each types of cells, the glasses could potentially reduce the need for additional surgery and spare patients from stress and expense.

Layar remains one of the best–known and most frequently downloaded augmented AR browsers for smartphones. With over 35 million downloads to date, it was one of the first apps to demonstrate the potential of AR. In a joint project with the ReShape Innovation Center in Nijmegen, The Netherlands, Dutch citizens can see exactly where semi–automatic defibrillators are located by using Layar on their smartphones. In an emergency the camera in the phone guides them to the closest device. Similar apps could be used with AR glasses or contact lenses.

Have you ever had a bad experience when a nurse had trouble finding a vein when attempting to take a blood sample? Success doing this is purely based on experience. Being able to spot an available vein would make this process more convenient and less painful. A new wearable, Eyes–On™ Glasses, uses imaging technology to find the location of the most suitable vein. The device is readily used in physician offices, clinics, and hospitals.

The success of such a technological breakthrough depends on the quality and quantity of applications available for the specific device. To help start–ups focusing on using Google Glass in healthcare join accelerators and incubators, Palomar Health and Qualcomm Life teamed up to build an incubator for developers called Glassomics.

The launch of the prototype already raised ethical and privacy concerns. What happens, for example, with private data when Glass is lost or stolen? How does the public react to the knowledge that it can record videos any time? Motorists have been reportedly pulled over for driving while wearing the Glass. Las Vegas casinos have banned the use of Google Glass even before its release. These examples show how far we still are from implementing it in practice.

From glass to contact lens and beyond

In one of his talks in 2013, Babak Parviz, an electrical engineer at the University of Washington, proposed using contact lenses for continuous body monitoring. Given that contact lenses are used by more than 100 million people, it is a good candidate for a continuous sensor. Lenses could contain miniature glucose sensors, for example, along with readout circuits and an antenna. Such a system could remotely powered by radio frequency broadcast, making it wake up, take a measurement, and send the data back before powering itself down.

Eyes–On™ Glasses on a nurse.

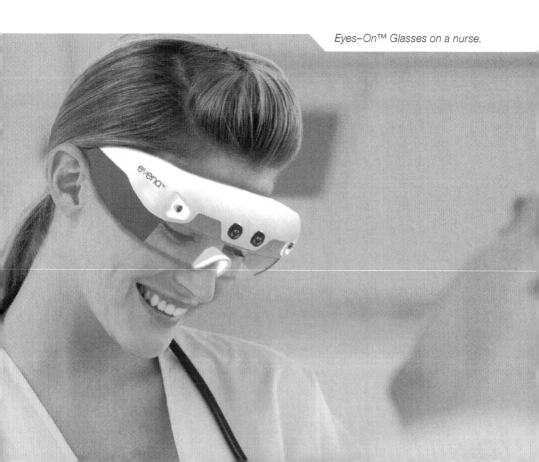

Google Glass can be controlled through voice and hand gestures. In the future contact lens sensors would be controlled with brain waves. Given developments in this area, the idea is quite plausible. The potential leveraging power of AR is huge enough that medical professionals should address patient privacy first, and justify its use in practice with evidence.

Lenses made of graphene, a special form of carbon, could make possible the manufacture of smart contact lenses, or ultra–thin devices whose infrared camera would extend users' vision to spectrums that are not visible to the human eye. Moreover, future contact lenses will not only allow us to look into a world augmented with additional information, but might also constantly measure and log health parameters.

According to the US Patent & Trademark Office, Google is working on a multi–sensor contact lens that would work with Google Glass, other wearables, Android smartphones, smart televisions, Google Now, and similar devices. By blinking, it will enable a user to turn the page of a book or proceed to the next song. Ultimately, it may be possible to insert a screen into the lens. But this will take years to fulfill.

Eventually hardware will probably not be needed to add data. Screens and keyboards will be projected on the wall or on a table, making it straightforward and accessible anywhere in clinical settings. Holographic keyboards hovering in front of the user will next make us forget about smartphones and tablets. The data will be stored only in the cloud. Small devices will probably replace personal computers and laptops, and not need traditional accessories such as keyboard and mouse. With ultra–high definition video streams and 3D binaural audio, online consultations will sound like real life. Gesture–sensitive interfaces similarly to those seen in the movie "Minority Report" will make interaction with big data commonplace. With virtual reality and increasingly sophisticated holograms, the practice of medicine will be re–invented.

New diseases resulting from excessive use of virtual reality (VR) in gaming and business can be expected. For example, virtual post–traumatic stress disorder (v–PTSD) which occurs in gamers wearing VR masks who participate in enormous virtual battles such as "Call of Duty." Their symptoms may be exactly the same as those in soldiers who fought in real wars. On the positive side, VR could be employed in psychotherapy. People will be able to virtually visit distant places or other worlds that they would never be able to experience in real life. Anxious patients could go through an upcoming operation step–by–step, or choose a hospital based on its "virtual experience" package.

Popular and intensive VR applications might induce some people to live their lives in the virtual world. The popularity of Second Life, one of the earliest VR environments online, decreased over time because it could not improve on the experience. But what if VR chambers become commercially available, allowing users to feel the world while sitting at home in a chair? They might live an entirely digital life, shop, meet others, and even work in an artificial environment. How would these possibilities change society? What could we do to persuade people not to switch from real life to a virtual world?

The first bi-directional brain–machine interfaces allowed monkeys to use a brain implant to control a virtual hand and also get feedback that tricks their brains into feeling the texture of virtual objects. Building on this, an Ottawa-based company called Personal Neuro is exploring the possible benefits of Google Glass analyzing the electrical activity of the brain, the electroencephalogram (EEG). We might not be far from controlling wearable devices with our thoughts.

Using such solutions in the operating room would take medical specialties to the next level. Currently, surgeons use cautery in which an electrical current heats tissue to make incisions with minimal blood loss. The intelligent iKnife goes one step further by analyzing the vaporized smoke by mass spectrometer to detect what molecules are in the biological sample. Doing so, it can identify in real-time whether the tissue is malignant or not. There is no need to send a biopsy specimen to the pathology lab.

A clinic in Germany started experimenting with a tablet-based AR application. During operations, surgeons can perform more precise excisions because they are guided by the patient's radiology images, which lets them see through anatomical structures.

Opportunities are almost endless. With the development of Google Glass, Sony's Morpheus, and Oculus Rift which was acquired by Facebook in 2014 for $2 billion, medical applications will likely expand in the coming years. After being sold to Facebook, the Oculus Rift team predicted that over the next 10 years, virtual reality will become ubiquitous, affordable, and transformative. There is still time to live up to these expectations.

Score of availability: 4

Focus of attention: Medical professionals more than patients

Websites & other online resources: GlassOmics (http://glassomics.com/), Google Glass applications (http://glass–apps.org/)

Companies & start–ups: Evena Medical (http://evenamed.com/), Google Glass (http://www.google.com/glass/start/)

Books: The Google Glass Revolution by Samuel Cole; Augmented Reality: An Emerging Technologies Guide to AR by Kipper & Rampolla

Movies: The Terminator (1984), Predator (1987), Minority Report (2002), Iron Man (2008), Avatar (2009), Surrogates (2009)

Trend 5. Telemedicine and Remote Care

Hugo Gernsback was a pioneer in both radio and publishing. He designed the first home radio set and published dozens of magazines in the early 1900s. He wrote an article about the future of radio telecommunication in the February, 1925 issue of Science and Invention. The device was the "teledactyl" (tele means far, dactyl means finger in Greek) and was meant to allow doctors to see and touch their patients through a viewscreen with robotic arms that was kilometers away. He predicted that the practice of medicine would look much different by the 1970s. From their offices doctors would diagnose and treat patients in their homes via machines and devices that worked through radio waves. He described the device in details.

"The doctor of the future, by means of this instrument, will be able to feel his patient, as it were, at a distance. The doctor manipulates his controls, which are then manipulated at the patient's room in exactly the same manner. The doctor sees what is going on in the patient's room by means of a television screen. Every move that the doctor makes with the controls is duplicated by radio at a distance. Whenever the patient's teledactyl meets with resistance, the doctor's distant controls meet with the same resistance. The distant controls are sensitive to sound and heat, all important to future diagnosis."

The idea of the teledactyl demonstrates how the doctor–patient relationship could take place at a distance. Actually, the first complete tele–surgical operation using a surgical robot was performed by a team of French surgeons located in New York on a patient in Strasbourg, France over a distance of several thousands of kilometers in 2001. It was called the Lindbergh operation named after American aviator Charles Lindbergh who was the first person to fly solo across the Atlantic Ocean. From one perspective, partial loss of the human touch is inevitable. But medical practice does not have to go entirely digital. When there is already an established relationship between patient and the doctor, a digital interaction can save time and effort for both parties.

From another perspective, the shortage of doctors is global. Solving this will require extensive use of digital methods. In the United States alone, the shortage of doctors is predicted to rise to 130,000 from the current 60,000 by 2025; and Africa has 25% of the worldwide disease burden but only 3% of the health workers. It is almost impossible to train all the physicians that will be needed.

To tackle this iRobot and InTouch Health announced in 2013 an autonomous remote–presence robot called RP–VITA. The FDA cleared its use in monitoring surgical patients before, during, and after their operations. It cannot perform remote operations given that it has no manipulating appendages, although extendable pan, tilt, and zoom lenses could allow collaboration between a remotely–located surgeon and one on site. Such a device could travel autonomously to destinations where doctors are in short supply.

Acute Care RP–VITA® by InTouch Health.

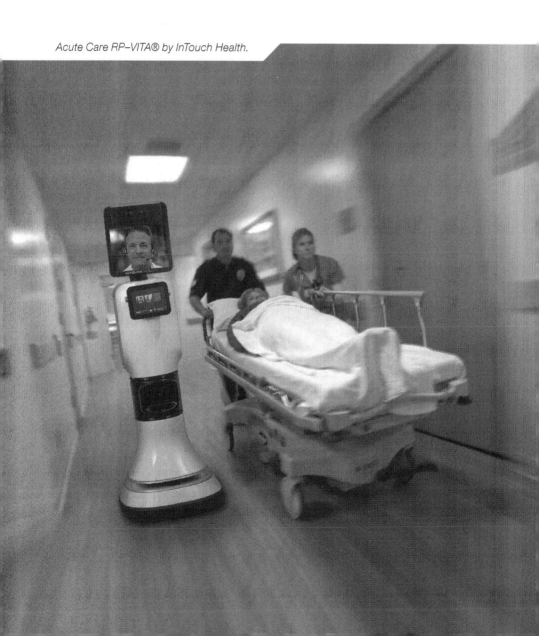

Dignity Health in the US uses similar video–conferencing machines that move on wheels and project the physician's face on a large screen. These robots have cameras, microphones, and speakers. According to Alan Shatzel, medical director of the Mercy Telehealth Network, the robot can be at the bedside in minutes no matter where the patient is located. For the physician operator, it feels like being with the patient in the room. Nothing can replace in–person care, but as Shatzel described, it is the next best thing.

For the last century illness triggered the same scenario. The doctor was summoned; he arrived at the house and made a quick assessment; and then he either prescribed a therapy or admitted the patient to the hospital. Telemedicine may prompt the first real change when a doctor is available only through online channels and a webcam. In the not–too–distant future telemedicine could evolve to generate a holographic image making the doctor's presence in the patient's home almost real. Only the remote touch remains to be worked out.

In the video game industry, a concept called force feedback has been used since the 1990s that lets users feel wobbles when driving on rough terrain in a car racing game. In California, I had a chance to use an educational device that simulated taking a biopsy. The force feedback let me feel the skin resistance when I administered a virtual injection. Glove–based feedback systems already exist to give users a remote sense of touch.

House calls of the 21st century

In its 2014 e–health report Deloitte called e–visits the house calls of the 21st century. It predicted over 100 million electronic visits globally in 2014, saving more than $5 billion comparing to the cost of in–person doctor visits. It saw 2014 as an inflection point when costs, quality of care, advances in telecommunications, and professional attitudes would drive their adoption. Their message to policy makers worldwide:

"As e–visits are proven and adopted in the developed world, and as the necessary infrastructure is deployed in the developing world, they are likely to offer affordable primary medical and diagnostic care to very large populations that do not have access today."

In 2010 the Hawaii Medical Service Association, the state's largest health plan covering over 700,000 citizens, was the first insurer to make the online resource of American Well available to its members. Those insured had the chance to talk with a doctor via a web camera. The remote doctor could send notes to the local one who might be unavailable. Individuals who were not members of the health plan could still use the service on a for–payment basis.

HealthTap is a service where patients pose a question to a panel of doctors. The initial query is free; follow up questions incur a charge. The site claims to have served more than 1.3 billion individual questions and saved over 13,000 lives. Commenting on the service, the American Medical Association warned that Internet should "complement, not replace, the communication between a patient and their physician." It pointed out that online health portals do not take a history, conduct a physical exam, or monitor the suggested treatment. Using such information in isolation could pose a threat to patients.

Some large corporations have tried to develop telemedical services. In November 2013, Google launched Google Helpouts as a successor to Google Answers. It let experts charge clients per session, per minute, or both; with Google initially to take a cut of 20%. Inasmuch as improving telehealth is a Google priority it waived its 20% fee for all healthcare related questions, and ensures that its video interchanges are compliant with HIPAA (Health Insurance Portability and Accountability Act).

Years ago, Maayan Cohen discovered that her healthy, young boyfriend had brain tumor. She found herself sitting in waiting rooms with stacks of papers that created confusion and a feeling of lack of control. Had she received all the results of tests, drugs, treatment, and medical history? Around this time Maayan met Ziv Meltzer, who was suffering from stomach pains no doctor could diagnose. They understood each other perfectly, left their jobs, and launched Hello Doctor, an online service and mobile application designed to manage and make sense of medical records.

Ziv Meltzer explained the background of HelloDoctor to me. In the company, everyone is a patient. The more patient information they collect and can share, the more they can help. HelloDoctor now focuses on collecting, organizing, and managing medical records because for many people that is where the greatest the pain is.

Video consultation is becoming a routine part of care offered by the Stanford Hospital & Clinics. Patients can schedule video visits through the hospital's website; provide information in advance; and at the appointed time meet with the doctor in a web-based videoconference from a computer equipped with a webcam.

While the number of similar services continues to grow, there is a need for a connection hub for doctors and medical records. In 2005, Ryan Howard saw a need for affordable, easy-to-use technology that met the needs of small medical practices. Howard quit his job, sold his car and house, and launched Practice Fusion. Before he had been in a serious motorcycle accident and in massive debt, but decided to use the settlement cash from his accident to pay the salaries of three employees. In 2014 the company has more than 110,000 medical professionals and handles more than 80 million patient records.

The ultimate goal of gathering big data in electronic medical records (EMR) ¬managed by professionals, and personal health records (PHR) updated by patients is creating smart alerts in natural language. That is, the system would understand the actual meaning of words and expressions in the records, thereby making it simpler to intervene in a patient's affairs when needed.

At the TED 2014 conference in Vancouver, Canada, Larry Page, CEO of Google gave an interview in which he mentioned electronic medical records years after Google Health, the company's early effort, was shut down. He said we could save a hundred-thousand lives this year if people would share the information of their medical records with the right people in the right ways.

Such innovations try to bring healthcare services to the patient's home. Examples include the HealthSpot station, which looks like doctor's office in a box. It is a telehealth system intended for large institutions and features medical diagnostics, face-to-face dialogue, and electronic health records with privacy. By sitting inside the box, patients can send information related to a physical examination through different kinds of cameras.

Medtronic, the largest medical device maker in the world, develops and provides insulin pumps, glucose monitors, and heart devices that can transmit patient data to a secure server. For diabetes, they eventually want to provide a patient's entire care team with continuous real-time glucose therapy information to avoid life-threatening high or low glucose conditions.

Microsoft has used all its main health and communication products to transform its Kinect device into a telehealth tool for physical therapy by combining the motion-tracking abilities of the Kinect, Skype, and Microsoft's cloud-based HealthVault EMR. Patients see exactly what they should do during their physical therapy session. Results are uploaded to the cloud, and session efficacy can be logged and shared.

These kinds of devices and services serve to connect patients to doctors when in-person care is not possible. Wouldn't this be a milestone? Patients should be able to download their own medical records. Medical professionals should be able to communicate and consult with each other without limitations. Everything seems to indicate that medical expertise as well as laboratory tests will soon be accessible from home. Due to the shortage of doctors worldwide and the lack of access to medical care in underdeveloped regions, connecting patients to physicians online will receive more and more attention. Telemedicine encourages patients to take more responsibility for their own care; but it does not mean the end of the doctor-patient relationship or personal contact. It should be considered an additional element that makes the relationship even more effective.

Score of availability: 8
Focus of attention: Patients
Websites & other online resources: International Society for Telemedicine & eHealth (http://www.isfteh.org/), The American Telemedicine Association (http://www.americantelemed.org/)
Companies & start-ups: In Touch Health (http://www.intouchhealth.com/), American Well (http://www.americanwell.com/), Practice Fusion (http://www.practicefusion.com/home.php)
Books: Telemedicine and Telehealth: Principles, Policies, Performance and Pitfalls by Darkins & Cary; Connected Health: How Mobile Phones, Cloud and Big Data Will Reinvent Healthcare by Ranck; The Creative Destruction of Medicine by Topol
Movies: Logan's run (1976)

Trend 6. Re-thinking the Medical Curriculum

I graduated from medical school in 2009. Looking back at my time as a medical student, I mostly used relatively old-fashioned books and anatomical atlases. In my later years I began to discover useful social media channels and online resources as well. It was hard to study anatomy and similarly difficult subjects by traditional means. Considering the various solutions and tools that could be useful in medical education nowadays, I do not know how I managed with only printed books.

The medical curriculum is supposed to train students to become healthcare professionals, and prepare them for practicing medicine. The problem is that the medical curriculum worldwide, almost without exceptions, focuses on today's technology and how doctors should deal with today's patients. But both technology and the general needs of patients change quickly.

Usually it takes 4 to 6 years to become a doctor, and another 5 to 10 years to become a specialist. Trying to remember what the world looked like 4 or 6 years ago I recall no widespread use of smartphones, tablets, Google Glass, social media, or artificial intelligence. That is how much the world can change in a few years' time. The rate of change is even faster now. Current curriculum does not prepare students for these even though new applications and technologies are becoming a crucial part of the medical profession. It is time to change and actually re-think the basics of what we call medical education.

As a first step, I launched a course at the University of Debrecen in 2008 that focused on meaningful and safe use of social media for medical students. Since then, the course has moved to Semmelweis Medical School in Budapest, Hungary, and been fully enrolled. The course covers the use of search engines, Facebook, Twitter, Youtube, blogs, and more in a medical setting. We are preparing students for the digital world. My teaching motto is "If you want to teach me, you first have to reach me". When students filled online surveys about their digital habits, and it turned out all of them used Facebook, I launched a Facebook challenge in the form of a page where every day I posed questions about the topics covered in the lectures. Students could compete for bonus points during the semester. It has been a huge success according to students.

The knowledge imparted in this course is called digital literacy. After I presented my experience with this curriculum at Stanford Medical School, a physician based in London wanted to visit Budapest once a week during the

The main page of The Social MEDia Course.

semester in order to take the course in person. There was nothing similar in the United Kingdom. It was the final sign that underscored the need for an online course that would present topics in detail; include hand–outs, study guides, and references; and a test with gamification pertinent to each lecture. This is what I created in 2012 under the name The Social MEDia Course. Since then, thousands of students and doctors (more of the latter than students), started the course. Hundreds acquired the "Ultimate Expert" badge and certification. But it is not enough to focus only on social media and mobile health. We need to prepare students for the world they will face when they actually start practicing medicine. In 2014, a pilot course was launched at Semmelweis Medical School with the mission of giving students a set of skills with which they will be able to navigate the sea of new technologies and the ocean of medical information. Called "Disruptive Technologies in Medicine," this course introduces them to personal genomics, telemedicine, 3D printing, regenerative medicine, imaging health, robotics, and artificial intelligence.

Such initiatives should be welcome by all medical schools in order to let students acquire skills that were not important before but they will have to use while practicing medicine in the near future.

Besides these prospective changes, there are numerous reasons why being a medical student should be a good experience nowadays. Online networks dedicated to focused topics on Twitter, Google+, Facebook and the blogosphere are capable of many things: filtering the most relevant news when network members trust one another; help crowdsource complicated clinical/scientific questions; create learning groups without geographical limits; and give access to global experts and projects.

The typical curriculum requires students to study texts and data by heart without proper reasoning and understanding the logic behind it. Instead, study through serious diagnostic games has clear advantages. The "Healing Blade" card game takes the player into a world of sorcery and creatures where real-world knowledge of infectious diseases and therapeutics play a pivotal role in the winning strategy. "Occam's Razor" is a real diagnostic card game released by NerdCore Medical. The company also releases Manga Guides to physics, statistics, and biochemistry. It successfully crowdfunded a game on Kickstarter surpassing the original goal of $25,000 with $98,113. The "Bacterionomicon" is an artbook bestiary based on the characters of the "Healing Blade." It has entries for 41 "Lords of Pestilence" covering infectious

Cards about characters representing bacteria and antibiotics in the game of NerdCore Medical.

bacteria, and 27 "Apothecary Healers" representing antibiotics.

It has never been so easy to gather required information in an automatic way. Subscribing to medical RSS feeds; checking news on Feedly.com or PeRSSonalized Medicine (perssonalized.com); setting up automatic Google Alerts (alerts.google.com) for different search queries; receiving peer reviewed papers from Pubmed.com by e-mail; and following citations by Google Scholar (scholar.google.com) have all become effortless, efficient ways of filtering an ever-increasing amount of medical information.

New resources started to appear to facilitate student learning. I had a chance to try The Anatomage Table at the Singularity University, and wish I could have used it in medical school. It is an anatomy visualization system on a human-sized screen for educational purposes, and it is being adopted by many of the world's leading medical schools and institutions. This virtual cadaver combines radiology software with clinical content that lets users visualize any anatomical structure from any angle.

BioDigital Systems recently introduced a virtual human body as a web-based platform with the intent of providing a searchable, customizable map of the human body. John J. Qualter from the New York University School of Medicine helped design the 3D installation. He describes it as a living digital textbook.

The University of Arizona College of Medicine announced an exclusive collaboration between the medical school and SynDaver Labs, a Florida-based company. The company has been producing synthetic cadavers that have a heart that beats and pumps blood, and a liver that can make bile. It has also created the world's most sophisticated synthetic human tissues and body parts. It could simultaneously assist students and reduce or eliminate the need for live animals, cadavers, and human Standardized Patients (the latter are actors trained in a script).

Without doubt, the future belongs to interdisciplinary innovations. For example, neurosurgeons at the University of California, San Diego School of Medicine and UC San Diego Moores Cancer Center use magnetic resonance imaging (MRI) guidance for delivering gene therapy directly into brain tumors. This way, the rest of the brain remains unaffected and the risk of the procedure is minimized. Another company, MRI Interventions, has developed and is commercializing systems to enable minimally invasive procedures under real-time MRI-guidance. The ClearPoint system for real-time, MRI-guided minimally invasive brain surgery is FDA-cleared, CE-marked, and currently installed in 29 hospitals. It is being used for direct drug delivery, laser ablation, and drug delivery for patients suffering from Parkinson's disease, dystonia, epilepsy, brain tumors, and more.

Specialists look at the same medical problem from different angles. Because current medical education encourages specialization, social media and other digital technologies can help bring about new ways of collaboration. Combining knowledge from multiple specialties and with computing could result in optimal outcomes for patients.

It is time to re-create the basics of the medical curriculum and re-think how we train future medical professionals who should be not only web-savvy and tech-savvy, but also have the skills to navigate an exponentially changing world of medical technology and information. Their primary goal of treating patients with empathy means that a well-designed balance is needed.

How to design a new curriculum

Some say that medical education has not really changed since the last paradigm shift in 1910 when the Flexner Report, a book-length study of the state of medical education in the US and Canada, advised medical schools to raise their admission and graduation standards, and stick to the protocols of mainstream science in teaching and research. Students today still have to become professionals who care for their patients; are able to collaborate with other disciplines and ancillary caregivers; are creative and critical thinkers; and are motivated to grow constantly as life-long learners.

I had a long talk with Jur Koksma, Assistant Professor at the Radboud University Medical Center, about these issues and the future of medical curriculums when I was a PhD opponent during a thesis defense in the Netherlands.

At Radboud University Medical Center, they are currently working on a revolutionary new medical curriculum. The educational vision behind this transformation has been inspired by people all over the world who want to improve people's lives through healthcare and education. It is based on two pillars that Koksma described.

"First of all, we want to bring students and patients together in realistic learning environments. Students should be 'learning professionals' who start learning by doing from the very first moment they enter the

curriculum. On the very first day students will talk to patients and hear their stories. This way, patient stories will set the narrative in motion that is a doctor's education. Students take genuine responsibility in professional practice, and after such shorter or longer periods of immersive learning, reflect on those practices and on their own competency and related professional learning goals. This is the didactic backbone.

The second pillar besides professional, practice based learning is the didactic principle of self directed learning. Students, as learning professionals, take responsibility for their own learning paths. They organize and manage their own education and, within certain boundaries, get to decide on the contents of their program. In that sense we try to maximize opportunities for personalized education, giving each and every person a chance to become the best doctor they can be on the basis of their unique talents and motivations. We are getting rid of a one size fits all approach in patient care. Let's also do this in medical education."

In this system, each student has a personal coach. They work with a so-called open space technology in which students themselves decide what will be addressed when students and teachers meet. Currently, biomedical and medical students also work as consultants for pharmaceutical companies in an attempt to come up with innovative ideas. These young students still have a lot to learn, but it seems they learn very quickly when under pressure.

Future medical schools will make global digital classrooms possible. The quality of different curriculums should be balanced given the wide access to information and educational resources online. No old books, no cadavers pickled with formaldehyde, no lack of information or educational resources should be issues that future medical schools have to face. Students will train collaboratively with other healthcare professionals, mirroring the cross-disciplinary approach that will be integral to the clinical environment of the future. Enhanced technology will allow for more efficient referrals, faster consultations, and more thorough transitions of care. As a result, providers can spend more time nurturing a strong relationship with their patients. Digital platforms, from IBM's Watson supercomputer to wearable devices, will take part in training students from day one.

Being a successful doctor is not a sprint race, but a marathon. The current examination systems do not really address the skill sets today's medical professionals should acquire. A better option might be to let students advance at their own pace and be examined when they have mastered the material. The Clayton Christensen Institute for Disruptive Innovation in San Mateo, California calls this competency–based learning, which is tailoring an educational program and curriculum for each student. If course materials are available online, students can be assessed individually. Knowing when a particular student is likely to perform to his or her full potential on a given exam might be attainable only by analyzing the student's answers with artificial intelligence.

As a whole, the curriculum must be able to address current needs and the ever–changing skill set needed for medical professionals to provide excellent care and use innovative technologies at the same time. It will be a struggle, but never in the history of education have we had so many opportunities to take the medical curriculum to the next level.

Score of availability: 4
Focus of attention: Medical students
Websites & other online resources: The Social MEDia Course
(http://thecourse.webicina.com/)
Companies & start–ups: Nerdcore Medical
(http://www.nerdcoremedical.com/), Anatomage (http://www.anatomage.com/),
Pocket Anatomy (http://www.pocketanatomy.com/), Osmosis
(https://www.osmosis.org/)
Books: Medical Education for the Future by Bleakley, Bligh & Browne; Understanding Medical Education: Evidence, Theory and Practice by Swanwick
Movies: The Doctor (1991)

Trend 7. Surgical and Humanoid Robots

Ever since I was a kid I have been constantly improving cognitive skills from speed to focus by using video games. I have tried almost all gadgets. I was therefore not surprised at how easy it was to use a daVinci surgical robot. At the 2013 Futuremed course in California I grabbed the joystick controls, stepped on the pedals, and looked into a viewfinder at a three-dimensional, high-quality image sent back by multiple cameras. I could move around tiny objects gripped by miniature but precise robotic arms.

My instructions for what to do exactly came from Dr. Catherine Mohr, the Director of Medical Research at Intuitive Surgical, and an expert in the fields of robotic surgery and sustainable technologies. She was standing behind me watching what I actually did on a screen. I told her about this book, and she found the time to share her views with me. The reason why I wanted to include her stories in this book is not only her knowledge and experience in this field, but also her similar ideas about technical developments for improving healthcare.

"In the fall of 2013, I was asked to partake in a debate at the Oxford Union. The proposition was "this house believes that the technology revolution will solve the global healthcare crisis". As a physician and a technologist, people were very surprised that I was arguing in opposition to this statement. But although I am a true believer in technology, and the power of technology to transform health care, I firmly believe that technology is a tool in our hands, and that the future of medicine will be humans wielding those tools wisely."

The history of robots and digitization in medicine does not go back very far. An early IBM 650 computer was used to scan medical records for subtle abnormalities in the 1950s; the first computer-assisted program for radiating brain tumors called the Gamma knife was introduced in 1974; the daVinci surgical robot system was launched in 1999; and the Robotic Arm Interactive Orthopedic System for use in partial knee and total hip surgery was introduced in 2004. Since then, development has been extraordinary.

Now, surgeons can control robotic arms and other functions on a control panel in the operating room or remotely through a transatlantic connection. The attention of the surgeon is an obligatory feature in robotic-assisted surgery. The equipment is designed to enhance the skill and experience of human surgeons.

Fully automated surgical robots have not yet arrived. Dr. Mohr has considered the issue of autonomy in the use of future medical robotics.

"Robots generally imply autonomous or semi–autonomous motion and decision making, and many of the devices that we think of as robots in medicine and surgery are instead "telemanipulators". With a telemanipulator, the physician's and surgeon's movements and judgment are being implemented through an electromechanical intermediary, but the human remains firmly in control."

The daVinci system, called Xi©.

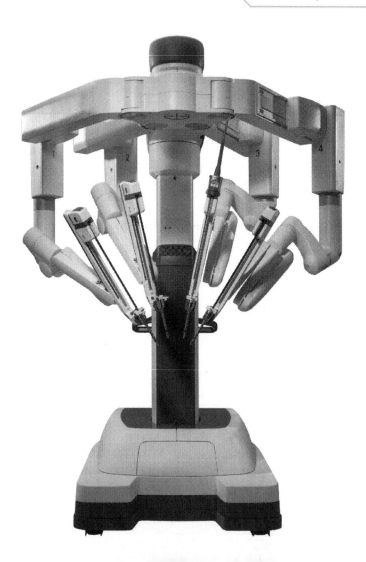

The new version of the daVinci system, called Xi, was released by Intuitive Surgical in 2014. It was designed to allow four–quadrant access to the abdomen, making workflow much easier for surgical procedures such as colorectal surgeries. The scope can be moved from robotic arm to arm, changing the surgeon's point of view without having to re–dock the robot. This allows the surgeon to move back and forth easily in a much wider surgical field than has been possible before. This capability will open up many more areas of general surgery to robotics, and allow more patients to get minimally invasive surgeries. It is even getting less invasive with the adoption of the single incision platform option.

Other areas for improvement include making the scale of operation smaller so that manipulations that are on the edge of a surgeon's capability become more comfortable and precise. Fluorescence imaging is another application. Blood vessels, lymph nodes, and the bile duct can be clearly delineated with dyes that fluoresce under ultraviolet light, making it helpful in many types of surgeries.

Obstacles for wider adoption

One of the obstacles to the wider adoption of surgical robots that must be overcome is correcting the perception of robot autonomy. People are justifiably nervous about surgery performed by a pre–programmed device. They are afraid of the idea of a robot being in control. Consider the case of current orthopedic robots where the cutting paths are predetermined. The robot either executes the plan or provides a haptic guide to the cutting, but a human surgeon is responsible for the planning. The patients are less apprehensive given that they perceive a human in control, not a machine.

Another obstacle is misunderstanding of the economics of robotics. According to Dr. Mohr, people look at the cost of a technology and assume that it simply adds to the cost of doing a procedure. This leads to the perception that robotics raise healthcare costs without adding value equal to or greater than that cost. In reality, robots are enabling surgeries that were formerly done through big open incisions to be done through tiny ones. And while the cost of the technology adds to the cost of the surgery itself, the decreased hospital stay, reduced complications, and lower rates of readmission lead many hospitals to save far more money with the use of the technology than they spend on it.

Another challenge facing any company bringing new technology into the healthcare field is regulatory. Regulatory agencies must strike a careful balance between promoting and protecting the public health. When promotion is emphasized, new technologies and drugs with the potential to improve patient well-being are enthusiastically adopted at the real risk of letting some technologies through that turn out to have negative effects. When protection is emphasized, new technologies are assumed to be bad until proven advantageous, and fewer new innovations survive the regulatory process. For a proper balance between promotion and protection, society needs a mature relationship between risk and benefit.

I discussed the potential of using advanced robotics in medicine, as well as the obstacles that must be overcome with Professor Blake Hannaford, Director of the Biorobotics Laboratory at the University of Washington. He worked on the remote control of robot manipulators at NASA's Jet Propulsion Laboratory; was awarded the National Science Foundation's Presidential Young Investigator Award; and is considered an expert of surgical biomechanics and biologically based design of robot manipulators.

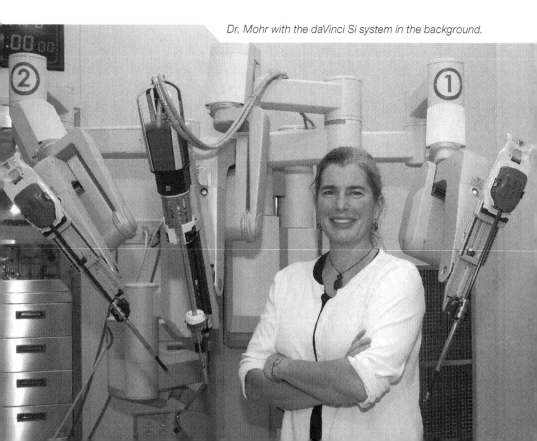

Dr. Mohr with the daVinci Si system in the background.

"As with all medical devices, there is a rigorous trade-off between innovation because of technical possibilities and the duty to apply the most proven methods to each patient. Wider adoption of medical robots requires advances on both fronts. In the clinic, we need to find and validate applications in which the patient has a better and safer outcome with robotic assisted treatment. On the engineering side, we need advances on software architectures for reliable integration of robotic algorithms with teleoperation."

When we talked, he was particularly excited about a project funded by the National Institutes of Health at the Biorobotics Laboratory. In collaboration with the Fred Hutchinson Cancer Research Center they aim to make tumors fluoresce when labeled with a molecule extracted from scorpion toxin. More fluorescence imaging agents will be available on the market soon which would make it simple to see directly where the cancer is and help surgeons avoid nerves and blood vessels.

They also work on developing a robust developers' community that promotes the use of open-source software that is now used at eleven universities worldwide. It is not known how open-source software will flow through the regulatory system, but the FDA is studying the attractive idea that bugs in open-source software can be found and repaired more easily than in software developed by large companies shielded with numerous patents. Researchers think that developing a clear regulatory framework for open-source medical software, including hybrids of open- and closed- source software, as well as longitudinal studies of new robotic assisted procedures that show clinical benefits are much needed to strengthen the power of advanced robotics in the operating room.

An important goal is to feel what the robot touches, which means getting useful haptic feedback from the patient tissues to the surgeon's hands. According to Professor Hannaford, haptics technology has matured a lot in the last ten years, but still struggles to find a robust market niche. Haptic feedback from surgical robotics is in great demand, and will be available eventually. It is still not clear, however, how to certify haptic feedback as completely safe and stable. In the future, surgeons might sit in special chairs, receiving a clear, three dimensional picture of what the robotic arms see in detail, thus be able to control tiny movements in great precision from a distance. In underdeveloped regions, surgical robots could be deployed so that operations are performed by surgeons who control the robots from thousands of kilometers away.

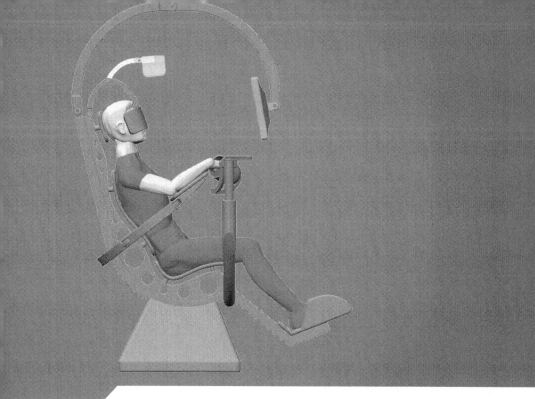

Concept art and a prototype of how future robots with telecommunication systems could be used by medical professionals.

In a chapter he wrote in Medical Devices: Surgical and Image Guided Technologies, Professor Jacob Rosen at the University of California, Santa Cruz, identified three trends which may lead to a revolutionary breakthrough in surgical robotics. First is an effort to reduce invasiveness, which will minimize trauma to surrounding tissue, reducing the risk for infection, and result in speedier recovery and shorter hospitalizations.

The second trend is improvements in visualization. Endoscopic cameras, along with new imaging modalities, provide a view and representation of anatomical structures.

The third trend concerns the level of automation and how much surgeon control is needed to execute the surgical procedure. In 2007, a research program called "Trauma Pod" funded by the Defense Advanced Research Projects Agency (DARPA) demonstrated that the operating room can be fully automated without the need for actual human presence. The surgeon directed the surgical robot via telepresence; the sterile nurse was replaced by a tools changer, an equipment dispenser, and a robotic arm, whereas the circulating nurse was replaced by an information technology system that tracked the tools and supplies used throughout the procedure.

Understanding the value of robotics

Dr. Mohr thinks that even with robotic manipulators, the operating room will never be fully robotic. There are so many tasks involved in keeping a patient stable during surgery that there is little value in building a robot for tasks that humans do better and with great versatility. Humans outdo robots in many areas, and will certainly continue to do so when versatility and adaptability is required.

The cost effectiveness of including new services and technologies like robotics in everyday healthcare is still not clear to anyone but a hospital Chief Financial Officer. While both patients and physicians tend to value technology and embrace it when it leads to better outcomes, neither patients nor physicians in the US healthcare system have access to data regarding the cost side of the equation. It is therefore very difficult to make cost effective decisions such as those Dr. Mohr described. In recent years she has seen the rise of the educated patient who advocates for himself and asks for minimally invasive or robotic surgery. Many procedures happen to be cost effective, but motivated patients still have little understanding of the economics.

By understanding surgical robots more, it will be apparent that they enhance the surgeon's capabilities rather than replace them. Such robots can potentially lend a surgeon dexterity, vision, and navigational guidance that are beyond what is possible by the unaided human. Like other cases of disruptive technology, understanding that the surgeon is still in control will go a long way toward easing the public's uneasiness about robotics.

According to these experts, there is huge value in making devices smaller than a millimeter in diameter. Containing robust moving parts, they would move into micro–scale manipulations while still being strong enough to interact with tissues. The ultimate goal that Dr. Mohr shared with me is to get better, more accurate, and early diagnosis of cancer so that we can operate when they are surgically curable. Achieving this could make cancer a speed bump in someone's life, not a life–changing tragedy.

Robots among us

There are many examples now how robots could play a role in medicine and generally in people's everyday lives.

Telenoid R1, designed by the Osaka University and Advanced Telecommunications Research Institute International, is a teleoperated android robot developed to transmit an individual's presence. It appears and behaves as a minimalistic persona, allowing viewers to feel as if an acquaintance far away is next to them. A remote presence might be a grandchild for the elderly with whom they can communicate in a natural setting. Another potential companion, Actroid, also developed by Osaka University, is a type of humanoid robot that has a visually strong human–likeness modeled on an average young woman of Japanese descent. It can mimic such lifelike functions as blinking, and breathing, and is able to recognize speech and respond in kind.

The Vasteras Giraff is a mobile communication tool similar to Skype that enables the elderly to communicate with the outside world. It is remote controlled and has wheels, a camera, and a monitor. The Aethon TUG is an automated system that travels through hospital corridors and moves medication, linens, food, and supplies from one space to another. It even navigates elevators. New models serving quite different purposes come out almost every month now.

Atlas is 1.83 m tall, weighs 150 kg, is made of graded aluminum and titanium, can walk on rough terrain, withstand being hit by projectiles, and balance on one leg. It costs about $2 million. It is a bipedal humanoid that Boston Dynamics presented during a 2013 conference. Inspired by the 2011 Fukushima Daiichi nuclear disaster, six different teams will compete in the 2014 DARPA Robotics Challenge to test the robot's ability to perform tasks such as including getting in and out of a vehicle, driving it, opening a door, and using a power tool. In the near future its sensate hands will enable Atlas to use tools designed for human use. By having cameras and intelligent software it can perform environment–dependent tasks such as identifying the piece of wood it was told to pick up and then stooping down to grab it.

Nine customers took a seat at "Robots Bar and Lounge" in Ilmenau, East Germany while a humanoid robot called Carl measured out spirits into cocktail shakers and engaged them in limited conversations. The robot was built by mechatronics engineer Ben Schaefer at H&S–Robots. He has spent 23 years in the field using parts of disused industrial robots from the German firm KUKA.

A robot companion developed by H&S–Robots.

Veebot, a California-based start-up, combined robotics with image-analysis software to draw blood from patients safely. The machine restricts the patient's blood flow, an infrared light shines on the skin, and a camera searches for a vein. Then it checks the vein via ultrasound to make sure it is on target. In less than one minute, it draws blood. Its success rate is about 83 percent, the same as humans. They are aiming at 90 percent before moving to clinical trials.

A company based in Israel, Given Imaging, developed the first pill cameras that can be swallowed and send information to a receiver outside the body. Several research groups are working on making these capsules self-maneuvering. A European collaboration of researchers called ARES is currently testing a way for multiple capsules to automatically snap together. It means capsules could be assembled into a more complex device once safely in the stomach after each is swallowed individually. Such capsules could perform a different task such as imaging, providing power, or taking samples. Inside the stomach the capsules would link together to create a snake-like device that slithers through the intestines, performing tasks that are more complex than those that can be performed by a single capsule or several free-floating ones.

In the distant future, medical drones could deliver supplies and drugs to conventionally unreachable areas. For example, 85% of roads are inaccessible during the wet season in sub-Saharan Africa, cutting off the population, and hindering transportation of medical supplies. The list of examples could go on almost without end.

Medical robotics is still a young, unexplored field made possible by technical improvements over the past couple decades, meaning that the potential benefits provided by such robots are not fully understood. They have only gone through a few generations, one can make although educated guesses about the influence of robots on medicine in the near future such as better medical outcomes, tissue engineering, gene therapy, and rapid interventions.

A fundamental challenge with automated robotic surgery is decision-making. Like surgeons now, a robot has to be able to spot a vein, know to avoid it, and to detect if it starts bleeding. Guang-Zhong Yang at Imperial College London thinks that aiming for fully autonomous surgical robots is not the right approach. Due to the fact that people are pretty good in terms of decision-making and learning; while robots are good at doing precise movements, a combination of both could be the solution.

In support of this notion the National Robotics Initiative is already underway-"co–robots acting in direct support of and in a symbiotic relationship with human partners." The question here is whether we will be able to control robots without untoward consequences. The famous science fiction writer Isaac Asimov anticipated the need for basic rules when he formulated his Three Laws of Robotics in his 1942 story "Runaround."

1. A robot may not injure a human being or, through inaction, allow a human being to come to harm.

2. A robot must obey the orders given to it by human beings, except where such orders would conflict with the First Law.

3. A robot must protect its own existence as long as such protection does not conflict with the First or Second Law.

Much later Asimov added a "zeroth" law that said "a robot may not harm humanity, or, by inaction, allow humanity to come to harm."

The paper that won an award at the 2014 IEEE International Conference on Human–Robot Interaction described robots communicating with people by human–like body language, gestures and cues. The authors think this is a crucial step to placing robots in homes where they might have a better, more natural interaction with people. Such efforts are needed to close the gap between people and the robots they create.

Score of availability: 5

Focus of attention: Medical professionals

Websites & other online resources: The Society of Robotic Surgery (http://www.srobotics.org/), Medical Robots News by IEEE (http://spectrum.ieee.org/robotics/medical–robots)

Companies & start–ups: H&S Robots (http://www.hs–robots.de), Boston Dynamics (http://www.bostondynamics.com/), da Vinci Surgery (http://www.davincisurgery.com/)

Books: I, Robot by Asimov

Movies: Prometheus (2012), Ender's Game (2013)

Trend 8. Genomics and Truly Personalized Medicine

I was about to become a medical student when the completion of the Human Genome Project was announced. The genetic information of a person's DNA was finally made available. I remember being thrilled at the opportunities that advances of genomics could provide humanity with. When I was working on my PhD, the Personal Genome Project garnered worldwide attention by aiming to sequence and publicize the complete genomes and share the medical records of 100,000 volunteers. Since the completion of the Human Genome Project in 2003, we have envisioned an era of personalized medicine in which everyone receives customized therapy and personalized dosages.

According to the Personalized Medicine Coalition (PMC) there are so far only about 150 cases in which personal genomics can be applied. These are based on evidence. As we move forward, we will increasingly have opportunities to use DNA analysis at the patient's bedside. This should be an obligatory step before actually prescribing any medications. Doing so means that patients would get a drug and dosage exactly customized to their unique genomic, thus metabolic background. Fast, accurate, and widely available DNA sequencing will be needed to reach this goal.

During my PhD thesis defense I was fortunate to have on my board of opponents Joel Dudley, PhD, Assistant Professor of Genetics and Genomic Sciences and Director of Biomedical Informatics at Mount Sinai School of Medicine. He and his team in New York work on one of the most exciting projects in systems biology, bioinformatics, and genomics. When I asked him where he thought the field of genomics was heading, he openly talked about his own medical conditions and their relation to his genome.

"I think that one way that innovative technologies can help keep the human touch in medicine is by helping patients feel understood. One example is that I have Crohn's disease, which is an inflammatory bowel disease. I am pretty open about this when I give talks and then I show how having my whole genome sequenced helped me understand my disease and also helped me with choosing the right therapy. I have mutations in the TPMT gene that would suggest I would have increased side effects if I were to take 6–mercaptopurine, which is commonly prescribed for Crohn's disease. I think that human diseases are so complex and their manifestations in individuals are often so unique

that individuals affected by disease are often seeking to have the unique and personal characteristics of their disease understood."

He mentioned how he helped individuals with Crohn's disease better understand their condition by identifying mutations in their genome sequence that are likely affecting their disease either through modified drug response or different progression. He thinks that once a patient is given the DNA evidence proving that they are indeed challenged with a specific disease– and have a specific name of the parts of their genes that are broken– it can be comforting. It can also help them build stronger ties within a community of similarly affected individuals.

He sees parallels with the autism gene panels now offered at Mount Sinai. Autism is a puzzling disease with a strong genetic component, yet parents and affected individuals often have to fight misconceptions or overly simplistic models of the disease that are held by doctors and family members. Through Dr. Dudley's tests some of these individuals will find that they have specific genetic mutations linked to autism. Such hard biological evidence can be a tremendous relief to families because it can explain their daily struggles, and they can show this evidence to others.

Dr. Dudley has firm views about the challenges genomics face in its quest to becoming widely adopted. Current EMR systems do not fundamentally understand genomic information, and vendors are not motivated to solve this problem. One reason why physicians limit their engagement with genomic information is that they traditionally have not had much formal training in either genomics or its effect on developing diseases.

At Mount Sinai School of Medicine they developed the CLIPMERGE platform to help EMRs make intelligent use of genetic information in prescribing drugs. In oncology, which has a growing catalog of cancer–causing mutations, Foundation Medicine is offering targeted genomic tests to guide clinical decisions; unfortunately, it is necessary to sequence entire cancer genomes to do this.

Dr. Dudley's team uses state–of–the–art methods in genomics and systems biology to analyze specified networks of similar medical conditions while keeping traditional values in mind.

"The problem with that is that we've forgotten what Greek physicians knew thousands of years ago, and that is the fact that the human body is a complex adaptive system with many connected dynamic components interacting and communicating on multiple levels—not only within the body, but also with the external environment. One hallmark of a complex adaptive system like the human body is that you cannot understand the whole by looking at individual parts and that the whole is always greater than the sum of the parts. In this light, the fact that medicine and biology are so siloed into domains or disease–focused specialties is, in my opinion, ridiculous, because that is not how it is in the human body. No disease manifests in isolation from the rest of an individual's physiology."

In the future, Dudley hopes it will be possible to define disease in terms similar to GPS coordinates. An individual's disease could be classified numerically in relation to other patients or diseases according to similarities with other patients or diseases. Partnerships with patients must be built where we can collect and analyze the streams of real–time information sent by consumer biosensors, and help predict when individuals are at increased risk. By prevention we shift our focus from disease treatment to maintaining human health and vitality.

Genome data for everyone

I envision a day when it will be quite common to have our genomes sequenced. The magic number will be 7 000 000 000 (global population) times 3 000 000 000 (number of base pairs in our DNA) equaling $2,1 * 10^{19}$ which is the number of base pairs that should soon be available. Based on trends in other industries such as mobile phones, I think the cost of sequencing a human genome will be close to zero, while the analysis needed to draw conclusions useful to medical decisions will be expensive.

Dr. Dudley agrees with me about the cost of sequencing, but he expects genome interpretation to eventually be free. Models will appear in which making huge investments in better genome interpretation tools or web services will be worthwhile because they will enable the collection of valuable information from a large population, capture attention, and somehow monetize that attention.

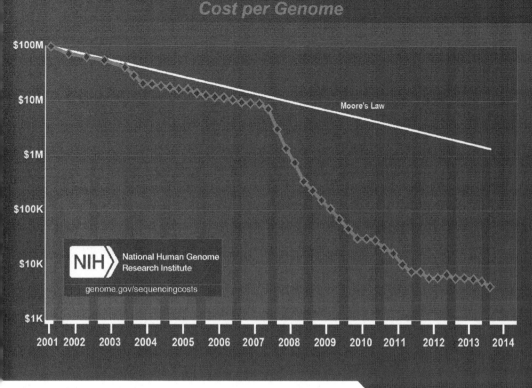

Typical cost of sequencing a human–sized genome over time on a logarithmic scale, as of 21 May 2014 estimated by the National Human Genome Research Institute.

Unfortunately, the broader clinical utility of genomics has not been firmly established yet. Examples exist in pharmacogenomics, covering the response given to particular drugs; and oncology where genomic information has strong scientific and clinical support for informing clinical decisions. But without established clinical usefulness backed by evidence, third–party payers will not be amenable to reimbursing the costs of applying genomics technologies.

In 2009 I was invited to the Science Foo Camp at the headquarters of Google, called Googleplex. There I met Professor George Church, world–famous Harvard professor of Genetics. I asked for his thoughts on the future of genome sequencing, and he scheduled a long call so we could discuss this, and the mission of this book, at length.

"The human touch is there, it has worked for long, sitting by the patient's bedside and trying to lift their spirits. Although with the advances of human genomics, parts of the process have become automated, medical professionals cannot practice the way they used to, it is no longer the same human contact that we had before. Patients usually get interested in new technologies first; therefore there is a constant request that physicians start using them. Medical professionals don't have to get detailed training about how magnetic resonance imaging works, they just need to know why it works."

Thousands of things can be done in genetics. But its real promises have not yet arrived. Professor Church explained that educating the general public and medical professionals is the biggest next step. With preventive medicine, people could be proactive in taking care of their own health rather than being reactive as we are now.

He questioned the quality of data obtained and used in genomics, though he was optimistic in envisioning portable DNA sequencing with smartphones; new kinds of eyeglasses that can see allergens and pathogens in the environment, and thereby change the way we work, go to school, or live our lives. The first GPS devices were hard to use and too complicated. But as the industry improved, instructions became simple enough for people to navigate smoothly. The same scenario can be expected in genomics. What is needed though, according to Professor Church, is better software.

Genomics can change lives

I have had genomic tests identifying some of the mutations I carry as well as partially sequencing my genome with three companies. Navigenics, Pathway Genomics, and Gentle provided me with a thorough analysis and a huge text file that contains my genomic information. It gave me a clear picture about how such services operate, and I probably experienced what other consumers went through. I simply opened the company's website, ordered my test, received a sampling tube a week later, and provided saliva sample. Certain companies require customers to provide almost 10 ml of saliva, a challenging process that can take half an hour. I sent the sample tube back and was notified of the results by e–mail.

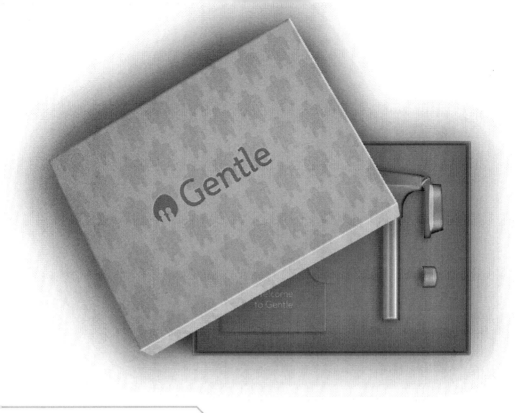

The sampling kit from Gentle.

With a few exceptions such as carrier status for rare conditions or certain pharmacogenomic features (meaning what drugs I am sensitive to), the information provided was not useful. Certainly it did not influence any of my medical decisions, except Gentle that provided definite answers to my questions. Accordingly, I was not surprised that the FDA warned the Google–backed company 23andMe to stop performing what it regarded as a medical test without its approval, and without physician oversight. The service had to change the way it analyzed and released consumers' genomic data. Given constant improvements, the service should become better and better over by time.

Recent news reports highlight the growing importance of genomics. Anne Morriss gave birth to a boy with a rare genetic disease, MCAD deficiency, which affects fat metabolism. It turned out that her sperm bank donor carried a rare genetic mutation for it just like she did. The unfortunate experience led her to launch a new company, Genepeeks, with a scientist at Princeton University. It takes the DNA of sperm donors and recipients and creates "virtual babies" or in–silica offsprings that can be screened for genetic diseases. They hope to make the technology available to any couple trying to conceive.

For about 25 years, it has been known that traces of fetal DNA can be detected in a pregnant woman's blood. A study in The New England Journal of Medicine recently demonstrated how DNA sequencing can detect an extra copy of a chromosome with remarkable accuracy, heralding perhaps a new era in prenatal DNA testing. Out of 1,914 young, healthy pregnant women, just eight fetuses had an extra chromosome. The test detected them all. What if in the future we could predict all diseases, main features of a child and even complex traits the live offspring will have to deal with? Would it lead to a genetic discrimination before birth?

I called Edward Abrahams to discuss such issues and the future of genomics. He is the President of the PMC launched in 2004 to educate the public and policy makers. It aims to promote new ways of thinking about healthcare, and represents over 225 innovators, academic, industry, patient, provider, and payer communities. In the 3rd edition of "The Case for Personalized Medicine", the PMC described a bright future involving genomics and big data:

"Imagine a physician sitting down with his laptop and a morning cup of coffee. On a website that he uses to help manage his practice, an alert pops up. It tells him that a series of studies have demonstrated a connection between multiple rare mutations found in 10 percent of people and the likelihood that they might convert to type 2 diabetes. Nearly all of his patients have had their entire genome sequenced and entered into their electronic medical record – a process that takes only a week, costs a few hundred dollars, and is reimbursed by insurance companies because of the many benefits it provides to lifelong health management.
He conducts a quick search of his 2,000 patient database and finds about 80 who are at risk. To half of those patients, he sends a strong reminder and advice on diet and lifestyle choices they can take to avoid the disease. To the other half, whose medical records reveal pre–diabetic symptoms; he sets up appointments to consider more proactive treatment with drugs that can prevent the onset of disease."

Abrahams told me that after the Human Genome Project was completed expectations were unrealistic. This often happens with technological breakthroughs. But over time that breakthrough is likely to transform the practice of medicine. It takes a long time to change regulatory patterns, and everything that needs to be addressed, but that is what PMC was created to do. Unfortunately, progress has been only incremental in taking products using genomic information to the market.

He believes that more evidence is needed showing that targeted therapies and personalized medicine can not only improve patient outcomes, but also save money when incorporated into the health system over the long term. If researchers can show that this is true, then they will have a much better argument to make to payers.

PMC's hope is that a more efficient system will appear by targeting therapies and thus avoiding inefficient side effects. A second purpose of the PMC is education given that most of the public and many providers do not really understand what this is really about. The PMC hopes that when people do understand how it works, both stakeholders can benefit. Sequencing costs will drop to zero. In twenty years we will stop talking about personalized medicine as it will no longer be anything special.

Oxford Nanopore, a UK–based company, released its MinION sequencer in 2013. It can read short DNA fragments, exists on a USB drive sized device, and can perform the actual sequencing on a laptop. Although it fell short of its originally high expectations, the device is proof of concept that we can bring genomic sequencing to the masses.

QuantuMDx, a new player on the market that lets any laypeople run DNA analyses, tried to crowdfund its development on Indiegogo. Its founders envisioned a handheld DNA laboratory device in every bathroom cabinet for at–home testing for ailments such as flu.

Showcasing how genomics could transform society, researchers at Penn State and the Catholic University of Leuven developed a statistical model for mapping facial features using racial, gender, and genetic markers. Now it is almost possible to create accurate mugshots using only DNA. Envision a crimeless world in which whoever leaves DNA behind can be traced easily in seconds.

It should not be surprising that Craig Venter, one of the fathers of modern genomics, described a really interesting method in his recent book, Life at the Speed of Light. He claimed to have built a prototype of a "Digital Biological Converter" that would allow biological teleportation.

One could receive DNA sequences over the Internet and synthesize proteins, viruses, and even living cells meaning the teleportation of life. The prototype can only produce DNA currently, not proteins or living cells. But given the history of Venter's previous ventures one can expect it to advance soon. It could not only teleport vaccines, antibiotics or insulin to long distances, but even provide patients with personalized drugs right away. This is the quest personalized medicine has to take on by using more and more advanced genomic analyses. Our blueprint, known as the DNA, is heavily responsible for making us different individuals; therefore it should start playing a much bigger role in making diagnoses and prescribing customized treatments in the near future.

Score of availability: 6

Focus of attention: Researchers and patients

Websites & other online resources: The Personalized Medicine Coalition (http://www.personalizedmedicinecoalition.org/), GenomeWeb (http://www.genomeweb.com/), PHG Foundation (http://www.phgfoundation.org/)

Companies & start-ups: Oxford NanoPore (https://www.nanoporetech.com), Gentle (https://gentlelabs.com/)

Books: Exploring Personal Genomics by Dudley & Karczewski

Movies: Gattaca (1997), Splice (2009)

Trend 9. Body Sensors Inside and Out

What do we do when we need to measure different health parameters? We go to a lab and provide blood sample; or to the hospital where they measure blood pressure, ECG, and perform other diagnostic tests. After that we wait and bring the results to the doctor to discuss the next step. If we need a radiology imaging or a laboratory test, it might take a lot of time due to waiting lists worldwide. When I wanted to get my DNA sequenced I provided saliva sample and sent it to direct–to–consumer genomic companies that gave me online access to the results a few weeks later. They even provided a genetic counselor to interpret the data for me over the phone.

There are only a few medical parameters that people have been able to measure at home by themselves. Blood pressure and blood glucose levels are prime examples. We rely on healthcare institutions to obtain data about our own body. But for how long?

What if medical professionals focused on solving this shortcoming instead of spending time and energy on obtaining whatever data is required for solving a medical problem? What if blood tests, biomarkers, imaging, or simply blood pressure values were available right away?

This notion has driven the development of newer kinds of sensors that can be embedded, implanted, or worn in order to measure health parameters in a way that hasn't been accessible before. Fitness and sport have been two areas that have put the most pressure on developers to come up with sensors that can ease, gamify, and improve an individual's health.

A massively increasing number of gadgets, solutions, and technologies now make such measurements possible, convenient, and simple. It will be a challenge to find a balance between using an increasing amount of personal tech and only that we actually need. During one of my talks I took an ECG with my smartphone using FDA–approved AliveCor. Afterwards a colleague told me that his wife would do an ECG on herself every 5 minutes if she had the device. Overuse is normal during the hype phase.

Downloads of smartphone medical apps declined after their initial release. In this spirit I remain confident we will find a proper balance for a technology's use over time. Wearing hundreds of health trackers should not be the solution even though insightful trackers add value to our lives. The best scenario might be to include tiny sensors in clothing and accessories–contact lenses or rings–making the measurement of health data elegant and invisible compared to a Holter ECG monitor that is worn for 24 hours.

According to Nielsen's 2013 Connected Life Report 15% of consumers who know the term "wearable" are wearing one. Of those who owned such a device, 61% owned fitness wristbands and 45% owned smartwatches. Costs per person need to go down to encourage mass adoption of these devices, which is exactly where the industry is heading.

In 2013, 96% of all connected wearable devices were activity trackers, 3% were smartwatches, and 1% were smart glasses. Tellingly, 82% of users believe that wearable tech has enhanced their lives. By 2017, 64 million shipments of such devices are expected (8 times larger than in 2012). Global spending on wearable technology is estimated to be $19 billion by 2018.

PSFK, a content network, released "The Future of Wearable Tech," which identified several possible inventions that let users feel one another from afar. A smart ring might let us feel a user far away; earbuds might monitor a wearer's mood and select the next song to match it. Zoomable contact lenses could assist patients with degenerative retinal disorders; low-voltage electronic make-up could activate gadgets by predetermined facial expressions; and ingestible password pills developed by Motorola and Proteus Health could let us log into websites or devices only by being in the proximity of the device.

Sensors can be embedded in tissue (pacemaker), ingestible (smart pills), epidermal (smart skin or digital tattoo), wearable (clothing or jewelry), and external (traditional blood pressure monitors and smartwatches). As their number is increasing quickly, 2014 might be a turning point when health wearables become mainstream and most people acknowledge the advantages this range of gadgets might offer.

Wearing invisible sensors

Given that wearable sensors will influence daily life, they have to be tiny, practically invisible, and yet technically accurate. Once I watched a presentation by Professor Takao Someya, PhD, of The University of Tokyo. He is the Project Director of Someya's Bio-Harmonized Project. His team has been working on the first flexible wireless sensor that can function as electrical Band-Aids or diapers.

His goal is to develop electronic devices that interface with living bodies, taking advantage of features of organic molecules. Such devices can be fabricated using biocompatible inks, creating circuits with millions of soft biosensors that can safely communicate with biological tissue.

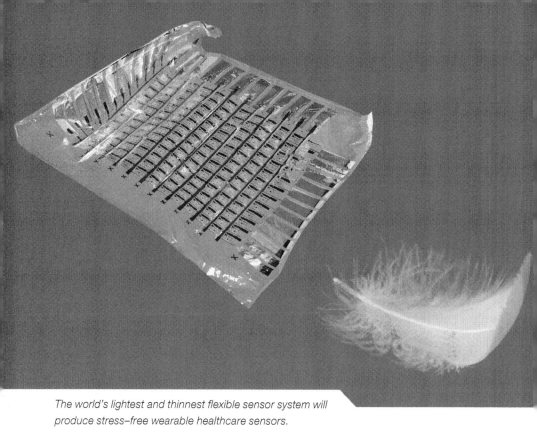

The world's lightest and thinnest flexible sensor system will produce stress–free wearable healthcare sensors.

When rigid materials are implanted into biological tissue they cause inflammation. This barrier hinders embedding sensors such as blood glucose detectors for long periods. In order to overcome this, Someya's team has focused on biocompatible organic semiconductors as opposed to conventional inorganic materials such as silicon. Potential developments include smart catheters, wheelchairs, and flexible health sensors that can constantly monitor certain parameters.

Professor Someya described the goal of his research:

"These probes will be able to sense the electrical and chemical signals of the billions of neurons which exist inside the human brain, and will enable high–resolution visualization of real–time neuron activities. By utilizing novel organic bio–devices, we aim to complete a visualization of complicated neural networks, and subsequently, a visualization of the activities of a whole brain that is an aggregation of billions of neurons."

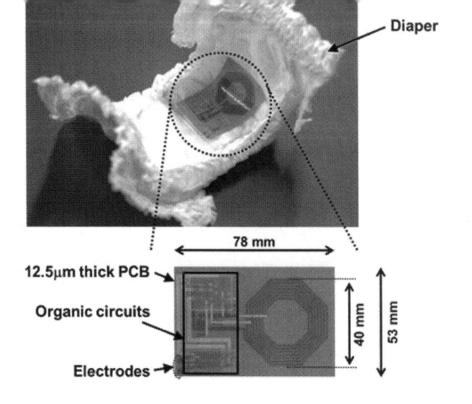

The world's first soft wireless organic sensor system detects liquid and wirelessly transmits data. The sensor is powered wirelessly and can be mounted to diapers or Band–Aids for disposable use.

Imagine that such sensors in the body and implanted in everyday devices could revolutionize the way we collect information about our health. Measuring easily quantifiable data is the gateway to better health. The future belongs to digestible, embedded, and wearable sensors. The latter works like a thin e–skin. These sensors will measure vital signs and important health parameters 24 hours a day, transmitting data to the cloud and sending alerts to medical systems, for example, when a stroke is happening real time. It will call the ambulance and transmit pertinent data.

One can swallow digital sensors that gather and store data to an external device. In gastrointestinal diseases, for example, swallowing a device that included a video camera could render an instant diagnosis by combining lab results with colonoscopy pictures.

Recently, Equivital provided the Oxford Kidney Unit with data to support the development of a tool that would prevent adverse events in patients with kidney failure who were undergoing haemodialysis (a method used to remove waste products such as creatinine, urea and free water from the blood). Equivital developed a sensor that continuously monitors vital signs including pulse oximetry, oxygen saturation, and core temperature. These are known risk factors for adverse events of dialysis. The company develops other applications for medical, pharmaceutical, and military use as well.

A thin sensor wore like a digital tattoo measuring health parameters.

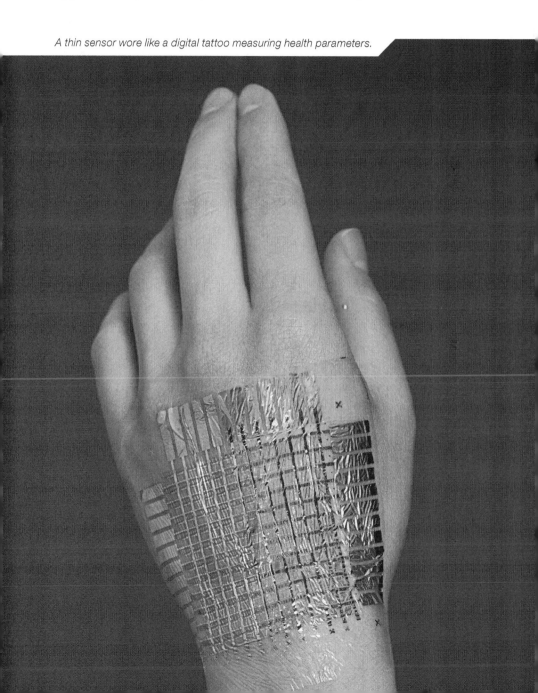

MC10, based in Cambridge Massachusetts, has developed a platform that combines conventional electronics with novel mechanics. It enables a new generation of thin electronic systems for sports, fitness, cosmetics, healthcare, energy and defense. They demonstrated their first product at the CES conference. It featured skullcap electronics to measure the impact force an athlete sustains during contact sports. It thus suggests whether or not players have received a potentially dangerous blow to the head. The company tirelessly develops silicon devices thinned to a fraction of the width of a human hair, uses stretchable metallic interconnects, and elastic rubberlike polymers to form complete powered systems that sense, measure, analyze, and communicate information.

A Japanese mobile carrier and materials developer Toray announced a joint project Hitoe (Japanese for "one layer"), a cloth containing nanofibers coated in a transmittable layer. Using electrodes, the clot can measure pulse and even metrics resembling a cardiogram with the plan to transmit the data to the smartphone of the owner of the smart cloth. This was considered one of the first steps in designing a new kind of clothing.

The "digital tattoo" developed by MC10.

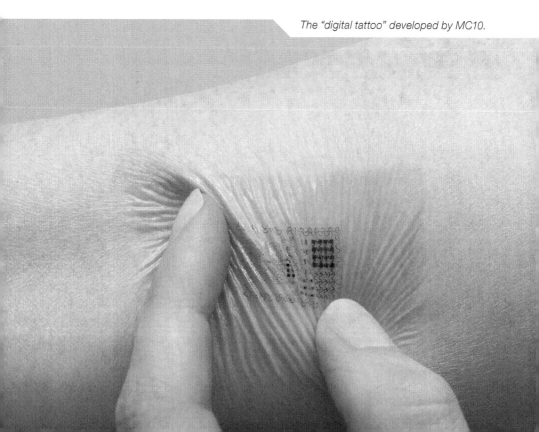

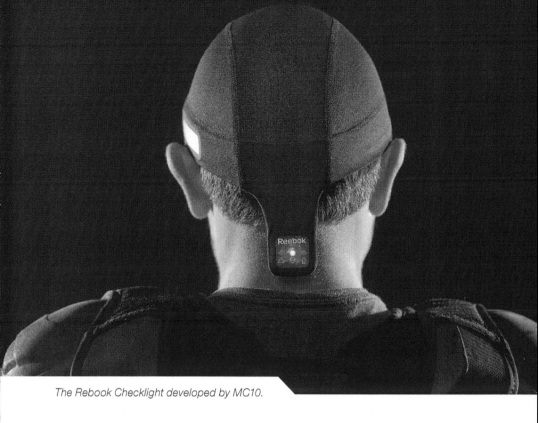

The Rebook Checklight developed by MC10.

Designer Kerri Wallace recently created a shirt that responds to body heat, and what mood that person is in. Workout gear developed by Radiate Athletics reports visual activity levels of the wearer in real–time. The company ithlete aims to tell users when to train more, and when to rest based continual heart rate monitoring.

HexoSkin has developed the first electronic shirt that tracks movement, respiration, and pulse. Users such as professional athletes, astronauts, and sport enthusiasts put the shirt on, plug in the device, and see their body metrics displayed on a smartphone right away. These statistics are uploaded to the user's online account and generate detailed recommendations on training and general health. Feedback on physical activity, stress, sleep quality, nocturnal breathing, and heart rate are all expensive at the moment, but a decline is expected in coming years.

The smart bra has successfully been tested in over 500 patients to date. It shows a 74% correlation to actual cancer stages in all types of breast tissue. Smart shoes connected to a smartphone guide the user to where he wants to get. Be prepared when famous fashion designers start to focus on such innovations.

Constantly monitoring our health?

Scanadu, founded in 2011 and based at the NASA Ames Research Center in Mountain View, California, finished a successful crowdfunding campaign that raised $1.66 million from 8,800 backers to develop medical technology devices for consumers. The prototype of the first product, the Scanadu Scout, is a portable device that measures parameters such as temperature, heart rate, blood oxygenation, respiratory rate, ECG, and blood pressure. It was shipped to backers in March, 2014, and the company plans to make the device available for consumers in the first quarter of 2015.

A rival Wi–Fi enabled sensor developed at National Taiwan University can be embedded in a tooth cavity and measure jaw movements, drinking, chewing, coughing, speaking and even smoking. The results are wirelessly transmitted. If the sensor receives all the appropriate inputs it can potentially curb assorted addictions, from smoking to drinking alcohol excessively.

A company called iHealth Lab is working on an ambulatory blood pressure monitor, wireless ambulatory ECG, and a wearable pulse oximeter that could be used in ambulances. Kolibree has developed a smart toothbrush that monitors brushing habits and helps users improve their dental health. A vitamin–sized ingestible pill camera is PillCamSB weighing less than 4 grams was approved for human use by the FDA. It can monitor pressure, pH, temperature, gastrointestinal motility, and detect ulcers, early signs of tumors, and bleeding within the small bowel. Sensors for almost any health parameter and any body part are becoming available. The developments described above have hit the market only in the last one to two years.

In addition to digestible and wearable sensors, imagine similar wireless technology providing real–time data from an artificial pancreas or recording brain waves constantly. Medtronic is a company a thirty–year history of innovation in diabetes technology. It brought the first insulin pump to market in 1983. In 2013, the FDA approved their fully automated "artificial pancreas," a device that closely mimics the insulin delivery of a working pancreas by continuously monitoring glucose levels and adjusting insulin delivery, all with little or no patient interaction.

Retinal implants that restore sight are already on the market. Second Sight makes an implant that includes a video camera and transmitter in a pair of glasses. Video images are converted into a series of electrical pulses transmitted wirelessly to an array of electrodes laying on the surface of the

The Scanadu Scout.

retina. The pulses stimulate the retina's remaining healthy cells, which relay them to the optic nerve.

Transparent 1–micron thick circuits embedded in a polymer membrane can be used in contact lenses to monitor the buildup of pressure in the eye for those with glaucoma, or continuously measure blood glucose levels in tears for diabetics. The technology is getting closer to making 24/7 monitoring a reality and matter of choice for patients. A skin patch dispenses drugs continuously and can determine when to stop. It can release therapeutic agents based on a patient's body temperature. Such patches could become entirely wireless and brought to the market in less than five years.

Wearable devices could use biometrics besides facial structures, expressions, DNA, or iris patterns. A Canadian start–up, Bionym, has developed biometric identification using the unique patterns of a user's ECG, which varies according to the size, shape, and position of the heart in one's body.

Leslie Saxon from the University of Southern California's Keck School of Medicine addressed the possibility of wearing more and more sensors in and on our body. A baby born five or ten years from now could be tattooed with an integrated circuit at birth that could monitor ECG, physical activity, nutritional status, sleep duration, breathing rate, body temperature, and hydration, all generating a huge amount of data that can be used in health management, disease prediction, and even monetization for large healthcare companies. The data could be transmitted to smartphones or tablets. Applications would give parents and pediatricians insights into the baby's health and condition in real–time. The same scenario is available for adults, especially soldiers or athletes. She warned, however, that we must be cautious. The point is "using machines to amplify their humanity, not to scare the heck out of them".

Daniel Reed, a frequent government advisor on science and technology policy, addressed the growing importance of wearables in 2013. He said that even though everyone is different, today's medical treatments are still quite generic. In a few years, we may have wearable and perhaps implantable metabolic diagnostics constituting an early health warning system.

Max Knoblauch, a reporter of Mashable.com, was not persuaded by the wearable revolution and Quantified Self movement. He therefore measured numerous daily parameters for 30 days, which he called the most miserable, self-aware 30 days he has ever spent. He used MyFitnessPal to track running, Sleepbot to track sleeping habits, and Fitbit to measure his physical activity. Some results were obvious while a few things were a surprise such as having a normal sleeping schedule. He learned that while the wearable revolution is here, we still have to wait for the right gadgets to appear that combine the many existing trackers into one. As if to underscore this, a recent study concluded that one-third of wearable device owners a stopped using them within six months.

Dr. Kamal Jethwani from the Center for Connected Health in Boston believes that the goal should not be to make people wear a activity tracker for a whole year, but to wear it when it is meaningful. There will be unintended consequences in the future with wearable devices, but this future can be human centric if we, at the level of the whole society, focus on the real potentials and risks. This is a discussion we all have to initiate now.

Score of availability: 5

Focus of attention: Patients

Websites & other online resources: Crunchwear (http://www.crunchwear.com/)

Companies & start-ups: MC10 (http://www.mc10inc.com/), Equivital (http://www.equivital.co.uk/), Scanadu (https://www.scanadu.com/)

Books: Sensor Technologies: Healthcare, Wellness and Environmental Applications by McGrath & Scanaill

Movies: Minority Report (2002), The Avengers (2012)

Trend 10. The Medical Tricorder and Portable Diagnostics

There was an imaginary device called the medical tricorder on the 1960s television show "Star Trek." Used by Dr. Leonard McCoy, it instantly diagnosed an infinite number of medical conditions. A detachable, high-resolution, hand-held scanner sends life-sign information to the tricorder itself, which can check all organ functions and detect the presence of dangerous organisms. An additional feature not relevant to the mission of this book is its data banks on non-human species that make it possible to treat other life-forms as well.

For decades the tricorder has been an element of science fiction, but it seemed it might be reality soon when the Qualcomm Tricorder X Prize was announced in 2012, promising to award $10 million to the first team to build a medical tricorder. Over 230 teams from 30 countries entered the competition. The prize guidelines require that the device should diagnose 15 different medical conditions ranging from sore throat, sleep apnea, to colon cancer across 30 people in 3 days through a consumer friendly interface.

Nowadays, we are getting closer to the tricorder becoming an everyday item. As our smartphones become increasingly small, handheld medical laboratories it seems we do not have to look much further. With over one billion smartphones and 3 billion mobile phones worldwide, they have begun to play an important role in determining how we communicate, shop, or find new contacts. Almost all medical issues have a relevant smartphone application, and the number is still growing.

An estimated 500 million smartphone users, including medical professionals, consumers, and patients, will be using a healthcare-related application by 2015. Half of the more than 3.4 billion smartphone and tablet users will have downloaded mobile health applications by 2018.

The potential medical use of such smartphone applications and devices is clearly described by a story about Dr. Eric Topol, chief academic officer of Scripps Health, who was on a flight from Washington, DC to San Diego when the pilot asked whether there was a doctor on board. A passenger had severe chest pains. Topol put his iPhone into the AliveCor ECG bracket, performed an ECG and concluded that the patient was probably having a heart attack. An emergency landing followed and the patient survived.

According to Dr. Topol, the smartphone will be the hub of the future of medicine serving as a health-medical dashboard. He is famous for saying that

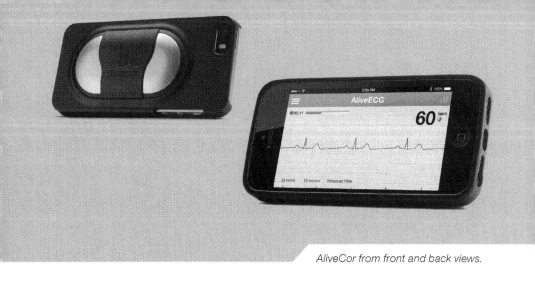

AliveCor from front and back views.

these days he prescribes a lot more applications than medications to his patients.

The founder and Chief Medical Officer of the company behind AliveCor is Dr. David E. Albert whom I met at the NASA Research Park in Moffett Field, California in 2013. Since then, I have been teaching medical students to use AliveCor and other portable devices in practice. Dr. Albert told me the device has been used more than a dozen times in–flight to make diagnoses from myocardial infarction to atrial fibrillation.

"Many arrhythmias have been captured by patients. Atrioventricular Nodal Reentry Tachycardia (AVNRT) in a young man who had a Fontan procedure at birth is one example where two 2–week Holter studies did not find anything. Six months after carrying our device, the young man had AVNRT at 250 beats per minute and was converted with adenosine at an emergency room with a definitive diagnosis. Probably as important are all the episodes of non–arrhythmias which are confirmed by a physician remotely and enable the prevention of an expensive emergency room visit."

The product's global roll to many markets with the same type of professional services that they have in the US could be a next step. As proof, they recently announced the integration of ECG data into Practice Fusion. Further integration of such portable diagnostic devices into EMRs is expected soon.

Another example is the iBGStar, the first blood glucose meter that can be connected to the iPhone and iPod. It is supported by an iOS application and measures blood glucose levels simply by inserting a test strip into the device, which is connected to the iPhone or iPod.

Clinical laboratory and radiology at home

Complicated methods for identifying microbes or measuring biomarkers have been the domain of laboratories equipped with expensive machines. Now this is moving to our homes. Biomeme designed a small, low–cost device that allows smartphone users with minimal laboratory skills to detect numerous diseases by replicating DNA. This is now only available in laboratories worldwide through expensive qPCR (quantitative polymerase chain reaction) machines that can amplify and quantify a DNA molecule.

An "optical lab on a chip" developed by researchers at UCLA measures 170,000 different molecules from cancer markers to insulin levels by using changes in light intensity. Only 7.5 cm high and weighing 60 grams, the device is able to detect viruses and single layer proteins down to 3 nanometers of size.

One of the largest European "lab on a chip" initiatives included thirteen partner institutions from eight countries. Its mission was to develop a portable laboratory that could deliver fast, low–cost, and reliable diagnostics. The project is called Labonfoil and received €5.3 billion in research funding from the European Union. The portable lab uses three 'smart cards' and a reader for analyzing the data, which can then be forwarded wirelessly to a computer, tablet, or smartphone.

With a few drops of blood, the first card can identify a specific protein whose presence is known to increase when cancer recurs. The second smart card can detect pathogens such as bacteria and viruses in food. The third card analyses phytoplankton concentrations in a sample of sea water.

A smart card of Labonfoil.

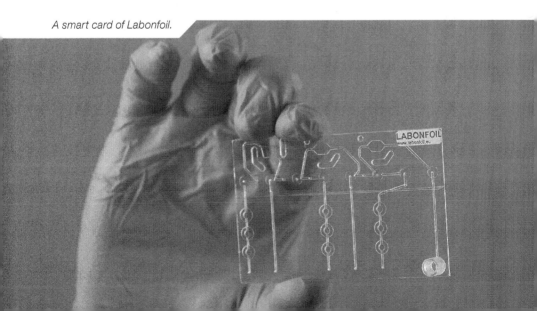

Northeastern University professor, Tania Konry, developed a small portable instrument called ScanDrop that can detect a variety of biological specimens. It contains a chip made of polymer or glass connected to equally tiny tubes. The extremely small–volume liquid sample such as water or biological fluid interacts with microscopic beads that in turn react with the lab test's search parameters including antibodies or cancer biomarkers.

If the device is clinically approved it might make it possible for lay people to carry out simple diagnostic procedures at home using their own smartphone. A smartphone application developed by University of Cambridge researchers turns a smartphone into a portable medical diagnostic device using colorimetric tests. After testing urine, saliva or other bodily fluid samples with a colorimetric test, the patient can take a photo of the test strip with the smartphone's camera and the Colorimetrix app analyzes the results by comparing them with pre–recorded calibration data.

Bringing radiology devices to patients' homes would likewise have clear benefits. About 60% of the world did not have access to ultrasound when the MobiUS SP1 was announced. It is an ultrasound device that can be used with a smartphone. Images are shared wirelessly, it has a storage capacity of 8GB, and it is portable and easy–to–use.

A cardiac intervention that uses MRI and CT machines to scan a patient's heart, create a model via 3D printing, and make a metallic mesh sleeve that can be implanted in the patient's chest was recently developed. This can be paired with a smartphone providing real–time and constant information about the heart and its health.

Evidence–based and customized Mobile Health

The number of medical mobile applications has been rising for years, although persuading users to keep using the apps is a challenge. The question is not whether such applications could be used in the practice of medicine or delivery of healthcare, but which ones and to what extent can be useful. Evidence based background is needed for implementing mobile apps in the clinical settings. In 2013, the FDA finally issued guidance that might facilitate the process, and encourages the development of mobile medical apps "that improve health care and provide consumers and health care professionals with valuable health information." Additionally, the FDA has a public health responsibility to ensure and oversee the safety and effectiveness of medical

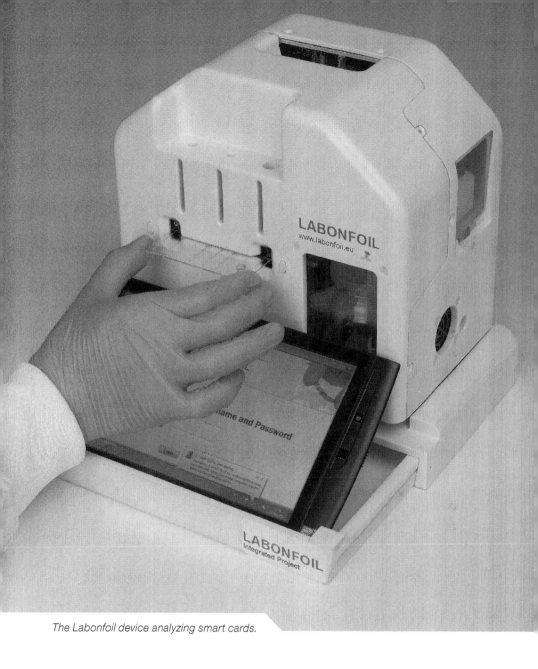

The Labonfoil device analyzing smart cards.

devices, which now include medical smartphone applications as well.

The first prescribed mobile application with health implications that is reimbursed by health insurance was launched in 2014. The Caterna Vision Therapy application is reimbursed by a German health insurance with 8.65 million Germans insured in partnership with a nationwide association of eye care centers. Since the 1st of April 2014, eye specialists have been prescribing it to patients.

pApp on different platforms.

A growing problem is that patients and doctors find it harder and harder to choose the right app for their health management or work. Doing a search for a medical condition or specialty yields a long list of applications from which it is extremely hard to choose quality ones. Patients and caregivers can become better at that in the same way they learned to assess the quality of books, then websites. But it takes time. Regulation of medical apps that does not limit their capabilities would have benefits for all stakeholders.

Customized mobile apps such as the pApp could address this issue by letting doctors create mobile apps for their patients without knowing anything about mobile app development. They choose what functions (so-called bundles) the app should have, and the patient can download the app right away.

In the future as smartphones and tablets become common modalities, they will be equipped with display screens that can be rolled up like a scroll or folded like a wallet, making the devices easy to carry around. In-built projectors, seamless voice control, 3D screens, and holograms might represent the future of smartphones.

One possible direction might be the integration of health devices into smartphones instead of downloading apps on them. Apple introduced the iOS8 operating system and new devices that can measure basic health parameters. It is rumored that Apple is moving into the field of medicine with big announcements coming in 2014. These rumors mostly focus on a smartwatch that could monitor several health parameters from body temperature to pulse through a user interface that Apple usually designs. Similar to the case of the first iPhone, it could break the barriers for wider adoption of mobile health tracking.

There might be a time when clinical laboratories will vanish and be replaced by small, handheld, medically efficient devices that anyone can use without prior training. Measuring health and blood parameters could become a common and cheap process for even laypeople.

Score of availability: 7

Focus of attention: Patients and medical professionals

Websites & other online resources: Qualcomm Xprize (http://www.qualcommtricorderxprize.org/), iMedicalApps (http://www.imedicalapps.com/)

Companies & start–ups: Happtique (http://www.happtique.com/), AliceCor (http://www.alivecor.com/)

Books: The Next Web of 50 Billion Devices: Mobile Internet's Past, Present and Future by Ahmad

Movies: Star Trek (TV series)

Trend 11. Growing Organs in a Dish

In 2013, a survey of more than 2000 US adults by the Pew Research Center provided a picture of how people think about living much longer lives. Surprisingly, 60% of responders do not want to live past 90, and 30% do not want to live past 80. A slight majority said that if new medical treatments slowed the aging process and allowed the average person to live to at least 120; it would be "a bad thing for society". The more a person associates medical treatment with higher quality of life and the more one associates longevity with productivity, the more they favor life extension. The reason behind the survey results probably lies in the perception that aging is a devastating process and people cannot yet think clearly about the potentials of regenerative medicine to improve the quality of life.

When it becomes possible to grow new organs and replace old ones, rejuvenate the whole body or cure diseases with stem cell therapy, this perception is likely to dramatically change. Being able to help patients with chronic organ failure and solve the shortage of donor organs is something that scientists in regenerative medicine are all striving for. Regenerative medicine is an emerging field that has the potential to revolutionize several types of treatments from heart disease to neurodegenerative disorders; eradicate the organ donor shortage problem; and completely restore damaged tissues such as muscles, or tendons.

After watching Professor Anthony Atala's fascinating talk at TEDMED in 2009 about how his state-of-the-art lab grows human organs from muscles and blood vessels to bladders, I knew I had to talk with him to get the latest updates about this field. Professor Atala is the editor of several peer-reviewed journals and the leader of teams that focus on innovative topics from nanotechnology to growing human tissues. He is the Director of the Institute for Regenerative Medicine at Wake Forest Baptist Medical Center, has led US national professional and government committees, has ten clinical applications of technologies that were developed in his laboratory, has edited thirteen books, published more than 300 articles, applied for or received over 200 national and international patents; and is also a practicing surgeon. There is not enough room to list all his achievements.

He shared with me how he regards new treatments and technologies, and the patient-physician interaction:

"Obviously, our goal as physicians is to heal. But all physicians have been the position where everything available to us is still not enough to help the patient. I direct a team of more than 300 scientists working to develop new technologies – namely cell therapies and replacement tissues and organs – to fill some of this void. Many people say what we're doing sounds like science fiction. But all of these technologies are actually based on the body's innate ability to heal itself.

As "high–tech" as these treatments are, I do not believe they create distance between physicians and patients. Instead, they serve to deepen the bond. Being able to offer a patient a new treatment strengthens the physician–patient relationship. After all, hope of getting better is the reason they first put their trust in us."

He thinks a key to solving medical and scientific problems that seem futuristic now is the "need" as the driving force behind innovation that can lead to new treatments. Scientists and physicians should constantly ask themselves whether there is a better way to do this or how they can solve this problem.

The 3D printer at work on a kidney scaffold.

A bladder scaffold being seeded with cells.

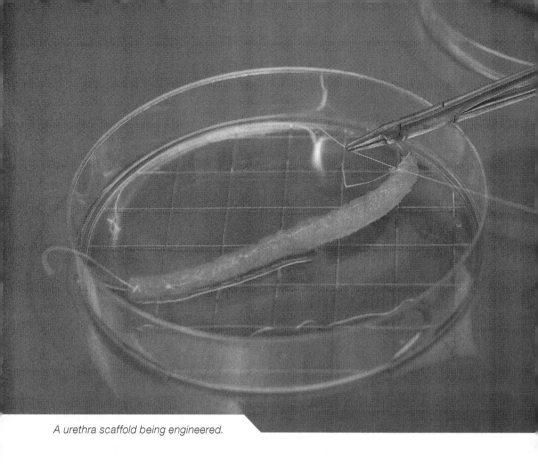

A urethra scaffold being engineered.

"Perseverance is also the key. If it does not work the first time, we need to try a different approach. Of course, there are many practical considerations involved in taking a new treatment from idea to reality, including the cost to develop and test new therapies, regulatory pathways and the ability to commercialize and make them widely available. But to me, the desire to solve problems and the drive to keep at it are at the heart of finding solutions."

Their goal at the institute is simply to develop new treatments to improve the lives of patients, although Professor Atala thinks it is best not to have pre-conceived notions about future directions, because that way they remain open to possibilities that their work uncovers. For example, maybe the entire kidney does not have to be replaced in patients with kidney failure. Researchers should not be wedded to that goal while ignoring other possibilities. Their focus is on the final goal of making the patient feel better, not on a particular way of making that happen.

As regenerative medicine is still a relatively new field of science, scientific progress alone will not drive the field forward. Manufacturing challenges and regulatory hurdles will also need to be successfully addressed.

In the 1980s Professor Robert Langer at MIT and surgeon Jay had the idea of combining 3D synthetic polymer scaffolds with cells in order to create new tissues and organs. While they were met with great skepticism

Some scaffolds and organ prototypes that were printed with a 3D printer.

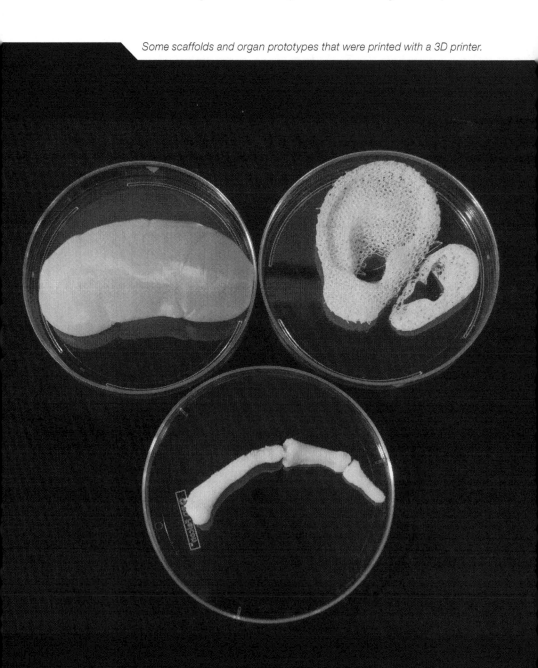

and it was difficult to secure government funds, they managed to license the patents to companies, which provided them with funding for additional research. The idea has since become a cornerstone of tissue engineering and regenerative medicine, resulting in the creation of artificial skin for burn victims and, hopefully soon, whole organs. Professor Langer is known all over the world as a pioneer in the field of tissue engineering.

His research led to the invention of biodegradable polymer that could be placed inside a cancerous growth to deliver regular doses of medication to the target site, thus creating a safer and more effective process than typical chemotherapy. His three-dimensional polymer scaffolds have also been used by scientists to grow human cells in various configurations. A famous example is an ear grown in the lab.

At various stages of his scientific career he opted to face challenges that seemed impossible and about which the research community was skeptical. He and his team currently have many patents and FDA-approved products. When I asked him about the key for solving medical/scientific problems that seem too futuristic now, his response was direct and on the spot: "Believing that you can."

Total biocompatibility of implanted materials, the prevention of rejection by the host, and successful vascularization and innervation of implants are important areas to develop. There is work to be done.

The world of stem cells

Most adult stem cells are able to differentiate into only a limited number of specialized cell types, while embryonic stem cells (ESCs) are pluripotent meaning that such cells can differentiate into any cell types. The research around ESCs has bumped into ethical concerns as the derivation of ESCs requires the destruction of a blastocyst, an early-stage embryo that some people consider to be a viable form of life. Despite this, this area of science could make significant advances in the future years.

Stem cell research was revolutionized in 2006 when Dr. Shinya Yamanaka invented induced pluripotent stem cells ("iPS). These cells can then be rebooted to the so-called "stage zero" of life that is similar to their state after fertilization. Therefore, these stem cells are genetically reprogrammed to behave like embryonic stem cells and can be transformed into new tissues or organs. The first clinical trials are now using iPS cells to cure age-related macular degeneration by reconstituting retinas and improving eyesight. If results are promising, it might soon be possible to be cured of Alzheimer's disease or cancer.

Researchers in Singapore developed a process whereby it is possible to derive adult stem cells from small samples of blood for stem cell reprogramming rather than using current invasive methods of obtaining bone marrow. Reprogrammed stem cells were transformed into human heart muscle cells that were even rhythmically beating.

Policy makers have substantial responsibility given that there are more and more stem cell clinics falsely claiming to offer safe and effective therapies for illnesses ranging from cardiovascular to Parkinson's disease.

In 2013, a University College London team made a new nose for a British man who lost his to cancer. Stem cells were obtained from the patient's fat tissue and grown in the lab for two weeks before being used to cover the nose scaffold. The new nose was implanted into the man's forearm so skin would grow over it. It is one of the several labs worldwide that are working on the futuristic idea of growing custom-made organs in the laboratory settings. So far, they have been able to make tear ducts, blood vessels, and windpipes, but researchers are optimistic that they can soon make more types of transplantable body parts. According to the team, it is like making a cake but using a different kind of oven.

University of Edinburgh researchers announced in 2014 that cells taken from humans were reprogrammed into stem cells and then grown into Type O red blood cells. It was the first time blood has been manufactured to appropriate quality and safety standards for transfusion into a human being. It might open the way to artificial blood soon.

In 2014 scientists succeeded in regenerating a living organ, the thymus, which produces immune cells. If the technique proves to be safe, it could pave the way for new therapies for people with damaged immune systems and genetic conditions affecting thymus development. Moreover, University of Cambridge researchers were able to identify ways to speed up the cellular processes by which human nerve cells mature. Functional nerve cells could be generated from skin cells and show the same functional characteristics as mature cells found in the body.

The ultimate goal is to grow new organs by printing them out in 3D in a fast, efficient, and safe way. A group named OxSyBio aims at developing 3D printing techniques to produce tissue-like synthetic materials for wound healing, drug delivery, organ repair and replacement. The technique they developed allows them to 3D print synthetic tissue–like materials from thousands of tiny water droplets each coated with a thin film mimicking a living cell's external membrane.

Although it seems most people do not want to live past 90 or 100 years, they will soon have to face that opportunity due to the rapid advances of regenerative medicine.

Score of availability: 3
Focus of attention: Researchers
Websites & other online resources: Centre for Regenerative Medicine (http://www.crm.ed.ac.uk/about/what–regenerative–medicine), Wake Forest Institute for Regenerative Medicine (http://www.wakehealth.edu/WFIRM/)
Companies & start–ups: Organovo (http://www.organovo.com/)
Books: Principles of Regenerative Medicine by Atala, Lanza, Thomson & Nerem; Regenerative Medicine Applications in Organ Transplantation by Orlando
Movies: Terra Incognita: The Perils and Promise of Stem Cell Research (2007)

Trend 12. Do–It–Yourself Biotechnology

One of the most inspiring stories in science and biotechnology recently belongs to Jack Andraka. I met him in the Netherlands and in California, as we both gave speeches at the same events. Imagine a young teenager sitting in the cafeteria focusing on his upcoming speech but being kind to the many people who approach him only to say hello. He told me he had been interested in biosensing and learning about ways to detect environmental contaminants until the age of 13 when a close family friend who was like an uncle to him, passed away from pancreatic cancer.

He was confused, sad, and did not even know what a pancreas was, much less what pancreatic cancer was. He decided to turn to our era's simplest information resource, the Internet, to figure things out. His parents used to go to the library to do research and they told him of horror stories of spending hours looking in the card catalog and tracing down books only to find them missing from the collection.

He agrees with me that technology does connect us more now, and he was able to teach himself a lot because of the Internet, starting with Wikipedia, reading the bibliography and then the articles in those entries he was interested in. He printed out papers to read later in bed. He was taking a high school introduction to biology class in 8th grade when he had an epiphany moment:

"I was reading a paper on single walled carbon nanotubes while I was half listening to my teacher talk about antibodies. Suddenly I had an idea! What if I combined what I was reading about (nanotubes) with what I was supposed to be learning about (antibodies) and created a sensor to detect pancreatic cancer?"

Obviously, it was not that simple and he had lots more work to do, but thanks to modern technology he was able to learn what is needed to develop an experimental design. His mother told him a lab was definitely needed given that his design looked a lot more complicated than his previous experiments. He sent out many e–mails and got many rejections, which helped him learn to write better and more interesting messages. Finally, he got a chance to work under Anirban Maitra, Professor of Pathology at Johns Hopkins School of Medicine who was a huge inspiration to him.

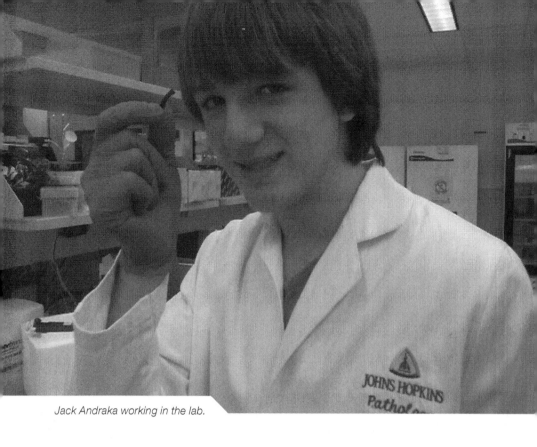

Jack Andraka working in the lab.

According to Andraka, the pancreatic cancer test he designed is 168 times faster, 1/26,000 as expensive (costing around three cents), and over 400 times more sensitive than the current diagnostic tests, and takes only five minutes to run. As a result, he won the 2012 Gordon E. Moore Award, the grand prize of the Intel International Science and Engineering Fair.

The method he worked out is truly innovative but has not been published yet in peer reviewed journals. Andraka discussed it with me saying that he was mostly concerned about seeing if the project would work; and after talking with his mentor and other high ranking scientists, he has learned that more work is needed before publication. Still, he cannot wait to move the project forward so the knowledge can help people. Currently, he is in talks with biotechnology companies to take over the work and further develop it.

He became an example for thousands of kids globally who have amazing ideas in science and medicine but do not want to go through the traditional (and slow) steps required. Instead, they try to find a solution right now by using all the connected opportunities they can find. Andraka answers questions from kids every day through e-mail and Skype and told me he loves the energy, optimism, and excitement they bring to science and math. It is a great time to be a kid with big ideas because they are able to learn so much quickly and connect with one another and with experts easily. Mostly he tells them that if a 15 year old who did not even know what a pancreas was could create a sensor to detect cancer, just imagine what they can do.

He thinks it is important to keep raising awareness for more funding for research and to keep pushing for open access to scientific journals so that citizen scientists can learn and help innovate. After finishing high school, he hopes to attend a university and be able to continue researching and learning.

With fellow student Chloe Diggs, he recently took the $50,000 first prize in the Siemens "We Can Change the World Challenge" by developing a credit card–sized biosensor that can detect six environmental contaminants: mercury, lead, cadmium, copper, glyphosate, and atrazine. The idea came after learning about water pollution in a high school environmental science class. It costs $1 to make and takes 20 minutes to run, making it 200,000 times cheaper and 25 times more efficient than comparable sensors.

Jack Andraka meeting Barack Obama, President of the US.

He is the perfect example how young scientists and science wannabes have the potential to contribute to research by simply having access to online databases, scientific information, and methods, as well as being open to innovation.

In a final example, and hopefully there will be more and more of these, Nathan Han won the Intel Science Fair in 2014 by developing an algorithm that is 81% accurate in identifying breast cancer-causing mutations, while the accuracy rate of existing algorithms is about 40%. The 15-year-old from Boston, US has been fascinated with bioinformatics, and chose to work out a new software for the mutation analysis of BRCA1, one of the most studied genes in the human genome, when a close friend's mother was diagnosed with ovarian cancer.

Biotechnology labs in the community

The first labs of the so-called Do-It-Yourself Biology community, a grassroots movement which was initiated to let students and others interested in biotechnology use professional laboratory equipment for their experiments, was launched in 2008. These enthusiasts seek to popularize biotechnology in the way that programmers popularized computing from their garages in the 1970s. Along with equipment, these labs provide a wellspring of biotech outreach and education. Local groups of DIY BIO are available from the US and Europe to Asia and Oceania.

BioCurious, a hackerspace for biotech, opened in 2011 with the mission statement that innovations in biology should be accessible, affordable, and open to everyone. They are building a community biology lab for amateurs, inventors, entrepreneurs, and anyone who wants to experiment with friends. They provide a complete working laboratory and technical library; equipment from fluorescent microscopes to PCR machines; materials; co-working space; and a training center for biotechniques. It was the first community biotech lab to crowdfund its start-up costs, the first to build a bioprinter, the first to sprout a company that Kickstarted almost half a million dollars. They are said to struggle with funding now, however.

The first time I came across The International Genetically Engineered Machine (iGEM) competition was when students working in the lab where I did my PhD decided to compete with one of their ideas. I learned that the Foundation behind iGEM is dedicated to education and competition, advancement of synthetic biology, and the development of open community and collaboration. It spun out of MIT in 2012 thus becoming an independent nonprofit organization

The logo of diybio.org..

located in Cambridge, Massachusetts. It began in January 2003 with a month–long course at MIT where students designed biological systems to make cells blink. It later grew to a summer competition with 5 teams in 2004, 13 teams in 2005, and gradually to 245 teams in 2012 and 2013.

Student teams are given a kit of biological parts at the beginning of the summer from the Registry of Standard Biological Parts. Working at their own schools, they use these parts and those of their own design to build biological systems and operate them in living cells. The project design and competition format provided an exceptionally motivating and effective teaching method. Students have created a rainbow of pigmented bacteria; an arsenic biodetector that responds to a range of arsenic concentrations in order to help under-developed countries detect arsenic contamination in water. They also developed BactoBlood, a cost-effective red blood cell substitute constructed from engineered bacteria. The system is designed to safely transport oxygen in the bloodstream without inducing sepsis, and to be stored for prolonged periods in a freeze-dried state. There is no limit to the teams' creativity.

Such community labs give youngsters interested in biotechnology and scientist wannabes a chance to test their ideas, conduct research, and get it to the final stage by making the results commercially available. This is the scenario that should be globally available to everyone with a good idea.

Biotech startups revolutionizing medicine

Elizabeth Holmes founded a company, Theranos, with her tuition money after dropping out of Stanford. The company develops a radical blood-testing service that requires only a pinprick and a drop of blood to perform hundreds of lab tests from standard cholesterol checks to sophisticated genetic analyses. This way, the results can be faster, more accurate, and cheaper than conventional methods. A motivation behind launching the company was her fear of needles, the only thing that actually scared her. Imagine how much more information such a test could provide if results would be better visualized and more informative. The same kind of data can be interpreted in different ways today due to the lack of quality in data visualizations.

Nanobiosym is dedicated to creating a new science that emerges from the holistic integration of physics, biomedicine, and nanotechnology. Examples include a portable nanotechnology platform that can rapidly and accurately detect genetic fingerprints from any biological organism, thus empowering people worldwide with rapid, affordable, and portable diagnostic information about their own health. The Cambridge, Massachusetts based company claims to have a diagnostic test that can detect the presence or absence of a disease's pathogen within an hour.

A company called uBiome is a microbiome sequencing service that provides information and tools for exploring microbiomes of customers who buy the service online. Based on research conducted the Human Microbiome Project, the company performs large-scale microbiome studies. Knowing the genomic background of our microbiome combined with our own genome and health information could yield a new way of identifying diseases and prescribing therapies.

Additionally, several recent studies focused on changing the basics of biology and taking biotechnology to the next level. Our DNA consists of 4 letters called nucleotides. In 2014, synthetic biologists at the Scripps Research Institute in La Jolla, California created cells with an expanded genetic alphabet that included two more letters, opening the door to a huge range of novel molecules. They have spent 15 years developing this new DNA whose sequences spell out instructions for making proteins. The next step is to determine whether cells can also transcribe the unnatural base pairs into RNA, and, ultimately, use them to make proteins.

At the same time, Autodesk, the design and engineering software company in California, created a synthetic bacteriophage, or virus, and then 3D printed the result. According to Andrew Hessel, an expert in this field, there is now the possibility that anyone can write software for living things with bio-code known as DNA. Completing the project took two weeks and about $1,000 compared to the multi-billion dollar efforts in the history of genomics.

Biotechnology has been one of the most promising areas of research in medicine, and it has not even shown its true potential. Re-thinking the basics of biology might have unknown consequences which we are not prepared for. The biotech industry has also been a key target for investors in the past couple of years, and it still could not take its deserved position, even though it has the potential to significantly change the way medicine is practiced through new solutions and by iterating the basics of biology.

Score of availability: 5
Focus of attention: Researchers
Websites & other online resources: iGEM (http://igem.org/), DIYBio (http://diybio.org/), BioCurious (http://biocurious.org/)
Companies & start-ups: Theranos (http://www.theranos.com/), Nanobiosym (http://www.nanobiosym.com/), uBiome (http://ubiome.com/)
Books: Culturing Life by Landecker, A Life Decoded by Venter; Life at the Speed of Light by Venter
Movies: Jurassic Park (1993)

Trend 13. The 3D Printing Revolution

A 14–month–old baby in the US had so many heart defects that it made the upcoming operation difficult. To better prepare in detail, hospital officials at Kosair Children's Hospital in Louisville, Kentucky contacted the J.B. Speed School of Engineering, where a polymer model of the baby's heart was created with a 3D printer. This provided vital insight ahead of surgery. Once the cardiothoracic surgeon had a model he knew exactly what he needed to do. The model allowed him to reduce the number of exploratory incisions and the overall operating time. This is just one example of how 3D printers could assist medical professionals.

3D printing fashions a three–dimensional object from a digital model by laying down successive layers of various materials. 3D printing could contribute to regenerative medicine, replacement surgery, operation planning, and many more ideas presented in this chapter.

Kaiba Gionfriddo was born prematurely in 2011. After 8 months his lung development caused concerns, although he was sent home with his parents as his breathing was normal. Six weeks later, Kaiba stopped breathing and turned blue. He was diagnosed with tracheobronchomalacia, a long Latin word that means his windpipe was so weak that it collapsed. He had a tracheostomy and was put on a ventilator––the conventional treatment. Still, Kaiba would stop breathing almost daily. His heart would stop, too. His caregivers 3D printed a bioresorbable device that instantly helped Kaiba breathe. This case is considered a prime example of how customized 3D printing is transforming healthcare as we know it.

In 2013 I spoke at Futuremed, which was organized by Singularity University. There I encountered 3D printing in person. I held a 3D–printed human jaw in my hands that had been printed out based on a patient's radiology scan.

Increasingly more objects can be made with 3D printers, and the biotechnology industry is keenly aware of the potential of this technology. Printing medical devices, living tissues, then eventually cells and pharmaceuticals might not be far away from everyday use. Parts such as bionic ears and simple organs might be printed at the patient's bedside, while printing transplantable human organs could eradicate waiting lists. Technological issues such as lack of available models or blueprints will be solved through crowdsourced and open–access databases from communities of designers.

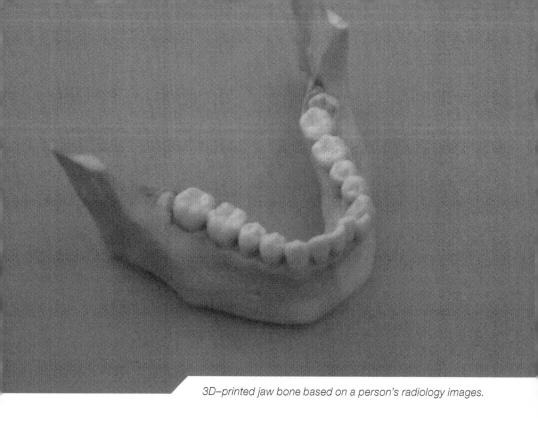

3D–printed jaw bone based on a person's radiology images.

3D printing to go mainstream

I've been following the articles of Michael Molitch–Hou for years. He's a Senior Writer at 3D Printing. He was one of the first experts I contacted to ask about this rapidly evolving industry.

"What I believe has really driven the 3D printing boom so far, though, is the open source movement around 3D printing that resulted from the expiration of important patents. Though Adrian Bowyer in the UK and Hod Lipson in the US were working on their open source 3D printers before the expiration of a key fused deposition modeling (FDM) patent owned by Scott Crump, inventor of FDM and founder of Stratasys, in 2009, it wasn't until after this patent expired that the movement exploded, fueling the entire 3D printing industry.

Once DIYers were making and, eventually commercializing their own 3D printers, they started to spread. They were way cheaper than any large manufacturer would have allowed and people could buy them in *kits and assemble their own for around $1,000 or so. Then, the media caught wind of it and, years later, you're writing a book that discusses how it impacts medicine."*

Therefore Molitch–Hou believes there needs to be a significant change in patent laws before the 3D printing industry can really take off. Imagine what would happen if pharmaceutical companies made the formulas for their drugs open source and publicly available, thereby allowing amateur scientists to synthesize medications, or small manufacturers to produce generic drugs at a fraction of the regular cost. If companies such as Organovo decided to release their designs as open source, than it might be possible for amateurs to 3D–print human tissues.

Aside from 3D–printed organs, he anticipates large, fast, multimaterial 3D printers to be invented soon. It could look like a single, robotic arm the size of a medium–sized construction vehicle. Or it could be an enormous gantry system able to extrude multiple materials. Molitch–Hou would also love to see electronic components entirely printed by 3D. If this were possible along with making 3D–printed metal components, we might be able to design a fully self–replicating 3D printer. The RepRap project was meant to explore possible designs for such a device. A preliminary study has already shown that using RepRaps to print common products results in economic savings.

The holy grail of 3D printing is printing molecules. If it were possible to determine the molecular makeup of an object and program it into the printer, we could produce endless copies of a living entity. Most likely we are not yet ready for that kind of development.

3D printing has grown from niche manufacturing to a $2.7 billion industry. As one of the key players of this new market, Organovo has over $24 million in equity precisely in order to attempt the manufacture of biomaterials and even artificial organs. Mike Renard in Commercial Operations spoke to me about their plans.

"We are working to provide better testing models for drug scientists with the goal to produce better and safer new medicines, at a lower total cost to develop. There are many stories of drugs failing too late in the discovery process, costing hundreds of millions of dollars with nothing to show for the effort. Moreover, there are examples of drugs that get to market, only to be recalled or restricted in their use because of life threatening complications for certain patients.

This area of science has great potential to be improved. Further, 18 people die each day in the US waiting for a possible life saving/extending tissue transplant. Other people live with a variety of chronic conditions due to various system failures, degenerative processes and metabolic deficiencies. The demand for functional tissue as a therapy alternative far exceeds the supply that will ever be available through current donor programs."

Printing living tissue compared to inanimate 3–dimensional objects is an enormous step even if technical improvements increasingly promise to make it a reality. Tissues in nature are three dimensional. They have defined architectures and repeating patterns. And they are made up of different cell types whose arrangement is critical to proper tissue function, as well as overall health of the system. 2D cell cultures and single cell lines are not capable of reproducing this complex native biology.

The Novogen MMX Bioprinter® prints fully human, architecturally correct 3D tissue in a variety of different formats, in this particular case into multi–well plates. Bio–ink or hydrogel can be dispensed from each of two print heads.

Left: A histological stain of bioprinted human liver tissue showing hepatocytes, hepatic stellate, and endothelial cells in an organized structure with the cell density and tight junctions of that found in native tissue. Right: Bioprinted human liver tissue in 3 dimensions.

Areas where printed living tissues could be used are expanding fast. One promising area is to create diseased tissues for research purposes. Having life–like disease models outside the body that behave like disease inside the body opens entirely new research avenues into the mechanisms of disease. These potential discoveries may fundamentally change how we target and design treatments, and how treatments may someday be personalized to an individual's phenotypic expression of a specific disease.

3D printing everything

The list of objects that have been successfully printed demonstrates the potential this technology holds for the near future.

Tissues with blood vessels: Researchers at Harvard University were the first to use a custom–built 3D printer and a dissolving ink to create a swatch of tissue that contains skin cells interwoven with structural material interwoven that can potentially function as blood vessels.

Low–Cost Prosthetic Parts: Creating traditional prosthetics is very time–consuming and destructive, which means that any modifications would destroy the original molds. Researchers at the University of Toronto, in collaboration with Autodesk Research and CBM Canada, used 3D printing to quickly produce cheap and easily customizable prosthetic sockets for patients in the developing world. Basically, they scan a damaged limb using Xbox Kinect, design the parts digitally, and then send the model to the printer which manufactures the socket in a few hours using polylactic acid, a thermoplastic that is easily modifiable with heat. The cost with this method is under $10. If we merge 3D printing with open source templates that anyone can manufacture, distribute, and modify, then a new era of cheaper prosthetics for amputees around the world could begin.

Drugs: Lee Cronin, a chemist at the University of Glasgow, wants to do for the discovery and distribution of prescription drugs what Apple did for music. In a TED talk he described a prototype 3D printer capable of assembling chemical compounds at the molecular level. Patients would go to an online drugstore with their digital prescription, buy the blueprint and the chemical ink needed, and then print the drug at home. In the future he said we might sell not drugs but rather blueprints or apps. While this could make prescription drug distribution more efficient, a danger is that unscrupulous people will steal the designs and raw supplies in order to print out whatever drugs they want at home. This could become a regulatory nightmare, far worse than printing out guns. It will also restructure the pharmaceutical industry and biotechnology as we know it.

Tailor—made sensors: Researchers have used scans of animal hearts to create printed models, and then added stretchy electronics on top of those models. The material can be peeled off the printed model and wrapped around the real heart for a perfect fit. The next step is to enhance the electronics with multiple sensors. This demonstrates the promise of a new kind of personalized heart sensor.

Bone: Professor Susmita Bose of Washington State University modified a 3D printer to bind chemicals to a ceramic powder creating intricate ceramic scaffolds that promote the growth of the bone in any shape.

Heart Valve: Jonathan Butcher of Cornell University has printed a heart valve that will soon be tested in sheep. He used a combination of cells and biomaterials to control the valve's stiffness.

Ear cartilage: Lawrence Bonassar of Cornell University used 3D photos of human ears to create ear molds. The molds were then filled with a gel containing bovine cartilage cells suspended in collagen, which held the shape of the ear while cells grew their extracellular matrix.

Medical equipment: A clinic in Bolivia 140 kilometers from the nearest city prints out splints and prostheses when supplies are low. The cost per piece runs about 2 cents for the plastic. This might allow developing nations to circumvent having to import large numbers of supplies. Already, 3D printing is occurring in underdeveloped areas. "Not Impossible Labs" based in Venice, California took 3D printers to Sudan where the chaos of war has left many people with amputated limbs. The organization's founder, Mick Ebeling, trained locals how to operate the machinery, create patient–specific limbs, and fit these new, very inexpensive prosthetics.

Tamperproof cable tether: Biomedical technician Steven Jaworski at Brookhaven Memorial Hospital designed a cable tether that holds together huge amount of wires and printed it out 3D using Makerbot, saving the hospital considerable money.

Cranium Replacement: Dutch surgeons replaced the entire top of a 22 year–old woman's skull with a customized printed implant made from plastic.

Tumor Models: Researchers in China and the US have both printed models of cancerous tumors to aid discovery of new anti–cancer drugs and to better understand how tumors develop, grow, and spread.

Eye: Fripp Design and Research in the United Kingdom aims to print out 150 prosthetic eyes in an hour. Mass production not only promised to speed up the manufacture of eye prostheses, but also significantly lower the costs. Additionally, customers can choose the color of the prosthesis.

Synthetic skin: James Yoo at the Wake Forest School of Medicine in the US has developed a printer that can print skin straight onto the wounds of burn victims.

Organs: Organovo announced in 2013 that their bioprinted liver assays were able to function for more than 40 days. Organovo's top executives and other industry experts suggest that within a decade we will be able to print solid organs such as liver, heart, and kidney. Hundreds of thousands of people worldwide are waiting for an organ donor. Imagine how such a technology could transform their lives.

To illustrate the big picture Molitch–Hou shared with me the story of Liam, a US child born with amniotic band syndrome. This results in only the partial formation of the fingers. Meanwhile, in South Africa, a woodworker named Richard Van As had his fingers severed in a woodworking accident. Both faced the costs of modern prosthetics, which for Richard might be $10,000 for a finger alone.

Elsewhere, an automation technician named Ivan Owen posted a YouTube video of a mechanical hand prop he had made for Halloween. Richard came across the video and subsequently asked if Ivan could construct a prosthetic arm with fingers for him. Living on opposite sides of the globe they communicated by Skype. MakerBot donated a MakerBot Replicator to each of them, which allowed them to print iterations of their prosthetic prototypes back and forth to each other until Richard got a good fit.

When Liam's father heard about their project he asked Ivan and Richard to help him construct a prosthetic hand for his son. After trial and error, Liam's dad was able to 3D print a set of plastic fingers good enough to grasp

A boy with a cheap prosthetic device printed out in 3D with RoboHand.

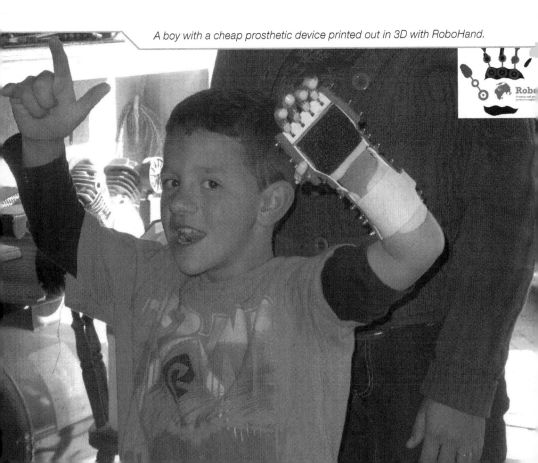

objects. This story of prosthetic hands has since become widespread, so much that Richard has started an organization called RoboHand that works to help people like Liam and himself print affordable prosthetics. RoboHand has begun developing a low–cost printed leg prosthesis. Richard has even worked with "Not Impossible Labs" and his efforts have inspired other organizations, such as e–Nable, to also pursue the 3D prosthesis printing.

The key here is the price difference of prosthetics created by different methods. For the cost of a myoelectric device that take signals from muscle fibers in the arm and send them to the fingers, one can print out 840 3D hands. Robohand has already enabled 200 people to use these inexpensive but very functional prosthetics. Its designs are obviously open source. 3D printing will soon be mainstream. The concept shows how it can revolutionize several elements of worldwide healthcare so long as regulatory and technical difficulties can be overcome.

Score of availability: 4

Focus of attention: Patients and medical professionals

Websites & other online resources: 3D Printing News

(http://3dprintingindustry.com/medical/),

The Cronin Group (http://www.chem.gla.ac.uk/cronin/)

Companies & start–ups: MakerBot (http://www.makerbot.com/),

3Dsystems (http://www.3dsystems.com/)

Books: MAKE, Ultimate Guide to 3D Printing 2014 by Frauenfelder

Movies: Iron Man 2 (2010)

Trend 14. Iron Man: Powered exoskeletons and prosthetics

On a sunny day in November, 2013 I attended the Europe Summit organized by the Singularity University in Budapest at the amazing venue of the Franz Liszt Academy of Music. We listened to Amanda Boxtel, who got paralyzed from a spinal cord injury in a ski accident in Aspen, Colorado in 1992. She told us how she felt after getting the diagnosis of never being able to walk again and how she refused to stop dreaming. Since then, she has established adaptive ski programs, carried the Olympic torch, organized disabled rafting expeditions, and even conducted research in the Antarctica. She has also become one of the ambassadors of an innovative company called Ekso Bionics.

Ekso Bionics was launched in California in 2005 with a brave mission to design and develop powered exoskeletons that could make walking possible again for paralyzed people. A powered exoskeleton is a mobile framework that a person wears. It contains motors or hydraulics that deliver part of the energy needed for limb movement.

Their exoskeletons are used by individuals with various degrees of paralysis and stemming by a variety of causes. By the end of 2012 Ekso Bionics had helped individuals take more than a million steps that would not otherwise have been possible. Boxtel is one of ten Ekso Bionics test pilots who received a customized exoskeleton. According to Boxtel, the project "represents the triumph of human creativity and technology that converged to restore my authentic functionality in a stunningly beautiful, fashionable and organic design."

The exoskeleton she wore at the conference was custom designed using precision 3D printing. Body scans helped the designers mold the robotic suit to her measurement. They then coupled the suit with mechanical parts and controls. This process usually takes about three months.

Designers had to face various challenges, such as whether paralyzed people can feel or not because undetected bruises can become infected. Boxtel's suit which was designed to fit her body with Velcro straps. This allows her skin to breathe so that she can walk without sweating too much.

Other challenges included the problem of power supply, joint flexibility, error control to detect invalid movements, and customization. Yet what better to illustrate the progress made than to have an individual in an exoskeleton making the kick–off at the football World Cup taking place in Brazil in 2014?

Amanda Boxtel standing in the 3D printed Ekso hybrid robotic suit in Budapest on the Heroes' Square.

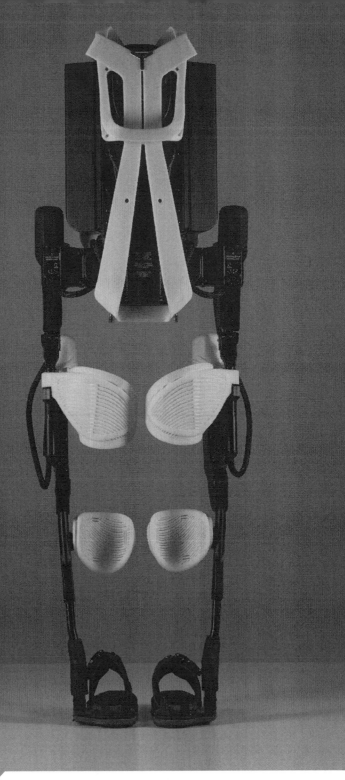

Full 3D Printed Ekso Suit by 3D Systems.

I discussed the future of Ekso Bionics with its Chief Technology Officer, Russ Angold. He has held assorted engineering positions at several companies, and works closely with the Lockheed Martin Corporation in licensing Ekso technology. He described the huge attention around the product:

"It is really interesting that we had over 3000 different individuals in our database in less than 2 years. The device is helping a lot of people who otherwise could not work, or their therapy would take a long time. Our job is giving them the technology that allows them to stay healthy and live a full life."

Ekso Bionics is working to make its technology available to more individuals ever since it started focusing on spinal cord injury. They now want to expand it to other conditions; and even add developments therefore the device could accommodate to those patients who have, for instance, 100% strength on one side and paralysis on the other. In considering cost one must factor in its value in reducing secondary complications such as urinary infections or chronic pain.

Angold pointed out that any new technology faces obstacles, and that paralysis can be emotionally trying for patients. While the company is careful not to overpromise what the device can do, they are working to gain great acceptance among medical professionals and patients who can benefit from their exoskeletons.

Architect Robert Woo had an accident that left him quadriplegic. His arms recovered in time, but both legs remained paralyzed. He felt useless and wanted to die. Turning to the Internet he came across a robotic exoskeleton called ReWalk developed by Argo Medical Technologies in Israel. He applied for their research program and trained in their use. Typical patients need twenty to seventy sessions to learn how to use these wearable robots. Woo mentioned how thrilling it was to be able to again stand next to his wife and give her a hug, and to walk with his children to the park. These are things that people take for granted, but which he has missed very much.

Italian engineers at the Perceptual Robotics Laboratory developed what they called a Body Extender, a robot that can help move heavy objects as an exoskeleton by lifting about 50 kilograms in each of its hands. It is claimed to be the most complex exoskeleton yet built. It can be used for assembling complicated products such as aircrafts; rescue victims after an earthquake or moving rocks away. We have not even begun to see the real potential of exoskeletons.

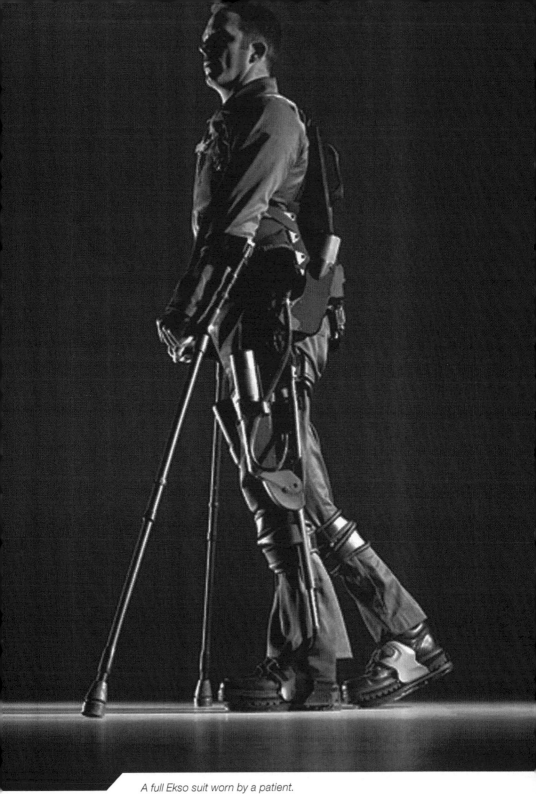

A full Ekso suit worn by a patient.

Customizing prosthetics

Hugh Herr, who directs the Biomechatronics research group at MIT's Media Lab, gave an amazing TED talk in 2014. Herr lost both his legs in a climbing accident 30 years earlier. He spoke of his plan to make flexible, smart prosthetics cheaper and widely available for those who need them. His team is pioneering a new class of smart biohybrid prostheses and exoskeletons for people with physical disabilities. It builds prosthetic knees, legs, and ankles that fuse biomechanics with microprocessors in order to restore normal gait, balance, and speed. They may even enhance biological functions including strength or speed. At the end of his talk came a surprise. Ballroom dancer Adrianne Haslet–Davis, who lost her left leg in the 2013 Boston Marathon bombing, performed on stage for us for the first time since her accident.

The Rehabilitation Institute of Chicago (RIC), designers at Vanderbilt University and prosthetics company Freedom Innovations reached a breakthrough by creating artificial limbs that allow amputees to walk up stairs, rotate an ankle, and navigate sloped terrains merely by thinking about it. A brain–controlled bionic leg is clearly a huge step in the future. RIC has been working on this since 2005. Using their innovation in 2012, Zac Vawter climbed over 2000 steps to the 103rd floor of Chicago's Willis Tower after losing his leg four years earlier in a motorcycle accident.

In 2014, the prosthetic won FDA approval for use in rehabilitation facilities, but not yet for personal use at home. Companies, researchers, and patients are petitioning the FDA to approve home use as well.

A San Francisco based company, Bespoke Innovations, went further in customization to make beautifully designed prosthetics based on the patient's needs and personality. Scott Summit, the designer at Bespoke, explained that in single amputees, the remaining leg is scanned and mirrored to give the correct geometry.

Athlete Jozef Metelka lost his leg in a 2009 motorbike accident and now has 12 different prosthetics that serve different functions from mountain biking and skiing to snowboarding and rollerblading. Each was designed by specialists at Pace Rehabilitation in the United Kingdom.

Another athlete, Mike Schultz, was a top professional snowmobile racer when his accident resulted in an amputation above the knee. With the help of the FOX Company that makes shock absorbers and racing suspensions, he designed and manufactured the prototype of the so–called "Moto Knee".

A customized prosthetic for a football player.

He later won multiple X–Games Gold Medals in the adaptive snow cross and motocross categories by using his own invention. The company he founded, Biodapt, sold over 100 of his extreme–sports prosthetics to other amputees so they could get back into the games they loved.

The real challenge for such companies is to design devices that can almost perfectly mimic the complex movements of hands and legs. Based on their i–limb technology, Touch Bionics introduced a prosthetic hand that allows individual fingers to move independently. Not only can the thumb rotate, but an iPhone app lets users control grip patterns as well. By clicking on the screen they can choose whatever grip patterns they prefer to use a mouse or to type, for instance. Life becomes much easier.

A photo from 1890 shows a little girl with prosthetic legs that seemed to be too modern compared to the technological advancements of that time. Many thought the photo was a hoax, but the photo was credited to James Gillingham, a well–respected shoemaker in 19th century England. He began making artificial limbs after a local man lost his arm in 1863. It is stunning how much this area has developed since then. And the end is not even near.

A customized prosthetic for a man who likes to ride his motorcycle.

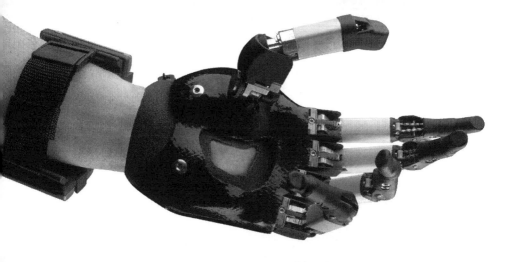

State–of–the–art prosthetic hands by Touch Bionics.

Neuroprosthetics

The ultimate goal is to make touch–sensitive prosthetic limbs that provide its wearer with real–time information via a direct interface with the brain. In one study, researchers identified brain patterns of neural activity that occur during natural object manipulation, and managed to induce the same areas by artificial manipulation. An interdisciplinary team of experts from academic institutions, government agencies, and private companies work on creating prosthetics that would restore natural motor control and sensation as a part of Revolutionizing Prosthetics, a DARPA project.

Something similar happened in the movie "The Empire Strikes Back" as Luke Skywalker received a complete prosthetic arm with a sense of touch after losing his arm in a battle.

Dennis Aabo Sørensen who lost his left hand in a fireworks explosion many years ago could tell what he was touching with his prosthetic hand again at the age of 36 because now it is possible to attach wired pressure sensors in the fingers of an artificial hand to sensory nerves in the upper arm. He could feel the shape and surface texture of the objects he touched. His first reaction was amazement at being able to feel something he had not felt in many years.

Medical professionals and engineers at the RIC have developed artificial limbs that can respond to a patient's thoughts. Computer chips implanted into the prosthetic limb are connected to sensors that pick up motor signals from the nerves that formerly made the hand move. To accomplish this, surgeons first had to reroute the nerves to large muscles at the end of the stump so that those muscles amplify the nerve signals. The strengthened nerve signals can then be detected by the prosthetic sensors which send them to motors that move the hand.

The ethical dilemmas

Bertolt Meyer, an academic known as "the bionic man," has had a cutting-edge £40,000 artificial forearm and hand since 2009. In 2013, he raised concerns about scientists and engineers launching technological advances on the open market without a prior ethical debate. He fears that who can afford it will be unfairly augmented and have an advantage over those who cannot. When this becomes apparent to everyone, he thinks a mass market for bionic enhancement will develop.

Meyer authored the documentary "How to Build a Bionic Man", in which he reveals how his own old prosthesis made him feel ashamed, while the newer one gives him confidence when out in public.

What happens to society when such artificial limbs start to offer truly augmented human capabilities? An example for this is the case of Professor Gil Weinberg who has created a robotic drumming prosthesis that can be attached to amputees. A drummer who now wears this additional drumstick can use the prosthesis and make it improvise while he is playing.

Another example is Matthew James, born with dysmelia, a congenital disorder causing deformed limbs. James wrote to his favorite Formula One team, Mercedes, at age 14 that he was ready to display their logo on his prosthesis if they could support him financially. He received £30,000 but was not taken up on his offer of advertising space. This story shows that the implementation of such innovations in the everyday lives cannot depend purely on individual entrepreneurship.

These devices are extremely expensive at the moment. Jose Delgado Jr. was born without a left hand. His health insurance covered the cost of a $42,000 myoelectric device. He recently received an offer from 3DUniverse to print out a Cyborg Beast prosthetic hand. Such open source printed hands are used in the Robohand project as well. Delgado was surprised that the 3D hand turned out to function better than the myoelectric device, so he decided to keep using it. It is true that the plastic used in 3D printing is easy to break, but it is a simple matter to print out a new one. The cost is almost nothing compared to conventional prosthetics.

Being born without a limb or losing one in an accident will soon not be a major disadvantage. As technology improves at a fast rate, these may even augment normal human capabilities. The real question facing us is not whether technology will be able to help such patients, but how to persuade healthy people in the near future not to change their own limbs to smart, state–of–the–art prosthetics.

Score of availability: 4

Focus of attention: Patients

Websites & other online resources: International Society for Prosthetics and Orthotics (http://www.ispoint.org/)

Companies & start–ups: Bespoke Innovations (http://www.bespokeinnovations.com/), Robohand (http://www.robohand.net/), Ekso Bionics (http://eksobionics.com)

Books: Powered exoskeleton 39 Success Secrets: 39 Most Asked Questions On Powered exoskeleton – What You Need To Know Paperback –by Horn

Movies: The Matrix Reloaded (2003), Avatar (2009), Iron Man 2 (2010), Elysium (2013), Edge of Tomorrow (2014)

Trend 15. The End of Human Experimentation

Today, new pharmaceuticals are approved by a process that culminates in human clinical trials. The clinical trial is a rigorous process from development of the active molecule to animal trials before the human ones, costing billions of dollars and requiring many years. Patients participating in the trial are exposed to side effects, not all of which will have been predicted by animal testing. If the drug is successful in trial, it may receive approval, but the time and expense are present regardless of the trial outcome.

But what if there were another, safer, faster, and less expensive route to approval? Instead of requiring years of "ex vivo" and animal studies before human testing, what if it were possible to test thousands of new molecules on billions of virtual patients in just a few minutes? What would be required to demonstrate such a capability? At the very least, the virtual patients must mimic the physiology of the target patients, with all of the variation that actual patients show. The model should encompass circulatory, neural, endocrine, and metabolic systems, and each of these must demonstrate valid mechanism–based responses to physiological and pharmacological stimuli. The model must also be cost efficient, simulating weeks in a span of seconds.

Such simulations are called computational cognitive architectures, although the current ones actually lack a comprehensive representation of human physiology. A truly comprehensive system would make it possible to model conditions, symptoms, and even drug effects. To order reach this brave goal, every tiny detail of the human body needs to be included in the simulation from the way our body reacts to temperature changes to the circadian rhythms of hormone action.

HumMod is a simulation system that provides a top–down model of human physiology from organs to hormones. It now contains over 1,500 linear and non–linear equations and over 6,500 state variables such as body fluids, circulation, electrolytes, hormones, metabolism, and skin temperature. HumMod was based on original work by Drs. Arthur Guyton and Thomas Coleman in the early 1970's.

Over the last forty years Coleman has taken their work and expanded it, first with a DOS based program called Human, then as a Windows based one called Quantitative Circulatory Physiology which is freely available and written in C++ programming language which made coding physiology challenging. Over the last eight years Dr. Robert Hester has directed the development of HumMod in tackling such issues, and now the physiology component is written in a format called XML.

Researchers' focus has been to create HumMod People, a population model of HumMod that allows for the simulation of "humans" with different physiological responses. This work can potentially help us understand how a human population responds differently to certain pathologies or drugs. Ongoing research in this field suggests that it will soon be possible to mimic the human body in simulation. I contacted Hester to get his expert opinion.

"We believe that there is a major problem with the way that physiological models have been developed. Our methods have been to start at a top level, with what may be considered initial crude descriptions of the physiological pathways. Then we add detail to these "crude" mathematical descriptions, thus refining the model. The benefit of this is that we develop an integrative model of human physiology. Other designs start at a lower level, such as biochemical and molecular simulation, and try to fit these models together. We believe there are several challenges with this type of simulation. One is that there is not sufficient experimental human data that will allow one to understand the biochemical pathways under a variety of conditions."

In the last few months they have been working with a company developing a device to monitor congestive heart failure in an attempt to predict when the patient should see their physician rather than go to an Emergency Room or be admitted to the hospital. Their patient model has a variety of pathologies and has generated simulations over a two–month period of operation. The company compared the resulting data to the human data to determine whether they were collecting the appropriate parameters.

HumMod was licensed from the University of Mississippi to commercialize the software and get funding to continue the project. It is now turning in different directions. The first is medical education. A browser version of HumMod is being developed to help students at all levels understand basic physiology. Programming patient scenarios and implementing HumMod into medical mannequins to provide realistic physiological responses can better train medical and nursing students to manage patients for the long term. Conducting physiological and clinical research is another obvious application.

As Dr. Hester indicated, the implementation of personalized medicine would certainly require such a physiological model.

"The idea that each of us is just like the other and should be treated (clinically) like anyone else is obsolete now. If our assumption is correct, that the equations underlying physiology are sacrosanct but that the coefficients (parameters) capture the differences in individuals. With a large enough "library" of patients, observations from a single patient can marginalize the library to a similar population. As observation continues, the larger pool might be winnowed down to a "most expressive" model, which might then be used as a basis for planning treatment, diet, exercise regimen, or any other aspect of health. The idea, while years from any kind of implementation, is intuitively clear."

Many elements from energy balance to neural signals still need improvement in order to make HumMod capable of simulating chronic conditions and complicated protocols. Generating large data sets will require appropriate software for proper analyses, but beyond these issues the long–term goal of the HumMod project is to model human physiology from birth to death.

HumMod is not the only effort in this area. The Avicenna project, partially funded by the European Commission, aims to construct a roadmap for future "in silico" clinical trials, which would make it possible to conduct them without actually experimenting on people. Other projects use real models instead of computational ones. A liver human organ construct, a physical object that responds to toxic chemical exposure the way a real liver does, was designed at the Gordon A. Cain University. The goal of the five–year, $19 million multiinstitutional project is to develop interconnected human organ constructs that are based on a miniaturized platform nicknamed ATHENA (Advanced Tissue–engineered Human Ectypal Network Analyzer) that looks like a CPR mannequin.

It would then be possible to test molecules without risking the toxic effects on humans, and to monitor fluctuations in the thousands of different molecules that living cells produce and consume. The beauty of this project is its plan to connect their working liver device to a heart device developed by Harvard University. If successful, they hope to add a lung construct in 2015 that is being developed at Los Alamos, and a kidney designed by the UCSF/ Vanderbilt collaboration by 2016, thus building the first physiological model of a human being piece by piece.

Simulating organs on chips

Simulating human physiology does not necessarily require building organs the same size as living human ones. Their physiology can be modeled more easily. A technique called organ–on–a–chip simulates the activities, mechanics, and physiology of entire organs and organ systems. An individual organ–on–chip is composed of a clear flexible polymer the size of a computer memory stick that contains hollow microfluidic channels lined by living human cells. The chips provide a literal glimpse into the inner workings of human organs given the transparent nature of the microdevices. Organs and structures including heart, lung, kidney, artery, bone, cartilage, and skin have been simulated by microfluidic

Designing a whole body biomimetic device will potentially correct one of the most significant limitations on organs–on–chips: the isolation of organs.

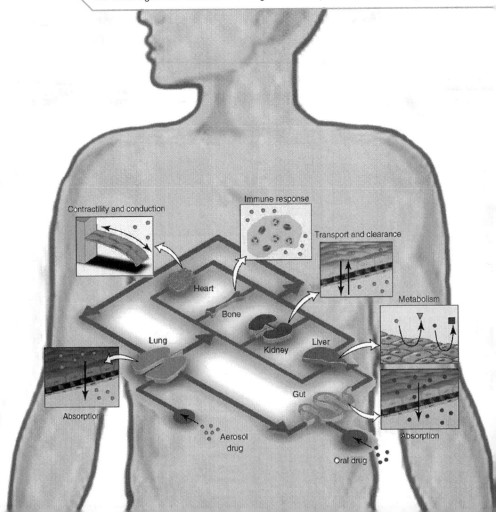

devices. They can let pharmaceutical companies measure direct effects of one organ's reaction on another. However, because the system becomes more complex as the design expands, as do the challenges that grow with it.

The Wyss Institute and a team of collaborators seek to link ten human organs-on-chips to imitate whole-body physiology. The instrument will control fluid flow and cell viability while permitting real-time observation of the cultured tissues and analysis of complex biochemical functions. This instrument will be called human-on-a-chip. It could be used to assess new drug candidates and provide critical information on their safety and efficacy. In 2014, the Wyss Institute created a bone-marrow-on-a-chip that reproduces the structure, function, and even cellular make-up of this complex human tissue. It will be a test tool for researchers studying the effects and toxicity of new drugs. Moreover, it could be used to maintain a cancer patient's bone marrow temporarily while undergoing radiation or chemotherapy that commonly destroys the tissue.

A revolutionary aspect of this new bone-marrow-on-a-chip is that it can actually generate blood cells in an artificial circulatory system which itself could supply the network of other organs-on-chips. Both the FDA and DARPA have provided funding for these efforts. Ultimately such devices could replace animal testing of new drugs and environmental toxins as well as accurately modeling human diseases.

Organ-specific features that can be modulated in human physiological models.

Organ	Demonstrated organ-specific features
Liver	Serum protein synthesis, liver zonation
Lung	Airway closure and opening, inflammation, alveolar-capillary interface
Kidney	Molecular transport
Gut	Intestinal absorption
Bone	Lacuna-canicular network
Breast	Cancer metastasis
Brain	Formation of new blood vessels in tumors

Another example from Georgia Institute of Technology is a device that mimics blood flow through narrowed coronary arteries in order to assess the effects of anti-clotting drugs such as aspirin. A study concluded that while aspirin can prevent dangerous blood clots in some patients at risk for thrombosis, it may not be effective in those merely with narrowed arteries. Given that doctors have a huge range of drugs from which to choose, such benchtop diagnostic devices could help save lives by preventing heart attacks while also lowering healthcare costs.

In 2014 tissue containing an individual's specific genetic disorder was replicated in the laboratory for the first time. Harvard scientists in collaboration with the Wyss Institute and others obtained skin cells from a patient with Barth syndrome, a rare cardiac disorder for which there is no known cure. They transformed the skin cells into stem cells that carried the mutation by using chips with human extracellular matrix proteins that mimicked the natural environment. The heart tissue grew out of these cells produced only weak contractions similarly to the weak heart muscle in Barth's syndrome. They concluded that we cannot really understand the meaning of a single cell's genetic mutation until a large chunk of organ is built and makes it possible to see how it functions or malfunctions.

Microengineered cell-culture systems mimicking organ physiology can be used to develop disease models that are relevant to people and more predictive of drug efficacy and toxicity while also providing better insights into the mechanism of drug action. We might discover new routes of drug delivery; analyze populations with different genetic backgrounds; determine pharmacokinetic properties of various compounds; even conduct clinical trials using microengineered models.

In 2014, the Insigneo Institute built a fully computer-simulated model of human physiology for personalized healthcare. "The Virtual Physiological Human" is intended to circumvent issues of clinical trials and animal testing by simulating the outcomes of therapies for patients. What they are working on could be vital to the future of healthcare. Without in silico medicine, organizations will be unable to cope with future demand. The Virtual Physiological Human will be a software-based laboratory for experimentation and treatment that can save time and money and lead to superior treatment outcomes.

If all the data on a patient were added to their simulation, it could make predictions about the given individual's status and future health outcomes, thus ushering in an era of truly individualized medicine. The team is also working on VIRTUheart for assessing coronary artery disease, a neuromuscular model for predicting treatment for Parkinson's disease, MySpine focusing on disc degeneration, and Mission–T2D that models a patient's risk of developing type 2 diabetes.

These examples show that an in–silico human is not going to appear in the next few years, but only in the distant future. We might not have the chance in our lifetimes of having simulated copies of ourselves model the illnesses we will develop. If we had them now, we could stop human experiments with new drugs and compounds that might be toxic; stop using animals during early stages of such trials; be able to predict treatment outcomes and the onset of disease before symptoms develop. All this would lead to a revolution in healthcare from the perspective of decreased costs and saving lives with computer models.

Score of availability: 2
Focus of attention: Researchers
Websites & other online resources: The Wyss Institute (http://wyss.harvard.edu/), Hummod (http://hummod.org/), Avicenna (http://avicenna–isct.org/)
Companies & start–ups: Virtual Physiology (http://www.virtual–physiology.com/)
Books: Handbook of Virtual Humans by Thalmann & Thalmann
Movies: S1m0ne (2002), The Congress (2013)

Trend 16. Medical Decisions via Artificial Intelligence

In 2011, people witnessed an interesting and at the same time weird competition on the television quiz show Jeopardy. It featured the two best players in the history of the show, Ken Jennings, who had the longest unbeaten run of 74 winning appearances, and Brad Rutter, who had earned the biggest prize of $3.25 million. Their opponent was a huge computer with over 750 servers and a cooling system stored at a location so as not to disturb the players. The room–sized machine was made by IBM and named after the company's founder, Thomas J. Watson. It did not smile or show emotion, but it kept on giving good answers. At the end, Watson won the game with $77,147 leaving Rutter and Jennings with $21,600 and $24,000 respectively.

Watson is perhaps the most important supercomputer, and one of the first to enter the artificial intelligence (AI) market in our time. Its success depends on how it acquires new knowledge. Martin Kohn, medical director of IBM Watson, explains that its training is an ongoing process, and it is rapidly improving its ability to render reasonable recommendations that oncologists, for example, think are helpful. Watson is also said to ascertain quickly what it does not yet know. Siri, the intelligent assistant in Apple's iOS, on the other hand, simply looks for keywords to search the web, and lists options from which one can choose.

What even the most acclaimed professors know cannot match cognitive computers. As the amount of information they accumulate grows exponentially, the assistance of computing solutions in medical decisions is imminent. While a physician can keep a few dozen study results and papers in mind, IBM's Watson can process more than 200 million pages in seconds. This remarkable speed has led to trying Watson in oncology centers to see how helpful it is in making treatment decisions in cancer care. Watson does not answer medical questions, but based on data it comes up with the most relevant and likely outcomes. Physicians make the final call. Computer assistance can only facilitate the work of physicians, not replace it.

IBM's chief of research said that what first hit them about Watson was its list of endless opportunities, because as the concept it represents can be applied to almost any situation. Initially the team chose medicine for obvious reasons. Imagine how useful Watson could be by suggesting diagnoses and treatment options. Watson could be the perfect tool to navigate decision trees

IBM Watson.

used by cancer specialists that weigh treatment options involving radiation, surgery, and countless numbers of chemotherapy drugs. It can read the world's medical journals, digest patient histories, keep an eye on the latest drug trials and new therapies, and even state–of–the–art guidelines in less time than it takes a physician to drink a cup of coffee. And it constantly keeps on learning.

Not surprisingly Watson has been tested in 2012 in different settings such as the Memorial Sloan Kettering Cancer Center. Simultaneously, Wellpoint, a large health insurer in the US, began using a Watson computer to speed up the authorization of medical procedures. Sometimes they refer to this transition as Watsonizing.

Watson's work with clinicians demonstrates how it could potentially transform healthcare. For more than a year, Watson has been trained in science and medicine by feeding it medical textbooks, peer reviewed journals, patient histories, and treatment guidelines. At Memorial Sloan–Kettering doctors used a tablet application to access the computer through the cloud. They input data or ask questions. Because Watson understands natural language, a query about a cancer treatment, for example, makes Watson note keywords, the particular type of cancer, and the genomic variant of the tumor. Using massively parallel processors, Watson then reviews millions of relevant pages of text, studies, patient's history, and much more in seconds. It generates hypotheses for treatment, suggesting options with varying levels of confidence on the tablet app. The doctor then makes the call by weighing the options.

According to Sloan–Kettering, it would take at least 160 hours of weekly reading just to keep up with the medical literature. As a result only around 20% of what doctors use when diagnosing and deciding on treatments relies on trial–based evidence. As Wellpoint officials noted, Watson's correct diagnosis rate for lung cancer is 90%, compared to 50% for human doctors.

Herbert Chase, a professor of clinical medicine at Columbia University who consulted with IBM during the development of Watson, said it is not humanly possible for a doctor to keep up to date of the current literature. He described a good case in which Watson turned out to be highly useful.

"I'll give you an example of a test we thought up for Watson. A patient was pregnant, had Lyme disease, and was also allergic to penicillin. And Watson came up with a drug. The first thing I thought was Watson made a mistake. That drug can't be given to someone allergic to penicillin. My knowledge was about five years old. And in the past couple of years, all the muckety–mucks had reviewed all the studies and had concluded yes, you can give that drug to someone who's allergic to penicillin."

A clinician researcher at the MD Anderson Cancer Center started one of her leukemia patients on a standard course of chemotherapy. The patient then developed a potentially life–threatening complication called tumor lysis syndrome that if not treated proactively can cause kidney failure, heart attack, or even death. Watson alerted her to the complication and let her take action immediately. That is how AI can assist medical professionals.

It is also used in clinical research such as a project in which the genomes of twenty five patients with a form of brain cancer are being sequenced. The data will be sent on to Watson. Watson's learning model can discover associations faster than researchers can. It can also prioritize the combinations of drugs and let physicians make better choices of what drug to use first.

Patients tend to believe their doctor knows everything. But that cannot be the case given that acquiring enough knowledge today is humanly impossible. The use of AI is relevant and almost inevitable, and should not destroy the traditional doctor–patient relationship.

The cost beyond

I recently came across a fascinating study that concluded it is cheaper to make a diagnosis with the help of AI than without it. Using 500 randomly selected patients for its simulations, physician performance and patient outcomes were compared to AI's sequential decision–making models. It turned out that there was a great disparity in the cost per unit of outcome change. The AI models cost $189 whereas treatment–as–usual cost $497.

I contacted one of the study authors, Casey Bennett from the Centerstone Research Institute, Nashville and he gladly shared the details and reasoning behind their work.

"On a personal level for me, one of the main drivers for my work was watching my grandparents as they aged and went into nursing homes due to various healthcare issues. Should they go on a medication/ treatment or not? It worked for 60% of people, but it may not for them. Will it cause dramatic side effects? Will those side effects be tolerable? Can we actually make them better? Are the potential long-term complications (and/or costs) worth it?"

Comparison of outcomes and costs of AI and treatment–as–usual.

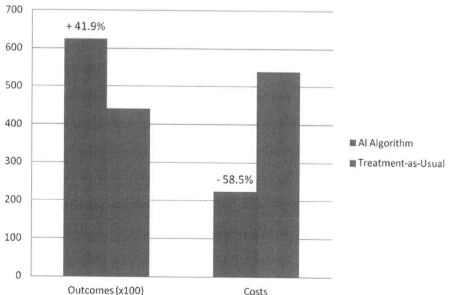

In medicine, physicians often make educated guesses. When you see your friends and family facing that, it becomes scary. For Bennett, the real goal of clinical AI should be to empower people – patients and clinicians alike – to give them the tools and information they need to make the best decisions they can. While he thinks there will always be a place for autonomous AI, humans can never be taken out of the equation completely. Getting machines and people to work together brings out the best in both.

Obstacles to overcome still include the fact that these technologies do not actually mirror the way we think about problems. This causes cognitive dissonance that often makes it hard for people to work with machines. Bennett and colleagues have faced challenges over the last few years in deploying AI and other innovative technologies in real–world clinical practice. But they managed to find a way.

Serious ethical concerns exist regarding AI's use in medicine. A frequent one is responsibility. Who is liable if a clinical AI makes a huge mistake? As in similar technologies such as surgical robots, medical professionals always make the final call, so this is not really an open question. Another issue is the means by which new guidelines and recommendations from evidence–based medicine get incorporated into clinical AI systems. This is critical if they are to meet clinical standards of care.

Dr. Stanley M. Shapshay questioned whether AI would actually be the future of medicine. He is concerned that advanced computer technology or AI needs to be evaluated and potentially integrated into modern medicine while serving as an aid and not a physician substitute. The therapeutic value of the physician–patient encounter is powerful medicine that is not replaceable by intelligent machines.

In 2014 Modernizing Medicine was the first EMR system to implement IBM's Watson. Imagine the possibilities when Watson gets integrated into more and more medical informatics systems.

Watson was given access to the Urban Dictionary in an attempt to help it learn slang, and thus be more facile with conversational language. It gradually picked up expressions such as "OMG" (Oh, my God), "hot mess," and even vulgar words. Although it is a natural language processer, it is unable to distinguish between slang and profanity. When it began using obscenities the team had to develop a filter to keep Watson from swearing, and purged the Urban Dictionary from its memory. Is there a point at which we will be unable to stop AI from learning more and more?

The friendly or unfriendly AI

If you ask people their views on AI most will think of science fiction movies–the Hal 9000 in "2001: A Space Odyssey" or Samantha in movie "Her". But AI is literally all around us in cars, appliances, smartphones, Amazon's software that predicts what you may want to purchase next, and Apple's voice–activated Siri. Companies such as Google, Facebook, and Netflix have been heavily investing in deep learning technology for years.

Most evolving areas of medicine generate huge amounts of information. The challenge is not only how to analyze the data but also how to deal with the sheer amount of it first. Using only one quarter capacity of the supercomputer called Beagle at Argonne National Laboratory in Illinois – in reference to the ship that accompanied Charles Darwin on his journey in 1831 – the simultaneous analysis of 240 full genomes took only two days, significantly accelerating the speed of research.

In 2009, IBM's 'Blue Brain' project tried to run a simulation of 1.6 billion neurons and nearly 9 trillion synaptic connections (the size of the cat's brain). It took 600 seconds to simulate 1 second of brain activity by using one of the world's most powerful supercomputers that had 147,456 processors. The human brain with its hundred billion neurons and well over a hundred trillion synapses is far more complex. Computational power obviously has to keep markedly improving year after year.

Another self–learning supercomputer called Nautilus had access to millions of newspaper articles starting from 1945. Using this huge amount of information about past events the computer quite successfully came up with suggestions on what would happen in the future, such as accurately locating Bin Laden.

Supercomputers that constantly develop and learn cannot by themselves give us the answers to questions humanity has been asking for millennia. Human–computer teams most likely hold the most promise for the future, an idea underscored in "Hype Cycle for Emerging Technologies," a report that Gartner published in 2013. In it, vice president and Gartner fellow Jackie Fenn summarized potential scenarios of human–technical interaction.

"By observing how emerging technologies are being used by early adopters, there are actually three main trends at work. These trends are 'augmenting humans with technology — for example, an employee

with a wearable computing device; machines replacing humans — for example, a cognitive virtual assistant acting as an automated customer representative; and humans and machines working alongside each other — for example, a mobile robot working with a warehouse employee to move many boxes."

Negative consequences in the long term might include a schizophrenic robot, one of which was actually simulated by researchers at the University of Texas. When they overloaded the computer with many stories, it claimed responsibility for a terrorist act and warned the researchers about setting off a bomb. When University of Georgia researchers presented an experiment in which they taught a group of robots to cheat and deceive, they showed that the robot had developed its own strategy by trial and error.

Robots with even minimal intelligence can also be ruthless. Scientists at the Laboratory of Intelligent Systems put a group of robots in a room that contained elements such as "food" and "poison". The closer a robot was to "food", the more points it collected. The robots were able to turn off their lights if needed. After several rounds almost all of the robots turned off their light, refusing to help one another in this way.

Nothing in AI has far led to a really intelligent entity in the way that most people think of one. But it is going to happen sooner or later. There might soon be an AI system that can design better, ultra-intelligent systems that we will not understand at all. What would the incentive be for such a system to be friendly to us? Do we want our cars to have their own opinions and make their own decisions that overrule ours? AI experts such as James Barrat and cosmologist Stephen W. Hawking tried to initiate a public discussion about the dangers an unfriendly AI would cause to society.

Truly successful AI must go through the Turing test, first proposed by Alan Turing, the famous mathematician and computer scientist. It is based on the disputed assumption that if a person cannot tell the difference between another human and the computer based on interaction, then that computer must be as intelligent as a human. While certain chatbots such as Eugene that simulated a 13-year-old Ukrainian boy were said to pass it, actually no AI systems has passed it yet. Although there is no reason to believe it will not happen soon.

One influence that might facilitate the way towards friendly and useful AI is the new A.I. XPrize challenge. In March of 2014, Chris Anderson and Peter Diamandis announced the A.I. XPrize, a modern-day Turing test to be awarded to the first AI to walk or roll out on stage and present a TED Talk so compelling that it commands a standing ovation from the audience. The rules are still being finalized, but looking back at the success of the Ansari X Prize that led to the first non–governmental launch of a reusable manned spacecraft, expectations are high.

Score of availability: 3

Focus of attention: Medical professionals

Websites & other online resources: BBC Future (http://www.bbc.com/future/tags/artificialintelligence), Xprize (http://www.xprize.org/prize–development/life–sciences)

Companies & start–ups: IBM Watson (http://www.ibm.com/smarterplanet/us/en/ibmwatson/)

Books: Neuromancer by Gibson; Our Final Invention: Artificial Intelligence and the End of the Human Era by Barrat

Movies: Forbidden Planet (1956), 2001: A Space Odyssey (1968), The Terminator (1984), A.I. Artificial Intelligence (2001)

Trend 17. Nanorobots Living In Our Blood

As part of an 1871 thought experiment the Scottish physicist James Clerk Maxwell imagined tiny "demons" that could redirect atoms one at a time. But the term molecular engineering was actually coined by MIT professor Arthur Robert von Hippel in the 1950s. On the evening of December 29, 1959, the famous physicist Richard Feynman described in his after–dinner lecture at the annual meeting of the American Physical Society how the entire Encyclopaedia Britannica could be written on the head of a pin, and how all the world's books could fit in a pamphlet.

Continuing the thought experiment, Kim Eric Drexler, an MIT undergraduate in the mid–1970s, envisioned that molecule–sized machines could manufacture almost anything. Drexler first published his ideas in a 1981 journal article. In a later book, he described nanotechnology's future role in revolutionizing other areas of science and technology that would lead to breakthroughs in medicine, artificial intelligence, and astronomy. His idea of an "assembler" could "place atoms in almost any reasonable arrangement," thus allowing us to build almost anything that the laws of nature will allow. Assemblers would moreover be capable of replicating themselves. In this way the overall number of assemblers could grow exponentially, allowing for the production of enormous objects.

Then in 1991 carbon nanotubes were discovered, which are about 100 times stronger than steel only one–sixth their weight, and have unusual heat and conductivity characteristics. The Juno spacecraft currently on its way to Jupiter uses carbon nanostructure composite to provide electrical grounding, discharge static, and reduce weight. From the beginning it was imminent that this technology would be used in medicine. Nanomedicine denotes using the properties developed by a material at its nanometric scale of 10–9 m.

In the wildest futuristic scenarios, tiny nanorobots in our bloodstream could detect diseases. After a few decades they might even eradicate the word symptom inasmuch as no one would have them any longer. These microscopic robots would send alerts to our smartphones or digital contact lenses before disease could develop in our body.

We are closer to these futuristic ideas than one might think. Nanosize robots, tiny cameras, special capsules used for targeting drug delivering, and magnetic nanoparticles for cancer therapy have already been developed by chemists, engineers, and biologists. Some of these applications are

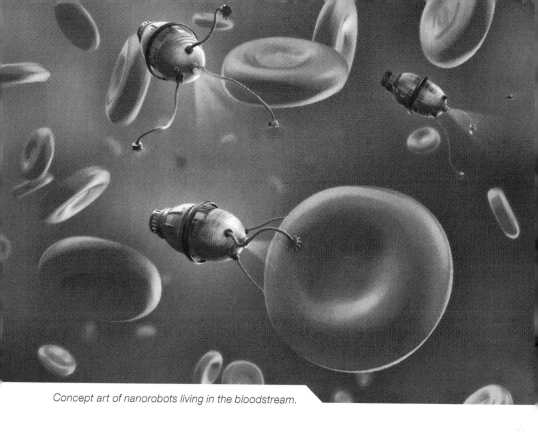
Concept art of nanorobots living in the bloodstream.

currently in testing period on animals or humans; some are already available to physicians. According to The European Technology Platform on Nanomedicine nanomedicine in 2014 has more than seventy products in clinical trials that cover major categories of disease such as neurodegenerative, musculoskeletal, and inflammatory. It already has seventy–seven marketed products from nano–delivery (44) and pharmaceutical (18), to imaging, diagnostics, and biomaterials (15).

An example of how it can change medicine is the placement of synthetic nanomotors inside living human cells and controlling them magnetically through ultrasonic waves. According to the leader of the research team it may be possible in the future to use synthetic nanomotors to studying cell biology in new ways. Nanomotors could also be used to treat cancer and other diseases by mechanically manipulating cells from the inside. These could perform intracellular surgery or deliver drugs directly to living tissues.

Nanomotors surprisingly have little effect on the cells at low ultrasonic power, but at increased power they move around, bump into cell structures, and can homogenize the cell's contents or puncture the cell wall. Their work could make the 1966 movie "Fantastic Voyage" real by having nanomotors circulate in the body, communicate with one another, make diagnoses, and administer therapy—all without human interaction. In the movie the medical staff boards an experimental submarine which is then drastically miniaturized and injected into a patient in order to destroy a life–threatening blood clot in his brain.

The submarine today is called clottocyte nanorobot. It functions similarly to platelets that stick together to form a blood clot that stops bleeding. Such nanorobots could store fibers until they encounter a wound, and then disperse them to create a clot in a fraction of the time that platelets do. Blood–related microbivore nanorobots act like white blood cells, and could be designed to be faster and more efficient at destroying bacteria or similar invasive agents. Bacterial or viral infections could be eliminated from someone in a matter of minutes as opposed to the days required for antibiotics to take effect. Nanobots would also not have their potential side effects.

Respirocyte nanorobots that act like red blood cells would have the potential to carry much more oxygen than natural red blood cells do for patients suffering from anemia. They might also contain sensors to measure the concentration of oxygen in the bloodstream. One day blood may become both a repository and symbiosis of nanorobots and our human cells.

Endless opportunities

Plenty of concepts have demonstrated how nanotechnology can transform medicine and healthcare from the basics. What if instead of general therapies cellular–repair nanorobots could perform surgical procedures more precisely by working at the cellular level?

Vaccine delivery with microneedle patches could provide cheaper, simpler, and safer methods of delivery compared to traditional administration that requires skilled professionals and runs the risk of infection. Microneedles at micron–scale are coated with a dry formulation of vaccine that dissolves in the skin within minutes after applying the patch. It has been shown that measles vaccine can be stabilized on microneedles and is comparably effective to the standard subcutaneous injection.

Creating drugs that directly attack cancer cells without damaging other tissues has been proven to be a safe method in treating cervical cancer. Swedish researchers have developed a technique that uses magnetically controlled nanoparticles to force tumor cells to self–destruct without harming surrounding tissue radiation and chemotherapy do. It is primarily intended for cancer treatment, although it could be used for other diseases including type 1 diabetes.

Looking ahead we might develop programmable nanoparticles that deliver insulin to initiate cell growth and regenerate tissue at a target location. In surgery, programmable nanoparticles could be injected into the bloodstream to seek out and remove damaged cells, grow new cells, or perform other procedures.

In neurodegenerative diseases such as Parkinson's, nanodevices could deliver drugs, implant neurostimulators, or transport intelligent biomaterials across the blood–brain barrier in order to direct regeneration within the central nervous system. Nanosponges circulating in our bloodstream could absorb and remove toxins. Nanobiopsy could make it possible to extract cellular material such as subpopulations of mitochondria and make them available for analysis. Nanodevices could measure insulin levels and deliver insulin to cells where it is needed. Whole–body imaging of fat distribution via nanoparticles would be possible, and artificial pancreas might also be in sight based on these potential developments.

Just as mice injected with nanomaterials have regained the ability to use paralyzed limbs, mobilizing stem cells through nanomaterials at an injury site could shorten recovery time. Novel implant materials and surfaces could prevent common implant infections. The list of opportunities is literally endless, and this is only the beginning.

One of the most forward–thinking experiments proved that DNA–based nanorobots can be inserted into a living cockroach and later perform logical operations upon command such as releasing a molecule stored within it. Such nanorobots, also called origami robots given that they can unfold and deliver drugs, could eventually be able to carry out complex programs including diagnoses or treatments. One of the most astonishing feats is the accuracy of delivery and control of these nanobots, which are equivalent to a computer system. A question that needs to be addressed soon is how our natural immune system will react to an army of nanorobots.

The first DNA nanodevice that survived the body's immune defense was created in 2014. It might open the door to smart DNA nanorobots using logic to spot cancerous tissue, and manufacture drugs at the desired location. Microscopic containers called protocells could detect pathogens in food or toxic chemicals in drinking water.

In the future, cloaked nanorobots could deliberately activate the immune system in order to fight cancer or suppress transplant rejection. Patients with cancer and other diseases would benefit from precise, molecular–scale tools in simultaneously diagnosing and treating diseased tissues. A huge step in this direction is making DNA nanoparticles endure in the body and not get destroyed by the immune system.

According to optimistic futurists, nanomedicines like smart drugs will lead to the prevention of all illnesses, even aging, making us superhuman from many perspectives.

Forming a new community

I spoke with András Paszternák, PhD, founder of The International NanoScience Community, about the steps nanotechnology might take to become a reality.

He sees cost as the key obstacle to wider adoption. When investors see high returns, then nanotech medical products will reach patients. It will take some time until nanotech is to all hospitals and doctors, but a huge boom is anticipated in the next three to five years. Questions remain open regarding nanoparticles that already have been added to cleaning materials and food additives. What are the potential risks of such devices entering our lung or heart?

Paszternák learned that connection and communication among scientists is a major issue. He therefore launched NanoPaprika in order to address this.

"We have today 7500 members coming from more than 80 countries. Thanks to Nanopaprika, several students have found PhD and postdoctoral positions or information about new nanotech developments. Senior researchers have met talented students; shared news about their results and found new collaboration partners. Nanopaprika is like an open source channel to connect nano addicted people and share the latest news in our scientific field."

Several limitations and threats will ensure nanomedicine is incorporated slowly into our everyday lives. There are technical issues about how nanorobots might navigate, sense their surroundings, and move through the body; how they might detect problems and communicate with one another; and what their biocompatibility is as they interact with the body.

Although the scenarios described above might sound positive, there is a range of serious threats that they pose. Bioterrorism is one, which might gain access to the "weapons" that are already inside us. If it is possible to hack pacemakers, it is certainly possible to hack nanodevices as well. Discussing these dangers as well as potential ways it could disrupt and support today's diagnostic and treatment options might help us prepare in time.

Score of availability: 1

Focus of attention: Patients and medical professionals

Websites & other online resources: Nanomedicine EU Platform (http://www.etp–nanomedicine.eu/public), The Foresight Institute (http://www.foresight.org/), NanoPaprika (http://www.nanopaprika.eu/)

Companies & start–ups: NanoBio (http://www.nanobio.com/), 3M (http://solutions.3m.com/), P2i (http://www.p2i.com/)

Books: The Invincible by Lem; The Diamond Age by Stephenson

Movies: Fantastic Voyage (1966), Star Trek: The Next Generation (1987–1994), Ghost in the Shell (1995), The Day the Earth Stood Still (2008)

Trend 18. Hospitals of the Future

Hospitals and healthcare institutions worldwide will face a huge transition from being a place where people go when they are sick to a place where they can make sure they are on the right track for preventing diseases and living a healthy lifestyle. The architecture, delivery process of healthcare, waiting rooms, and timetables all have to dramatically change in order to successfully serve patients and medical professionals.

At the end of the 19th century, medical care became too complex to be delivered at home, and it shifted to centralized facilities. At a time when traveling even moderate distances was laborious and expensive compared to the cost of hospital care it turned out that it was cheaper to build a hospital in every town. In the US, the number of hospitals grew from 178 in 1873, to 4,300 in 1909, 6,000 in 1946, 7,200 by 1970, and finally down to 5,700 today. Nowadays, innovative technology allows same–day surgeries in which patients enter and leave the hospital the same day. Still, the facilities do not represent the most modern ideas in delivering care.

Providing an identical range of services in every hospital regardless of actual needs in a given population does not bode well for future healthcare systems worldwide. Creating networks of institutions focusing on different aspects of medicine might be a better solution.

A typical hospital room has hardly changed since post–World War II years, even though its design is crucial from the perspective of patient recovery and avoidable infections. The patient room of the future should be designed to serve as a safe, private, comfortable, and connected place for healing. A non–profit organization in New York, NXT Health, designed and funded such a prototype intended to reduce infections, falls, errors and ultimately costs.

The proposed room covered all the aspects described above. A canopy above the bed houses electrical, technical, and gas components, even a noise–blocking system. A Halo light box can be programmed for mood and light therapy, and also serving as screen to display clouds or the sky. The head panel contains equipment that can measure almost any health parameter unobtrusively while continually logging results. The footwall features a screen for entertainment, video consultations, and accessing whatever information the patient needs.

Floors are made of low–porosity rubber that does not need chemical sealers and does not trap bacteria and other substances. It case of a fall it

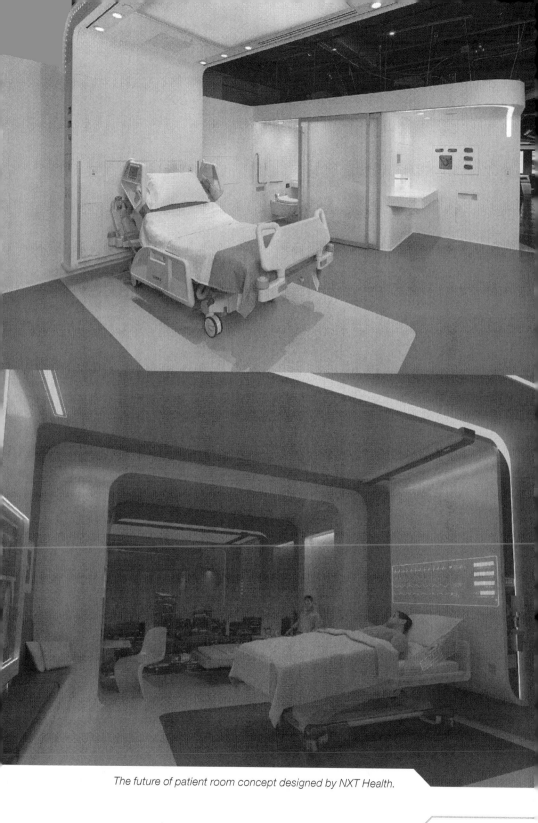

The future of patient room concept designed by NXT Health.

reduces impact. To reduce potential infections all surfaces are made of solid materials that are often used in kitchen countertops. A light at the entrance reminds staff to wash their hands before entering the room. Information and data can be added to patient records here as well as at a control panel.

Lessons for designing future hospitals

The Walnut Hill Medical Center in Dallas has been referred to as the Apple experience hospital due to its design and innovative nature. Potential employees must take a psychological exam, and the application process is exceptionally tough. Patient greeting begin in the parking lot with complementary valet service. Inside, the staff follows the Ritz Carlton "15–5" rule meaning that a hospital employee must smile at the patient from 15 feet and greet them with a warm hello at 5 feet. All employees are trained to communicate properly with patients and their families. Patient rooms feature large windows that provide natural light and pleasuring views. Richly colored wood and earth tones compliment the interior. At admission, patients receive tablets that are loaded with videos, reading materials, and tools to make it easier to communicate with staff and stay updated on their condition.

Hospitals of the future will generate positive feelings based on colors and architecture. Facilities for fitness, wellness, and prevention will be available. Gamification will play an important role in motivating patients to pursue a healthy lifestyle by rewarding them when following the therapy they agreed upon. Eliminating identification mistakes through positive patient identification by augmented reality and bionic tags holds obvious advantages. Virtual procedures and real–time consultations will become part of the daily routine.

AI will soon organize all the details of the healthcare system. It will direct people when and where to go by analyzing their records, and automatically responding to doctors' notes and prescriptions. Waiting lists will be eliminated. Patients will be able to download data from their wearable health trackers before seeing the doctor. Medical records and archives will be digitalized, and new information will be stored in the cloud in a safe, efficient format. 3D printers will print out medical equipment or even prostheses when needed.

Big data might become our doctors in the future, or at least play a much more important role in the practice of medicine and the development of therapies than it does today. Like what Netflix, Google, Amazon, and Facebook do today, using big data will be the next big step in changing the basics of healthcare.

Technology	2014	2030
Archives	Big space	Stored in the cloud
Diagnostics	In hospital	Home diagnostics
Waiting room	Big	Non-existing
E-consultation	Baby steps	Everyday

Main differences between hospitals today and in the future.

In the basement office of Jeff Hammerbacher at Mount Sinai's Icahn School of Medicine, a supercomputer called Minerva named after the Roman goddess of wisdom and medicine was installed in 2013. In addition to being a researcher, Hammerbacher co–founded software companies such as Cloudera and Demeter to better store, process, mine, and build data models. In just a few months Minerva generated 300 million new calculations to support healthcare decisions.

Dr. Joel Dudley, director of biomedical informatics at the Icahn School of Medicine, was depicted in the chapter about personalized medicine. He said that what they are trying to build is a learning healthcare system.

"We first need to collect the data on a large population of people and connect that to outcomes. Let's throw in everything we think we know about biology and let's just look at the raw measurements of how these things are moving within a large population. Eventually the data will tell us how biology is wired up."

When they assembled and analyzed the health data of 30,000 patients who volunteered to share their information, it turned out that there might be new clusters or subtypes of diabetes.

By analyzing huge amounts of data it might be possible to pinpoint genes that are unique to diabetes patients in these different clusters, providing potentially new ways to understand how our genomic background and environment are linked to the disease, its symptoms, and treatments.

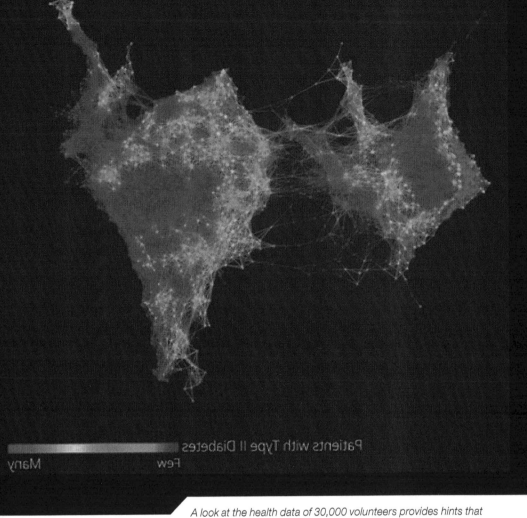

Patients with Type II Diabetes

Few   Many

A look at the health data of 30,000 volunteers provides hints that we know less than we realize about diabetes and its subtypes.

Their goal is to enroll 100,000 patients in the so–called BioMe Biobank, funded by The Charles Bronfman Institute for Personalized Medicine. It owns a large collection of plasma samples and large–scale genomic data stored in a way that protects patients' privacy but allows researchers to analyze the data.

Methods and technology already exist, although these are not widely used. The biggest obstacle is usually data access.

A way through which the whole concept of hospitals could be reimagined is by engaging members of healthcare communities. For 24 hours on January 9, 2013, the Institute for the Future hosted such an experiment under the name "Future of the Hospital." Its purpose was to generate ideas about how to reinvent the hospital experience. It was run on IFTF's Foresight Engine, an online crowdsourcing platform designed to engage people from all over the world in participatory forecasting through a three–step process of scenario development, community engagement, and analysis of themes that emerged from the forecasts. As a result, more than 600 people from five continents participated, including hospital executives, architects, nurses, doctors, and computer scientists. The discussions generated over 4,500 ideas.

In 2013, "Intel Health Innovation Barometer" was released by Intel Corporation indicating that patients' healthcare needs worldwide are principally focused on technology and personalization. Traditional hospitals, according to 57% of people, will be obsolete in the future. Not surprisingly, 84% of people would be willing to share their personal health information to advance care and lower costs; more than 70% are receptive to using toilet sensors, prescription bottle sensors, and swallowed health monitors; 72% would be willing to see a doctor via video conference for non–urgent appointments; and 66% said they would prefer a care regimen designed specifically for them based on their genetic profile. These are the expectations the hospitals of the future must meet.

In 2012, the Royal College of Physicians established the Future Hospital Commission to provide recommendations drawn from the best of hospital services, taking examples of existing innovative, patient–centered services to develop a comprehensive model of hospital care that meets the needs of patients. Their report, published in 2013, mentioned the word technology only twenty–seven times throughout the 180 page report. Future hospitals will revolve around wearable devices and advanced technologies even though it will still be possible to maintain the in–person doctor–patient relationship by making the hospital experience a truly rejuvenating and positive one.

Score of availability: 3
Focus of attention: Patients and medical professionals
Websites & other online resources: American Hospital Association (http://www.aha.org/)
Companies & start–ups: NXT Health (http://nxthealth.org/)
Books: Lean–Led Hospital Design: Creating the Efficient Hospital of the Future by Grunden
Movies: Elysium (2013)

Trend 19. Virtual–Digital Brains

The brain is a unique organ, the most developed organ in the universe with some very interesting features based on psychological studies. In a classic study, students found a boring task more interesting if they were paid less to take part. The unconscious mind reasoned that if they did not do it for money they must have done it because it was interesting. Multi–tasking skills, hallucinations, obedience to authority (e.g. the Milgram Experiment), and the placebo effect all underscore what a special system we have to deal with when researching the brain.

Japanese scientists could map one second's worth of activity in the human brain with K computer, the fourth most powerful supercomputer in the world. It has 705,024 processor cores and 1.4 million gigabytes of random access memory (RAM) at its disposal. Simulating the neural network of 1.73 billion nerve cells and 10.4 trillion synapses requires such petascale computers; simulating the whole brain at the level of individual nerve cells and their synapses will probably be possible with exascale computers within the next decade.

Stanford University announced in 2014 that it has been working on a circuit board that can mimic the behavior of the human brain. The so–called Neurogrid circuit is now able to replicate the processes of 1 million human neurons, resulting in computer chips that are 9,000 times faster than a desktop computer. The human brain consumes only three times as much power as NeuroGrid with 80,000 times more neurons than that. Their long–term goal is to develop this technology further so that its prosthetic interaction with the human mind could look like science fiction. One of the lead researchers said that due to exponentially powerful technologies which are transforming our sphere of possibilities, we are no longer subject to Darwinian natural selection. We will be able to extend our reach.

The Human Brain Project, funded by the European Commission, aims at building a completely new computing infrastructure for neuroscience and brain–related research, catalyzing a globally collaborative effort to understand the human brain and its diseases and, ultimately, to emulate its computational abilities. The project involves hundreds of researchers and will cost an estimated €1.1 billion. Sebastian Seung and his team work on mapping the brain's connectome under the OpenWorm project. Their mission is to simulate a nematode worm in a computer. In 2014, European scientists produced the first ultra–high resolution 3D scan of the entire human brain. In the US, President Barack Obama recently approved a $100 million brain mapping initiative. These examples show that the pace at which brain research is moving forward is extraordinary.

IBM's Cognitive Computing Group has developed chips that can simulate how neurons and their connections work by being able to simulate the creation of even new connections. A chip called "SYNAPSE" can simulate 256 neurons with about a quarter of a million synaptic connections. The project's long–term goal is to simulate 10 billion neurons with their 100 trillion connections, representing approximately the power of the human brain but using less and less power.

In the 19th century, punch cards were used to control automatic textile looms, enter data and commands into computers from 1896 and were used well into the 1970s. Keyboards were only introduced in the 1960s, as well as the first mouse in 1963 containing a block of wood with a single button and two gear–wheels. The first optical mouse appeared in 1980, multitouch was introduced in 1984; and natural user interfaces such as the Nintendo Wii or Microsoft Kinect were released in the 2000s. These are the ways we have been expanding our minds in the form of communicating with digital devices. The next logical step is designing brain–computer interfaces that could be controlled by thought.

We are getting closer to understand in detail how the brain really works. It is the biggest quest humanity has ever gone on. Simpler obstacles and almost unsolvable technical difficulties are on the way.

Measuring EEG at home

In 1924, Hans Berger recorded the first human EEG measuring the faint electrical signals that brains emit while thinking, sleeping, moving, or meditating. Since then, being able to accurately and comfortably measure EEG even at home has been the focus and it is not as simple as it might sound.

Ariel Garten is the perfect example for how an inter–disciplinary background of neuroscience, fashion design, and psychotherapy can help solve global problems and develop innovative solutions. I discussed the possibilities with her right after ordering my own Muse, the brain sensing headband with seven sensors, five on the forehead and two SmartSense

Ariel Garten, co-founder and CEO of InteraXon, wearing Muse: the brain sensing headband.

conductive rubber ear sensors, that was designed to detect and measure brain activity even though neurologists are generally critical of such applications and warn about the risk of overstating what these devices can do. The measurements can be accessed on a tablet or smartphone via Bluetooth. Muse's EEG sensors detect the spontaneous activity of neurons that generate electrical frequencies.

Garten's mother is an artist. Her enormous oil paintings inspired Garten to launch a clothing line in high school, and then open Toronto Fashion Week with her own line. After that, she worked in the scientific lab of Professor Steve Mann, pioneer of cybernetics and wearable computers, and was interested in mind–technology interaction. There, she and her colleagues got the idea of using brain activity to trigger musical playback. Not long after, she co–founded InteraXon with Trevor Colemen and Chris Aimone and went on to develop Muse, the brain–sensing headband.

"It was really challenging for me to find out about a staff member of ours was suffering from stress and anxiety. She started working with Muse, doing daily sessions. She came back to me a week ago telling the whole story of how Muse had helped surpass her emotional challenges. I'm continuously amazed at the power and potential of brain–computer interfaces."

An early prototype involved a levitating chair which would rise toward the ceiling accompanied by a satisfying sound effect only if the user managed to slip into a state of relaxation by wearing the EEG headband similarly to other biofeedback sensors. In 2012, they finished a successful Indiegogo crowdfunding campaign raising almost $300,000, surpassing its original goal of $150,000. It might have potential for treating attention deficit hyperactivity disorder known as ADHD; it has a potential benefit for epilepsy; could teach people to focus attention, decrease pain, increase cognitive function, emotional intelligence, memory, and athletic performance; and decrease stress and depression.

On the 1st of May, 2014, they started shipping Muse to thousands and thousands of individuals who want to measure their brain waves at home. Mine is also on the way.

As Garten sees this area, technological breakthroughs will be a driving force. An ever–increasing database will generate a vast amount of data as more and more people use it. Low cost headsets will democratize the technology market. Now citizen scientists, developers, and researchers can create applications themselves.

EEG is measured in microvolts compared to the thousand times more millivolts of ECG, but muscle noise can obscure the tracing therefore educating users to make the data clear is crucial. This already happened in the 1950s as part of the standard technique for EEG technicians. Being calm or doing exercises show when the mind is active or in rest. Muse gives a score based on which users can train themselves how to rest or focus better. It takes time for people to learn about new wearable devices and the potential outcomes these might provide. Security and keeping privacy information safe are also issues. Garten has already addressed these concerns.

"One and a half years ago people were surprised when I described Muse to them, now they cannot wait to try it themselves. Education is the key to let people know what data they can obtain by using such a device. Also, users must be ensured the data are kept private by using encryption technology; moreover it only measures trends in brain activity."

As a big fan of any open source movement, I tried to find an initiative with a similar mission of making EEG measurement simple and accessible to anyone worldwide. The challenge is that untrained people cannot distinguish artifact from actual brain waves therefore they need to know how to reduce impedance in the electrodes and to make all the electrodes equal. Anyone can learn this, but it takes time and can hardly be done via the Internet or without certain equipment. The OpenBCI (Open Brain–Computer Interface) project has the goal to tackle such issues. Conor Russomanno and Joel Murphy had a successful Kickstarter campaign raising twice the amount of $100,000 as they originally sought. The aim was to develop, with some funding help from DARPA, an affordable 8–channel EEG signal capture platform, an open–source brain–computer interface kit that gives anybody an access to their brain wave data. In 2014, OpenBCI launched a 3D–printable helmet–like EEG device to let anyone customize and print their own. It took seven hours to print the prototype. With all related files published online, people can build their own.

I asked Conor Russomanno, who also teaches a course called "The Digital Self" at Parsons School of Design, to describe the path the OpenBCI movement is walking on now.

"The quest is to help solve the biggest mystery, the real background of cognitive disorders. Miracles take place when technology makes it possible to get the information that we actually need. The technical implications of BCI might not be obvious to people (except hackers and developers), although it has the potential to make huge impacts on our everyday lives."

Measuring EEG is the only solution to non–invasive BCI, but practicability is the real challenge. There are great devices such as Neurosky, Interaxon, and Emotiv already available on the market, although it will still take effort and time to find the optimal level between being functional and wearable at the same time. He thinks that this is going to be an extremely lucrative industry in 5–10 years. Imagine a healthcare system with personalized medicine based on EEG measurements and live feedback.

"For higher resolution data, more electrodes are needed. The more data, the better. With practical or applied EEG, you are trying making inferences about neural networks and processes inside the brain by looking at electrical charges of the scalp. It's similar to looking at waves crashing on the beach and then making inferences about plates are shifting or winds are blowing in the middle of the ocean."

Measuring the brain waves of Conor Russomanno of OpenBCI.

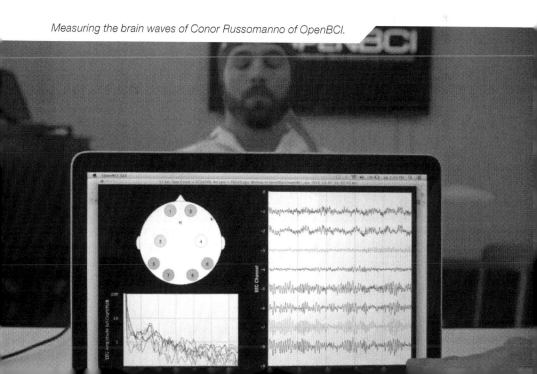

There are several obstacles to overcome for developing better BCI platforms. The first is to understand and accept that the brain does not necessarily work like a computer. Second, the brain is more than a network of neurons. There other types of cells such as glia making up 15% cells in the brain that are involved in vital background communication in the brain but neither are electric nor synaptic. Finally, much better technology is needed for thoroughly analyzing brain activity.

As a futuristic scenario, Government Works Inc, is working on BCI headsets to be used for lie detection and criminal investigations. The company claims that the technology can tell whether a person has knowledge of certain information or events.

Controlling neurons with optogenetics

When the interdisciplinary research journal Nature Methods chose optogenetics in 2010 as the "Method of the Year" across all fields of science and engineering, and when it was also highlighted in "Breakthroughs of the Decade" in the journal Science, it became clear that optogenetics belongs to the top trends in the future of medicine.

Optogenetics is a neuromodulation technique combining methods from optics and genetics to control the activity of individual neurons in living tissue. It does this by introducing genes that code for light–sensitive proteins. This way, certain genes can be turned on and off only using light. From another perspective, it provides a way to control the brain and behavior through light. A crucial element of the method is how the beam of light gets through the skull. Usually, lab mice undergo stereotaxic surgery to mount an LED light or optical fiber. Different types of neurons can be selectively turned on, offering excellent spatial resolution. It could allow much more precise manipulation of the brain than implanted electrodes, drugs, or transcranial electromagnetic stimulation do.

Physicist Leonard Mlodinow, who has also been a screenwriter for television series such as Star Trek: The Next Generation, said a Nobel Prize in this area is not far off, and that "optogenetics is destined to change the way we treat mental illness, and eventually, even, the way we understand ourselves as human beings."

Optogenetics shows the potential to provide new therapies for several medical conditions such as epilepsy, Parkinson's disease, obsessive–

compulsive disorder, schizophrenia, depression, and various kinds of addiction. A recent study reported the ability to create false memories in mice. This is the first time fear memory has been generated via artificial means. By the time we clearly understand the placebo effect, false memories of taking drugs could be implanted in patients, tricking them into believing that they have taken the drug.

When MIT's Ed Boyden, author of a famous article describing the methods and future developments of optogenetics, was asked about the potential benefits, he described a few futuristic scenarios.

"First, there is fundamental understanding of the brain, which has humanistic and philosophical implications. As an example, a group at Caltech used an optical fiber together with optogenetic tools in a deep part of the brain, making it sensitive to light. When they illuminated this region, the animals became aggressive. If we can understand the neural basis of violence or aggression, it might do a lot to explain more difficult aspects of human behavior, and maybe we can get a handle on some of these mysteries.

Another application is clinical; can we find ways to treat patients? Over a quarter of a million people have some kind of neural implant already. If we can use light to more specifically activate a set of neurons, maybe we could treat patients suffering from Parkinson's, chronic pain, deafness, or other conditions."

Dealing with pain is a global issue for millions of people. Optogenetics might help them as well. A Stanford University research group injected a virus containing the DNA of an opsin, a protein found in light–sensitive cells of the retina, into the paw nerves of mice. A few weeks later, only nerves involved in pain contained the genes coding for opsin present in their DNA. It seems possible now to give a mouse an injection, and two weeks later shine a light on its paw to change the way it senses pain. This method might be able to test rapidly new pain relieving medications and, as a truly futuristic scheme, allow doctors to one day use light to relieve pain.

The ultimate goal is to develop newer forms of opsins with different properties that respond to different colors of light, making optogenetics enter a Technicolor age. Actually, an MIT team has already discovered a new protein reactive to red light, as well as the fastest light–reacting protein discovered so far, thus further improving the potential of optogenetics.

While this technology may provide nearly endless applications for medical conditions, a major obstacle in making it practical is being able to deliver the light to the cells, because tissue is usually in the way. Recently, a new hydrogel implant that can be used to both shine light and sense its presence deep within the body was created.

Another problem is transferring animal results to human. Genetic material has to be added to brain cells that we would like to control in order to be able to turn them on and off through light. While demonstrated in mice, genetic engineering in human neurons is not yet an option.

Finally, we need to understand the neural background of the medical conditions mentioned above in order to know exactly which neurons or neural circuits are over- or under-active, and make them normal again.

Brain implants and neuroenhancement

Kevin Tracey decided to become a neurosurgeon when he was 5 and his mother died as a result of an inoperable brain tumor. His grandfather explained to him that surgeons tried to take the tumor out but could not separate the malignant tissue from healthy neurons. Then he wanted to solve problems that were insolvable. He later became a pioneer in bioelectronics. In 2011, his company SetPoint Medical began the world's first clinical trial to treat rheumatoid-arthritis patients with an implantable nerve stimulator. He thinks that instead of drugs, treatment one day might be delivering a pattern of electrical impulses. Such an innovation will replace the drug industry.

There have been and current exist efforts in which people try to electrically stimulate their brain in order to have better memory or focus better. Brent Williams, an engineer, built a home device for brain stimulation for a total cost of $20 in 2012. He connected a simple circuit to two kitchen sponges soaked in saline using alligator clips and positioned them to his head with a sweatband. One sponge was placed above his right eyebrow and the other on the left side of his forehead. The battery got into place; he turned a small dial, and sent an electric current into his brain. Since then, he has been electrifying his brain two to three times a week. He does it for about 25 minutes in the evening while reading on the couch. Williams got the idea from a news story about how Air Force researchers were studying whether brain stimulation could reduce pilot training time which might sound like how characters did that in the movie "The Matrix".

Neuroenhancement or using drugs to improve functionalities of the brain raises serious ethical concerns. A new initiative by the European Commission, the Neuroenhancement Responsible Research and Innovation project, aims to get scientists and the public discussing the related issues about these emerging technologies. Neuroenhancement was originally designed to help impaired patients, but now it is used to enable healthy humans to become smarter, faster, or even more charming.

When I contacted Dr. Gary Marcus, at New York University and Dr. Christof Koch at the Allen Institute for Brain Science, they directed me to their recent article that covered the whole topic of future brain implants and enhancement in detail. They said that brain implants today are where laser eye surgery was decades ago, and that it will advance significantly in the upcoming years.

Imagine a retinal chip giving you perfect eye sight or the ability to see in the dark; a cochlear implant giving you perfect hearing; a memory chip giving you almost limitless memory. Such brain implants will not be the first neuroprosthetics given that those have been around commercially for three decades. Examples include cochlear implants, and now retinal implants which were first approved by the FDA in 2013. Implants used in Parkinson's disease send electrical pulses deep into the brain, activating some of the pathways involved in motor control. Such future implants must be non-toxic and biocompatible. There are technical difficulties as well, but like the smartphone industry, experts expect to find solutions to these issues soon.

Connecting brains and computers

Duke University neuroengineers designed a brain–machine–brain interface to be tested on monkeys, and established a direct link between a brain and a virtual body. The virtual body was controlled by the animal's brain activity, while its virtual hand generated tactile feedback information which was signaled back to the brain. Monkeys could explore virtual worlds and objects while actually feeling them.

University of Reading researcher Dr. Kevin Warwick managed to control machines and communicate with others using only his thoughts with a cutting–edge neural implant. In 1998, Warwick, who earned the nickname "Captain Cyborg" from his colleagues, implanted a transmitter in his arm to control doors and other devices; then in 2002 he decided to implant electrodes directly into his nervous system in order to control a wheelchair with his thoughts and allow a remote robot arm to mimic the actions of his own arm.

Having a goal of helping voiceless patients communicate as a next, and very brave, step, Warwick implanted a chip into the arm of his wife to link their brains together through the Internet, creating the world's first electronic brain–to–brain communication. When she moved her hand three times, he felt three pulses and recognized that his wife was communicating. He is optimistic that mind–to–mind communication will become a commercial reality in the next one or two decades. When Cathy Hutchinson, paralyzed years earlier by a brainstem stroke, managed to take a drink from a bottle by manipulating a robot arm with only her brain and a neural implant in 2012, the path became clear for future research.

An obvious question is when it will become possible to improve or even control our dreams? A company called Remee is developing a sleep mask designed to increase the frequency of dreams. Light technology is hidden in the mask, which can produce customizable light patterns that the user's dreaming mind learns to recognize. A lot more research can be expected in this area.

When neuroscientists are able to scan the brain in high spatial and chemical resolution designing math models for all the brain cells, digital brain emulations could be created. Such embodied emulations would be able to perform tasks that humans are bad or slow at. Some experts say that one day these emulations might outnumber humans, leading to a new kind of society. Robin Hanson from Oxford University's Future of Humanity Institute envisions that "because emulations are easily copied, you could train one to be a good lawyer and then make a billion copies who are all good lawyers." It would certainly transform society into something new and unknown.

A movement called Transhumanism with California roots going back to the 1980s, and science–fiction writers such as Isaac Asimov and Julian Huxley (who coined the word himself in 1957), now has now over 10,000 members who are ready to download their neural data and live forever in digital form, leaving this biological waste we call the human body behind.

In the future, we might see near–invisible cell powered sensors; wireless non–contact EEG devices; and emotional or thought reading solutions based on EEG. The most important aspect is making sure it is being used in the right way; a constitution of what should and should not be done is therefore very much needed. We are now standing at a critical point in evolution that could tip entirely to technology rather than humanity with the focus on our most complicated organ. A public discussion initiated in time could allow us to win and possibly find a balance between eliminating mental disorders and using brain-computer interfaces.

Score of availability: 2

Focus of attention: Patients

Websites & other online resources: The Human Brain Project (https://www.humanbrainproject.eu/), OpenBCI (http://www.openbci.com/), Optogenetics @ Stanford (http://www.stanford.edu/group/dlab/optogenetics)

Companies & start–ups: Interaxon (http://www.interaxon.ca/), Remee (http://sleepwithremee.com/)

Books: How to Create a Mind by Kurzweil; Brain–Computer Interfaces: Principles and Practice by Wolpaw & Wolpaw

Movies: The Terminal Man (1974), eXistenZ (1999), The Matrix (1999), Upldr (2013), The Machine (2013), Transcendence (2014)

Trend 20. The Rise of Recreational Cyborgs

On the 8th of October in 2016, Zurich, Switzerland will host the first championship sports event under the name Cybathlon for parathletes using high–tech prostheses, exoskeletons, and other robotic and assistive devices. This is going to be the first event of its kind. According to their website:

"The main goal of the Cybathlon is to provide a platform for the development of novel assistive technologies that are useful for daily life. Through the organization of the Cybathlon we want to help removing barriers between the public, people with disabilities and science."

It is the goal of the Swiss National Science Foundation in the frame of the National Competence Center in Research of Robotics to disseminate research to the public, removing barriers between science, the general public, and people with disabilities. I contacted Professor Robert Riener, one of the organizers, to ask about his personal motivation and again, there was a personal story behind it.

"My personal story is that I met so many people with disabilities who were not satisfied with the assistive technology currently available. E.g. bionic upper arm devices are not fulfilling the real needs, have too short battery power or cannot carry high load/weight. Other technologies such as powered–exoskeletons are still too bulky and too slow, and wheelchairs can still not go over steps. The Cybathlon should lead to new technologies in the long run that are much better, functional in daily life, thus leading to a real acceptance and therefore to an improvement of quality of life."

He agreed that new technology must always be safe and ethical. But the main goal is to provide assistive devices that really help handicapped people in daily life, and allow them to participate in a competition that could not do at all with conventional or no technology. This potential advantage, he added, even justifies a minimum level of risk, which always exists when using novel technologies.

Participating teams, which will try out their technology in a rehearsal in Zurich in the fall of 2015, will compete in six disciplines:

- Brain Computer Interface Race: Contestants will be equipped with brain–computer interfaces that will enable them to control an avatar in a racing game played on computers.

- Functional Electrical Stimulation Bike Race: Contestants with complete spinal cord injuries will be equipped with Functional Electrical Stimulation devices, which will enable them to perform pedaling movements on a cycling device that drives them on a circular course.

- Leg Prosthetics Race: It will involve an obstacle course featuring slopes, steps, uneven surfaces, and straight sprints.

- Powered Exoskeleton Race: Contestants with complete thoracic or lumbar spinal cord injuries will be equipped with actuated exoskeletal devices, which will enable them to walk along a particular race course.

- Powered Wheelchair Race: A similar obstacle course featuring a variety of surfaces and environments.

- Arm Prosthetics Race: Pilots with forearm or upper arm amputations will be equipped with actuated exoprosthetic devices and will have to successfully complete two hand–arm task courses as quickly as possible.

A cyborg, which is short for "cybernetic organism", is a person with both organic and mechanical parts such as biomaterials and bioelectronics. Enormous progress in microelectronics and semiconductor technology has made it possible for electronic implants to control, restore, or improve bodily functions. Examples include cardiac pacemakers, retinal implants, hearing implants, or implants for deep brain stimulation in cases of pain or Parkinson's disease. Bioelectronic developments can be combined with robotics to result in highly complex neuroprostheses. All these aim at restoring lost or damaged human functionalities.

By the time technology gets better at this, which it is constantly, a clear trend seems to be enhancing those human features and capabilities. It is not hard to envision a new generation of recreational cyborgs who become cyborgs with perfect eyesight or hearing only because they want to and because they can afford it.

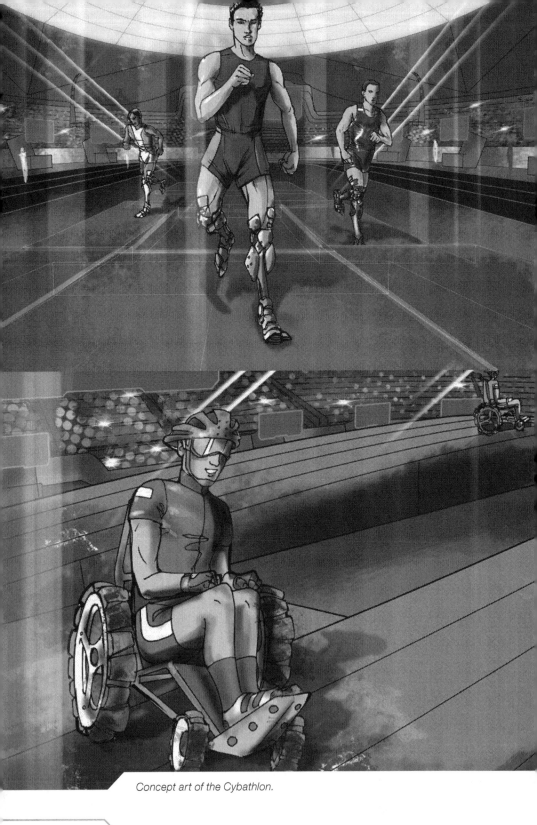

Concept art of the Cybathlon.

The first cyborg ever

One morning in 2004, University of Toronto Professor Steve Mann was awakened by a car that smashed into the corner of his house. He tried to speak with the driver but the driver sped off, striking Professor Mann and running over his right foot. He had been working on wearable devices for 35 years and was wearing his computerized–vision system that gives him a better view of the world. The impact injured his leg and broke the wearable computing system which normally overwrites its memory buffers rather than permanently recording images. But as a result from the vehicular damage, it saved pictures of the license plate and driver who was later identified and arrested.

In the 1970s, Professor Mann explored different ways to design wearable devices when most computers were the size of large rooms and wireless data networks were unheard of.

"The first versions I built sported separate transmitting and receiving antennas, including rabbit ears. Nearly everybody around me thought I was totally loony to wear all that hardware strapped to my head and body. When I was out with it, lots of people crossed the street to avoid me. The future of computing was as much about communications between people wearing computers as it was about performing colossal calculations."

In 1995, he was first to have a passport photo showing him as a cyborg even though he rejected the term "cyborg" as being too vague. He has been working on wearable computing devices since high school in the 1980s when his mission was to create a "digital eye". The Institute of Electrical and Electronics Engineers (IEEE) referred to him as the father of augmented reality and wearable computing. His High Dynamic Range imaging invention is used in nearly every commercially manufactured camera including the iPhone.

In his own Eyetap wearable computer, three simultaneously captured images at different exposures are combined in real–time to produce a view of the world that is as rich in details that can be produced by the human eye. By capturing over a dynamic range of more than a million to one, the user can see details that cannot be seen by the human eye or any currently existing cameras. He and others have been working on an eyeborg system that includes an implantable camera in the prosthetic eye.

Professor Steve Mann on his passport in 1995 (left), and with one of his prototypes in 1980 (right).

He was also first to make a clear distinction between surveillance (when people are being monitored from a higher authority) and inverse surveillance, for which he coined the word "sousveillance" (when cameras are worn by people). He has written many times that cameras would soon be everywhere, raising positive and negative consequences.

In 2012, Professor Mann wrote about an experience in which he was kicked out of a McDonald's in Paris after employees asked him to remove his headset that could record photos and videos from his point of view. McDonald's issued a statement confirming that he had been ejected, but denied that there was physical contact. Professor Mann, however, released a photo which appears to show an employee grabbing his glasses. He, his wife, and their two children were in line to purchase food when an employee told them that cameras were not allowed. Although Professor Mann presented a doctor's note stating he needs to wear his headgear, employees crumpled up his doctor's note and then allegedly pushed him out the door and onto the street, damaging his gear in the process.

He only asked McDonald's not to prohibit or attack vision research inasmuch as his glasses are designed to eventually help people with vision and memory problems. His case shows with clarity the potential dangers people who wear such technologies will have to face. He also described in one of his papers that wearable device recordings can be similar to human memory, and therefore public establishments should not discriminate against people whose memories are captured by computer devices. He envisions a future in

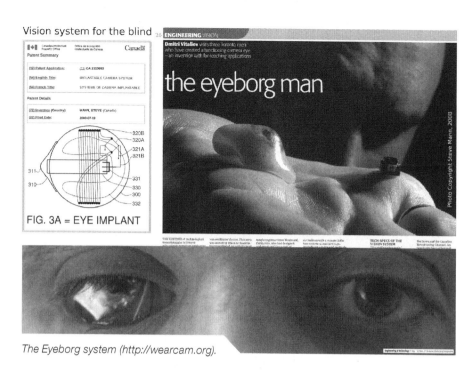

FIG. 3A = EYE IMPLANT

the eyeborg man

The Eyeborg system (http://wearcam.org).

which people from Alzheimer's patients to healthy adults can use wearable technology as extended memory without being harassed.

Why would society be biased against people who decide to augment their lives with technology in the form of wearable computing or sensors? This is already happening, and there is no reason to think that the number of cyborgs will not increase dramatically in time. Neil Harbisson, for example, recently became one of the first people in the United Kingdom to have a passport photo illustrating his cyborg nature. The color–blind artist wears a head–mounted device called an eyeborg that allows him to see color, and he wants to help other cyborgs like himself gain more rights.

The Most Connected Man

Chris Dancy is usually referred to as the world's most connected man. He has between 300 and 700 systems running and collecting real–time data about his life at any given time. He started five years ago when he noticed his doctor having a hard time keeping up with his health records. Since then, he has lost 45 kg or 100 pounds, and learned to meditate. He told me he is now more aware of how he responds to life and is ready to take steps to adjust to his environment. He has also formed better habits thanks to the feedback he is constantly getting from the devices. He gladly shared his views with me.

"We all have beliefs about our lives and our choices. Seeing the data about our lives and choices helps us convince ourselves of relationships we believe we see. With very simple data, for instance, sleep, it's easy to fall into confirmation bias. When you add more data sources such as ambient noise, phase of the moon, air quality, temp, etc it becomes much easier to try to prove your answers WRONG, instead of proving them RIGHT."

Dancy uses a variety of wearable technology from the fitness tracker Fitbit to the Pebble smartwatch, weighs himself on the Aria Wi–Fi scale, and sleeps on a Beddit mattress cover to track his sleep. When I asked him about people's general view about his life, I was not surprised by the experience he's had.

A concept art picture about the most connected man, Chris Dancy.

"Right now it's a bit silly. They either understand and see that my work could profoundly impact humanity, or they think I'm a "gadget nut". Additionally some people on the internet are so very cruel with personal attacks."

He thinks if Apple or Samsung were to add a "health" app, it would be game over for others. Samsung S5 will measure heart rate out of the box. Apple iOS8 will include a health package called "HealthKit,", and the iPhone 5s ships with the m7 chip that is already tracking a person's movements. What is still needed is an awareness of massive tracking and how people could choose to use it for their health and future goals.

In the near future consumers will measure as much data as possible about their health, lifestyle, and other parameters at home rather than in healthcare institutions, and use that data in their health management. Dancy's general view is that within two years most consumers will be in charge of their own health data and many medical decisions, and lower cost insurance

A summary of what parameters and elements
Chris Dancy measures and logs on a daily basis.

will be available to those who do this work. As soon as a $100 genetic test is available most people will use their genetic data to manage much of their decision making. He expects to see this common behavior by 2018.

He is looking forward to certain technological developments such as disposable sensors that track motion, skin response, room temperature, humidity, and more, revolutionizing health for people with low income, change the way we experience movies, theme parks, and our very relationship with the people and systems we interact with. Smart clothing that could give us a memory of events from their perspective. Imagine a prom dress that could be so much more magical if it had the ability to collect the experience. But the key is the ultimate health application programming interface as a way for these devices, sensors, services, and applications to talk to one another. Until then, he keeps on measuring a lot of parameters to improve his life.

Augmenting human capabilities

It will soon be possible to be faster, jump higher, think more rationally, be better at drawing, or have perfect eyesight as technological advances make these happen in coming years. What happens when such augmentation becomes commonplace or when we are able to augment even intelligence nobody knows. Moving health disadvantages to normal has been the focus of modern

Chris Dancy in October of 2012 (left) and in October of 2013 (right).

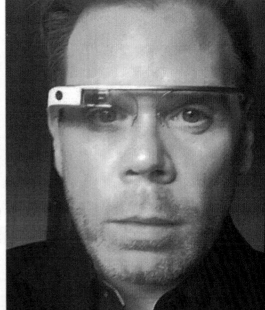

medicine. But the upcoming era will be dedicated to actually augmenting these. At what point is there an increased risk of losing what makes us human? When DARPA announced the creation of its Biological Technologies Office, an effort to "explore the increasingly dynamic intersection of biology and the physical sciences", it became clear that we are not far from creating "transhuman soldiers". Quadriplegic volunteers who partially or totally lost the use of all their limbs agreed to undergo brain surgery to have a small array placed on the surface of their brains that picked up neural signals for motor control. They learned to use them to control sophisticated robotic arms. It was a connection between the human brain and the rest of the world.

Does it really matter to what extent we implement technologies in our bodies if it can prevent or cure diseases? Would anyone oppose the extensive use of innovative technologies if it eradicated diseases? Imagine a fully automated "artificial pancreas" that closely mimics the insulin delivery of a working pancreas using technology that continuously monitors glucose levels and adjusts insulin delivery with minimal or no patient interaction. Imagine how the lives of diabetic patients worldwide could improve.

The real challenge is not the advancement of technologies as it is going forward. But from what point should it be considered a threat to humanity instead of a gift? Determining this will be a huge test.

The rise of recreational cyborgs will not only generate new technologies for longevity, but will initiate a dramatic change in the basic structure of society.

Score of availability: 2
Focus of attention: Patients
Websites & other online resources: Cybathlon
(http://www.cybathlon.ethz.ch/), Chris Dancy (http://www.chrisdancy.com/),
Prof. Steve Mann (http://www.eecg.toronto.edu/~mann)
Companies & start–ups: Glance (http://www.glanceapp.info/)
Books: Machine Man by Max Barry
Movies: I, Robot (2004), RoboCop (2014)

Trend 21. Cryonics and Longevity

Benjamin Franklin wrote in one of his letters in 1773 that he lived "in a century too little advanced, and too near the infancy of science" that he could not be preserved and revived to fulfill his desire to see and observe the state of the United States of America in a hundred years' time. Epic movies such as "2001: A Space Odyssey", "Aliens" or "Prometheus" all featured people preserved at low temperatures to survive a long space flight and later get reanimated. Cryotherapy has been used to treat skin conditions such as warts, moles, and skin tags. Whole body cryotherapy in specially designed chambers has been used as a rehabilitation method for athletes.

In real life, over 270 people have undergone cryopreservation since it was first proposed in 1962. That means they are frozen with the hope that healing and resuscitation may be possible in the future, although many scientists are skeptic about the idea.

Suspended animation was first tried on pigs (which are physiologically very similar to people) in 2002. Researchers replaced the pig's blood with a cold saline solution, cooling the pig's temperature to 10 Celsius (50F). Its injury was treated, and the pig was gradually warmed back up by replacing the saline with blood again. Despite being dead for a few hours, the pig's heart started beating on its own, and it had no apparent physical or cognitive impairment.

Similar saline–cooling procedures were used to reanimate people who have been recently declared dead. This was the background for research performed in Pennsylvania in May, 2014 to test a new method of freezing gunshot victims while doctors tried to save their lives. It is called emergency preservation and resuscitation. All the patient's blood get replaced with cold saline, which rapidly cools the body and stops almost all cellular activity. It remains to be proven whether the method is safe for wide use in emergency departments.

Regulations in this area are tricky as cryopreserving someone before they die can be considered murder. In the US, cryonics can only be legally performed after individuals have been pronounced legally dead.

The Cryonics Institute in Clinton Township, Michigan stores hundreds of cryopreserved people and animals along with DNA and tissue samples. Sub–zero temperatures halt cells from sustaining further damage from external sources. It costs thousands of dollars upon death, plus a one–time membership fee to get cryopreserved. On their website a buyer's guide and a book called "Cold Facts" are available, including details about preparing for the cryopreservation.

Critics have hit cryogenics hard from many perspectives. Bioethicists said that unless it is technically possible to replace all of the water left in a body's cells with glycol, an odorless, colorless, liquid material used in industrial applications like antifreeze formulations; unfreezing a frozen corpse will rupture the cell walls, ensuring that patients become a so–called "corpsesicle". For the moment, cryogenics remains an area of science fiction.

Transhumanist and philosopher Zoltan Istvan went further in arguing that "parents should have the legal right to painlessly put their extreme special needs children into a cryogenic state while they are biologically healthy and have years left on their lives". Such a point of view demonstrates that society has to start discussing these issues now.

How long can we live?

Hendrikje van Andel–Schipper was born in 1890 and died in 2005 at the age of 115. She left her body to science to find out how she remained in relatively good health for so long. Scientists found that about two–thirds of her white blood cells had been made by only two stem cells, meaning that she had "a superior system for repairing or aborting cells with dangerous mutations." To find the biological reasons for longevity, the Archon X Prize, a $10 million challenge, aimed at sequencing the DNA of 100 centenarians rapidly, accurately, and inexpensively. The centenarians donated their DNA to find out whether they have rare genes that may protect them from age–related diseases.

Due to aging, more and more solutions have to be worked out specifically for elderly people. The Stanford Center on Longevity launched a student contest in 2014. Contestant entries included "Automated Home Activity Monitoring", a system for detecting patterns of daily living and generating a call for help when necessary; "Caresolver", a caregiver platform to give caregivers support and facilitate coordination with a larger caregiving team; "Confage", an engaging gaming experience that teaches older users how to better use touch screen devices; or the winner "Eatwell", a tableware set specifically designed for the needs of people with Alzheimer's.

The science of life extension has many names from anti–aging medicine and indefinite life extension to experimental and biomedical gerontology. The point is that some people would like to live longer lives, and research has been generating a vast amount of data in recent years. Approaches might involve anti–aging drugs, vitamin supplements, repairing cells one by one by nanotechnology, cloning replacement parts, genetic modification, or the ultimate step of mind uploading in digital format.

A 2013 research poll in the United States found that 38% of Americans would want life extension treatments while 56% would reject them. What is surprising is that only 4% consider an "ideal lifespan" to be more than 120 years. The longest anyone has been definitively proven to live is 122 years. Jeanne Calment's birth records confirm her birth in 1875. She died in 1997. A person born today can expect to live more than 70 years based on today's actuarial tables. But globally that person will be able prolonge his life span to more than 100 years in a few decades. The first human who will live robustly to age 150 is already alive today.

Joel Garreau, author of Radical Evolution: The Promise and Peril of Enhancing Our Minds, Our Bodies—and What It Means to Be Human, sketched four possible scenarios for longevity. In scenario A, the exponential increases in biological, genetic, neurological, information, nano, and implant technologies will have relatively minor impact on current trends in lifespan, health span, costs, hospitals, and health insurance. In scenario B, such advances in genetics, robotics, information, and nanotechnology will succeed in increasing lifespan but largely fail to increase health span. Scenario C features advances in personalized medicine, tissue engineering, organ regeneration, implants, and memory enhancement as well as novel means of peering into the body along with major interventions in heart disease, diabetes, and cancer. Scenario D depicts an immortality that requires technology to advance faster than we age.

Aubrey de Grey is a British theoretician of gerontology and Chief Science Officer of the SENS Research Foundation. He suggested that a cure for aging is within reach in our lifetimes, while the majority of scientists disagree. He put forth his views in Strategies for Engineered Negligible Senescence, a research and advocacy program that aims to tackle issues related to aging. He says that aging is barbaric and should neither be allowed or accepted. To allow people to die is bad, and this is why he works to cure aging. He donated $13 million to the SENS Foundation after his mother died and left him an inheritance of roughly $16 million.

In the early 2010s, companies riding the tech wave have turned their attention to prolonging life. In 2013, Google announced the launch of a brand new company called Calico whose mission is to tackle aging and illness as well as to take a big-data approach to speed healthcare discoveries. The CEO is Art Levinson, chairman of Apple and former CEO of the biotech pioneer Genentech. The company has been persuading renowned scientists to join their efforts, although it is not clear what they actually plan to do.

In 2014, a new company was established by J. Craig Venter, leader of the private team that sequenced one of the first two human genomes, along with Peter Diamandis and Robert Hariri. The mission of "Human Longevity, Inc." is to help researchers understand diseases associated with age-related decline. To achieve this, the DNA of subjects from children to centenarians will be decoded and compiled into a database to include details on both genome and microbiome. They hope to sequence the genomes of over 100,000 people per year, with the intent of making "100-years-old the new 60."

Score of availability: 1

Focus of attention: Patients

Websites & other online resources: Cryogenics Society of America (http://www.cryogenicsociety.org),

SENS Research Foundation (http://www.sens.org/)

Companies & start-ups: Calico (https://en.wikipedia.org/wiki/Calico_(company)), Human Longevity Inc. (http://www.humanlongevity.com/)

Books: Countdown to Immortality by FM-2030, Schnall & de Grey

Movies: 2001: A Space Odyssey (1968), Alien (1979), Prometheus (2012)

Trend 22. What Will a Brand New Society Look Like?

The technologies, trends, and changes we've discussed make it evident that society as a whole will undergo serious and sometimes dramatic changes in the coming years. I have had very interesting talks with ethicists, philosophers, and those representing new concepts in medicine. For instance, I discussed the relationship between the human touch and disruptive technologies with Dr. Mairi Levitt, bioethicist at Lancaster University in the United Kingdom. She has firm beliefs about the changing status quo.

"I agree that innovative technology does not necessarily mean the human touch is removed but that is what seems to have happened so far. I think the human touch is now delivered by different lower status people (if at all). Perhaps innovative technology has worked best when the human touch is less relevant e.g. creating new artificial limbs, or better hip replacements.

The human touch– answering bells when patients ring, listening and responding to patient needs, sitting with new mothers to help them breast feed, feeding patients who can't feed themselves etc. – seem to become low status tasks compared with anything more high tech and are carried out when there is time by those on the lowest rung of the job hierarchy. High tech seems to equate with high status."

Dr. Levitt thinks there will be no major problems in technologies gaining acceptance if they can be presented as prolonging lives, improving treatment, and making life easier for caregivers. The real problem will be how the health service can afford them, and how to make the right decisions on priorities so that low tech treatments that help people are not neglected. She argued that the upcoming waves of technological change in medicine could be dangerous if medical students are encouraged to get excited about technology rather than about helping those who are ill. Medical education has to make sure that it trains good medical professionals who can secondarily deal with technology.

Judit Sándor, Director of the Center for Ethics and Law in Biomedicine at CEU, noted that what seems like enhancement for a medical professional may not look like that from the patient's point of view. What is desirable for one person may be entirely inadequate to another.

"If classifications are merely techno–centric or pathological, important aspects of fundamental rights may be ignored or simply neglected. Therefore I believe that policies should aim, first and foremost, to restore the dignity and liberty of the people affected. This might only involve the goal to increase physical accessibility to the workplace and to sensitize the work environment for someone who is now considered disabled. One should never view, however, (bio)technological enhancement as a tool for substituting the missing social solidarity."

While ethicists help us discuss the issues that extensive use of technologies in medicine might cause, the question is how to predict the next trends, or how to choose those that seem to have the most potential. Ian Pearson is a well–known futures consultant and sci–fi author who made plenty of successful predictions in You Tomorrow. He provided me with amazing suggestions when I started my journey as a medical futurist. He has definite theories about how hard it is to predict the future.

"Picking up on advances on making connections between nerve tissue and electronics, linking that to activity in skin patches monitoring blood properties, and factoring in ongoing miniaturization, you can easily make a short term prediction that we'll have plasters being used routinely to monitor health in hospital wards, a mid–term prediction that we will soon be able to use electronics on thin membranes or even in the skin surface to record and replay sensations, or display our current health state.

In fact, it was already possible to make such a long term prediction in 2001 when we first understood that we could print electronics on paper and that electronic signals could be transmitted via the skin. So depending what level of technology you consider, it is possible to look further into the future."

As advanced technology takes over more of diagnosis and treatment, human caregivers at all levels will migrate more toward the emotional interface role. He envisions that caring will resume its place as the most important role a nurse performs, for example, while doctors will dispense more advice for prevention and self–care. Machines will do most of the analysis. Advancing technology will encourage humans to focus on the human side and let machines do the work. Recognizing that advanced technology actually humanizes people will lead to the better acceptance of technology, and appreciation for the partnership of man and machine.

Technosexuality and beyond

A man named Davecat lives with his wife and mistress, both of whom are Synthetiks—specially designed, life-sized Dolls. Accordingly, Davecat calls himself a technosexual. In this book one of my goals was to demonstrate how society might change due to emerging technologies. While some will not understand how Davecat thinks about his partners, his story represents perfectly the diversity of concepts and theories that will arise in the next couple of years.

One of the reasons he agrees to make media appearances with his wife Sidore and their mistress Elena is to expose the general populace to the concept of Synthetik humans. Incidentally, Synthetik is a catch-all phrase that he started to use to describe both passive artificial companions, such as love dolls, and active ones such as Gynoids and Androids. Because Dolls are becoming increasingly realistic, humanoid robotics is advancing, and society's mindset is broadening, he believes we will see more and more Synthetiks in the next couple of decades. He told me he does what he does to affirm it is not only possible to lead a reasonably fulfilling life with artificial partners, but that he will not be the only one doing so in time.

"Being an iDollator has improved my life, without question. Having Sidore and Elena has enabled me to meet all sorts of interesting people, both within and outside the iDollator community, and make great friendships. As iDollator culture straddles the line between 'lifestyle' and 'hobby', I believe the same can be said once people are able to have their own Gynoid or Android partner.

Technosexuals will be able to get together and show off their artificial partners, and at the same time, learn new and interesting things pertaining to that world, much as people do when they get together for vintage car meets or those who collect Bakelite radios, for example. Synthetiks, and by extension, technology, genuinely do bring individuals together. To those with the right mindset, it dispels loneliness and fosters an amazing sense of community."

People's general view about his life is a three-way split, he says. There are those who think that silicone companions is intriguing and unique; those who already know about Synthetiks through media sources and think having

Davecat with his wife Sidore.

an artificial partner is for losers or perverts; and those who never heard of Synthetiks before encountering him.

"I think one of the reasons that detractors react as they do is due to jealousy. They may have gone through a series of unfulfilling relationships themselves, and seeing someone in love with a Synthetik companion may be upsetting to them. I'm always trying to convince those on the fence about Synthetiks, of course. Both Sidore and I get our fair share of people speaking ill of us, either directly to us or behind our backs on the Internet, but thankfully, we get more responses from supportive individuals, and a handful from those who have seen us on whatever documentary or television segment, saw how contented we are, and decided to save up for a silicone companion of their own. "

He agreed that with the right sort of AI programming a person could fall in love with an operating system. Videogames currently exist for handheld systems in Japan that simulate virtual girlfriends, and they are quite popular. Having a humanoid robot that resembles a human would be a sufficient draw for many people, but bestowing that robot with AI would lead to a new society. Anything that can simulate a flesh–and–blood human without any of the flaws or capriciousness of one would definitely be appealing to those who seek that quality. But what about those who are uncomfortable with such humanoids?

Davecat told me he can picture scores of lonely people, whether unlucky in romance, having trouble fitting in society, or elderly people who simply want someone to speak to – better yet a Gynoid or Android with the ability not only to listen but respond – would be a genuine benefit to thousands of individuals.

This story is merely one example of what changes and new concepts society will soon have to face and cope with. In the future we can expect a whole range of new attitudes, roles, and jobs that might sound weird today. A "Healthcare Navigator" might assist patients in accessing information they need in the jungle of healthcare systems. An "End of Life Therapist" might help in planning for the years before a client's death. A "Robot Counsellor" might help wealthy individuals who are looking to purchase robots for their homes determine which model is best suited to a family's needs.

What happens to the millions of prosthetics, breast implants, and pacemakers now in use after someone dies raises not only ecological problems but also represents the range of new problems that must get dealt with. Breast implants and replacement hips are currently not removed at death as there is no clear reason to do so. But cremation is a different issue. Titanium or cobalt implants do not burn up, and any batteries will explode when heated.

To tackle this problem the Dutch company Orthometals collects about 250 tons of such metals every year from crematoriums around Europe. It sells them to automobile and aeronautical industries. A second–hand implant may be the only way that millions of people can afford this life–saving equipment, and so the charity Pace4Life collects functioning pacemakers from funeral parlours for use in India.

With new concepts, technologies, and solutions, what now seem fantastic possibilities will be accompanied by genuine threats to humanity. It is our choice how far we go.

Score of availability: 1

Focus of attention: All of us

Websites & other online resources: The World Future Society (http://www.wfs.org/)

Companies & start–ups: –

Books: Society and Technological Change by Volti; Shaping Technology / Building Society by Bijker & Law

Movies: Metropolis (1926), Blade Runner (1982), 1984 (1984), Bicentennial Man (1999)

Part III: Preparing For the Future of Medicine

Keep yourself up–to–date

No matter how you are related to healthcare, following the main trends of medicine has advantages such as keeping you in the loop of important developments. Try to be up–to–date by using digital methods: subscribing to quality resources and news sites via RSS, or transforming your social media channels into news streams. For example, it took me several months to hide the contacts on Facebook who never post useful articles, and begin to follow pages that covered my favorite topics. Now my Facebook stream is a pure gold mine of relevant information like Twitter and Google+ are. Curation does not only apply for content, but for contacts as well.

Medicalfuturist.com features curated news about the future of medicine every day. It also offers this as a free daily newsletter. Examples of websites covering topics about the future include IO9.com (http://io9.com/tag/futurism), Kurzweil AI (http://www.kurzweilai.net/), and the World Future Society (http://www.WFS.org).

Embrace digital

Whether you like it or not, the world is becoming more and more centered on technologies. It does not necessarily mean that everyone has to agree with all the upcoming changes, or that our lives will all become centered around digital from now on, but accepting the increasing importance of digital is a useful thing to do. Many patients will require a different, more human–based perspective from their caregivers. The needs of these patients, even if the world is fully technological, will have to be addressed. Constantly look for solutions to improve one's practice as a medical professional or one's health as a patient. Time management and certain online solutions might save you a lot of time every week. Embrace digital comfortably and only use techniques that make your life easier and your work more efficient.

Read, listen and watch

No other time of entertainment history has produced as many movies, interviews, and television shows as we have today, or led to the creation of books meant to initiate discussions about the future. Movies such as "Her" (2013) or "Gattaca" (1997), and books such as *Physics of the Future* by Michio Kaku, and Our *Final Invention* by James Barrat speak about ethical issues and considerations we will have to start discussing soon.

Look outside of medicine

Keeping an eye on only medical–related developments will cause you to miss opportunities developing in other industries but which could easily be applied to medicine. What if the next announcement that has a chance to revolutionize a medical specialty comes from nanotechnology, the energy sector, or robotics? Keeping an open eye and informing oneself about concepts not specifically related to medicine could avoid this. IBM's Watson supercomputer or the first nanotubes were not designed with medical applications in mind. But these could still contribute to the advancement of medical technology.

Avoid hype

Hype in medicine has never done anything meaningful. Too much hype can hurt a research area when people realize that the high expectations generated in the early phases have not been met. It took years to get over the hype about smartphone applications. Now, instead of downloading a lot of medical apps, people have gradually learned to choose only the pertinent ones. Evidence backed by massive data is needed for any sensible use of digital solutions in medicine. Checking these studies and papers gives a picture about key research areas. Use Pubmed.com or Google Scholar (scholar.google.com) for this purpose.

Extrapolate from today's trends

Strategically analyze trends and extrapolate the future in a meaningful way. Checking the online resources, databases, books, and movies I have suggested after every trend can help gather more relevant details. Being hungry for new information will be a key feature in the future, and the amount will grow exponentially day by day. Identify which trends seem relevant to your needs. Try to become almost an expert in that. Trend watching is not enough; but knowledge is needed to make your own assessment about technologies, as well as skills that let you choose which trends are the most important ones.

Forget about the ultimate solution

There are movements and philosophies that highlight one concept or approach even though it is highly unlikely that one solution will lead to a prosperous future. A network of interconnected people, devices, and concepts is intended to solve global issues. It is advisable not to trust just one movement or philosophy such as transhumanism or singularitarians. The most plausible solution will be a mix of all the concepts trying to describe the coming decades. Be skeptical and analytical before accepting major philosophies about the future. In the history of mankind the number of new philosophies has never increased as fast as it is doing no. But it has never been easier to learn more about them.

Don't get scared by the growing importance of technology

Sometimes, the development of various technologies shows a world that is far away from our ideal, but as history has shown it is not common for a particular technology to revolutionize our way of living in a short amount of time. It took over a decade for the Internet to reach its current status; driverless cars have not yet appeared on the roads despite driving millions of miles without incident; and augmented reality devices such as smart glasses or Google Glass have not yet changed the way surgeons teach medical students at thousands of medical schools even though they have been around for years. Such changes will happen eventually, but in medicine and healthcare it takes time to implement change. We need it to properly adjust to new needs.

Don't overestimate technology

When the Human Genome Project was completed people expected that the practice of medicine would be revolutionized within years. It took over a decade to implement the first genomic variants in medical decision making, and it is still a slow and ongoing process. When the iPhone appeared physicians and patients looked forward to using them at home for medical purposes. It took almost a decade for the first evidence–based medical application to get accepted by insurance companies. Technology alone will not provide solutions to the major problems that healthcare institutions face worldwide. It can provide us with tools and opportunities, but nothing more.

Don't give up if you lack IT skills

A lot of medical professionals, particularly older ones, have told me they have given up on keeping track of new technologies because sometimes they even have a hard time turning on a computer. For them, forthcoming solutions will be a huge help given that IT equipment is expected to become simpler in the coming years. By being able to input data into medical records on holographic keyboards and simple user interfaces instead of suffering with antiquated systems will facilitate the job for those who now struggle with technologies.

Fight to keep the human touch

Even though I might sound optimistic given the preface and introduction to this book, the quick rise of technological advances shows the promise of removing the human element in medical practice. This scenario largely depends on how we tackle the challenges we will soon face. Let's find solutions that enable, moreover require, the human touch. While healthcare will become more efficient, medicine will still be centered on people communicating with each other.

Accept mutual relationships

Without a public acceptance of the mutual relationship between using disruptive technologies and maintaining the human touch, the coming waves of changes will only lead to strife. If conservative stakeholders of medicine only want to keep the human touch and spread a feeling of fear against technologies, or if technologists overpromise new devices and techniques, then the outcome will be the least desirable for us all. There must be a balance between these approaches, and I remain confident that by learning about both sides it will become possible to prepare for that balance over time.

Prepare others for the changes

Even in 2014 it is relatively rare to read or watch news segments that depict future technologies and how they could be used in medicine. It is still a big deal when someone mentions longevity, nanotechnology, or surgical robotics in a television program. There is only a small set of online resources covering these issues, their ethical considerations, and potential threats. What would help is discussing such ideas and directions with one another. Spread the word, ask questions, and engage people who are interested in the amazing intersection of technology and the practice of medicine.

Predicting the future of medicine is challenging

Medicine and healthcare represent unique fields that are based on very specific rules, and where new methods and treatments are added to an old basic structure. Nobody can predict the future of medicine in detail, although extrapolating to upcoming years based on current trends is one possible way. As a proof, in the 18th century French painters were asked to paint what the world would be like in the year 2000. Checking the results you will realize these artists had pretty crazy ideas, as well as they hit the nail with some others such as teleconferencing or fast vehicles. However, they made mistakes assuming that education would be like putting books into a machine that would transfer the knowledge into the minds of students. While it would be beneficial, the approach works better for IBM's Watson than it does for people. As these research trends are constantly evolving, repeated evaluation of the choices we've made is necessary to make sure that the picture we have about the future is still relevant.

Communicate and crowdsource

The end of this book should mean the beginning of many discussions. The whole community talking about the future is interested in your opinions concerning trends that shape the future. Given that a goal of this guide is to initiate public discussions, please feel free to use the #medicalfuture hashtag on Twitter, as well as any blogs and other social media channels to express your thoughts. Influence decision makers if your idea can make a change. Be bold and feel free to crowdsource solutions to complicated problems; use the power of the masses and crowdfund if you have a good idea without the required financial background. There are no limitations for good ideas any more.

Conclusion

"There is nothing like a dream to create the future."
-Victor Hugo

Futurists such as Ray Kurzweil and Ian Pearson usually talk about one of the final inventions of mankind, the digital brain. By the time we understand how the brain works neuron by neuron on small and large scales, we should be able to download our thoughts, our mind, and our memories and live forever in this digital brain. While it won't happen any time soon, I feel that the digital brain has already been invented in my professional life. I call it social media.

Online, I have access to a large repository of expert minds in my fields of interests. I can count on them whenever I need answers or basic information about scientific, medical, or clinical issues. I live within a huge network of people with whom I can communicate constantly. Back when I had a complicated question as a medical student I could ask my professors, fellow students, and maybe make a few phone calls. But often I was alone without an answer. It was a terrible feeling to be left alone when making important decisions. I never wanted to feel that way again. Therefore I spent years creating online networks on my blog, Google+, Facebook, Twitter, and Linkedin to assure that professionally I would never be alone again. Making it possible for every medical professional and patient to say the same line: I'm never alone. This might be the biggest invention in the history of medicine.

Innovation happens faster than ever. Huge companies and start-ups are eager to revolutionize small or large segments of medicine. Patients are becoming e-patients who persuade their doctors to move closer to the digital world. By educating students and medical professionals over time, we can give them the skills to save time in their practices and to be better guides for their patients in this digital jungle. Recent examples have demonstrated the potential and power of technology, and how it can give us better opportunities to connect, learn, and improve as people. What is still missing is a comprehensive, extensive, and public discussion that includes ethicists and representatives of all groups in order to cover the major issues about to shape the future of healthcare and medicine. This book was meant to initiate such debates and, hopefully, it is just the beginning.

Based on the trends and technologies presented in this book, we can assume that no matter how important a role technology will play in our lives, human touch is and will always be the key in the doctor–patient relationship. Even though the waves of change coming towards us will be huge, and the effects may be devastating, medicine can not only survive but a new system of healthcare and a new way of practicing medicine will be born if all the stakeholders are prepared. Each can make its own assumptions, and acquire whatever skills are needed to adjust to this ever–changing new world. I think we have time, and that it is still possible.

I hope that this book will help people prepare for the amazing yet uncertain future of medicine, as well as a new world of healthcare that optimistically leads to an era when a guide is not needed any more.

Acknowledgements

Ernest Hemingway who won the Nobel Prize in Literature in 1954 said in his acceptance speech that "Writing at its best is a lonely life." I'm very thankful to my wife who made sure this does not apply to me. I'm grateful to my family for bearing with me throughout the long months while I was writing. And I'm pleased to have my friends who kept on sending me amusing e-mails when they knew I was working hard.

Many thanks to Lucien Engelen for writing the foreword for this book; and for providing me with a lot of suggestions and advice over the years.

This book would not be the same without the amazing editorial work of Dr. Richard E. Cytowic; the cover art of Szilvia Kora; and the interior design of Roland Rekeczki.

I cannot be thankful enough to all the experts who agreed to be interviewed for this book, including Jason Berek-Lewis, Dr. Christian Assad-Kottner, Denise Silber, Dave deBronkart, Jared Heyman, Alexander Ryu, Isabel Hoffmann, Mathias Kück, Dr. Rafael Grossmann, Ziv Meltzer, Dr. Arun Mathews, Kimble L. Jenkins, Sarah Doll, Dr. Jur Koksma, Prof. Blake Hannaford, Dr. Catherine Mohr, Prof. Jacob Rosen, Dr. Joel Dudley, Prof. George Church, Dr. Edward Abrahams, Prof. Takao Someya, Dr. Dave Albert, Prof. Robert Langer, Prof. Anthony Atala, Jack Andraka, Michael Molitch-Hou, Mike Renard, Russ Angold, Prof. Robert Hester, Dr. Casey Bennett, Dr. András Paszternák, Conor Russomanno, Ariel Garten, Prof. Robert Riener, Chris Dancy, Prof. Steve Mann, Davecat, Ian Pearson, Dr. Mairi Levitt, Dr. Malia Fullerton, Prof. Judit Sandor, Prof. Ed Boyden and many companies and startups.

I also appreciate the music that helped me write for long hours provided by the Focus@Will team and the songs composed by Cliff Martinez.

Illustration Sources

Page 7: E–Patient Dave deBronkart

Page 16: Wellapets

Page 22: Fotografie Katharina Jäger ©2011

Page 26: TellSpec

Page 28: HapiFork

Page 29: Dr. Rafael Grossmann

Page 33: Eye–On Glasses

Page 38: InTouch Health

Page 45: NerdCore Medical

Page 51: [2014] Intuitive Surgical, Inc

Page 53: Dr. Catherine Mohr

Page 55: Prof. Blake Hannaford, University of Washington, and Prof. Jacob
        Rosen, University of California, Santa Cruz.

Page 58: H&S–Robots

Page 64: National Human Genome Research Institute

Page 66: Gentle

Page 72: Takao Someya

Page 73: Takayasu Sakurai & Takao Someya

Page 74: Takao Someya

Page 75: MC10

Page 76: MC10

Page 78: Scanadu

Page 81: AliveCor

Page 82: Courtesy of Labonfoil EU Project 224306.

Page 84: Courtesy of Labonfoil EU Project 224306.

Page 85: pApp

Page 88: Prof. Atala, Wake Forest Institute for Regenerative Medicine

Page 89: Prof. Atala, Wake Forest Institute for Regenerative Medicine

Page 90: Prof. Atala, Wake Forest Institute for Regenerative Medicine

Page 91: Prof. Atala, Wake Forest Institute for Regenerative Medicine

Page 96: Jack Andraka

Page 97: Jack Andraka

Page 99: License: Creative Commons Attribution–ShareAlike 3.0 Unported License.

Page 105: Organovo

Page 106: Organovo

Page 109: Robohand.

Page 112: 3D Systems

Page 113: 3D Systems

Page 115: Ekso Bionics.

Page 117: Courtesy 3D Systems.

Page 118: Courtesy 3D Systems.

Page 119: Touch Bionics.

Page 125: Timothy.ruban on Wikipedia; license: Creative Commons Attribution–Share
Alike 3.0 Unported.

Page 130: User:Clockready on Wikimedia Commons, license: Creative Commons
Attribution–ShareAlike 3.0 Unported

Page 132: Casey C. Bennett & Kris Hauser [2013] "Artificial intelligence framework for
simulating clinical decision–making: A Markov decision process approach."
Artificial Intelligence in Medicine. 57(1): 9–19

Page 144: NXT Health

Page 147: Li Li, Mount Sinai Icahn School of Medicine, and Ayasdi

Page 151: InteraXon

Page 154: OpenBCI

Page 163: D'Arc. Studio Associates Architects

Page 165: Steve Mann, (2013). "Veillance and Reciprocal Transparency: Surveillance
versus Sousveillance, AR Glass, Lifeglogging, and Wearable Computing"
Proceedings of the IEEE ISTAS 2013, Toronto, Ontario, Canada, pp1–12.

Page 166: http://wearcam.org

Page 167: Chris Dancy

Page 168: Chris Dancy

Page 169: Chris Dancy

Page 178: Itagaki Azusa

Page 178: Itagaki Azusa

References

Introduction
Pew Research, 15 Theses About the Digital Future
http://www.pewinternet.org/2014/03/11/15-theses-about-the-digital-future/

Empowered Patients
Yahoo Finance, Genentech and PatientsLikeMe Enter Patient-Centric Research Collaboration - http://finance.yahoo.com/news/genentech-patientslikeme-enter-patient-centric-130000088.html
Crowdmed, https://www.crowdmed.com/how-it-works?category=patient
Crowdsourcing A Mom's Medical Diagnosis: Help is needed!
http://scienceroll.com/2012/07/02/crowdsourcing-a-moms-medical-diagnosis-help-is-needed/http://artisopensource.net/
Research Conducted Using Data Obtained through Online Communities: Ethical Implications of Methodological Limitations, PLoS Med. 2012;9(10):e1001328
Accelerated clinical discovery using self-reported patient data collected online and a patient-matching algorithm, Nature Biotechnology 29, 411-414 (2011) doi:10.1038/nbt.1837
http://www.ted.com/speakers/dave_debronkart

Gamifying Health
Do We Have a Winner? Gamification in Healthcare http://www.healthbizdecoded.com/2013/05/do-we-have-a-winner-gamification-in-healthcare/
Wired, Can Gamification Help Fix One of the Biggest Health Problems You've Never Heard Of? http://insights.wired.com/profiles/blogs/seeking-solutions-to-the-biggest-problem-you-ve-never-heard-of#axzz2wujFwuqb
From gamification to personalized medicine, here's a list of companies pitching at IMPACT http://medcitynews.com/2013/10/want-know-pitching-impact-check-list/
12 Surprising Gamification Stats for 2013 http://www.getmoreengagement.com/gamification/12-surprising-gamification-stats-for-2013
Gamification: Still the Future of Fitness?
http://dailyburn.com/life/tech/gamification-future-of-fitness/
Playing for better health with BioGaming http://blogs.msdn.com/b/healthblog/archive/2014/03/24/playing-for-better-health-with-biogaming.aspx
Wired, Forget the Quantified Self. We Need to Build the Quantified Us http://www.wired.com/2014/04/forget-the-quantified-self-we-need-to-build-the-quantified-us/
Alternate Reality Game Will Turn You Into a Fitness Maniac

http://www.fastcodesign.com/3028503/alternate-reality-game-will-turn-you-into-a-fitness-maniac

Wikipedia, Re-Mission, https://en.wikipedia.org/wiki/Re-Mission

PSFK Future Of Health Report (slideshow)

http://www.slideshare.net/PSFK/psfk-future-of-health-report-33393202

Serious Games Transforming Health Through Challenging Conversations

http://seriousgamesmarket.blogspot.fr/2014/04/serious-games-transforming-health.html

Nintendo Wii rehabilitation („Wii-hab") provides benefits in Parkinson's disease. Parkinsonism Relat Disord. 2013 Nov;19(11):1039-42.

The Nintendo Wii as a tool for neurocognitive rehabilitation, training and health promotion, Computers in Human Behavior Volume 31, February 2014, Pages 384-392

Mobile Health News, Eight ways the Microsoft Kinect will change healthcare

http://mobihealthnews.com/25281/eight-ways-the-microsoft-kinect-will-change-healthcare/

Science Daily, Wii-playing surgeons may improve performance on laparoscopic procedures http://www.sciencedaily.com/releases/2013/02/130227183500.htm

How do you solve a problem like medication non-adherence?

http://www.bcmj.org/blog/how-do-you-solve-problem-medication-non-adherence

Why the University of Washington Wants Its Surgeons to Play Videogames

http://allthingsd.com/20130911/why-the-university-of-washington-wants-its-surgeons-to-play-videogames/

Medical News Today, Researchers use Lumosity to identify early cognitive impairment in cirrhosis patients http://www.medicalnewstoday.com/releases/273503.php

Eating in the Future

5 Futuristic Food Trends

http://abcnews.go.com/Health/futuristic-food-trends/story?id=20954898#5

Business Insider, This Test-Tube Burger Could Literally Save The World

http://www.businessinsider.com/cultured-beef-burger-could-save-the-world-2013-8

R.I.'s Food Innovation Nexus seeks to create foods to treat medical conditions

http://www.providencejournal.com/breaking-news/content/20131229-r.i.s-food-innovation-nexus-seeks-to-create-foods-to-treat-medical-conditions.ece

BBC Future, The future of food

http://www.bbc.com/future/story/20140206-the-future-of-food

14 Reasons to Be Hopeful About the Future of Food

http://foodtank.com/news/2013/10/fourteen-reasons-to-be-hopeful-about-the-future-of-food

Engadget, Foodini is a 3D printer for everything from burgers to gnocchi

http://www.engadget.com/2014/03/27/foodini/?ncid=rss_truncated

The Guardian, Food trends in 2014: from digital dining to healthy junk food
http://www.theguardian.com/lifeandstyle/2014/jan/06/food-trends-2014-digital-dining-healthy-junk-food
Technology at the dining table, Spence and Piqueras-Fiszman Flavour 2013, 2:16
The Elderly Get the First Taste of 3D Printed Future Food
http://3dprintingindustry.com/2014/04/14/3d-printed-future-food
IEET, Future Technology Could Eliminate the Need to Eat Food
http://ieet.org/index.php/IEET/more/pelletier20130107
The Atlantic, The Man Who Would Make Food Obsolete http://www.theatlantic.com/health/archive/2014/04/the-man-who-would-make-eating-obsolete/361058/
Will Stem Cell Burgers Go Mainstream?
http://www.iflscience.com/plants-and-animals/will-stem-cell-burgers-go-mainstream
IO9.com, Could Soylent really replace all of the food in your diet?
http://io9.com/could-soylent-really-replace-all-of-the-food-in-your-di-510890007

Augmented Reality and Virtual Reality
Science Daily, Special glasses help surgeons ,see' cancer
http://www.sciencedaily.com/releases/2014/02/140210184257.htm
Medgadget, Google Glass App Turns Anyone Into Rapid Diagnostic Test Expert
http://www.medgadget.com/2014/02/google-glass-app-turns-anyone-into-rapid-diagnostic-test-expert.html
10 ways Google Glass could show up in everyday medical care http://www.mlive.com/news/grand-rapids/index.ssf/2014/01/10_ways_google_glass_could_tra.html
Forbes, ,OK Glass, Save A Life.' The Application Of Google Glass In Sudden Cardiac Death http://www.forbes.com/sites/johnnosta/2013/07/06/ok-glass-save-a-life-the-application-of-google-glass-in-sudden-cardiac-arrest/
Medgadget, Google Glass Coming to Rhode Island Emergency Room to Help Diagnose Skin Conditions (VIDEO) http://www.medgadget.com/2014/03/google-glass-coming-to-rhode-island-emergency-room-to-help-diagnose-skin-conditions.html
Researchers develop Google Glass app that delivers instant analysis of point-of-care diagnostic tests http://www.imedicalapps.com/2014/03/researchers-google-glass-app-medical-diagnostic-tests/
Graphene smart contact lenses could give you thermal infrared and UV vision
http://www.extremetech.com/extreme/178593-graphene-smart-contact-lenses-could-give-you-thermal-infrared-and-uv-vision
Continuous Monitoring Contact Lenses - A Moonshot Proposal
http://www.engineering.com/DesignerEdge/DesignerEdgeArticles/ArticleID/6415/Continuous-Monitoring-Contact-Lenses--A-Moonshot-Proposal.aspx

The Next Web, How augmented reality is augmenting its own future
http://thenextweb.com/insider/2014/01/31/augmented-reality-augmenting-future/#!Bcn94
Facebook, Google, And Sony Are Getting Ready To Fight A Cyberpunk War
http://www.fastcodesign.com/3027921/facebook-google-and-sony-are-getting-ready-to-fight-a-cyberpunk-war
Daily Mail, Glass without the glasses: Google patents smart contact lens system with a CAMERA built in http://www.dailymail.co.uk/sciencetech/article-2604543/Glass-without-glasses-Google-patents-smart-contact-lens-CAMERA-built-in.html
Medgadget, Personal Neuro Seeks to Combine Google Glass with EEG [INTERVIEW]
http://www.medgadget.com/2014/04/personal-neuro-seeks-to-combine-google-glass-with-eeg-interview.html
Doctor Credits Google Glass For Saving This Patient's Life http://www.huffingtonpost.com/2014/04/10/google-glass-saves-life-steven-horng_n_5120371.html
Breastfeeding Mothers Getting Help From Google Glass?
http://scienceroll.com/2014/02/04/breastfeeding-mothers-getting-help-from-google-glass/
Wearable technology to improve education and patient outcomes in a cardiology fellowship program - a feasibility study, Health and Technology December 2013, Volume 3, Issue 4, pp 267-270

Telemedicine and Remote Care

Smithsonian.com, Telemedicine Predicted in 1925
http://www.smithsonianmag.com/history/telemedicine-predicted-in-1925-124140942/?no-ist
GizMag, iRobot receives FDA approval for physician avatar RP-VITA
http://www.gizmag.com/irobot-intouch-health-rp-vita-medical-fda-approval/25977/
When Life Gives You Lemons, Make Lemonade. When Life Gives You Cancer...
https://medium.com/personal-stories-about-healthcare/when-life-gives-you-lemons-make-lemonade-when-life-gives-you-cancer-b2c9a3d8aa6d
What is the future of telemedicine?
http://blog.econocom.com/en/blog/what-is-the-future-of-telemedicine/
These 4 Companies Could Alter the Future of Telehealth http://www.fool.com/investing/general/2014/02/06/these-4-companies-could-alter-the-future-of-telehe.aspx
Should It Really Take 14 Years to Become a Doctor?
http://www.slate.com/articles/health_and_science/medical_examiner/2014/03/physician_shortage_should_we_shorten_medical_education.html
The Guardian, Telehealth can play an important role in the future of healthcare
http://www.theguardian.com/healthcare-network/2013/nov/12/telehealth-important-role-future-healthcare

Deloitte, eVisits: the 21st century housecall http://www2.deloitte.com/content/dam/Deloitte/global/Documents/Technology-Media-Telecommunications/gx-tmt-2014prediction-evisits.pdf

Larry Page Makes the Case for Electronic Medical Records https://www.linkedin.com/today/post/article/20140322154035-19886490-larry-page-on-electronical-medical-records-ted

Robots let doctors ‚beam' into remote hospitals http://www.modernhealthcare.com/article/20131117/INFO/311169930

Venure Beat, Practice Fusion owes its success — and its culture — to a motorcycle crash http://venturebeat.com/2013/01/29/practice-fusion-owes-its-success-and-its-culture-to-a-motorcycle-crash/

IEEE, Remote tactile sensing glove-based system http://ieeexplore.ieee.org/xpl/articleDetails.jsp?arnumber=5626824

Physician Shortages to Worsen Without Increases in Residency Training https://www.aamc.org/download/153160/data/physician_shortages_to_worsen_without_increases_in_residency_tr.pdf

Global Challenges Facing Humanity http://www.millennium-project.org/millennium/Global_Challenges/chall-08.html

Re-Thinking the Medical Curriculum

UA College of Medicine Cuts Deal For Synthetic Cadaver http://www.tucsonweekly.com/TheRange/archives/2013/10/31/ua-college-of-medicine-cuts-deal-for-synthetic-cadaver

Medgadget, Virtual Reality Dissection System Helps Study Anatomy, Spare a Cadaver (VIDEO) http://www.medgadget.com/2014/04/virtual-reality-dissection-system-helps-study-anatomy-spare-a-cadaver-video.html

The New York Times, The Virtual Anatomy, Ready for Dissection http://www.nytimes.com/2012/01/08/business/the-human-anatomy-animated-with-3-d-technology.html

Medgadget, Real Time MRI Guidance and Visualization for Brain Surgery Using Clearpoint System: Interview with CEO of MRI Interventions http://www.medgadget.com/2013/11/real-time-mri-guidance-and-visualization-for-brain-surgery-using-clearpoint-system-interview.html

Surgical and Humanoid Robots

Jacob Rosen, Surgical Robotics - Chapter 5, In "Medical Devices" edited by Martin Culjat, Rahul Singh, and Hua Lee, John Wiley & Sons 2013 pp. 63-97.

Jacob Rosen, Blake Hannaford, Richard Satava, Surgical Robotics - Systems Applications and Visions, 1st edition 2011 by Springer, ISBN 978-1-4419-1126-1 http://www.springerlink.com/content/978-1-4419-1125-4#section=841753&page=1

Information Week, 10 Medical Robots That Could Change Healthcare
http://www.informationweek.com/mobile/10-medical-robots-that-could-change-healthcare/d/d-id/1107696?page_number=2
Here's a robot that can draw your blood
http://www.dvice.com/2013-7-28/heres-robot-can-draw-your-blood
Medical Robots: Current Systems and Research Directions, Journal of Robotics Volume 2012 (2012), Article ID 401613, 14 pages
Technology Review, Building a Self-Assembling Stomach-Bot
http://www.technologyreview.com/news/410857/building-a-self-assembling-stomach-bot/
Healthcare Innovation and the National Robotics Initiative
http://blog.larta.org/2013/08/28/healthcare-innovation-and-the-national-robotics-initiative/
Wired, Peering under your skin: the future of surgical robotics is virtual
http://www.wired.co.uk/news/archive/2013-06/11/robo-surgeons
Medgadget, Intuitive's New da Vinci Xi Robotic Surgical System Unveiled (VIDEO)
http://www.medgadget.com/2014/04/intuitives-new-da-vinci-xi-robotic-surgical-system-unveiled-video.html
Using Drones to Deliver Medical Supplies in Roadless Areas
http://engineering.curiouscatblog.net/2014/04/10/using-drones-to-deliver-medical-supplies-in-roadless-areas/
Medical News Today, Improving the human-robot connection
http://www.medicalnewstoday.com/releases/275441.php
Daily Mail, Carl the robot bartender serves customers at German bar
http://www.dailymail.co.uk/news/article-2379966/Carl-robot-bartender-pours-drinks-customers-German-bar.html

Genomics and Truly Personalized Medicine

Kurzweil AI, Craig Venter's 'biological teleportation' device
http://www.kurzweilai.net/craig-venters-biological-teleportation-device
Forbes, A DNA Sequencing Breakthrough That Many Expectant Moms Will Want
http://www.forbes.com/sites/stevensalzberg/2014/03/09/a-dna-sequencing-breathrough-that-many-expectant-moms-will-want/
Medgadget, Handheld DNA Analyzer Wraps Up Indiegogo Campaign: Interview with Jonathan O'Halloran, QuantuMDx's Chief Scientific Officer
http://www.medgadget.com/2014/03/handheld-dna-analyzer-wraps-up-indiegogo-campaign-interview-with-jonathan-ohalloran-quantumdxs-chief-scientific-officer.html
Penn State Researchers Create 3D Models from DNA Samples
http://3dprintingindustry.com/2014/03/31/3d-models-dna-penn-state-research

The Guardian, Startup offering DNA screening of ,hypothetical babies' raises fears over designer children http://www.theguardian.com/technology/2014/apr/07/disease-free-digital-baby-designer-children-fears

Personalized Medicine Coalition, The Case for 3rd Edition Personalized Medicine http://www.personalizedmedicinebulletin.com/wp-content/uploads/sites/205/2011/11/Case_for_PM_3rd_edition1.pdf

Body Sensors Inside and Out

A New Wi-Fi-Enabled Tooth Sensor Rats You Out When You Smoke or Overeat http://motherboard.vice.com/blog/a-new-wi-fi-enabled-tooth-sensor-rats-you-out-when-youre-smoking-or-overeating

Smart Embedded Devices: Here They Come http://biomedicalcomputationreview.org/content/smart-embedded-devices-here-they-come

Digestive Diagnostics: Portable, Wearable, Insideable http://ibs.aurametrix.com/2014/02/digestive-diagnostics-portable-wearable.html

IEEE, Putting Electronics in People http://spectrum.ieee.org/tech-talk/biomedical/devices/putting-electronics-in-people

Mashable, Lifelogging: The Most Miserable, Self-Aware 30 Days I've Ever Spent http://mashable.com/2014/03/20/lifelogging-experiment/

Health: Sensing Trouble http://therotarianmagazine.com/health-sensing-trouble/

The Verge, Smart skin patch knows when you need your meds http://www.theverge.com/2014/3/30/5558990/smart-skin-patch-knows-when-you-need-your-meds

Engadget, ,Wello' iPhone case can track your blood pressure, temperature and more http://www.engadget.com/2014/03/06/wello/

World Future Society, The Future of Biometric Identification and Authentication http://www.wfs.org/blogs/ian-pearson/future-biometric-identification-and-authentication

Medgadget, One Step Closer to the Artificial Pancreas: Interview with Medtronic's Dr. Francine Kaufman https://www.medgadget.com/2014/04/one-step-closer-to-the-artificial-pancreas-interview-with-medtronics-dr-francine-kaufman.html

CNN, FDA approves first bionic eye http://edition.cnn.com/2013/02/19/health/fda-bionic-eye/

The website of Takao Someya http://www.jst.go.jp/erato/someya/en/project

Engadget, Japanese ,smart clothing' uses nanofibers to monitor your heart-rate (video) http://www.engadget.com/2014/01/30/ntt-docomo-toray-smart-cloth/

Medical News Today, Online game helps doctors improve patients' blood pressure faster http://www.medicalnewstoday.com/releases/276932.php

The Medical Tricorder and Portable Diagnostics

A complete medical check-up on a chip
http://phys.org/news/2014-03-medical-check-up-chip.html
A Revolutionary Portable Lab for Rapid and Low-Cost Diagnosis http://www.mdtmag.com/news/2014/02/revolutionary-portable-lab-rapid-and-low-cost-diagnosis
Techcrunch, Biomeme Wants To Turn Your iOS Device Into A Disease-Detecting Mobile DNA Lab http://techcrunch.com/2013/08/07/biomeme-wants-to-turn-your-ios-device-into-a-disease-detecting-mobile-dna-lab/
The Economist, The dream of the medical tricorder http://www.economist.com/news/technology-quarterly/21567208-medical-technology-hand-held-diagnostic-devices-seen-star-trek-are-inspiring
Portable Lab Enables Fast Diagnosis of Medical and Environmental Conditions http://www.atelier.net/en/trends/articles/portable-lab-enables-fast-diagnosis-medical-and-environmental-conditions_427875
Diagnostics: A Focus on Imaging, Portability, and Regulations http://www.mdtmag.com/articles/2013/06/diagnostics-focus-imaging-portability-and-regulations
Science Daily, Biological testing tool, ScanDrop, tests in fraction of time and cost of industry standard http://www.sciencedaily.com/releases/2014/03/140326142305.htm
BBC News, ‚Star Trek' - The Tricorder
http://news.bbc.co.uk/dna/place-lancashire/plain/A55853012
51 digital health metrics in 2013
http://mobihealthnews.com/27638/51-digital-health-metrics-in-2013/
Wired, A Gold Gadget That Would Let You Stop Heart Attacks With a Smartphone http://www.wired.com/2014/04/clear-3-d-printed-defibrillators-can-shock-heart-without-pads
Techcrunch, Apple Introduces HealthKit For Tracking Health And Fitness Data http://techcrunch.com/2014/06/02/apple-ios-health/
iBGStar® Blood Glucose Meter http://www.bgstar.com/web/ibgstar

Growing Organs in a Dish

Fear of Immortality http://www.slate.com/articles/technology/future_tense/2013/08/aging_polls_and_life_extension_why_don_t_americans_want_to_live_longer.html
TED, Growing new organs
https://www.ted.com/talks/anthony_atala_growing_organs_engineering_tissue
Process Devised to Generate Stem Cells from Drop of Blood
http://sciencebusiness.technewslit.com/?p=17197
Scientific American, Future of Medicine: Advances in Regenerative Medicine Teach Body How to Rebuild Damaged Muscles, Tissues and Organs

http://www.scientificamerican.com/article/future-of-medicine-advances-regenerative-medicine-rebuild-damaged-muscles-tissues-organs/

The Future of Regenerative Medicine

http://www.huffingtonpost.com/andre-choulika/post_5200_b_3598945.html

World Future Society, Investing in the Future of Regenerative Medicine

http://www.wfs.org/blogs/james-lee/investing-future-regenerative-medicine

The future of regenerative medicine: Stem cell therapy may be approaching faster than you think http://www.sp-exchange.ca/2014/02/26/the-future-of-regenerative-medicine-stem-cell-therapy-may-be-approaching-faster-than-you-think/

Gel to heal divide between bones and surgical implants

http://www.rsc.org/chemistryworld/2014/04/gel-heal-divide-between-bones-surgical-implants

Science Daily, Living organ regenerated for first time: Thymus rebuilt in mice

http://www.sciencedaily.com/releases/2014/04/140408115610.htm

The Economist, Engage reverse gear

http://www.economist.com/news/science-and-technology/21600356-first-time-mammalian-organ-has-been-persuaded-renew-itself-engage-0

How these London scientists make body parts in a lab

http://dfm.timesherald.com/article/how-these-london-scientists-make-body-parts-in-a-lab/a0240fa12279467740adb7cfe4cef1ac

Gizmodo, British Scientists Say They've Created Artificial Blood for Humans

http://gizmodo.com/british-scientists-say-theyve-created-artificial-blood-1563033374

Technology Review, Implant Lets Patients Regrow Lost Leg Muscle http://www.technologyreview.com/news/526996/implant-lets-patients-regrow-lost-leg-muscle/

Kurzweil AI, Regenerating plastic material grows back after damage

http://www.kurzweilai.net/regenerating-plastic-material-grows-back-after-damage

Scientists Grow Functional Nerve Cells Using Stem Cells http://gadgets.ndtv.com/science/news/scientists-grow-functional-nerve-cells-using-stem-cells-528959

BBC Future, Will we ever... grow synthetic organs in the lab? http://www.bbc.com/future/story/20120223-will-we-ever-create-organs

Do It Yourself Biotechnology

Scientific American, DIY Biotech Labs Undergo Makeovers

http://www.scientificamerican.com/article/diy-biotech-labs-undergo-makeovers/

Wired, This Woman Invented a Way to Run 30 Lab Tests on Only One Drop of Blood

http://www.wired.com/2014/02/elizabeth-holmes-theranos/?cid=18964974

Biotech Alliance to Humanize Pig Lungs for Transplant

http://sciencebusiness.technewslit.com/?p=17636

Wired, Biologists Create Cells With 6 DNA Letters, Instead of Just 4
http://www.wired.com/2014/05/synthetic-dna-cells/
This Genius Kid Has Invented A Device That Quickly Detects Water Contaminants
http://www.fastcoexist.com/3030503/this-genius-kid-has-invented-a-device-that-quickly-detects-water-contaminants
This 15-Year-Old Came Up With Software To Hunt Down Cancer-Causing Gene Mutations http://www.fastcoexist.com/3031095/this-15-year-old-came-up-with-software-to-hunt-down-cancer-causing-gene-mutations

The 3D Printing Revolution

Technology Review, Artificial Organs May Finally Get a Blood Supply http://www.technologyreview.com/news/525161/artificial-organs-may-finally-get-a-blood-supply/
Medgadget, 3D Printing Low-Cost Prosthetics Parts in Uganda
http://www.medgadget.com/2014/03/3d-printing-low-cost-prosthetics-parts-in-uganda.html
Baby Heart Patient Saved by 3D Printing
http://3dprintingindustry.com/2014/02/25/baby-heart-3d-printing
Can you 3D print drugs?
http://theweek.com/article/index/246091/can-you-3d-print-drugs#axzz34Qnp52se
Popular Science, How 3-D Printing Body Parts Will Revolutionize Medicine
http://www.popsci.com/science/article/2013-07/how-3-d-printing-body-parts-will-revolutionize-medicine
Technology Review, Heart Implants, 3-D-Printed to Order
http://www.technologyreview.com/news/525221/heart-implants-3-d-printed-to-order/
How a Medical Clinic in the Bolivian Rainforest Might Use 3D Printing
http://3dprintingindustry.com/2014/02/18/medical-clinic-bolivian-rainforest-might-use-3d-printing
The Scientist, Organs on Demand
http://www.the-scientist.com/?articles.view/articleNo/37270/title/Organs-on-Demand/
Anatomically Accurate Aorta Cells 3D Printed at Sabancı University in Turkey
http://3dprintingindustry.com/2014/03/20/3d-printing-aorta-cells-turkey
Hospital Technician Tethers Cables & Saves Hospital Money with 3D Printing
http://3dprintingindustry.com/2014/03/23/hospital-technician-tethers-cables-saves-hospital-money-3d-printing
Mashable, 3D Printing Is a Matter of Life and Death
http://mashable.com/2013/09/05/3d-printing-healthcare/

Bone Replacements and Heart Monitors Spur Health Revolution in Open Source 3D Printing (Op-Ed) http://www.livescience.com/43787-bone-replacements-and-heart-monitors-spur-health-revolution-in-open-source-3d-printing.html

Bioprinting Infographic http://www.printerinks.com/bioprinting-infographic.html

22 Year Old Receives Complete 3D Printed Cranium Replacement http://3dprint.com/1795/22-year-old-receives-complete-3d-printed-cranium-replacement/

Medgadget, Scientists on Track to Assemble 3D Printed "Bioficial" Heart http://www.medgadget.com/2014/04/scientists-on-track-to-assemble-3d-printed-bioficial-heart.html

Bone replacements and heart monitors spur health revolution in open source 3D printing http://theconversation.com/bone-replacements-and-heart-monitors-spur-health-revolution-in-open-source-3d-printing-23789

3D Printed Osteoid Medical Cast - Heals Bones 80% Better http://3dprintboard.com/showthread.php?2918-3D-Printed-Osteoid-Medical-Cast-Heals-Bones-80-Better

Kurzweil AI, 3D-printed tumor model allows for more realistic testing of how cancer cells grow and spread http://www.kurzweilai.net/3d-printed-tumor-model-allows-for-more-realistic-testing-of-how-cancer-cells-grow-and-spread

CNN, Artificial eyes, plastic skulls: 3-D printing the human body http://us.cnn.com/2014/04/17/tech/innovation/artificial-eyes-3d-printing-body/index.html

3D Printing Organs, Blood Vessels and All, Takes a Big Step Toward Reality | Singularity Hub http://singularityhub.com/2014/05/05/new-method-to-produce-blood-vessels-in-lab-grown-organs/

Bioprinting a 3D Liver-Like Device to Detoxify the Blood http://www.jacobsschool.ucsd.edu/news/news_releases/release.sfe?id=1512

US FDA Wants An Open Dialogue About 3D Printing Medical Devices http://3dprintingindustry.com/2014/05/20/us-fda-wants-open-dialogue-additive-manufacturing-medical-devices

Life-cycle economic analysis of distributed manufacturing with open-source 3-D printers, Mechatronics Volume 23, Issue 6, September 2013, Pages 713-726

Researchers Have 3D-Printed Blood Vessels http://www.businessinsider.com/researchers-have-3d-printed-blood-vessels-2014-6

Iron Man: Powered exoskeletons and prosthetics

3D-printed exoskeleton helps paralyzed skier walk again http://www.cnet.com/news/3d-printed-exoskeleton-helps-paralyzed-skier-walk-again/

Human Exoskeleton, The 'Body Extender,' Is 'Most Complex Wearable Robot' Ever Built http://www.medicaldaily.com/human-exoskeleton-body-extender-most-complex-wearable-robot-ever-built-270576

CBS News, Paralyzed patients hope ReWalk exoskeleton gets approved by FDA http://www.cbsnews.com/news/paralyzed-patients-hope-rewalk-exoskeleton-gets-approved-by-fda/

Wikipedia, Powered exoskeleton https://en.wikipedia.org/wiki/Powered_exoskeleton

The Future Of Touch-Sensitive Prosthetic Limbs: Real-Time Sensory Information http://www.science20.com/news_articles/future_touchsensitive_prosthetic_limbs_realtime_sensory_information-122278

Bionic body no longer science fiction as researchers develop revolutionary new prosthetics, ways to restore sight http://news.nationalpost.com/2014/01/01/bionic-body-no-longer-science-fiction/

Wired, The Future of Prosthetics Could Be This Brain-Controlled Bionic Leg http://www.wired.com/2013/10/is-this-brain-controlled-bionic-leg-the-future-of-prosthetics/

BBC Future, Prosthetics: Meet the man with 13 legs http://www.bbc.com/future/story/20140123-the-man-with-13-legs

National Geographic, Revolution in Artificial Limbs Brings Feeling Back to Amputees http://news.nationalgeographic.com/news/2014/02/140222-artificial-limbs-feeling-prosthetics-medicine-science/

Medgadget, Touch Bionics Unveils i-limb ultra revolution Prosthetic Hand With iOS Control App (w/video) http://www.medgadget.com/2013/04/touch-bionics-unveils-i-limb-ultra-revolution-prosthetic-hand-with-ios-control-app.html

Medgadget, Self-Designed Prosthetic Knee for Extreme Sports: Interview w/Mike Schultz, Biodapt Inc. http://www.medgadget.com/2014/03/self-designed-prosthetic-knee-for-extreme-sports-interview-wmike-schultz-biodapt-inc.html

Medgadget, How Next Generation Bionic Devices Will Help Everyone Trek Through Life http://www.medgadget.com/2014/03/how-next-generation-bionic-devices-will-help-everyone-trek-through-life.html

Why The Future Of Prosthetics Is A Question Of Ethics http://www.psfk.com/2013/10/prosthetics-ethics.html

From Trauma to TED: Boston Marathon Survivor Adrianne Haslet-Davis on Recovery, Care, and Collaboration http://www.rwjf.org/en/blogs/culture-of-health/2014/04/from_trauma_to_ted.html

BBC News, Rise of the human exoskeletons http://www.bbc.com/news/technology-26418358

Kurzweil AI, Robotic prosthesis turns drummer into a three-armed cyborg
http://www.kurzweilai.net/robotic-prosthesis-turns-drummer-into-a-three-armed-cyborg
Man Compares His $42k Prosthetic Hand to a $50 3D Printed Cyborg Beast
http://3dprint.com/2438/50-prosthetic-3d-printed-hand/
Studio photograph of a young girl wearing a pair of artificial legs
http://www.ssplprints.com/image/102576/girl-wearing-two-artificial-legs-1890-1910
Engadget, FDA approves a life-like prosthetic arm from the man who invented the
Segway http://www.engadget.com/2014/05/09/luke-bionic-arm-approved-by-fda

The End of Human Experimentation

Wyss Institute, Three 'Organs-on-Chips' ready to serve as disease models, drug
testbeds http://wyss.harvard.edu/viewpage/484/
Wikipedia, Organ-on-a-chip https://en.wikipedia.org/wiki/Organ-on-a-chip
From 3D cell culture to organs-on-chips, Huh et al, Special Issue - 3D Cell Biology,
Trends in Cell Biology, December 2011, Vol. 21, No. 12
Artery chip shows aspirin can't prevent all blood clots
http://www.futurity.org/fake-arteries-show-aspirin-cant-prevent-blood-clots/
Kurzweil AI, Simulated human liver achieved in 'benchtop human' project
http://www.kurzweilai.net/simulated-human-liver-achieved-in-benchtop-human-
project#!prettyPhoto
Kurzweil, AI, Bone marrow-on-a-chip unveiled
http://www.kurzweilai.net/bone-marrow-on-a-chip-unveiled
The Independent, In silico: First steps towards a computer simulation of the human
body http://www.independent.co.uk/life-style/health-and-families/health-news/in-
silico-first-steps-towards-a-computer-simulation-of-the-human-body-9340781.html
Wired, Virtual Humans will help NHS predict your treatment
http://www.wired.co.uk/news/archive/2014-05/08/virtual-physiological-human
Harvard News, 'Heart disease-on-a-chip'
http://news.harvard.edu/gazette/story/2014/05/heart-disease-on-a-chip/
Microchip-like technology allows single-cell analysis
http://phys.org/news/2014-05-microchip-like-technology-single-cell-analysis.html
HumMod: A Modeling Environment for the Simulation of Integrative Human Physiology,
Front Physiol. 2011; 2: 12.

Medical Decisions via Artificial Intelligence

Is it possible to build an artificial superintelligence without fully replicating the human
brain? http://www.vitamodularis.org/articles/can_artifical_superintelligence_be_built_
without_replicating_the_human_brain.shtml

IBM Watson: The inside story of how the Jeopardy-winning supercomputer was born, and what it wants to do next http://www.techrepublic.com/article/ibm-watson-the-inside-story-of-how-the-jeopardy-winning-supercomputer-was-born-and-what-it-wants-to-do-next/#

IBM's Watson Is Learning Its Way To Saving Lives http://www.fastcompany.com/3001739/ibms-watson-learning-its-way-saving-lives By Jon Gertner

Medical News Today, Evaluating the expertise of humans and computer algorithms http://www.medicalnewstoday.com/releases/271345.php

Wired, Why Human-Computer Teams Hold the Most Promise for the Future http://www.wired.com/2014/02/human-computer-teams-hold-promise-future/

Gartner's 2013 Hype Cycle for Emerging Technologies Maps Out Evolving Relationship Between Humans and Machines http://www.gartner.com/newsroom/id/2575515

IBM, I'll take 'Business and Medicine,' Alex http://www.ibm.com/smarterplanet/us/en/innovation_explanations/article/rob_high.html?lnk=ushpcs2

Artificial Intelligence The Future of Medicine? JAMA Otolaryngol Head Neck Surg. 2014;140(3):191

Medical News Today, A supercomputer could change how diseases are treated http://www.medicalnewstoday.com/articles/272975.php

Wired, IBM's Watson is better at diagnosing cancer than human doctors http://www.wired.co.uk/news/archive/2013-02/11/ibm-watson-medical-doctor

Venture Beat, IBM Watson fires its own cancer-fighting 'moonshot' http://venturebeat.com/2013/10/18/ibm-watson-fires-its-own-cancer-fighting-moonshot/

MD Anderson Cancer Center to Use Watson to Help Battle Cancer http://asmarterplanet.com/blog/2013/10/md-anderson-cancer-center-plans-to-use-ibm-watson-to-help-eradicate-cancer.html

Can computers save health care? IU research shows lower costs, better outcomes http://newsinfo.iu.edu/news/page/normal/23795.html

Forbes, IBM's Watson Attempts To Tackle The Genetics Of Brain Cancer http://www.forbes.com/sites/matthewherper/2014/03/19/what-watson-cant-tell-us-about-our-genes-yet/

The New Yorker, Why We Should Think About the Threat of Artificial Intelligence http://www.newyorker.com/online/blogs/elements/2013/10/why-we-should-think-about-the-threat-of-artificial-intelligence.html

Stanford AAAI Talk: Positive Artificial Intelligence http://selfawaresystems.com/2014/03/24/stanford-aaai-talk-positive-artificial-intelligence/

Five Creepiest Advances in Artificial Intelligence http://www.learning-mind.com/five-creepiest-advances-in-artificial-intelligence/

IEET, The Singularity Is Further Than It Appears
http://ieet.org/index.php/IEET/more/naam20140327
Wired, Artificial Intelligence Is Now Telling Doctors How to Treat You
http://www.wired.com/2014/06/ai-healthcare/
Business Isnsider, IBM's Watson Supercomputer May Soon Be The Best Doctor In The World http://www.businessinsider.com/ibms-watson-may-soon-be-the-best-doctor-in-the-world-2014-4#ixzz34WADQJHn
IO9.com, IBM's Watson computer has parts of its memory cleared after developing an acute case of potty mouth http://io9.com/5975173/ibms-watson-computer-has-parts-of-its-memory-cleared-after-developing-an-acute-case-of-potty-mouth
IO9.com, A Chatbot Has ‚Passed' The Turing Test For The First Time
http://io9.com/a-chatbot-has-passed-the-turing-test-for-the-first-ti-1587834715
Medgadget, The First EMR to Integrate with Watson (INTERVIEW)
http://www.medgadget.com/2014/06/the-first-emr-to-integrate-with-watson-interview.html

Nanorobots Living In Our Blood

Top 10 developments in nanodermatology in 2013
http://nanotechportal.blogspot.hu/2014/02/top-10-developments-in-nanodermatology.html
Types of Nanorobots being Developed for Use in Healthcare http://www.dummies.com/how-to/content/types-of-nanorobots-being-developed-for-use-in-hea.html
Kurzweil AI, Robots in the bloodstream: the promise of nanomedicine
http://www.kurzweilai.net/robots-in-the-bloodstream-the-promise-of-nanomedicine
Science Daily, New nanoparticle that only attacks cervical cancer cells
http://www.sciencedaily.com/releases/2014/03/140314212122.htm
The Nanotechnology Revolution
http://www.thenewatlantis.com/publications/the-nanotechnology-revolution
Looking to the Future: Advances in Nanotechnology, an Interview with Travis Earles from Lockheed Martin http://www.azonano.com/article.aspx?ArticleID=3738
Kurzweil AI, Magnetically controlled nanoparticles cause cancer cells to self-destruct
http://www.kurzweilai.net/nanoparticles-that-cause-cancer-cells-to-self-destruct
Popular Science, Nano-Robots That Compute With DNA Installed Into Living Cockroach http://www.popsci.com/article/science/nano-robots-compute-dna-installed-living-cockroach
Superhumans Created by Nanotechnology within 30 years
http://www.thatsreallypossible.com/news/852/nanotechnology-superhumans/
Science Daily, Cloaked DNA nanodevices survive pilot mission
http://www.sciencedaily.com/releases/2014/04/140422100021.htm

Contribution of Nanomedicine to Horizon 2020 http://www.etp-nanomedicine.eu/public/press-documents/publications/etpn-publications/etpn-white-paper-H2020
Here's a Surprising Look at How Nanotechnology Could Reengineer Our Bodies http://www.policymic.com/articles/89803/here-s-a-surprising-look-at-how-nanotechnology-could-reengineer-our-bodies

Hospitals of the Future
In The Hospital Of The Future, Big Data Is One Of Your Doctors http://www.fastcoexist.com/3022050/futurist-forum/in-the-hospital-of-the-future-big-data-is-one-of-your-doctors
Forbes, Hospitals May Be Disappearing In The Era Of Health Care Reform http://www.forbes.com/sites/robertpearl/2013/11/14/hospitals-may-be-disappearing-in-the-era-of-health-care-reform/
Wired, What Would the Ideal Hospital Look Like in 2020?
http://www.wired.com/2013/07/hospital-of-the-future/
Op/Ed: Hospital of the Future Will Be a Health Delivery Network
http://health.usnews.com/health-news/hospital-of-tomorrow/articles/2014/01/14/oped-hospital-of-the-future-will-be-a-health-delivery-network
The Wall Street Journal, The Hospital Room of the Future
http://online.wsj.com/news/articles/SB10001424052702303442004579119922380316310
IFTF, Future of the Hospital: Foresight Engine Game & Public Analysis Report -
http://www.iftf.org/our-work/health-self/health-horizons/future-of-the-hospital-game-report/#sthash.XCTUJvBc.dpuf
The Future of Hospitals: Visions of the Healthcare Landscape in 2035
http://www.beckershospitalreview.com/leadership-management/the-future-of-hospitals-visions-of-the-healthcare-landscape-in-2035.html
Forbes, The Hospital Steve Jobs Would Have Built
http://www.forbes.com/sites/carminegallo/2014/03/26/the-hospital-steve-jobs-would-have-built/
The Future of Wearable Computing in Healthcare
http://www.mdtmag.com/blogs/2014/01/future-wearable-computing-healthcare
The Doctor's Office of 2024 — 4 Predictions for the Future
http://profitable-practice.softwareadvice.com/doctors-office-of-2024-0514/
The Charles Bronfman Institute for Personalized Medicine
http://icahn.mssm.edu/research/institutes/institute-for-personalized-medicine/innovation-and-technology/biome-platform

Forbes, Global Study Finds Majority Believe Traditional Hospitals Will Be Obsolete In The Near Future http://www.forbes.com/sites/theapothecary/2013/12/09/global-study-finds-majority-believe-traditional-hospitals-will-be-obsolete-in-the-near-future/

Virtual-Digital Brains
OpenBCI wants you to build products with brain waves and 3D printer http://www.3ders.org/articles/20140113-openbci-wants-you-to-build-products-with-brain-waves-and-3d-printer.html
How to Create a Mind, Kurzweil, 2012, Penguin Books, p. 195.
Supercomputer takes 40 mins to calculate a single second of human brain activity http://www.itproportal.com/2014/01/13/supercomputer-takes-40-mins-calculate-single-second-human-brain-activity/
Medgadget, Build Your Own Brain-Computer Interface with OpenBCI (INTERVIEW) http://www.medgadget.com/2014/01/build-your-own-brain-computer-interface-with-openbci-interview.html
IO9.com, What will life be like when digital brains outnumber humans? http://io9.com/what-will-life-be-like-when-digital-brains-outnumber-hu-1529764158
Meet the woman making brainwave control look more like meditation and less like the Matrix http://www.digitaltrends.com/computing/spotlight-on-ariel-garten-the-ceo-behind-interaxons-thought-controlled-brainchild/#!YW9Cm
Kurzweil AI, Real-time MRI-guided gene therapy for brain cancer http://www.kurzweilai.net/southern-californias-first-real-time-mri-guided-gene-therapy-for-brain-cancer
The Wall Street Journal, The Future of Brain Implants http://online.wsj.com/news/articles/SB10001424052702304914904579435592981780528
How the Human/Computer Interface Works (Infographics) http://www.livescience.com/37944-how-the-human-computer-interface-works-infographics.html
4 Hurdles to Making a Digital Human Brain http://www.livescience.com/37068-4-hurdles-digital-human-brain.html
IEET, Mind-to-mind thought talking possible by 2030, scientist says http://ieet.org/index.php/IEET/more/pelletier20140310
IO9.com, Would it be evil to build a functional brain inside a computer? http://io9.com/would-it-be-evil-to-build-a-functional-brain-inside-a-c-598064996/all
Meet the man building an AI that mimics our neocortex - and could kill off neural networks http://www.theregister.co.uk/2014/03/29/hawkins_ai_feature
Telegraph, ‚Transhumanists' are planning to upload your mind to a memory stick… http://blogs.telegraph.co.uk/technology/jamiebartlett/100013025/transhumanists-are-planning-to-upload-your-mind-to-a-memory-stick-and-extend-life-indefinitely-are-they-mad-dangerous-or-the-saviours-of-mankind/

Extreme Tech, Hackers backdoor the human brain, successfully extract sensitive data
http://www.extremetech.com/extreme/134682-hackers-backdoor-the-human-brain-successfully-extract-sensitive-data
CNET, High-tech headband reads your mind
http://www.cnet.com/news/high-tech-headband-reads-your-mind/#ftag=CADf328eec
10 of the Most Surprising Findings from Psychological Studies
http://expandedconsciousness.com/2014/05/03/10-of-the-most-surprising-findings-from-psychological-studies/#oq3ghvghoVEeWVYH.99
Wired, Inside the Strange New World of DIY Brain Stimulation
http://www.wired.com/2014/05/diy-brain-stimulation/
The Myths, Realities, and Ethics of Neuroenhancement
http://motherboard.vice.com/read/the-myths-realities-and-ethics-of-neuroenhancement
The New York Times, Can the Nervous System Be Hacked?
http://www.nytimes.com/2014/05/25/magazine/can-the-nervous-system-be-hacked.html?_r=0
The Computer That Replicates a Human Brain
http://www.thedailybeast.com/articles/2014/05/01/the-computer-that-replicates-a-human-brain.html
IO9.com, Biotech Breakthrough: Monkeys can feel virtual objects using a brain implant
http://io9.com/5846275/biotech-breakthrough-monkeys-can-feel-virtual-objects-using-a-brain-implant
Wired, Creating a ‚morality pill’ more a question of ethics than science
http://www.wired.co.uk/news/archive/2014-05/16/molly-crockett-morality-drug
Science, Creating a False Memory in the Hippocampus
http://www.sciencemag.org/content/341/6144/387
Medgadget, Optogenetics Researchers Stop Pain With a Beam of Light
http://www.medgadget.com/2014/02/optogenetics-spots-stops-pain-with-beam-of-light.html
Medgadget, Light-Guiding Hydrogel Brings Optogenetics Closer to Clinical Application
http://www.medgadget.com/2013/11/light-guiding-hydrogel-brings-optogenetics-closer-to-clinical-application.html
Medgadget, Optogenetics Now in Technicolor
http://www.medgadget.com/2014/02/optogenetics-now-in-technicolor.html
Scientific American, Why “Optogenetic” Methods for Manipulating Brains Don’t Light Me Up** http://blogs.scientificamerican.com/cross-check/2013/08/20/why-optogenetic-methods-for-manipulating-brains-dont-light-me-up/
The Brain Prize 2013: the optogenetics revolution, Trends in Neurosciences Volume 36, Issue 10, p557-560, October 2013
Interview: Ed Boyden on Optogenetics, Neuroscience, and the Future of Neuroengineering

http://blog.addgene.org/mits-ed-boyden-on-optogenetics-neuroscience-and-the-future-of-neuroengineering

Using Light To Control The Brain: How 'Optogenetics' Could Cure Alcohol Addiction http://www.medicaldaily.com/using-light-control-brain-how-optogenetics-could-cure-alcohol-addiction-265899

Wikipedia, Optogenetics https://en.wikipedia.org/wiki/Optogenetics

Method Man http://www.stanford.edu/group/dlab/papers/KD%20Nature%20Profile%202013.pdf

Independent optical excitation of distinct neural populations, Nature Methods 11, 338-346 (2014)

MIT discovers the location of memories: Individual neurons http://www.extremetech.com/extreme/123485-mit-discovers-the-location-of-memories-individual-neurons

IO9.com, A New Technique Could Erase Painful Memories -- Or Bring Them Back http://io9.com/a-new-technique-could-erase-painful-memories-or-brin-1585412300

Independent optical excitation of distinct neural populations, Nature Methods 11, 338-346 (2014)

The Rise of Recreational Cyborgs

Augmented 'Olympics': Championship for Robot-Assisted Parathletes Coming in 2016 http://www.factor-tech.com/health-augmentation/augmented-olympics-championship-for-robot-assisted-parathletes-coming-in-2016/

Quantigraphic camera promises HDR eyesight from Father of AR http://www.slashgear.com/quantigraphic-camera-promises-hdr-eyesight-from-father-of-ar-12246941/

Digital Destiny and Human Possibility in the Age of the Wearable Computer http://eyetap.org/cyborg.htm

IEEE, Steve Mann: My "Augmediated" Life http://spectrum.ieee.org/geek-life/profiles/steve-mann-my-augmediated-life

Exclusive: Cyborg Steve Mann Details Alleged McDonald's Assault http://blog.laptopmag.com/exclusive-cyborg-steve-mann-on-alleged-mcdonalds-assault

IO9.com, The first person in the world to become a government-recognized cyborg http://io9.com/the-first-person-in-the-world-to-become-a-government-re-1474975237

Mashable, Meet the ,Most Connected Man' in the World http://mashable.com/2014/03/13/most-connected-man-in-world-chris-dancy

Superhero Vision Coming in Graphene Contact Lenses? http://news.discovery.com/tech/biotechnology/superhero-vision-coming-in-graphene-contact-lenses-140319.htm

DARPA's new biotechnology lab will focus on cyborg tech http://www.dvice.com/2014-4-1/darpas-new-biotechnology-lab-will-focus-cyborg-tech

Medgadget, One Step Closer to the Artificial Pancreas: Interview with Medtronic's Dr. Francine Kaufman http://www.medgadget.com/2014/04/one-step-closer-to-the-artificial-pancreas-interview-with-medtronics-dr-francine-kaufman.html

IO9.com, DARPA's New Biotech Division Wants To Create A Transhuman Future http://io9.com/darpas-new-biotech-division-wants-to-create-a-transhum-1556857603/+georgedvorsky

Michigan Man Among 1st To Get ‚Bionic Eye' http://www.manufacturing.net/news/2014/04/michigan-man-among-1st-to-get-bionic-eye

Graphene Contact Lenses Let You See in the Dark http://nanotechportal.blogspot.ca/2014/05/graphene-contact-lenses-let-you-see-in.html?m=1

Steve Mann (2013). „Vision 2.0, My Augmediated Life", IEEE Spectrum, Volume 50, Issue 3, Digital Object Identifier: 10.1109/MSPEC.2013.6471058, pp42-47. See also „My Augmediated Life: What I've learned from 35 years of wearing computerized eyewear", http://spectrum.ieee.org/geek-life/profiles/steve-mann-my-augmediated-life

How McDonaldized surveillance creates a monopoly on sight that chills AR and smartphone development Steve Mann, 2012, 1010 (October 10) http://eyetap.blogspot.ca/2012/10/mcveillance-mcdonaldized-surveillance.html

Cryonics and Longevity

Wikipedia, Cryonics https://en.wikipedia.org/wiki/Cryonics

Cryonics Could Help Improve Some Lives in the Future http://www.psychologytoday.com/blog/the-transhumanist-philosopher/201405/cryonics-could-help-improve-some-lives-in-the-future

Wikipedia, Cryotherapy https://en.wikipedia.org/wiki/Cryotherapy

The Verge, Watch these men take care of the frozen dead http://www.theverge.com/2014/4/10/5599668/we-will-live-again-tribeca-film-festival-selection-about-cryopreservation

Cryonics and the search for 'something more' beyond death http://news.nationalpost.com/2013/10/25/cryonics-and-the-search-for-something-more-beyond-death/

Humans will be kept between life and death in the first suspended animation trials http://www.extremetech.com/extreme/179296-humans-will-be-kept-between-life-and-death-in-the-first-suspended-animation-trials

BBC Future, Human hibernation: Secrets behind the big sleep http://www.bbc.com/future/story/20140505-secrets-behind-the-big-sleep

Wikipedia, Life extension https://en.wikipedia.org/wiki/Life_extension

Drooling on Your Shoes or Living Long and Prospering? http://www.slate.com/articles/technology/future_tense/2013/09/four_scenarios_for_our_future_lifespans.html

With Calico, Google looks to make your lifespan its business http://www.extremetech.com/extreme/166858-with-calico-google-looks-to-make-your-lifespan-its-business
Immortality, biotechnology, and the woefully unprepared criminal justice system http://www.extremetech.com/extreme/178859-immortality-biotechnology-and-the-woefully-unprepared-criminal-justice-system
CNN, How Google's Calico aims to fight aging and ‚solve death'
http://edition.cnn.com/2013/10/03/tech/innovation/google-calico-aging-death/
Boosting Longevity with Massive Genome Sequencing and Cyborg Technology http://www.prophecynewswatch.com/2014/March18/184.html#9172ADeFRplrQoZV.99
Medgadget, Winners of Stanford Center on Longevity's Design Challenge Announced http://www.medgadget.com/2014/04/winners-of-stanford-center-on-longevitys-design-challenge-announced.html
Popular Science, Hints To Longevity Found In Blood Of 115-Year-Old Woman
http://www.popsci.com/article/science/hints-longevity-found-blood-115-year-old-woman
XPRIZE 100 Over 100 Candidates http://genomics.xprize.org/100-over-100
Strategies for Engineered Negligible Senescence https://www.fightaging.org/archives/2004/11/strategies-for-engineered-negligible-senescence.php
Interview with Aubrey de Grey, PhD
http://www.lef.org/magazine/mag2013/jul2013_Interview-with-Aubrey-de-Grey-PhD_01.htm

What Will a Brand New Society Look Like?

The Atlantic, Married to a Doll: Why One Man Advocates Synthetic Love
http://www.theatlantic.com/health/archive/2013/09/married-to-a-doll-why-one-man-advocates-synthetic-love/279361/
As Technology Marches Forward, Who Gets Left Behind?
http://footnote1.com/as-technology-marches-forward-who-gets-left-behind/
BBC Future, What happens to prosthetics and implants after you die?
http://www.bbc.com/future/story/20140311-body-parts-that-live-after-death
Mashable, 10 Crazy Jobs That Will Exist in the Future
http://mashable.com/2014/04/28/jobs-of-the-future